WORKING CLASSES

The PWS Series in Computer Science

WORKING CLASSES

Data Structures and Algorithms Using C++

RICK DECKER
STUART HIRSHFIELD

Hamilton College

PWS Publishing Company

I(T)P **International Thomson Publishing Company**

Boston • Albany • Bonn • Cincinnati • Detroit • London • Madrid
Melbourne • Mexico City • New York • Paris • San Francisco
Singapore • Tokyo • Toronto • Washington

PWS PUBLISHING COMPANY
20 Park Plaza, Boston, Massachusetts 02116-4324

I(T)P ™   International Thomson Publishing
          The trademark ITP is used under license.

For more information contact:

PWS Publishing Co.
20 Park Plaza
Boston, MA 02116

International Thomson Publishing Japan
Hirakawacho Kyowa Building, 31
2-2-1 Hirakawacho
Chiyoda-ku, Tokyo 102
Japan

Thomson Nelson Australia
102 Dodds Street
South Melbourne, 3205
Victoria, Australia

International Thomson Publishing Europe
Berkshire House I68–I73
High Holborn
London WC1V 7AA
England

International Thomson Editores
Campos Eliseos 385, Piso 7
Col. Polanco
11560 Mexico D.F., Mexico

Nelson Canada
1120 Birchmount Road
Scarborough, Ontario
Canada M1K 5G4

International Thomson Publishing Asia
221 Henderson Road
#05–10 Henderson Building
Singapore 0315

International Thomson Publishing GmbH
Königswinterer Strasse 418
53227 Bonn, Germany

Library of Congress Cataloging-in-Publication Data
Decker, Rick.
    Working classes: data structures and algorithms using C++ / Rick Decker, Stuart Hirshfield
        p. cm.
    Includes index.
    ISBN 0-534-94566-X
    1. C++ (Computer program language)   2. Data structures (Computer science)
I. Hirshfield, Stuart. II. Title.
QA76.73.C153D44   1996
005.7'3—dc20
                                                    94-43941
                                                    CIP

 This book is printed
on recycled, acid-free
paper.

Sponsoring Editor: Michael J. Sugarman
Developmental Editor: Mary Thomas
Production Editor: Abigail M. Heim
Marketing Manager: Nathan Wilbur
Manufacturing Coordinator: Lisa Flanagan
Editorial Assistant: Benjamin Steinberg

Interior Designer: Catherine Hawkes Design
Cover Designer: Julia Gecha
Cover Artist: Angela Perkins
Typesetter and Interior Illustrator: Electric Ink, Ltd.
Cover Printer: New England Book Components
Text Printer and Binder: Quebecor Printing/Martinsburg

Cover Image: The SteelTec™ product ©1993 by Remco Toys, Inc. All rights reserved. Used with permission.

Printed and bound in the United States of America.
95 96 97 98 99—9 8 7 6 5 4 3

For Natty, Adam, Ben, and Shauna

CONTENTS

**P A R T
T H R E E**   N O N L I N E A R   S T R U C T U R E S

5 RECURSION 183

6 TREES 223

9 UNORDERED COLLECTIONS 342

10 TRAVESTY: PUTTING IT ALL TOGETHER 391

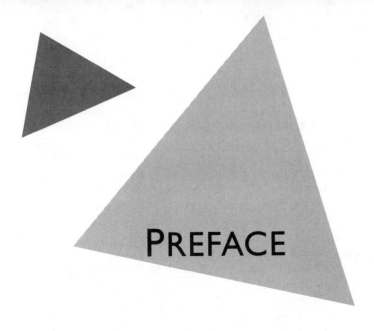

PREFACE

Over the years, we've had a number of students who have said, in one form or another, "I want to be a computer scientist because I really like programming and am very good at it." Of course computer scientists, both novices and seasoned veterans, are often called upon to write programs, but to equate computer science with programming is to confuse the product with the process. Being an excellent draftsman who can faithfully represent a scene on paper is no guarantee that your works will eventually hang in the Metropolitan Museum. It's a step in the right direction, but an artist must also have an intimate familiarity with the more general principles of composition, perspective, color and so on.

In essence, programming is little more than the efficient management of a particular kind of large intellectual process, and the guidelines for good programming are nothing but the application of common-sense principles that apply to any complex creative task. It goes without saying, though, that before you can think efficiently you have to have something to think *about*, which for our purposes means that in order to write good programs, you must have an idea about how information may be represented in a program.

Computer science is a young discipline, but has developed enough over the past few decades to gain a consensus about what should constitute the core data structures. In this book, we have tried to capture this core by providing what might be called the "classic" data structures—the most commonly applied methods for representing information in a computer program—along with the algorithms for manipulating this information. In terms of things to think about for programming, this book offers a collection of tools that should be part of the working knowledge of any programmer.

This book is not about programming, however. Computer science is a science, and as such mainly seeks a theoretical framework that can be used to describe the behavior of the objects under study, which in our case are computers and their programs. One of the objectives that have determined the form of the book is to provide a broad view of what a data structure really is. In our approach, data structures are not just a collection of ad hoc type declarations and function definitions, but rather any data structure is a particular instance of an abstract data type, which consists of (1) a set of positions and a set of elements associated with the positions; (2) a logical structure defined on the positions; and (3) a collection of structure-preserving operations on the positions and the elements they "contain."

We have chosen to define the structure of an abstract data type by specifying a structural relation on each set of positions. Doing so provides a natural progression of the chapters, where each new abstract data type is introduced by removing some of the structural restrictions from a prior type. Thus we begin with lists, whose structure is defined by a linear order, and progress to trees by removing the requirement that each position have a unique successor, then to directed graphs by removing the requirement of a unique predecessor, and finally to sets, where there is no structure at all on the positions. Throughout this process, we see that each new abstract data type still can be described by the threefold view of a collection of positions with a structural relation and a collection of structure-preserving operations.

Some History

After using Pascal in this course for five years, it was clear to us that, for all its strengths as a teaching language, Pascal is not the most felicitous choice as a vehicle for a course in data structures. An abstract data type is nothing more than a collection of data and operations on that data, and that, of course, is the definition of a class. When preparing to write the book you have before you, we considered several object-oriented languages and finally settled on C++, largely because of its popularity. We'd be the first to admit that C++ has its warts and blemishes, but in our opinion it is the appropriate choice at present.

The Audience

Though we did not set out to tailor this book to any preexisting curriculum, it turned out that it covers essentially all of CS2 and part of CS7, as described in the ACM Curriculum '78, and a subset of the union of CS2 and CO2, set forth in Norman Gibbs and Alan Tucker's 1985 Model Curriculum for a Liberal Arts Degree in Computer Science. The material contained here should be covered early in any computer science curriculum, and we have written this book for an audience of first and second year students in computer science who are familiar with C or (preferably) C++. For those readers whose background is Pascal, we provide a Pascal–C++ "dictionary" in Appendix A. A course in discrete mathematics is desirable as a pre- or corequisite for this material, but the relevant mathematical background is summarized in Appendices B and C for those who need it.

The Contents

Our intent has been to write a book that could be used as the basis for a semester-length course in data structures or advanced programming. Realizing that the subject matter of this book comes at an early stage in the education of a computer scientist, we included a number of mentions, necessarily brief, of some of the topics awaiting the student down the road. Most of the canonical sorting and searching algorithms are covered, along with mentions of computational complexity, compiler design, unsolvable problems, NP-completeness, and fundamental paradigms for algorithms. We believe that one can never have enough exercises—this book has 359, by actual count, and each chapter concludes with an optional Explorations section, where we treat interesting topics that extend the material of the chapter.

Chapter 1 covers some of the necessary preliminaries, such as program design, the definition of an abstract data type, and assertions and program verification. We begin by specifying an array as an abstract data type, and conclude with the *Number* ADT that represents integers of arbitrary size. **Chapter 2** describes the *List* ADT and continues the preliminary material of Chapter 1 by discussing parametrized classes and functions, big-O notation, and timing of algorithms. The chapter concludes with a discussion of memory management. In the Explorations section, we discuss sorted lists and searching, along with self-organizing lists.

In Chapters 3 and 4 we continue the investigation of linear data structures. **Chapter 3** covers strings and introduces the Boyer-Moore string search algorithm. **Chapter 4** covers the remaining standard linear structures, stacks and queues, motivating these by applications to manipulate postfix expressions. The Explorations cover stack-based maze traversal and a simple operating system simulation. Since a considerable number of queue applications involve simulation, Appendix C (Random Numbers and Simulation) may be useful at this point.

Chapter 5 provides a segue into nonlinear structures by introducing recursion and recursively defined data structures. Timing estimates for recursive algorithms are covered in depth, along with an introduction to LISP. We deal with Quicksort in the Explorations. Appendix B, which covers logarithms and exponentials, induction, and elementary combinations, is helpful supplementary material at this stage.

Chapters 6 and 7 cover trees. **Chapter 6** provides the necessary background on binary trees and their implementations, traversal algorithms, and treesort; and the Explorations discuss threaded trees, minimal-length codes, and tries. **Chapter 7,** which can be omitted if necessary, covers two extensions of binary search trees, namely AVL trees and B-trees.

Chapter 8 covers graphs and digraphs, along with a representative sample of graph algorithms for traversal, spanning trees, minimal-cost paths, minimal spanning trees, and an introduction to complexity theory through the Traveling Salesperson Problem. In the Explorations, we discuss topological sorting and applications of powers of the adjacency matrix.

Chapter 9, on sets, describes bit vector, list implementations of sets, dictionaries, and associations, and provides a comprehensive introduction to hashing. The chapter concludes with *PriorityQueue* ADT and heapsort. In the Explorations, we continue our discussion of hashing and introduce the *DisjointSet* ADT.

In **Chapter 10** we consider the problem of regenerating text from a large sample and trace the development of programs to solve this problem, using a real computer/compiler system to show how practical time and space constraints arise from choices of data structure.

Supplementary Material

In addition to the data disk (IBM PC compatible) included with this book, an *Instructor's Manual* is available from the publisher. A Macintosh version of the data disk is also available from the publisher.

Acknowledgments

A lot of people deserve praise for seeing this book through to completion. Thanks go to Billy Lim, *Illinois State University,* Barbara Boucher Owens, *St. Edward's University,* and Daniel Ling, *Okanagan University College,* for their thoughtful reviews; and to our students and colleagues for suggesting countless changes in earlier versions. Special kudos go to the folks at PWS Publishing, especially Mike Sugarman and Ben Steinberg (the Batman and Robin of publishing), Abby Heim (who held her nervous breakdown at bay throughout an insanely busy production process that included working on two of our books simultaneously), J. P. Lenney (for picking out great wines and picking up the tab), and Nathan Wilbur (for just being Nathan). Writing and producing a book is a task that rates up there on the discomfort scale with cholera, except that writing takes longer. It can never be called pleasurable, but the friendship and warmth of the PWS crew at least has made it bearable.

Rick Decker
Stuart Hirshfield

WORKING CLASSES

PART ONE

INTRODUCTION

1 PRELIMINARIES

Computer science is concerned with the study of problem solving with computers. Notice that we did not say that computer science *consists* of problem solving with computers, any more than mathematics consists of solving equations or music consists of producing notes. It is not enough to be able to answer the question, How do we solve a particular problem with the help of a computer? If it were, the study of computer science could stop after one or two introductory programming courses. Instead, the proper subject matter includes questions like the following:

1. What are the possible different ways to solve a problem?
2. How are the solutions for a particular problem related?
3. What technique is best for a particular problem?
4. What do we mean by a "best" solution for a problem?
5. In what ways are solutions for different problems related?
6. How do we verify that we have a solution for a problem?
7. What problems can and cannot be solved with a computer?

Although all of these questions contain the word *problem*, they all seek answers in a context that is broader than simply solving a particular problem. In fact, all of these questions (indeed, all of the questions of computer science) are different aspects of the same fundamental question:

What *general principles* underlie the notion of problem solving with computers?

In this text, we will concern ourselves primarily with those aspects of this fundamental question that deal with the structure of the data in a program

3

and, in addition, with the techniques of manipulating that data in an efficient fashion.

 ## 1.1   ADTs: ABSTRACTION AND ENCAPSULATION

When we design a program, one of the most important parts of the process is our choice of data structures. When we refer to a **data structure**, we mean the way information is logically organized in a program, subject to the constraints given by the language we use to write the program. Suppose, for instance, that you had to produce a program that would perform arithmetic on very large integers. Now, C++ (or any high-level language, for that matter) has a number of built-in **data types**, such as integers, floating-point numbers, arrays, and pointers, but none of the data types provided by the language are themselves suited for the task we have in mind, mainly because C++ integers are restricted to a fixed number of (binary) digits, often 16 or 32. The largest number that can be expressed in 32 binary digits is a little more than 4 billion, which would be completely unsatisfactory for the kinds of calculations we want to perform, like computing the 129-digit number known as RSA-129, the result of the following multiplication:*

$$3276913299326670954996198819083446141317764296799294253979828853\overline 3$$
$$\times\ 3490529510847650949147849619903898133417764638493387843990820577$$
$$(= ???)$$

Clearly, to do the kinds of things we want, we must invent a data structure of our own, built out of the available C++ data types. One way of looking at this process is to observe that this problem—and, in fact, any but the most trivial kind of problem—requires us to *extend* the C++ language so that, at least in the context of our program, we can act as if C++ has built into it a data type that supports what is known as **multiprecision arithmetic**.

In an object-oriented language like C++, we might define a class, *DigitList*, that we would use to represent such long integers. One possibility might be to keep an array of *digits*, arranged in increasing order of their place values, along with three integers: *sign* (+1 for positive numbers and zero, –1 for negative numbers), *size* (for the number of digits in our number), and *max* (for the maximum possible numbers we can fit in our array before we have to replace it with a larger one). Figure 1.1 shows how a *DigitList* object might represent the number –716,448,909,312.

Having decided on the data structure, we would then write member and friend functions for the operations we want: We would overload the

---

* The number RSA-129 arose in a much more difficult problem than finding the product: The number was given and the challenge was to factor it into the two numbers we illustrate. It took over 600 people working together about eight months to find the factors.

FIGURE 1.1

A *DigitList* object representing −716,448,909,312

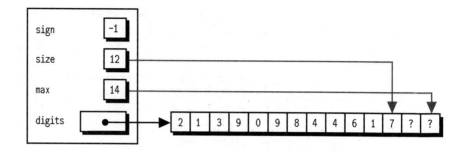

input/output operators, >> and <<, the arithmetic operators +, - (two forms, for negation and subtraction), *, and /, and comparison operators like == and <, and we would write the usual collection of constructors and a destructor. Having done that, we'd have a class that provides all the support our program needs. That's a pretty good job for an apprentice, but it's not the way a master programmer would attack the problem.

Abstraction

In computer science, as in most other fields, the difference between a novice and an expert is not so much a function of knowledge or intelligence as it is of wisdom gained from experience. To be sure, an expert in a field can call on a much larger collection of facts than the novice, but even more important is the way the expert's knowledge is categorized and arranged. The human mind is superbly adapted to recognize patterns and similarities in the information it receives and to make plans of action based on those similarities. For example, we don't have to devote a great deal of effort planning how to obtain a meal in an unfamiliar restaurant, because we recognize without much effort that this is just another instance of the category of Eating Out problems. While the details may be different tonight, we know what to do because we have worked through the solution to the Eating Out problem many times in the past; we have formed an *abstract* framework, in which every Eating Out problem is just a special case.

For someone just learning to write programs, every problem is new and every solution must be invented from scratch. For an expert, almost every problem is somewhat like one that he or she has seen before and so can be solved by suitable modifications of techniques that have proved effective in the past. Thus, the expert would recognize that the *DigitList* class has a great deal in common with the *List* structure: They both are containers for collections of objects (integers, in this case) arranged in a linear order (place order, in this case). While a *DigitList* requires operations (like addition) that are not available to users of the general *List* class, the expert recognizes that much of the work has already been done in the design of the *List* class.

Just as biologists identify certain common properties among animals to group them into genus categories—catlike, doglike, bearlike—computer scientists classify data structures into categories such as linear, hierarchical (treelike), and network (weblike) structures. Once we understand what these categories are, the properties they have in common, and how to implement them efficiently, much of the work of program design is done for us. For example, if we know about the linear abstract data type *List,* then it should make little difference whether the problem we want to solve involves employee records, patients waiting in a doctor's office, or multiple precision arithmetic, since all of these can be viewed as instances in which the information is organized in a linear order.

All of the abstract data types are derived from a single classification scheme describing what the objects of the abstract data type look like and what we wish to do with them. As a start, we can say that an **abstract data type,** which we will abbreviate as **ADT,** consists of the following:

1. A **structure,** the skeleton of the ADT, which is specified by:

    a. Two sets of underlying objects: a set, *Atom,* of the elements that make up the ADT and a set, *Position,* where, intuitively speaking, we will place the atoms
    b. A **structural relation** that describes how the positions are arranged

2. A collection of **operations** that can be performed on those elements

For example, we could specify the abstract data type *DigitList* as follows:

DigitList

Structure. The underlying set of atoms consists of the digits $0, \ldots, 9$. The underlying set of positions consists of an arbitrary (finite) set arranged in a linear order, one after the other. Each digit list is considered to represent an integer, equal to what one would have by considering the digit list in decimal place order.

Operations

DigitList(). Creates a list representing the number 0.

DigitList(long n). Creates a digit list from a long integer *n*.

DigitList(const DigitList& d). Copies the list *d*.

~DigitList(). Destroys the list.

DigitList& operator= (DigitList d). Overloads the assignment operator, copying *d*.

int operator== (DigitList d, DigitList e). Overloads the equality operator, returning 1 if and only if *d* and *e* represent the same number.

DigitList& operator+ (DigitList d, DigitList e). Overloads the assignment operator, returning a reference to a DigitList that represents the sum of the numbers represented by *d* and *e*.

. . . along with a number of other operations we omit here.*

Once we recognize that *DigitList* is just a special case of the ADT *List,* we gain several advantages. First, having implementations of *List* available saves us the trouble of designing our program from scratch; it's far easier to modify well-written code than it is to generate our own each time we need it. Doing this allows us to concentrate on the big picture rather than falling into the novice trap of constantly being bogged down in details. Second, knowledge is power. If we take the time to study the properties of abstract data types, it might just happen that we will learn something about one of them that later has some real practical value.

Reuse and Encapsulation

If we had a computer scientist grandmother, she might have given us the grandmotherly advice, "If it's good, it's worth keeping." This is another reason to study abstract data types. If, as we have indicated, the *List* ADT occurs so often in practice, it would make the programming process considerably simpler if we had an implementation of *List* available as a library for later use. Doing so represents a middle ground in language design. We want to extend our language to include higher-level constructs, but we don't want to be placed in the position of having to write a new language. In simple terms, we make our programming job as easy as we can by identifying and designing software modules we can **reuse.**

Our hypothetical computer scientist grandmother has even more to say on this subject: "If it's worth keeping, it should be easy to use." If, for instance, we perceive that the *List* ADT is going to be useful for a wide range of programs, we would like, as much as possible, to be able to plug it into any program with a minimum of effort. One of the things we especially want to avoid is having to make substantial modifications in a program just because we include an implementation of *List.* After all, the point is to make programming easier, not harder. The advantage of the ADT approach is that it encourages us to **encapsulate** useful code into chunks of logically related data structures and algorithms so that any fine-tuning we need to perform will be localized in the ADT and not spread throughout the rest of the program.

ADTs, OOP, and Things to Come

The real power of the **object-oriented programming** (OOP, for short) approach that we see in C++ and similar languages is that such languages include built-in mechanisms for specifying abstract data types. After all, a C++ class is a description of a collection of data, along with operations that may

---

* This is, we admit, an incomplete and inaccurate definition. We'll do it right in Section 1.5, but we didn't want to burden you with details at this stage.

be performed on the data, and that's exactly what we produce when we describe an ADT. Once we've written the *List* ADT as a Lists.h header file of declarations and a Lists.cpp file of function definitions, we can include these in a program and write the program exactly as if lists were part of C++.

In subsequent chapters, we will begin with a linear order as the structural relation, as in Figure 1.2, and gradually weaken the properties of the structural relation to produce less restricted structures. From linear structures we will remove the requirement of unique successors to produce **hierarchical** structures, such as the family tree in Figure 1.3, and from the hierarchical structures we will further remove properties to produce **network** (or **graph**) structures, such as the diagram in Figure 1.4. Eventually, we will arrive at the abstract data type *Set,* which has no structural relation at all on its elements.

1.2   ADT: *INTEGERARRAY*

The first abstract data type we'll consider in detail is based on a C++ data structure you've already seen: the array of integers. This may at first seem a bit like reinventing the wheel; after all, arrays of integers are already built into C++, so why not just use them as they are? There are two very good reasons. First, although you are likely quite proficient at using arrays, you probably haven't given too much thought to what they actually are in terms of a formal definition of the array data structure as an abstract entity. Second, the array structure that C++ provides has several shortcomings; for example, the array indices must start at zero. To represent an array of daily events in a year, we might find it useful to use indices 1 to 366. Since C++ arrays begin at zero, we either have to declare a type DayData[367] and never use index 0 or declare DayData[366] and subtract 1 from the day to get to the proper entry in the array. In addition, many C++ compilers don't check whether the indices you use are within the legal range (unless you tell the compiler to perform such checks for you). Finally, whenever you define an array, you should check whether the system was successful in allocating the necessary amount of space in memory. C++ won't do that checking for you, and trying to access an element in an array when there really isn't an array to access can cause all sorts of catastrophic (and hard-to-fix) consequences.

Our *IntegerArray* abstract data type should be easy enough to understand. The only apparent difference between this type and ordinary C++ arrays of integers is that we don't restrict ourselves to a starting index of zero. Instead, we allow the indices to be any interval of integers, from *lower* to *upper,* as illustrated in Figure 1.5.

FIGURE 1.3
A hierarchical
structure

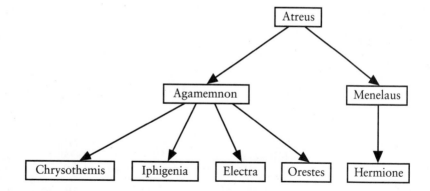

Throughout this text, we will specify each of our abstract data types in
C++ terms, but remember that an abstract data type is *abstract*; it isn't associated with any particular language. We couch our specification in C++ only
because the language is familiar and is well suited for description of ADTs.

IntegerArray

Structure. An array (of integers, in this case) consists of a collection of
positions, each of which "contains" a single array element. Each position has a unique *index*, which is an integer in a continuous range from
lower to *upper*, so for each index *i*, we will have *lower*≤*i*≤*upper*.

Operations

`IntegerArray()`. Constructs a one-element array with index value 0. The
element in position 0 is initialized to the value 0.

`IntegerArray (int up, int low = 0)`. Constructs an array of zeros with indices in the range `low`, . . . , `up`. This requires that *low*≤*up*.

`IntegerArray (int a[], int sz)`. Constructs an *IntegerArray* from an array
of integers. The array *a* is assumed to have indices 0, . . . , *sz*−1, as
will the newly constructed array.

`IntegerArray (const IntegerArray& a)`. A copy constructor, this constructs
a copy of the argument *a*.

FIGURE 1.4
A network structure

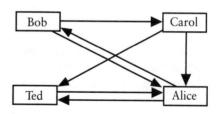

FIGURE I.5

The user's view of an
IntegerArray object

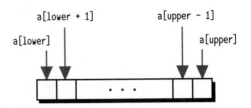

~IntegerArray (). The destructor. This deletes all positions in the array
and leaves *lower* and *upper* undefined.

void SetBounds(int up, int low = 0). Sets the upper and lower indices of
the array, keeping existing data in the old positions, where possible. Note that the new bounds may lie outside the range of the old
bounds (if *low* < *lower* or *upper* < *up*). In that case, the elements in
the new range are initialized to zeros.

IntegerArray& operator= (const IntegerArray& a). Makes this array into a
copy of the array *a* and returns a reference to the new copy.

int& operator[] (int i) const. The array is left unchanged, and a reference
is returned to the element in position *i*. This function requires that *i*
be a legal index, which is to say that we require *lower*≤*i*≤*upper*.

unsigned int Size() const. The array is unchanged, and the number of elements in the array is returned.

int Lower() const. Returns the lower index and leaves the array unchanged.

int Upper() const. Returns the upper index and leaves the array unchanged.

It is now easy enough to turn our specifications into a C++ class declaration. As you read the following header file, notice first that we have enclosed
it within compiler directives.

```
#ifndef INTARRAYS_H
#define INTARRAYS_H
        .
        .
        .
#endif
```

This common practice guards against possible link errors resulting from multiple declarations. We know that every C++ object must be declared before
being used, so in every file that used *IntegerArray*s, we would make the direc-

tive `#include "IntegerArrays.h"`. However, if our program consisted of several files, each of which used *IntegerArrays*, the resulting multiple declarations would lead to errors, since the linker isn't "smart" enough to realize that these multiple declarations are identical.* The directive `#ifndef INTARRAYS_H` instructs the system to check whether the identifier "INTARRAYS_H" has already been defined. If it hasn't, all the lines between `#ifndef` and `#endif` are inserted (since this is the first time the header file has been seen), including the directive `#define INTARRAYS_H`, which defines the term so that it will be recognized next time. However, if "INTARRAYS_H" has been defined, everything between `#ifndef` and `#endif` is ignored, so it will never cause a multiple-declaration error.

We have declared a friend function, `<<`, to allow us to display the contents of an array. Strictly speaking, this operator doesn't need to be a friend, since it could be defined in terms of the *IntegerArray* member functions. We included it, though, to relieve users of this class from the need to write their own output routines.

Notice that the functions *Size, Lower,* and *Upper* and the destructor are sufficiently simple that we have chosen to place their definitions in the header file. The `inline` compiler hint tells the compiler to consider simply placing the compiled code for an `inline` function in place of any function calls, but we use it more as a marker to the reader, since functions that are defined within a class declaration are automatically made `inline`. To save typing, we'll frequently omit the word in future declarations.

Finally, the private part of the class declaration includes the member data we need to implement this class. We keep two integers, *lower* and *upper,* to represent the bounds on the indices, and a pointer, *data,* to the array (in free store) where the elements themselves will be stored, as we illustrate in Figure 1.6. Of

FIGURE 1.6

Internal and external views of an *IntegerArray*

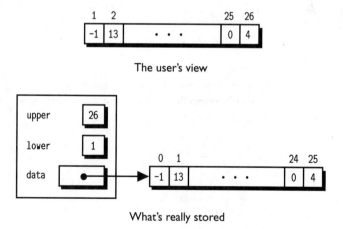

The user's view

What's really stored

---

* Some C++ compilers allow you to request that the linker recognize and ignore such multiple inclusions.

course, the *data* array is an ordinary C++ array with starting index 0, so we
have to do some arithmetic to make sure the indices match up as they should.
You should be able to convince yourself that if *a* is an *IntegerArray*, the element
a[*i*] will be stored in *a.data*[*i* – *lower*].

```
//================ IntegerArrays.h ===============
#ifndef INTARRAYS_H
#define INTARRAYS_H
// A class consisting of arrays of integers, with
// bounds-checking and careful memory management.
// An IntegerArray may have arbitrary upper and lower
// indices.  The array may be grown or shrunk
// by resetting the array bounds.
// NOTE: The upper bound in the constructor and in
// SetBounds is the upper index and not the size.  For
// example, a call to Array(10) will construct an
// 11-element Array with indices 0 .. 10.

#include <iostream.h>

class IntegerArray
{
    friend ostream& operator<< (ostream& os, const IntegerArray& a);
public:
    // Constructors, destructor
    IntegerArray();
    IntegerArray(int up, int low = 0);
    IntegerArray(int a[], int sz);
    IntegerArray(const IntegerArray& a);
    ~IntegerArray ()
        { delete[] data;} ;

    // Modifiers
    void SetBounds(int up, int low = 0);
    IntegerArray& operator= (const IntegerArray& a);
    int& operator[] (int i) const;

    // Access functions
    unsigned int Size() const
        { return (upper - lower + 1);} ;
    int Lower() const
        { return lower;} ;

    int Upper() const
        { return upper;} ;
```

ements to zeros, we set them to the values in the array *a*. We use *Assert* to check that we aren't given meaningless size argument, *sz*, for the array, but we have to leave to the caller the responsibility of ensuring that the size argument is less than or equal to the actual size of the array *a*, since there's no easy way we can check that. Notice that the copy constructor that follows this function is nearly identical, as you would expect, since they do the same thing with different arguments.

```
IntegerArray:: IntegerArray (int a[], int sz)
// Construct a from an array of ints,
// copying elements 0 .. sz - 1.
// NOTE: It is the responsibility of the client to ensure
// that sz is a legal size for a.
{
    Assert(sz > 0, "Impossible size in constructor");
    lower = 0;
    upper = sz - 1;
    data = new int[sz];
    Assert(data != 0, "Out of memory in constructor");

    for (int i = 0; i <= sz - 1; i++)
        data[i] = a[i];
}


IntegerArray:: IntegerArray (const IntegerArray& a)
// copy constructor
{
    lower = a.lower;
    upper = a.upper;
    data = new int[upper - lower + 1];
    Assert(data != 0, "Out of memory in copy constructor");

    for (int i = lower; i <= upper; i++)
        data[i - lower] = a.data[i - lower];
}
```

SetBounds is the most complicated of the *IntegerArray* member functions, largely because there are several ways the new and old bounds can be arranged. We begin by finding the intersection of the old and new ranges: We set *lowMax* to be the larger of the two lower bounds and *upMin* to be the smaller of the two upper bounds. Doing so, we know that the part of the original array that falls within the new bounds will be those positions in the range *lowMax*, . . . , *upMin*. We then allocate a new array and place the original elements where they belong. Finally, we fill any newly created array positions outside the intersection with zeros and make *data* point to the new array. Figure 1.7 illustrates how *SetBounds* works in one case.

FIGURE 1.7

An example of *Set-Bounds*

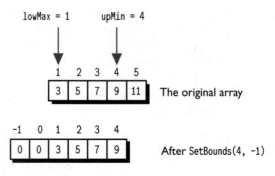

The original array

After SetBounds(4, -1)

```
void IntegerArray::SetBounds(int up, int low)
// Reset the upper and lower bounds, keeping any old
// data that falls within the new bounds and filling any
// new entries with zeros.
{
    Assert(low <= up, "Bad bounds in SetBounds");

    unsigned int newSize = up - low + 1;
    int* newData = new int[newSize];
    Assert(newData != 0, "Out of memory in SetBounds");

    int lowMax, upMin;
    // Find the intersection of old and new ranges.
    if (lower < low)
        lowMax = low;
    else
        lowMax = lower;
    if (upper < up)
        upMin = upper;
    else
        upMin = up;

    // Transfer data from old to new.
    for (int i = lowMax; i <= upMin; i++)
        newData[i - low] = data[i - lower];

    // Fill in new unassigned entries.
    for (i = low; i < lowMax; i++)
        newData[i - low] = 0;
    for (i = up; i > upMin; i--)
        newData[i - low] = 0;

    delete []data;    // Free up old data array,
    data = newData;   // and use the data in the new array.
```

```
      lower = low;
      upper = up;
}
```

As is usually the case, the definition of the assignment operator is almost identical to that of the copy constructor. One difference is that here we check whether the address of *a* is the same as this object. If so, we do nothing, since there's no need to assign to ourself. Otherwise, we destroy the existing *data* array and continue as in the copy constructor, trying to allocate a new *data* array and filling it with the elements of *a*. We finish by returning a reference to the object, so that multiple assignments like `array1 = array2 = array3` will act as they should.

```
IntegerArray& IntegerArray::operator=
                   (const IntegerArray& a)
// Assign one IntegerArray to another.  The object's
// bounds become those of the argument's.
{
    if (this != &a)  // no need to assign to self
    {
        lower = a.lower;
        upper = a.upper;
        delete []data;
        data = new int[upper - lower + 1];
        Assert(data != 0, "Out of memory in assignment");

        for (int i = lower; i <= upper; i++)
            data[i - lower] = a.data[i - lower];
    }
    return *this;
}
```

Finally, to make an *IntegerArray* object act like an ordinary C++ array, we overload the subscript operator []. After checking that the index *i* in the square brackets is legal for this array, all we do is return a reference to the corresponding element in the *data* array.

```
int& IntegerArray::operator[] (int i) const
// overload of subscript operator
{
    Assert((i >= lower) && (i <= upper),
           "Illegal array index in [ ]");

    return (data[i - lower]);
}
```

1.4 CS INTERLUDE: ASSERTIONS AND VERIFICATION

It goes without saying that when we write a program; we want to make it as error-free as possible. Less obvious, perhaps, is that this step should take place when we are thinking of how to write the program in the first place. Why bother, you may wonder, since we'll eventually run the program on a number of sample inputs to see that it works as it should? Testing is a good idea and should always be used, but it suffers from a serious shortcoming. For all but the simplest programs, the number of possible input combinations is so large that we can't be completely sure that a program will work correctly on all possible inputs. We are thus forced into a compromise position: We test a program on a "reasonably large" set of normal inputs and then test the program on a reasonably large set of "pathological" inputs. We might check to see that the program gracefully handles cases of no input, input that is negative when it should be positive, input that is at or beyond the largest values we ever expect to encounter, and so on. But even if a program works flawlessly on all test inputs, we have no guarantee that our test cases cover everything that could happen. There are plenty of documented cases of testing being insufficient, including the error that occurred on October 5, 1960, when the computerized United States radar defense system triggered an alert of a massive enemy attack because the rising moon was interpreted as a wave of incoming ballistic missiles. During the testing phase, everyone was thinking about missiles, and nobody thought to ask, "How will this program react to the moon?" The conclusion is obvious. In the words of Edsger Dijkstra, "Testing can reveal the presence of errors, but never their absence."

Instead of relying only on testing, we should do as much as is practical to **verify** that our program works as it should. Part of this verification is to write our program so that it is as robust as possible, able to handle situations beyond its control, like bad input, as gracefully as possible.

Assertions

We use assertions to increase program robustness. An **assertion** is a logical condition that is assumed to hold at some point of program execution. In a complete verification of a program, there would be an assertion before and after every statement describing the expected state of the program at that time, but we rarely achieve that degree of diligence. In practice, we identify potentially fatal conditions and use a function that takes action when disaster is about to strike.

Because such checking is so useful, we have invented two functions, *Assert* and *Warn,* and placed their descriptions in the files Assertions.h and Assertions.cpp, which we now describe.*

---

* We should mention that there is a C++ library, <assert.h>, that does somewhat the same thing, but not quite in the way we need.

```
//=============== Assertions.h ==============
#ifndef ASSERT_H
#define ASSERT_H

void Assert(int safeCondition, char* errMsg);
void Warn(int safeCondition, char* errMsg);
#endif
```

Assert first checks whether *safeCondition* is true. If it is, *Assert* does nothing. On the other hand, if *safeCondition* is false, *Assert* displays the error message and calls the function *exit* (declared in <stdlib.h>) to halt execution of the program.* *Warn* behaves similarly, but doesn't exit the program.

```
//=============== Assertions.cpp ==============

#include <stdlib.h>  // for exit()
#include "Assertions.h"

void Assert(int safeCondition, char* errMsg)
{
   if (!safeCondition)
   {
      cerr << "***Error: " << errMsg << endl;
      exit(1);
   }
}

void Warn(int safeCondition, char* errMsg)
{
   if (!safeCondition)
      cerr << "***Warning: " << errMsg << endl;
}
```

Verification

It's not always easy to look at a sequence of statements and figure out what they will do, much less prove that they act as designed. One technique that is often helpful is to use a collection of **memory snapshots,** in which we draw boxes representing the contents of variables and update the contents as each

---

* In some versions of C++, the integer argument to *exit* is displayed before the program terminates. This can be useful for debugging, since it can be used to provide information about where in the program *exit* was called.

statement is executed. Consider the following sequence of three assignment statements using integer variables *a* and *b*:

```
// Program segment S
a = a - b;
b = a + b;
a = b - a
```

We've departed from good programming practice here by deliberately making the variable names as unenlightening as possible. We've also chosen a particularly opaque collection of statements, just to make things more interesting.

To trace the execution of such a segment, we draw boxes for each of the variables, representing the memory locations corresponding to the variables. In the following diagram, we fill the *a* box with the unknown value *A* and put another unknown, *B*, in the *b* box. By doing this, we're saying, "We don't know what's in the *a* variable, nor do we care. We do know, though, that it is some integer, so we may as well represent it by *A*, to distinguish it from the variable *a*." We now execute each statement in turn, filling in the memory boxes:

$$a \quad \boxed{A} \qquad\qquad b \quad \boxed{B}$$

```
a = a - b;
```

$$a \quad \boxed{A - B} \qquad\qquad b \quad \boxed{B}$$

```
b = a + b;
```

$$a \quad \boxed{A - B} \qquad b \quad \boxed{(A - B) + B} \; = \; \boxed{A}$$

```
a = b - a;
```

$$a \quad \boxed{A - (A - B)} \; = \; \boxed{B} \qquad\qquad b \quad \boxed{A}$$

We can see that if we have *a* = *A* and *b* = *B* at the start, we'll wind up with *a* = *B* and *b* = *A* after executing the three statements. In simple terms, we've shown that the three statements of *S* swap the values of *a* and *b* for any initial values the variables may have.* In formal notation, we would write our **specification** for the program segment *S* as

```
{(a = A) && (b = B)}  S  {(a = B) && (b = A)}
```

where the notation {P} S {Q} is a short way of representing the sentence "If the **precondition** *P* is true before execution of statements *S*, then the **postcon-**

---

* Actually, that's not quite correct, since if *a* and *b* were very large at the start, the intermediate calculations might produce values that are out of the range of allowable integers.

dition Q will be true after execution." In cases where we make no particular assumption about the precondition P, we will use the form {true} S {Q}, since that's the same as saying, "If true is true (i.e., in any case), then Q is true after execution of S."

We've seen how to trace programs that are more or less static, but how do we guarantee that a loop does what we expect it to do? Showing the correctness of loops is, as you might expect, somewhat more complicated, but it is vitally important, since except in the simplest cases, it's generally not at all obvious what a loop does. If a loop performs a collection of statements repeatedly, modifying its variables as it goes, how can we know what will be true when repetition halts? We need to turn a dynamic situation, in which some action is performed an arbitrary number of times, into a static one, in which some assertion is true and remains so throughout. What we need is a logical expression that remains true at the end of each iteration through a loop. Then we'll have a single statement that, since it's true after each iteration, will also be true when the loop terminates. And that's exactly what we're looking for.

To show this principle in action, consider the following code, intended to produce the sum of the first n odd numbers, $1 + 3 + \cdots + (2n - 1)$.

```
int   sum = 0,
      i = 1;
while (i <= n)
{
   sum = sum + (2 * i - 1);
   i++;
}
```

If we try some sample executions with different values of n, we might notice that it appears that this segment concludes with $sum = n^2$. Can we prove that this is true in general? Yes, we can, because we're lucky enough to discover the **loop invariant** condition, $sum = (i - 1)^2$. This is certainly true before we enter the loop (when $sum = 0$ and $i = 1$), and the trace in Figure 1.8 shows that if the invariant is assumed true at the start of one iteration of the loop, then it will be true at the end of that iteration.

Now we can state what the loop does. If $sum = (i - 1)^2$ is true after each iteration of the loop, and the loop **exit condition** is $i > n$ (so, since the loop counts up, we have $i = n + 1$ when the loop quits), we may combine these two facts to show that after the loop is completed, we must have $sum = (i-1)^2 = ((n+1)-1)^2 = n^2$. Our loop calculates squares, as we guessed.[*]

The process we followed is a common one when tracing the action of loops. We'd be the first to admit that it's not a trivial process, but we'd also add that it's a process that can sometimes be very helpful. As you become

---

[*] The mathematically experienced reader might have observed that using loop invariants to prove an assertion about a loop is similar to a proof by induction.

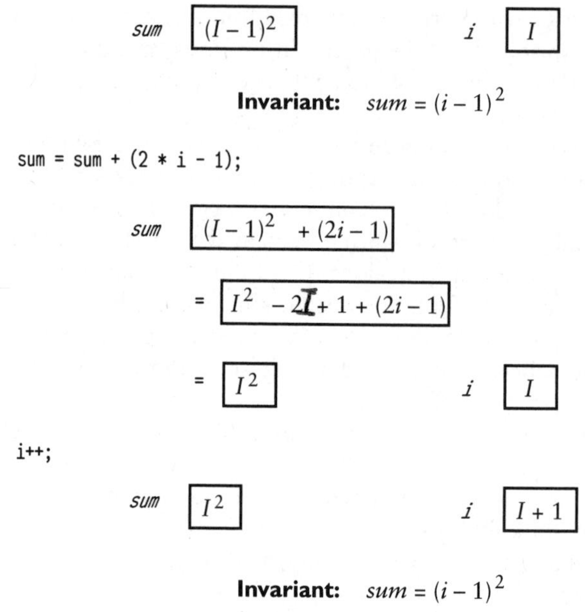

FIGURE 1.8

The loop invariant condition

sum $\boxed{(I-1)^2}$ $\qquad$ i $\boxed{I}$

Invariant: $sum = (i-1)^2$

sum = sum + (2 * i - 1);

sum $\boxed{(I-1)^2 + (2i-1)}$

$=$ $\boxed{I^2 - 2I + 1 + (2i-1)}$

$=$ $\boxed{I^2}$ $\qquad$ i $\boxed{I}$

i++;

sum $\boxed{I^2}$ $\qquad$ i $\boxed{I+1}$

Invariant: $sum = (i-1)^2$

more comfortable with loops, you'll find that you can often take a quick look at a loop and verify that it does what you expect it to do. You'll find, though, that there are times when a loop is not completely transparent. In these cases, the time taken to prove that a loop works correctly pays off as an investment in not having to find and fix errors after they occur.

There is a five-step process we can use to verify that a loop performs as specified. These five steps should be used when designing a loop, as well. While writing a loop, you should make sure that it will terminate. You should have a goal in mind for the loop, and you should write the loop body so that each iteration makes progress toward that goal. Finally, you should convince yourself that the goal will indeed be met when the loop terminates.

To demonstrate that a loop works correctly, follow these five steps:

1. Verify that the loop will eventually reach its exit condition.
2. Perhaps using examples as guides, try to find a condition that holds throughout the life of the loop. Look particularly for one that, when combined with the exit condition, will produce a statement that implies the intended goal of the loop.
3. Show that the condition is true before entering the loop.
4. Trace the loop body to show that if the condition is assumed true at the start of the loop body, then it will be true after the body.
5. Combine the loop condition with the exit condition to produce a statement that is true on completion of the loop.

We admit that complete verification of a program has some problems. First, it generally produces a proof that is at least as long as the program itself.

For very short functions, we can often tell that the program is correct by simple inspection, thereby saving the trouble of a formal verification proof. Second, verification is necessarily more of an art than a science, often requiring some cleverness on our part in finding loop invariants. It would be nice to produce an algorithm that, given a program and preconditions and postconditions, will always generate a proof that the preconditions guarantee that execution of the program will cause the postconditions to be true. Unfortunately (and somewhat surprisingly), that is an impossible task. Our view is that verification is like brushing after every meal: It's unquestionably desirable, but there are times when it's just more trouble than it's worth. The compromise between full verification and practical program design is to identify the potential disasters and use assertions to trap situations that, if allowed to continue, would render the program useless.

1.5 APPLICATION: MULTIPRECISION ARITHMETIC

In this chapter's application, we will use what we have learned about the *IntegerArray* ADT to finish the job we started in Section 1.1, namely, writing a package of routines to support arithmetic on integers of arbitrary length. Although it is clear that arrays are well suited for storing the digits in the number, you'll see that nowhere in the specification of the *Number* ADT is there any mention of arrays. That's as expected. An ADT's description shouldn't burden the reader with details of implementation.

Number

Structure. A *Number* object is an integer of arbitrary size and so has no structure in the conventional sense. For purposes of input and output, however, we will use the customary decimal notation, displaying a positive number as a sequence of digits

$$d_k, d_{k-1}, \ldots, d_2, d_1, d_0,$$

corresponding to the number that has the value

$$d_0 + d_1 10^1 + d_2 10^2 + \cdots + d_{k-1} 10^{k-1} + d_k 10^k$$

where each digit satisfies $0 \le d_i \le 9$. Negative numbers will be displayed in a similar way, with a leading minus sign.

Operations

Number(). Pre: true. (Remember, this means that there is no special precondition.) Post: This number represents the value 0.

`Number(long i)`. Pre: true. Post: This represents the integer *i*.

`Number(const Number& n)`. Pre: true. Post: This number represents the same value as *n*.

`~Number()`. Pre: true. Post: This number is undefined.

`ostream& operator<< (ostream& os, const Number& n)`. Pre: *n* is defined. (To simplify our specifications, we'll assume from now on the requirement that all function arguments are defined.) Post: *n* is unchanged. The decimal representation of *n* is inserted in the ostream *os*, and a reference to *os* is returned.

`istream& operator>> (istream& is, Number& n)`. Pre: *is* contains the decimal representation of a number. Post: *n* represents the number in the istream, and the corresponding characters have been extracted from *is*. The operator returns a reference to *is*.

`Number operator+ (const Number& n, const Number& m)`. Pre: true. Post: *n* and *m* are unchanged, and the operator returns a number representing the sum *n+m*.

`Number operator- (const Number& n, const Number& m)`. Pre: true. Post: *n* and *m* are unchanged and the operator returns a number representing the difference *n−m*.

`Number operator- (const Number& n)`. Pre: true. Post: *n* is unchanged, and the operator returns a number representing the negation, *−n*, of the argument.

`Number operator* (const Number& n, const Number& m)`. Pre: true. Post: *n* and *m* are unchanged, and the operator returns a number representing the product *n * m*.

(We leave specification of the operations /, %, ++, and -- as exercises.)

`int operator== (const Number& n, const Number& m)`. Pre: true. Post: *n* and *m* are unchanged, and the operator returns 1 if *n* and *m* represent the same number and 0 otherwise.

(We leave specification of !=, <, >, <=, and >= as exercises.)

`Number& operator= (const Number& n)`. Pre: true. Post: *n* is unchanged, and the operator returns a reference to a copy of *n*.

(We leave specification of +=, -=, *=, /=, and %= as exercises.)

`int Length()`. Pre: true. Post: Returns the number of digits in the decimal representation of this number.

It's worth observing that in the specifications for *Number*, we have used reference arguments for nearly all of our functions. You know, of course, that when we want a function to modify one of its arguments, the argument should be a reference. If the argument isn't to be modified, we could call it by value, as `Number n`, rather than going to the trouble of writing the argument as a reference to a constant object, `const Number& n`. The reason we encourage reference arguments for most functions is that many of the objects we'll be defining in this text will be fairly large; using references as a matter of course eliminates the hidden overhead of the system making a copy of the argument just so it can be passed to a function.

Declaring the *Number* Class

In the declaration file of the *Number* class, we have chosen to define many of the operations as friends rather than member functions. We did this primarily for comprehension. Remember that an object's member function has the object itself as an implicit first argument, whereas there are no implicit arguments for friend functions—what you see is exactly what's there. If we had overloaded the operator+ as a member function, we would have had to declare it as `Number operator+ (const Number& n)`, which obscures the fact that addition takes two arguments.

We have also declared three private auxiliary functions, *IsZero, AddPos,* and *SubPos*. We could have dispensed with the latter two at the cost of complicating the addition and subtraction operators. If you think about it, addition (and subtraction, for that matter) by the grade school algorithm is really a two-part process. We first have to look at the signs of the numbers. If they are the same, we can add in the usual way; but if they are different, we perform the appropriate subtraction rather than an addition. The functions *AddPos* and *SubPos* "separate out" the addition or subtraction of positive integers, leaving addition proper, for instance, just to check the signs and call the appropriate function.

Finally, the private part of the declaration contains the member data needed for this class: an *IntegerArray* to store the digits and an integer to store the number of digits in our number (which may not necessarily be related to the size of the *digit* array). In this implementation, we will store the sign of the number in *digit*[0], and for reasons of convenience, we will keep the actual digits in increasing place order, as we illustrate in Figure 1.9.

FIGURE 1.9

Our implementation of the *Number* representing −9312

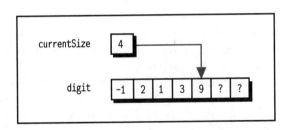

```
//================ Numbers.h ================

#ifndef NUMBERS_H
#define NUMBERS_H
#include <iostream.h>
#include "IntegerArrays.h"

class Number
{
    friend istream& operator>>
            (istream& s, Number& n);
    friend ostream& operator<<
            (ostream& s, const Number& n);

    friend Number operator+ (const Number& n, const Number& m);
    friend Number operator- (const Number& n, const Number& m);
    friend Number operator- (const Number& n);
    friend Number operator* (const Number& n, const Number& m);

    friend int operator== (const Number& n, const Number& m);

public:
    Number();               // Initialize a number to zero.
    Number(long i);         // Initialize/typecast long to Number.
    Number(const Number& n); // copy constructor
    int Length() const {  return currentSize;} ;

private:
    int currentSize;     // current number of digits (> 0)
    IntegerArray digit; // the digit array
    int IsZero() const
            { return (digit[currentSize == 0);} ;
    // Add two positive Numbers.
    void AddPos(const Number& n, const Number& m);
    // Subtract two positive numbers: n - m.
    void SubPos(const Number& n, const Number& m);
} ;
#endif
```

Notice that although they appear in the specification, there is no mention in the declaration of either an assignment operator or a destructor. That's because C++ will generate these functions for you if they're not declared. The generated assignment operator performs a memberwise copy of the class object, using any assignment overloads that have been declared for the member data. That's why we can get away with not writing an assignment here but couldn't with the *IntegerArray* class. We don't want just to copy the pointer to the *data* array; rather, we want to create a new array with the same values. The generated destructor, similarly, calls (or generates) destructors for all the member data, so it will call the destructor for *digit* that we defined in the *IntegerArray* class.

Finally, notice the definition of *IsZero*. To test whether a number is zero, we inspect the high-order digit, since the only possible representation for zero in this implementation is the number with *currentSize* = 1 and *digit*[1] = 0.

Defining the *Number* Class

The first function we define in Numbers.cpp is the friend overload of the insertion operator, >>. We begin by getting characters (up to the first return, which *getline* then discards) from standard input and placing them in the array *instr*. We then find the number of characters we read and place their numeric equivalents in the *digit* array.

```cpp
//================ Numbers.cpp ================

#include "Numbers.h"
#include <iostream.h>

istream& operator>> (istream& s, Number& n)
// NOTE: The Number must be sent as a reference,
// since it's modified as a side effect.
{
   const MAX_CHARS = 80;
   char instr[MAX_CHARS];
   // Fill the input array with null characters.
   for (int i = 0; i < MAX_CHARS; i++)
      instr[i] = '\ 0';

   s.getline(instr, MAX_CHARS);

   int isNegative = 0;
   if (instr[0] == '-')  // Test for negative input.
      isNegative = 1;

   i = 0;
   while (instr[i++])    // Find input length.
      ;
      // i now refers to the second null past the end.

   if (isNegative)
   {
      n.currentSize = i - 2;
      n.digit.SetBounds(n.currentSize);
```

```
        for (i = 1; i <= n.currentSize; i++)
            n.digit[n.currentSize - i + 1] = int(instr[i] - '0');
        n.digit[0] = -1;
    }
    else
    {
        n.currentSize = i - 1;
        n.digit.SetBounds(n.currentSize);
        for (i = 0; i < n.currentSize; i++)
            n.digit[n.currentSize - i] = int(instr[i] - '0');
        n.digit[0] = 1;
    }
    return s;
}
```

As is often the case, it is easier to define the insertion operator, <<. All we do is display a negative sign if the number is negative and then display the rest of the *digit* array, from highest place order to lowest.

```
ostream& operator<< (ostream& s, const Number& n)
{
    if (n.digit[0] < 0)
        s << '-';

    for (int i = n.currentSize; i > 0; i--)
        s << n.digit[i];

    return s;
}
```

We mentioned before that the addition overload leaves the actual addition or subtraction to the private functions *AddPos* and *SubPos*. All that addition does is check the signs of the numbers to be added and, depending on which of the four possible cases applies, call the appropriate function to finish the job. The subtraction operator is even simpler. Because we have a negation operator, all it takes to find the difference $n-m$ is to compute the sum $n+(-m)$.

```
Number operator+ (const Number& n, const Number& m)
{
    Number r;
    if (n.digit[0] > 0)
        if (m.digit[0] > 0)
            r.AddPos(n, m);        // n > 0, m > 0
        else
            r.SubPos(n, -m);       // n > 0, m < 0
```

```
      else
         if (m.digit[0] > 0)
            r.SubPos(m, -n);        // n < 0, m > 0
         else
         {
            r.AddPos(-n, -m);       // n < 0, m < 0
            r.digit[0] = -1;
         }
      return r;
}


Number operator- (const Number& n, const Number& m)
{
   Number r = n + (-m);
   return r;
}
```

One advantage of this **sign-magnitude representation** is that negation is trivial, requiring only that we invert the sign in *digit*[0]. The only other thing we do is check whether the number is zero and make sure that the sign is positive if it is (so we'll never display "–0").

```
Number operator- (const Number& n)
// Unary negation.  This does not change the value
// of its argument.
{
   Number r = n;                 // Copy n into the return value.
   if (r.IsZero())               // Handle zero separately.
      r.digit[0] = 1;
   else
      r.digit[0] = -r.digit[0]; // Flip the sign digit,

   return r;                     // and return the result.
}
```

To multiply two numbers, we use the algorithm we all learned in elementary school. The only difference is that we don't write down the partial products we get from each digit; instead we accumulate the partial products in a single number r, which eventually becomes the full product. Figure 1.10 illustrates one step in a typical multiplication, where we are about to include the contribution of the 7 in 847 and the 2 in 256. (For ease of reading, we haven't shown the sign digits of the numbers, and we have reversed the order of digits in all the numbers.) Notice that the ith digit of n and the jth digit of m influence the $(i+j-1)$th digit in the product.

We use a pair of nested loops, one running through the digits of n and the other running through the digits of m, to form the product, after using *SetBounds* to make r's *digit* array as large as it could possibly be. At each

FIGURE 1.10

One step in computing
847×256

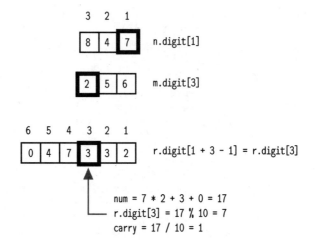

stage, we compute *num,* which is $n.digit[i] * m.digit[j] + r.digit[i+j-1] + carry$. We then use *num* % 10 to get the new *r* digit and *num*/10 to get the carry. We repeat this process for all possible digits and conclude by setting the *currentSize* of *r* to either *n.currentSize* + *m.currentSize* (if the last carry was more than zero) or *n.currentSize* + *m.currentSize* − 1 (if there was no final carry).

```
Number operator* (const Number& n, const Number& m)
// Multiplies two numbers.
{
   Number r;  // Initialize product to zero.

   // Handle zero product separately, since it's easy.
   if (n.IsZero() || m.IsZero())
      return r;

   // Make r as large as it could possibly be.
   r.digit.SetBounds(n.currentSize + m.currentSize);
   // Set sign of product.
   r.digit[0] = n.digit[0] * m.digit[0];

   // Multiply by elementary school algorithm.
   intnum = 0;
   for (int i = 1; i <= n.currentSize; i++)
   {
      int carry = 0;
      for (int j = 1; j <= m.currentSize; j++)
      {
         num = n.digit[i] * m.digit[j] + r.digit[i + j - 1] + carry;
         r.digit[i + j - 1] = num % 10;
         carry = num / 10;
      }
```

```
        r.digit[i + j - 1] = carry;
    }
    r.digit[n.currentSize + m.currentSize] = carry;

    // Adjust the size of the product if needed.
    if (carry > 0)
        r.currentSize = n.currentSize + m.currentSize;
    else
        r.currentSize = n.currentSize + m.currentSize - 1;

    return r;
}
```

Compared with multiplication, testing for equality is easy. Because we can subtract and test for zero, all we have to do is see if $n-m$ is zero. If it is, we know that $n == m$. Enough said.

```
int operator== (const Number& n, const Number& m)
// Compares two Numbers for equality.
// n == m iff n - m == 0
{
    Number temp = n - m;
    return (temp.IsZero());
}
```

The default constructor sets this number to zero. In the **initialization list** in the header, we call the constructor, *digit*(1), for the *digit* member datum to initialize it to a two-element array of zeros, indexed by 0 and 1 and we call *current*(1) to set the *current* member datum to 1. Having done that, all we have to do is set the sign digit, *digit*[0], of this number to 1.

```
Number::Number() : digit(1), current(1)
// Initialize a Number to zero.
{
    digit[0] = 1;
}
```

To construct a number from a long integer *i,* we extract the digits of *i* by repeatedly getting the quotient *i* % 10 and then removing that digit from *i* by using the expression *i*/10. For example, if we start with *i*=379, we see that *i* % 10 is the digit 9 and *i*/10 is 37. Repeating the process with 37 gives us the digit 7 and the new *i* of 3. The last iteration gives the digit 3 and the new *i* of 0, at which point we know we're done. Notice that we begin in the initialization list by calling the constructor for *digit,* setting the *digit* array to 21 zeros, which should certainly be large enough to hold the digits of any long integer we're given.

```
Number::Number(long i) : digit(20)
// Initialize this Number to a given long.
{
    // Set the sign digit.
    if (i < 0)
    {
        digit[0] = -1;
        n = -n;
    }
    else
        digit[0] = 1;

    // Fill the digit array.
    currentSize = 0;
    do
    {
        digit[++currentSize] = i % 10;  // Get the digit,
        i /= 10;                        // remove it from i.
    } while (i > 0);
}
```

The copy constructor has very little to do. In the initialization list, we call the copy constructor for the *digit* member datum, so all the function body has to do is copy the *currentSize* datum.

```
Number::Number(const Number& n) : digit(n.digit)
: digit(n.digit), currentSize(n.currentSize)
// Copy constructor.
{
}
```

Addition of positive numbers looks more complicated than it really is, mainly because addition has two phases: adding all digits in those places where both numbers have digits, followed by propagating the carry through the remaining digits of the longer number.

```
void Number::AddPos(const Number& n, const Number& m)
// For positive n, m, sets this object to n + m.
{
    int largeSize,      // size of the longer of n, m
        smallSize;      // size of the shorter of n, m
    if (n.currentSize > m.currentSize)
        largeSize = n.currentSize;
    else
        largeSize = m.currentSize;
    smallSize = n.currentSize + m.currentSize - largeSize;
```

```
    // Make this Number as large as it could become.
    digit.SetBounds(largeSize + 1);
    digit[0] = 1;     // Set the sign digit.

    int carry = 0, num = 0;
    // Add through the digits in the shorter number.
    for (currentSize = 1; currentSize <= smallSize; currentSize++)
    {
        num = n.digit[currentSize] + m.digit[currentSize] + carry;
        carry = num / 10;
        digit[currentSize] = num % 10;
    }

    // Now add the remaining digits in the longer number.
    for (currentSize = smallSize + 1;
         currentSize <= largeSize; currentSize++)
    {
        if (largeSize == n.currentSize)
          num = n.digit[currentSize] + carry;
        else
          num = m.digit[currentSize] + carry;
        carry = num / 10;
        digit[currentSize] = num % 10;
    }

    // Finally, propagate the last carry, if any.
    if (carry)
        digit[currentSize] = carry;
    else
        currentSize--;
}
```

Subtraction of two positive numbers is the most complicated of the *Number* member functions. Unlike addition of positive numbers, subtraction seems complex because it truly is. Think about it. Assume that we know how the digit manipulation part works. What still has to be done to compute $n-m$ for positive numbers?

1. Find out which number has more digits.

    a. If they have different lengths:

        i. If n is longer, remember that the sign of the result will be positive.
        ii. If m is longer, remember that the sign of the result will be negative.

    b. If they have the same length, find which represents a larger number.

        i. If they represent the same number, the difference is zero. Return zero.

        ii. If *n* is larger, remember that the sign of the result will be positive.

        iii. If *m* is larger, remember that the sign of the result will be negative.

2. Do the subtraction of (longer/larger)–(shorter/smaller).

    a. Construct the result, reserving as many digits as the larger/longer number.

    b. For the length of the smaller number, subtract digit by digit, borrowing as you go up in place value.

    c. For the remainder of the digits in the larger number, propagate the borrows until no borrowing is necessary.

3. Set the sign of the result.

4. The number may have shrunk during subtraction; that is, the difference may have fewer digits than the longer/larger number. If so, adjust the size of the result.

That's just what we do in the following function, as a careful perusal will verify. We leave as an exercise what it is that the variable *signDigit* does; but the rest of the function is just the C++ version of the preceding steps.

```
void Number::SubPos(const Number& n, const Number& m)
// For positive n, m, sets this object to n - m.
{
    //---------- Find the larger of the two arguments.
    int i, largeSize, smallSize, signDigit;
    if (n.currentSize != m.currentSize)
    {
        if (n.currentSize > m.currentSize)
            largeSize = n.currentSize;
        else
            largeSize = m.currentSize;
        smallSize = n.currentSize + m.currentSize - largeSize;
        signDigit = 2 * (largeSize == n.currentSize) - 1;
    }
    else
    {
        i = largeSize = smallSize = n.currentSize;
        // Starting from the high-order digit,
        // find the first place where the digits
        // are unequal.
```

```
      while ((i > 0) && (n.digit[i] == m.digit[i]))
        i--;
      if (i == 0)   // Difference is zero--dump out.
      {
        currentSize = 1;
        digit[0] = 1;
        digit[1] = 0;
        return;
      }
      else
        signDigit = 2 * (n.digit[i] > m.digit[i]) - 1;
  }


  // Subtract large - small in the conventional way.
  digit.SetBounds(largeSize);
  int borrow = 0,
      num;

  for (i = 1; i <= smallSize; i++)
  {
      num = borrow + signDigit * (n.digit[i] - m.digit[i]);
      digit[i] = (10 + num) % 10;
      if (num < 0)
        borrow = -1;
      else
        borrow = 0;
  }

  for (i = smallSize + 1; i <= largeSize; i++)
      if (signDigit == 1)
      {
        digit[i] = (10 + borrow + n.digit[i]) % 10;
        borrow = (((borrow + n.digit[i]) < 0) ? -1 : 0);
      }
      else
      {
        digit[i] = (10 + borrow + m.digit[i]) % 10;
        borrow = (((borrow + m.digit[i]) < 0) ? -1 : 0);
      }

  currentSize = largeSize;
  digit[0] = signDigit;

  // Tidy up if the number shrank during subtraction.
  while (digit[currentSize] == 0)
      currentSize--;
}
```

1.6 SUMMARY

An abstract data type is an abstraction of the means of organizing data in a program. The use of abstract data types provides a middle ground between an informal description of the logical arrangement of information and the data structures used for the storage of information in a program. An abstract data type consists of three aspects: (1) an underlying set, *Atom*, and a set, *Position*, of possible positions into which to place the atoms; (2) a collection of objects with a common internal structure; and (3) a collection of structure-preserving operations on these elements.

The C++ array type has several shortcomings, like lack of index verification and lack of careful memory management, which we addressed by defining the *IntegerArray* ADT. We used the class based on this type to implement the *Number* class and represent integers that were larger than we could deal with using the built-in C++ data types. This process exemplifies a standard practice in modern programming, namely, using the data types provided by the language to make structures that extend the language in ways that are useful for our applications. Object-oriented languages like C++ are particularly well suited for this kind of extension because they provide a class structure and generally a file organization that, respectively, allow us to abstract the important parts of a data structure and encapsulate these definitions for later use.

An important part of the programming process is to verify our programs as we are designing them. Using memory snapshots to hand-trace code and loop invariants to further help us show that loops do what they should is an indispensable part of the programming process. We should always test our programs on sample inputs, but testing is almost never a substitute for proving that a program is correct.

For an explanation of representing numbers, refer to Donald Knuth, *The Art of Computer Programming*, vol. 2, *Seminumerical Algorithms* (Reading, MA: Addison-Wesley, 1968). This three-volume set (more to come, we hope) is the standard reference in computer science. If you don't own all three, you should. For a readable account of RSA-129, see Brian Hayes, "The Magic Words are Squeamish Ossifrage," *American Scientist* 82 (July–August 1994): 312–316.

1.7 EXERCISES

1. Terry Winograd developed a program called SHRDLU that was intended to model a simple "world" consisting of children's blocks of various shapes and colors. Among other things, SHRDLU was designed to simulate manipulation of the blocks by picking them up and

placing them elsewhere. Give a specification of the abstract data type *Blocks,* keeping in mind such properties as color, shape, "on top of," and so on.

2. One way to describe the structure of a collection of positions in an ADT is to couch the description in terms of **successors** and **predecessors** of positions. We can illustrate this graphically, using boxes for positions and arrows for immediate successors, as shown here for a position with one predecessor and two successors:

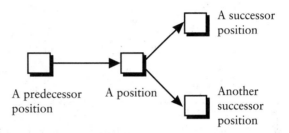

To describe the structure of an ADT, then, we provide a collection of properties that the predecessors and successors must satisfy. For example, in a linear structure like *List,* every position must have at most one successor and at most one predecessor.

a. Show that the single property we have just given for *List* isn't sufficient to describe a linear structure, by drawing pictures of structures that satisfy the property but shouldn't be called lists.

b. Give a collection of structural properties that will describe a linear structure.

c. A **totally binary tree** has a structure defined by the following rules:

1. There is exactly one position, called the **root,** that has no predecessor.

2. Except for the root, each position has exactly one predecessor.

3. Every position has either no successors or exactly two.

Draw pictures of some totally binary trees. How many positions can such an object have?

d. Give a condition on the positions of an object that will guarantee that the object is **connected,** in the ordinary sense of the term.

3. Continuing the investigation of Exercise 2, we can define the **ancestor** of a position by saying that x is an ancestor of p if and only if either (1) $x = p$ or (2) x is a predecessor to y and y is an ancestor of p. In the following structure (the **lattice** of divisors of 12, specifically), the ancestors of the position containing 2 are the positions containing 2 itself, 4, 6, and 12.

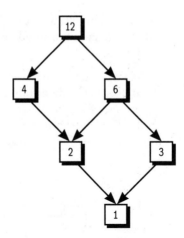

a. The **join** of two positions is defined to be the first common ancestor of the positions, so the join of 2 and 6 in the structure shown here is 6, and the join of 3 and 4 is 12. Give a precise definition of *join*.

b. In the structure shown here, every pair of positions has a unique join. That's one of the defining properties of a lattice structure and needn't be true in general. Draw a structure in which there are two positions that have more than one join.

c. Draw the lattice of divisors of 120 (counting 1 and 120, there are 16 divisors). If you're careful, you can draw it in a form that's as pretty as the picture shown here. It looks like a stack of three blocks.

d. For lattices of divisors, the value in the join of two positions has another name. If n and m are the values stored in two positions, what value is associated with their join?

4. Repeat Exercise 3 in reverse, defining x to be the **descendant** of p if p is an ancestor of x and defining the **meet** of two positions to be their first common descendant (you don't have to redraw the lattice of divisors of 120).

5. Provide definitions for the structure of the following ADTs.

a. *Set,* under the usual interpretation of the word.

b. *Bag,* also called **multiset**, which is similar to *Set,* except that elements are allowed to occur more than once in each object. Thus, $\{a, a, b, c, c, c\}$ is a legal bag, but would not be a legal set.

c. *Ring,* in which the elements are arranged in a circle. This is commonly used to handle jobs on several terminals that are waiting to use a single central computer. We often single out a position as the **current** one, where all insertion, inspection, and deletion take place. The current position can be moved by advancing it one place in the ring.

6. (a–c) Give a reasonable collection of operations on the structures in Exercise 5.

7. (a–c) Provide declarations of classes corresponding to the ADTs in Exercise 5.

8. Write a definition of the *IntegerArray* output operator << as an **external** function; that is, do what the user of this class would have to do if (1) we hadn't written the operator in our class and (2) the user was forbidden to modify our class.

9. Since we have such a nice array structure in *IntegerArray*, could we use it to save its own data? In other words, could we change the *IntegerArray* declaration's private part to look like this?

```
private:
    int   lower,
          upper;
    IntegerArray data;
```

10. Why does the *IntegerArray* subscript operator return a reference to an int? Why couldn't we just return the value in the *data* array?

11. Give the preconditions and postconditions for the following functions.
    a. `void Sort(IntegerArray& a)`, which sorts the elements of *a* in increasing order.
    b. `int Mindex(IntegerArray a, int from, int to)`, which returns the index of the minimal element in the part of the array *a[from]*, . . . , *a[to]*. If there is more than one smallest element, it doesn't matter which one's index is returned.
    c. `int FirstMindex(IntegerArray a, int from, int to)`, which returns the index of the minimal element in the part of the array *a[from]*, . . . , *a[to]*. If there is more than one, the smallest index of all minimal elements is returned.

12. (a–c) In the functions in Exercise 11, what calls to *Assert* would be appropriate?

13. Find the exit conditions of the following loops. In other words, tell what must be true upon exit from each loop. You may assume that all variables have been declared. Be careful. Remember, the loop body may modify the variables in the control expression.
    a.
```
while (i < 5)
{ . . . }
```
    b.
```
int i = -10;
while (i++)
{ . . . }
```

c.   do
```
{ ... }
while ((i < j) && (a[i] == 0));
```
d.
```
for (int i = 1; i < 20; i *= 2)
{ ... }
```

14. Find a simple way to describe what this code segment does, and use memory snapshots to prove that it does what you say it does. (The function *abs* returns the absolute value of its argument, so *abs*(3) is 3 and *abs*(−3) is also 3.)

```
p = (a + b + abs(a - b)) / 2;
q = a + b - p;
```

15. For the following loops, find the best loop invariants you can in that the loop invariant, together with the loop exit condition, will imply the postcondition. Prove that your invariant is indeed an invariant in that if it is true at the start of each iteration, it is then true after.

a.
```
int i = 0;
while (i < 10)
    i++;
// Post: i = 9
```

b.
```
int   found = 0,
      done = 0;
      i = 0;
while (!done)
{
  if (i > 100)
     done = 1;
  else if (a[i] == x)
  {
     done = 1;
     found = 1;
  }
  else
     i++;
}
// Post: (found && (a[i] == x)) || (!found)
```

c.
```
int min = a[0] + 1,
    i = 0,
where = i;
while (i <= to)
{
  if (a[i] < min)
  {
     min = a[i];
```

```
            where = i;
        }
        i++;
    }
    // Post: (0 ≤ where ≤ to) && (a[where] ≤ a[i], for
    // all i, 0 ≤ i ≤ to)
```

16. As we said, we invented the *Number* class because the C++ int and long types don't permit us to represent very large numbers. Precisely, what's the largest number that can be represented in 32 binary digits? Using the common form of representation, that's the binary number we'd write as a sequence of 32 1s—that is, 11111111111111111111111111111111.

17. Compute RSA-129.

18. Using the *Number* class, write and test programs that compute the following.

    a. 2^{512}. *Hint*: There is a way to do this that is not the first one you'd think of, but which is quite a bit faster than the obvious way.

    b. 100!, which is called "100 factorial" and is equal to $1 \times 2 \times \cdots \times 99 \times 100$.

    c. F_{100}, the 100th term in the sequence of *Fibonacci numbers*, which is defined by

    $$F_0 = 1, \quad F_1 = 1, \quad \text{and} \quad F_n = F_{n-1} + F_{n-2}, \quad \text{for } n > 1$$

    In other words, after the first two terms, each subsequent term is the sum of the two preceding ones. For example, the first few terms of this sequence are 1, 1, 2 (=1+1), 3 (=2+1), 5 (=3+2), 8, 13, 21, 34, 55, 89, 144. *Hint*: The apparently clever way of doing this is hideously inefficient.

19. In our implementation, how big is a *Number* object? In other words, how much memory is needed to store the representation of –9312? Assume that integers require 2 bytes and pointers 4.

20. In the description of the *Number* member function *SubPos*, there are five different cases for the inputs *n* and *m*. Give an example of each. For instance, the case where the numbers are equal could be illustrated by $n=123, m=123$.

21. In the definition of *SubPos*, what is the purpose of the variable *signDigit*? In particular, what's the reason for the statement

    ```
    subPos = 2 * (largeSize == n.currentSize) - 1;
    ```

22. Provide specifications for the *Number* operations we omitted in the text.

    a. !=, <, >, <=, >=

    b. /, %

    c. +=, -=, *=, /=, %=

    d. ++, -- (in both prefix and postfix forms. Deciding on the return type will probably be the hardest part of this exercise.)

23. (a–d) Provide C++ declarations for the operators of Exercise 22.

24. (a–d) Provide definitions for the operators of Exercise 22.

25. Write definitions for the following *Number* functions.

    a. `friend Number Abs(const Number& n)`, which returns the absolute value of n.

    b. `friend Number Random(int k)`, which returns a number of length k whose digits have been chosen randomly. *Hint*: Look up the definition of the function *rand* in `<stdlib.h>`. You might need to modify the argument list of *Random*.

    c. `friend int IsOdd(const Number& n)`, which returns 1 if n is odd and returns 0 otherwise.

    d. `friend Number Power(const Number& n, long p)`, which returns n^p. You may assume for this exercise that $p \geq 0$.

26. Discover another reason why we didn't overload + as a member function by writing the definition of the member function declared as

```
Number operator+ (const Number& n);
```

    Hint: There are several decisions you need to make here: Should + add n to this number or just return the result of adding n to this number? In each case, what would a call to this operator look like? How would you use this operator in a complicated expression?

27. **a.** Write the member function `Number Reverse()`, which returns the reverse of this number, so that if $n=4723$, $n.Reverse(\ )$ will return 3274.

    b. Use *Reverse* to write the function `int Palindrome(const Number& n)`, which returns 1 if and only if n is a **palindrome**, that is, if n reads the same left to right as right to left, as do 454 and 3553.

    c. An interesting problem that appeared on "Square One" (a Public Broadcasting System show about mathematics for kids) is the following: Take a starting number, add it to its reverse, and continue this process until the result is a palindrome. For example, starting with 95, we add it to its reverse to get $95+59=154$. Add this to its reverse and we get $154+451=605$. Add this to its reverse and we have $605+506=1111$, which is a palindrome, after three iterations. Write a program to count the number of iterations this process takes to produce a palindrome, and try it for some starting values. As a reality check, for the starting value 98 it takes 24 iterations and results in the palindrome 8,813,200,023,188. Don't even think about trying it on 295; if that ever results in a palindrome, the result is at least 4500 digits long.

d. (Unknown) Does the process in part (c) always result in a palindrome for any starting value? Send us a proof and we promise to share credit with you.

28. What changes would you have to make in *Number* to represent numbers in **base n,** so, for instance, a base-8 (or **octal**) number would be represented by a sum

$$d_0 + d_1 8^1 + d_2 8^2 + \cdots + d_{k-1} 8^{k-1} + d_k 8^k$$

For example, the number we represent as 233 would have the base-8 representation 351, since $233 = 3 \times 64 + 5 \times 8 + 1$.

29. In Exercise 28, we showed that 233 has base-8 representation 351. You can show that 351 (considered now as an ordinary base-10 number), is 15F in base 16 (using A, . . . , F to represent the "digits" 10, . . . , 15). Define a function $B(n)$ that carries out this process. Informally, we'd have:

```
char* B(char* n)
{
    Convert n to a base-8 number m;
    Consider m as a base-10 number and convert it
      to a base-16 number p;
    return p;
}
```

a. Show that $B(\text{``66''}) = \text{``66''}$.

b. Find some other digit strings, *s,* for which $B(s) = s$.

c. (Unknown) Find *all* digit strings, *s,* for which $B(s) = s$.

30. In the base *n* representation in Exercise 28, there is no reason why *n* must be a positive number. In particular, we could define base (–2) representation, writing each number as a sum of powers of –2:

$$d_0 + d_1 (-2)^1 + d_2 (-2)^2 + \cdots + d_{k-1} (-2)^{k-1} + d_k (-2)^k$$

where each digit d_i is either 0 or 1. For example, we could write 47 as 1110011, since

$$47 = 1 + 1 \times (-2) + 0 \times (4) + 0 \times (-8) + 1 \times (16) + 1 \times (-32) + 1 \times (64)$$

a. In base (–2) notation, count from –15 to 15.

b. Represent –47, 861, –1024, and 1722 in base (–2).

c. What numbers have base (–2) representation 110101, 111, 1111, and 101010100?

  d. Invent an algorithm for finding the base (–2) representation of a number. *Hint*: Consider the algorithm for finding the binary (base 2) representation.

  e. There's a very cute way to add numbers in this notation. Find it.

  f. A nice feature of base (–2) notation is that no number requires a minus sign. Invent an algorithm for negating numbers in this notation and use it to negate the numbers in part (c).

1.8   EXPLORATIONS

Representation of Integers

Our decision about how to represent integers in the implementation of *Number* was by no means the only possible one. The representation we chose is known as **sign-magnitude**, meaning that the digits represent the absolute value of the number and we keep an extra data member for the sign. This causes some difficulties in the implementation, since addition and subtraction have to be handled as separate cases. So? That's how we were taught in school, and Miss Pedicord wouldn't have lied to us. It happens, though, that there are equally good ways of representing integers, making use of the trivial observation that $-1 \times 10 = -10$. In our positional representation, this means that if we allow negative digits, we can express -4 as $(-1 \times 10) + 6$ or $(-1)\,6$, and observing that $-100 + 90 + 10 = (-1) \times 100 + (9) \times 10 + 10 = 0$, we can represent -67 as $(-1)\,3\,3$:

$$
\begin{array}{rccc}
 & (-1) & 9 & (10) \\
- & 0 & 6 & 7 \\
\hline
\end{array}
$$

$$
\begin{array}{rcccccc}
 & (-1) & 9 & (10) & = & & 0 \\
+ & 0 & (-6) & (-7) & = & + & (-67) \\
\hline
 & (-1) & 3 & 3 & = & & -67
\end{array}
$$

In this **tens complement notation**, we represent the negation of the number

$$d_k d_{k-1} \ldots d_1 d_0$$

by first **complementing** the digits, to form the number

$$\left(d_k - 9\right)\left(d_{k-1} - 9\right)\ldots\left(d_1 - 9\right)\left(d_0 - 9\right)$$

and then adding 1 to the complement in the usual way. In essence, we've moved the sign bit to the high end of the number, since a negative number will have -1 as its high-order digit and a positive number will have 0.

31. Demonstrate how tens complement notation works by giving the representation of −582, -9999, −1010, and −0.

32. What numbers are represented by these tens complement digit lists?

$$-1, 2 \quad -1, 9 \quad -1, 7, 8 \quad -1, 9, 9, 9 \quad 0, 0$$

33. The advantage of tens complement notation is that in addition and subtraction, we don't have to concern ourselves with the signs of the arguments.* Show that the ordinary addition algorithm can be used for subtraction by computing the following differences.

 a. $788 + (−582)$

 b. $401 + (−582)$

 c. $582 + (−582)$

34. Now multiply the numbers in Exercise 33 and show that multiplication works, too, regardless of the sign of the arguments (with a little care).

35. Think carefully about whether it's worth it to change *Number* to use this representation. Give reasons for and against.

36. Modify *Number* so that integers are represented internally in tens complement form. You might have to add some functions to the class and remove some that are no longer necessary.

Bit Vectors

A **bit vector** is an array where the elements can only have the values 1 and 0. Bit vectors are useful for a number of applications, such as representing sets of integers. For example, to represent a set chosen from the **universe** of possible values $n, \ldots, m$, we could use a bit vector $b[n], \ldots, b[m]$, where we indicate that j is in the set by setting $b[j] = 1$, and we indicate that j isn't in the set by setting $b[j] = 0$. For example, in the universe $1, \ldots, 32$, the set {1, 5, 19, 20, 23, 30} would be represented by the bit vector

   10001000000000000011001000000100

37. Give a specification of the *BitVector* ADT. Some operations you might want to include are Set(int i), which sets $b[i]$ to 1, Reset(int i), which sets $b[i]$ to 0, and Invert(int i), which changes $b[i]$ from 0 to 1 and vice versa. You might want to include structure-level operations such as

friend BitVector Union(BitVector a, BitVector b)

---

* This is why many computers represent numbers in **twos complement** form, using base 2 rather than base 10; since addition, subtraction, and negation are simple, it's easier to wire the hardware using this representation.

which sets *result*[*i*] to (*a*[*i*] || *b*[*i*]) for all possible *i*. Why, by the way, do we call this function *Union*?

38. Give a complete implementation of the class *BitVector*. Think about whether this should use *IntegerArray* as a member or whether it should be derived from *IntegerArray* as a base class.

39. Use *BitVector* to compute the primes ≤*n*. Recall that a **prime** number is a (positive) integer that is divisible only by itself and 1, so 7 is a prime but 6 isn't (since it's divisible by 6 and 1, but also by 2 and 3). We can do this by using the venerable **sieve of Eratosthenes**, using a bit vector *p*[2], ..., *p*[*n*], whose values are initially all 1s. To run the sieve, we do these steps:

1. Set *trial* to 2.

2. Repeat the following steps as often as needed:

     a. Set *p*[2 * *trial*], *p*[3 * *trial*], *p*[4 * *trial*], ... to zero (we're "crossing off" the elements that can't be primes).

     b. Find the next element after *p*[*trial*] that's not zero, and make that the new *trial*.

3. When the process is completed, the number *j* will be prime if and only if *p*[*j*] == 1.

     a. Before you implement this algorithm, discover the most efficient condition you can for the statement "as often as needed" in step 2.

     b. Produce a list of the 1229 primes less than 10,000.

     c. (Tricky) Many programs make use of a list of primes. Discuss whether it would be more efficient to have a file of primes in the decimal form

         2 3 5 7 11 13 17 19 21 23 29 31 37 . . .

     or in bit vector form

         110101000101000101010100000101000001 . . .

LINEAR STRUCTURES

2

LISTS

Entries in a telephone book, people waiting in a doctor's office, pieces of food on a shish kebab: All these have in common the property that they may be considered to have a natural linear order in that there is a "first" element, followed by a "next" element, which is itself followed by a "next" element, and so on, until the "last" element. This organization of a collection of elements in a linear order arises so frequently that we collect all such objects under the general heading of **lists**.

You'll see in later chapters that the *List* abstract data type is in many ways the fundamental structure of this entire text. Before we explore the *List* ADT, though, we should mention a somewhat subtle philosophical point that has some practical ramifications. There is no innate reason to single out lists for study; like all the structures we will consider in this book, we concentrate on lists and other ADTs not because they are natural objects in the way that planets, dogs, clouds, and trees are, but rather because they are convenient arrangements of information that we often use when we write programs. In that sense, lists in computer science are more like sonnets in the study of poetry because they both are formalizations of patterns of information that arise in the practice of our craft. For the same reason, there are no innately given operations on *List* objects. If you read five data structures texts, you will very likely find five different specifications of the *List* abstract data type, all basically similar but all differing according to the biases of the authors. Consequently, you shouldn't consider any of the *List* operations as set in stone. When designing your own *List* class, you should feel free to include operations that seem to you to be important and to remove operations that you consider inessential. After all,

49

the ability to work within a framework of rules and the wisdom to know when to bend or break the rules are what distinguish the novice from the expert.

 ADT: *LIST*

The structure of a *List* object is very similar to that of an array—a collection of elements arranged in a linear order. In every nonempty list there is a unique first element with no predecessor, immediately followed by a second, which is followed by a third, and so on, until the last element, with no successor, as we illustrate in Figure 2.1.

    The main difference between the *List* and the *Array* abstract data types is that lists do not permit access by a numbered index. Instead, each list has a *current position* that may change over time and that serves as the location where insertion, deletion, inspection, and modification of elements take place. This difference is reflected in the collection of operations available to users of a *List* object. Here is the specification of our version of the *List* ADT.

FIGURE 2.1

Lists and nonlists

These are lists:

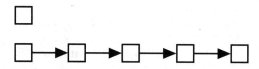

These are not lists:

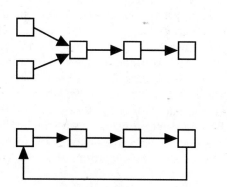

List

Structure. An arbitrarily large (finite) collection of positions in linear order. Each position contains an element of type T. Any nonempty list has one distinguished position, known as the *current position.*

Operations

List(). Pre: true. Post: The list is empty and the current position is undefined.

List(const List& s). Pre: true. Post: The list is a copy of *s*.

~List(). Pre: true. Post: The list is empty.

void Clear(). Pre: true. Post: The list is empty.

List& operator= (const List& s). Pre: true. Post: The list is a copy of the list *s*.

void InsertAfter(T e). Pre: true. Post: If the list was empty, it consists of a single position, containing the element *e*, and this position is now the current position. If the list was not empty, it now contains a new position (which is now the current position) and *e* is in that position. The new position is the successor to the old current position, which is circled in the following diagram.

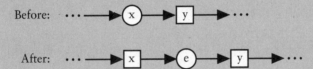

void InsertBefore(T e). Pre: true. Post: If the list was empty, it consists of a single position, containing the element *e*, and this position is now the current position. If the list was not empty, it now contains a new position (which is now the current position) and *e* is in that position. The new position is the predecessor of the old current position, as shown here.

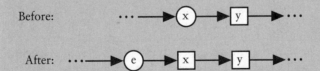

void Remove(). Pre: The list is nonempty. Post: The old current position is removed from the list. If the list had a single position, the current position is undefined. If the list had more than one position, the position preceding the old current position (if any) now precedes the successor to the old current position (if any). If the list had more than one position, the current position is the successor to the old current position, if there was one. Otherwise, the current position is the predecessor of the old current position. One possible case of this operation is illustrated in the following diagram.

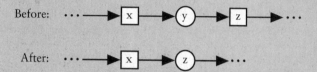

Before: $\cdots \longrightarrow$ x $\longrightarrow$ y $\longrightarrow$ z $\longrightarrow \cdots$

After: $\cdots \longrightarrow$ x $\longrightarrow$ z $\longrightarrow \cdots$

`void Head()`. Pre: true. Post: The current position is the first position in the list, if any; otherwise, the current position remains undefined.

`void Tail()`. Pre: true. Post: The current position is the last position in the list, if any; otherwise, the current position remains undefined.

`List& operator++ (int)`. Pre: The current position is defined and is not the last position in the list. Post: The current position is the successor to the old current position if there is one; otherwise, the list is unchanged.

`List& operator-- (int)`. Pre: The current position is defined and is not the first position in the list. Post: The current position is the predecessor of the old current position if there is one; otherwise, the list is unchanged.

`T Retrieve() const`. Pre: The list is not empty. Post: The list is unchanged, and the element in the current position is returned.

`void Update(T e)`. Pre: The list is not empty. Post: e is in the current position, replacing the element that was there.

`int Includes(T e) const`. Pre: true. Post: If e is in the list, returns 1 and sets the current position to that of the earliest instance of e. If e is not in the list, returns 0 and leaves the list unchanged.

`int Length() const`. Pre: true. Post: The list is unchanged, and the number of elements in the list is returned.

Most of these operations are self-explanatory, but there are a few tricky points that deserve mention. Note that we have two functions, the destructor and *Clear*, that apparently do the same thing. In fact, they do. In the next section, you will see that the body of the destructor consists of nothing but a call to *Clear*. We obviously don't need both functions, but many people find it awkward to make an explicit call to a destructor, preferring instead to have a named member function they can use. Note also that we have overloaded the postfix versions of the increment and decrement operators, ++ and --, so that we can, for instance, advance the current position of a list *s* by the expression s++. You may recall that the declarations of the postfix versions of these operators are distinguished from the prefix versions by a dummy int argument in the postfix versions.

Finally, it may seem somewhat redundant to include two insertion operations, but we have to have them both. Without *InsertBefore* we wouldn't be able to insert a new element at the head of the list, and without *InsertAfter* it would be impossible to insert a new element at the tail of the list.

Parametrized Classes

The *IntegerArray* class we defined in Chapter 1 suffers from a troublesome drawback. There's really no structural or operational difference between arrays of integers, arrays of characters, or arrays of any other type, but if we needed arrays of several types in a program, we would have to take the time to write a class definition for each kind of array we needed. Fortunately for us, the newest releases of C++ have a feature that takes care of this problem.

We may describe a **parametrized class** by preceding its definition by the phrase template<class T>. The parameter *T* stands for any type, either a user-defined class or a predefined type like int. For instance, we represent a collection of classes (of lists of elements of whatever type we wish) by using a parametrized class, *TList*, which we declare like this:

```
template<class T>
class TList
{
    // Declarations of friends, member functions,
    // and member data, as usual, using T for the element type.
} ;
```

Throughout the body of the class declaration, we are free to use the type parameter *T* just as we would use any type name, so we can declare the *Update* function, for instance, by writing

```
void Update(T x);
```

just as we would write void Update(int x) in an ordinary class declaration. Such a declaration serves as a template for an infinite collection of class declarations. In a program that uses a list of integers, we would refer to the type name *TList<int>*, and similarly, *TList<char>* would be the name of a type representing a list of characters. There is nothing special about our use of the name *T* for the type parameter; we could have called it *Element_Type*, if we had wanted to or used any other legal C++ identifier. Similarly, there's no special importance attached to the class name *TList*; we could have called it *PList* or *Foo*, if we had so desired.*

---

* We could have made the obvious choice of calling it *List*, except that some C++ implementations come with a *List* class built in, whose definition would conflict with ours.

Having defined a class template, we can use the angle bracket notation to refer to the type name, as we do when we declare the overload of the assignment operator:

```
TList<T>& operator= (const TList<T>& s);
```

This notation is a bit intimidating at first glance, we'll admit. Just keep in mind that *TList<T>* refers to "a list of elements of type *T*," so the operator declaration would be read as: "The operator = returns a reference to an object of type *TList<T>*. It takes as its argument a reference to a constant *TList<T>* object, here named *s*."

The following listing is the public part of the declaration of our parametrized class *TList*. We've left out the details of the part that is hidden from the users of this class, since that part will depend on the choices we make about how to represent lists internally. We will get to that in the next section, where we'll provide two different representations of the *List* ADT.

```
//=============== Lists.h ===============

#ifndef TLISTS_H
#define TLISTS_H
#include <iostream.h>

// Declaration of lists of elements of parametrized type

template <class T>
class TList
{
    // Display the list.
    friend ostream& operator<< (ostream& os, TList<T> s);

public:
    TList();                        // Construct an empty list.
    TList(const TList<T>& s);       // copy constructor
    ~TList();                       // destructor
    void Clear();                   // Delete all elements.
    // assignment overload
    TList<T>& operator= (const TList<T>& s);

    // Insert e after current position.
    void InsertAfter(T e);
    // Insert e at current position.
    void InsertBefore(T e);
    // Delete the node at the current position.
    void Remove();

    // Move current location to the head.
    void Head();
    // Move current location to the tail.
    void Tail();
```

```
// Move current to next position.
TList<T>& operator++ (int);
// Move current to prior position.
TList<T>& operator-- (int);

// Return the element at the current position.
T Retrieve() const;
// Store e in current location.
void Update(T e);
// membership test
int Includes(T e);
// Return the size of the list.
int Length() const;

protected:
// The List data members go here.
} ;
#endif
```

IMPLEMENTATIONS

There are two common ways to represent the *List* ADT: using an array to store the list data elements and using pointers to make a linked collection of data elements. Each approach has its advantages, and neither is better than the other for all applications. We'll discuss both and conclude this section with a discussion of their relative merits.

Arrays

The array implementation of *List* is the simpler of the two implementations we will discuss. We will maintain a pointer to an array (in free store), where the list elements are stored in order of their positions. Along with this, we will keep three integers: *size* will store the number of elements in the array, *max* will be equal to the largest possible number of elements the array can store, and *current* will be equal to the index of the element in the current position. Figure 2.2 illustrates how these hidden data members would be used to represent a *List* object.

```
T*    value;      // pointer to the array of positions
int   size,       // number of elements in the list (≤ max)
      max,        // size of the array
      current;    // current index in the array
                  // (0 ≤ current < size)
void Grow();      // Grow the array to twice its size.
```

FIGURE 2.2

Using arrays to represent lists

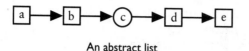

An abstract list

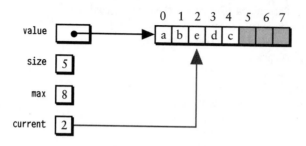

The list implemented with an array

Notice the function *Grow* in the class declaration. Because arrays have a fixed size and lists don't, we will need to be able to increase the size of the array in case an insertion would require more room than is currently available. It makes good design sense to hide *Grow* from the user of our *List* class, since it depends on our choice of implementation and so shouldn't be available to the user of the class.

Also, as you read the class definition, notice that the member functions are—like the *TList* class declaration itself—parametrized, so that they serve as templates for functions that use arbitrary types in their definitions. We parametrize functions in much the same way that we parametrized for classes: We precede the definition by the phrase `template<class T>` and then define the function as expected, using the type parameter T as we would any other type name. Consider, for example, the header of the definition of the assignment overload:

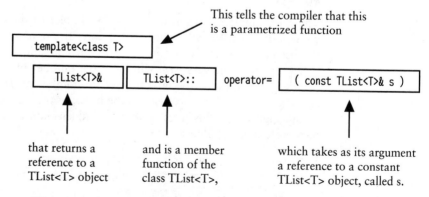

We admit that this is rather verbose, but it's not hard to understand if you keep in mind that except for the parameters, it's just like the header of every C++ function definition you've ever seen. We describe the return type, the owner of the function (if any), its name, and its argument list. If you look back at the header file for this class, you will notice that we didn't include the phrase template<class T> in the function declarations. We didn't need it because the entire class declaration was parametrized, so it was assumed that all member functions and friends mentioned in the declaration were also.

The first few functions of the array-based *List* class are quite simple, as you can see.

```cpp
//=============== ArrayLists.cpp ===============

#include "Assertions.h"    // for Assert, Warn
#include "ArrayLists.h"

template<class T> ostream& operator<< (ostream& os, TList<T> s)
// Display an entire TList, from first position to last.
// NOTE: This assumes the existence of an insertion.
// operator, <<, for the type T.
{
   for (int i = 0; i < l.size; i++)
      os << s.value[i] << '\ t';
   return os;
}


template<class T> TList<T>::TList()
   : size(0),
   max(10),
   current(0)
// Default constructor.  Builds an empty list,
// using an array of 10 elements.
{
   value = new T[max];
   Assert(value != NULL, "Unable to create a new list");
}


template<class T> TList<T>::TList(const TList<T>& s)
   : size(s.size),
   max(s.max),
   current(s.current)
// copy constructor
{
   // Set the member data of this list to
   // match those of the s list.
   size = s.size;
   max = s.max;
   current = s.current;
```

```
    value = new T[max];  // Try to make a new array.
    Assert(value != NULL, "Unable to construct copy");

    // Copy the values from the s list.
    for (int i = 0; i < size; i++)
        value[i] = s.value[i];
}


template<class T> TList<T>::~TList()
// Destroy the List.
{
    Clear();
}


template<class T> void TList<T>::Clear()
// Delete all nodes in the List.
{
    delete []value;
    size = max = current = 0;
}


template<class T> TList<T>& TList<T>::operator= (const TList<T>& s)
// assignment overload
{
    if (this != &s)  // Don't assign to yourself.
    {
        size = s.size;
        max = s.max;
        current = s.current;

        // Kill the old array and construct a new one,
        // filling it with s's values.
        delete []value;
        value = new T[max];
        Assert(value != NULL, "Unable to assign lists");

        for (int i = 0; i < size; i++)
            value[i] = s.value[i];
    }
    return *this;
}
```

The insertion routines are the first ones whose actions aren't completely obvious. To insert a new element in an array at the current position, we shift the elements from the current position to the tail up by one, thus making a "hole" where we can insert the new element. Note that the order of shifting is important: We must first move the tail element, then the next-to-last element, and so on, as in the following diagram. (What would happen if we shifted in the other order, from the current element to the end of the list?)

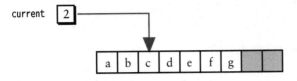

The original array

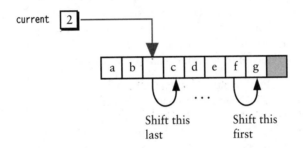

Shift this   Shift this
last   first

After shifting

Once we understand how to insert an element before the one in the current position, inserting an element after the one in the current position is trivial: All we have to do is advance the current position by one and then perform *InsertBefore* at the new location. In both routines, notice that we have to make sure there's enough room in the array for the new element and that after the insertion we have to increment the *size* member datum.

```
template<class T> void TList<T>::InsertBefore(T e)
// Insert e at the current position, shifting array
// elements to make room.
{
    if (size == max) // No room in the array,
        Grow();      // so make it larger.
    if (size > 0)
        for (int i = size - 1; i >= current; i--)
            value[i + 1] = value[i];
    value[current] = e;
    size++;
}
```

```
template<class T> void TList<T>::InsertAfter(T e)
// Insert e after the current position by moving current
// up one position and then inserting there.
{
    if (size == max)
        Grow();
    current++;
    InsertBefore(e);
}
```

Removing an element from the list is like inserting in reverse. After making sure there actually is something in the list to remove, we shift the elements after the current position *down* one slot, thus effectively removing the element at the current position. Just as it was with insertion, the order of shifting is important: We must shift the element after the current position first and the tail element last, just backward from the order we needed in insertion. Also, as we did with insertion, we have to remember to decrement the *size* member datum, reflecting the new size of the list.

```
template<class T> void TList<T>::Remove()
// Delete the element at the current position.
// If the list is empty, display a warning.
{
    Warn(size > 0,
        "Attempt to Remove an element from an empty list");
    if (size > 0)
    {
        for (int i = current; i < size - 1; i++)
            value[i] = value[i + 1];
        size--;
    }
}
```

The operations *Head, Tail,* ++, --, *Retrieve,* and *Update* are simple enough that they need no explanation, except perhaps to observe that ++ and --, like the assignment operator, return a reference to the list. We need a reference return value so that we can use the modified list in more complicated expressions like (theList++).Remove().

```
template<class T> void TList<T>::Head()
// Move current location to the head.
// Do nothing if the list is empty.
{
    current = 0;
}
```

```
template<class T> void TList<T>::Tail()
// Move current location to the tail.
// Do nothing if the list is empty.
{
   if (size > 0)
      current = size - 1;
}


template<class T> TList<T>& TList<T>::operator++ (int)
// Move current location to next position.
// Do nothing if current is at the tail of the list.
{
   if (current < size - 1)
      current++;
   return *this;
}


template<class T> TList<T>& TList<T>::operator-- (int)
// Move current location to previous position.
// Do nothing if current is at the head of the list.
{
   if (current > 0)
      current--;
   return *this;
}


template<class T> T TList<T>::Retrieve() const
// Return the element at the current position.
// Quit the program if the list is empty, since we can't
// return anything.
{
   Assert(size > 0, "Cannot Retrieve an element from an empty list");
   return value[current];
}


template<class T> void TList<T>::Update(T e)
// Store e in current location.
// Warn the user if the list is empty.
{
   Warn(size > 0,
        "Cannot Update an element in an empty list");
   if (size > 0)
      value[current] = e;
}
```

To test whether an element *e* is in a list, we perform a **linear search,** which means that we begin at the head of the list and inspect every element in turn, stopping our search as soon as we run out of elements to inspect or find an element that matches *e*. The function *Includes,* by the way, is a questionable candidate for inclusion as a member function of the *List* class. First, it could be defined in terms of other member functions (as we ask you to do in the exercises) and so is in a sense less "primitive" than the other list operations. Second, and even more troublesome, it could perhaps violate the design consideration of modularity. Suppose, for example, that we had a list of employee records. In that case, the type *T* might be a struct containing employee ID, name, address, pay rate, and so on. Suppose also that we wanted to be able to search our list for a particular ID. To do that would require us to compare records by ID, perhaps by overloading the inequality operator != for the struct *T*. The upshot is that we would have an operation in one class that required the existence of an operation in another class. Without compulsively careful attention to the documentation of the *List* class, a programmer might not catch this requirement, leading to possible headaches, at the very least.

```
template<class T> int TList<T>::Includes(T e)
// Returns 1 if and only if e is in the list.
// If found, set current to the location of the first
// instance of e.
// NOTE: This assumes the existence of an operator !=
// for the type T.
{
    int i = 0;
    while ((i < size) && (value[i] != e))
        i++;
    if (i < size)      // Found a match,
        current = i;   // so set current to the location.
    return (i < size);
}
```

The function *Grow* doubles the size of the value array by first allocating a new array of twice the size (also checking whether the allocation succeeded), pointed to by *newValue*. We then copy the existing elements into the new array, delete the existing value array, and finally make the *value* pointer point to the new array.

```
template<class T> void TList<T>::Grow()
{
    max *= 2;
    T* newValue = new T[max];
    Assert(newValue != NULL, "Could not Grow the list");

    for (int i = 0; i < size; i++)
        newValue[i] = value[i];
    delete []value;
    value = newValue;
}
```

The array implementation of *List* is easy enough to understand, but it does have some problems. First, not all operations run in constant time: As we have seen, insertion and removal of an element can take time proportional to the length of the list, since we have to shift all the elements after the current position. Another problem is that arrays in C++ must be **contiguous**, which is to say that the array takes up a single, potentially large block in memory. When we create a list or make a copy, we use *new* to find space in the free store for the new data array. Obviously, there may be times when there simply isn't room enough in memory to honor our request, so all we can do is abort the program. These problems can be cured (almost completely) by another implementation, but we pay for these solutions with greater complexity and a loss of some of the conceptual simplicity of arrays.

Linked Lists

Using *new* to allocate an array is somewhat like buying tickets to a show for yourself and 20 friends and requesting that all the seats be together. There may still be plenty of tickets available, but there may not be a block of 20 seats. If we define a collection of **nodes**, each containing a list element and a pointer to another node, we are in a position similar to purchasing 20 tickets and not being picky about everyone sitting together: As long as there's space available anywhere in memory, we will be able to store our list.

To use such a **linked list** implementation, we need another class in addition to the *List* class. The basic building block of the linked list implementation will be the node, which we declare as follows and illustrate in Figure 2.3.

```
template <class T>
struct Node
{
    Node() { next = NULL;} ;     // constructor
    T value;                     // data stored in a node
    Node<T>* next;               // pointer to next node
} ;
```

FIGURE 2.3

Nodes and linked lists

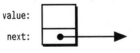

A single node

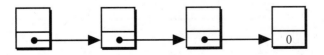

A collection of nodes, linked to form a list

In Figure 2.3, notice that we make use of the NULL pointer (i.e., a pointer with value 0) to mark the last node in our linked list. You will see shortly that this convention is quite useful when we **traverse** a list, using the *next* pointers in each node to track our way from each node to its successor.

Now that we see how a linked list will be arranged, how do we get access to the elements? A common strategy is to refer to a linked list by a pointer to the first node in the list. We'll do that, but we'll also expand on this idea by including some other useful information. We will represent a linked list by a **header record,** consisting of pointers to the first and last cells, along with an integer that contains the number of elements in the list. This information will be stored in the protected part of the linked list class, as shown here and illustrated in Figure 2.4.

```
protected:
    Node<T> *first,     // pointer to first node in the list
            *current,   // pointer to current node
            *last;      // pointer to last node in the list
    int     size;       // number of elements in the list
```

We must be especially careful when writing pointer-based algorithms because, unlike arrays, linked lists can occur in three logically distinct forms, depending on whether the list is empty, has a single cell, or has more than one cell. In writing routines for linked lists, we must be sure that our routines can correctly handle all possible cases. The three forms of linked lists are indicated in Figure 2.5.

```
//=============== LLists.cpp ===============

#include <stdlib.h>         // for exit, NULL
#include "Assertions.h"     // for Assert, Warn
#include "LinkedLists.h"
```

FIGURE 2.4

A linked implementation of *List*

An abstract list

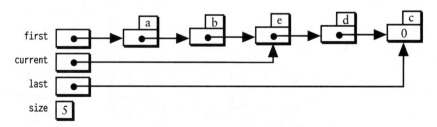

The list implemented as a linked collection of nodes

FIGURE 2.5

Three forms of linked lists

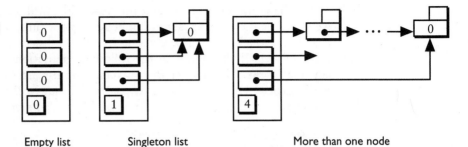

Empty list   Singleton list   More than one node

```
template<class T> ostream& operator<< (ostream& os, TList<T> s)
// Display an entire TList, from first position to last.
{
    Node<T>* p = s.first;
    while (p)
    {
        os << p->value << '\ t';
        p = p->next;
    }
    return os;
}
```

The definition of the overload of the output operator, <<, is instructive, because it embodies one of the fundamental linked list algorithms. To traverse the entire list, displaying the contents of each node, we use an auxiliary pointer, *p*. We begin by making *p* point to the first cell in the list. Then, as long as *p* is not zero (the NULL pointer), we display the *value* data of the node pointed to by *p* and advance *p* by making it point to the same cell as the *next* pointer. In this algorithm, *p* serves much the same role as the index in an array traversal: The statement p = p->next is very much like index++ in that it causes the reference to move to the next location in the list, as in Figure 2.6.

```
template<class T> TList<T>::TList()
: first(NULL), current(NULL), last(NULL); size(0)
// Default constructor.  Builds an empty list.
{     }
```

FIGURE 2.6

Traversing a linked list

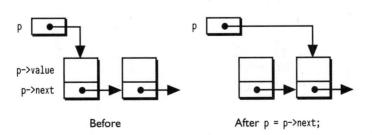

Before   After p = p->next;

In the copy constructor (and the nearly identical assignment overload), we again see the traversal algorithm in action, this time in two lists. The idea is simple enough. We traverse the list *s* and the list object itself in parallel. Look at steps 1 through 4 in the following definition and you'll see how copying works. The pointer *lptr* traverses the list argument *l*, and as each node is encountered, its value is copied into a newly constructed cell in the list we are making, which is itself traversed by the pointer *nptr*.

```
template<class T> TList<T>::TList(const TList<T>& s)
// copy constructor
{
    Node<T>  *lptr = s.first,
             *nptr;

    if (lptr == NULL)
    {   current = first = last = NULL; size = 0;}
    else
    {
        // Construct the first node in the list.
        nptr = new Node<T>;
        nptr->value = lptr->value;
        if (lptr == s.current)
            current = nptr;
        first = nptr;
        lptr = lptr->next;

        // Track through the remainder of the list,
        // copying nodes as we go.
        while (lptr)
        {
            // (1) Build a new node at the end of this list,
            nptr->next = new Node<T>;
            // (2) advance nptr to the new node,
            nptr = nptr->next;
            if (lptr == s.current)
                current = nptr;
            // (3) copy the s node value into the new node,
            nptr->value = lptr->value;
            // (4) and advance lptr.
            lptr = lptr->next;
        }
        nptr->next = NULL;
        last = nptr;
        size = s.size;
    }
}
```

We should mention a caution concerning this copying algorithm (and the array version, too, as a matter of fact). Notice in step 3 that we assign the values from the *s* list into the list we are making. This seems to be just what we should do, but there's a potential problem hidden here. The list elements can be any type *T* whatsoever, *including pointers*. But when we copy pointers, we don't copy their targets. If *T* was a pointer type, then, the copy constructor and the assignment overload would lead to two lists whose elements point to the same objects (known as a **shallow clone**), as shown in Figure 2.7. This **aliasing** is generally not what we want to happen, since a change of any of the targets of one list would result in an invisible change to the targets of the other. In the exercises, we ask you to consider how you might solve this problem.

The destructor and the *Clear* function embody another common linked list operation: removing a node from a list. When removing a node from a list, we don't want to lose our access to the list; instead, what we want is to "point around" a node prior to deleting it. *Clear* accomplishes this by keeping two pointers as the list is traversed. We use the *current* pointer and a pointer called *nptr*, writing our algorithm so that *current* points to the node *after* the one pointed to by *nptr*. In that way, *current* provides us with an entry into the remainder of the list, so we can delete the node pointed to by *nptr* without losing the list.

```
template<class T> TList<T>::~TList()
// Delete all nodes in the List.
{
    Clear();
}

template<class T> void TList<T>::Clear()
// Delete all nodes in the List.
{
    Node<T>* nptr = first;
    current = first;
```

FIGURE 2.7

Copying pointers produces aliases

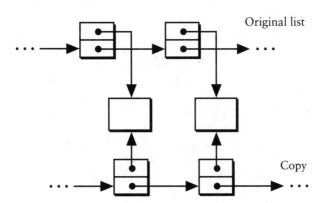

```
      while (current)
      {
         current = current->next;
         delete nptr;
         nptr = current;
      }
      first = current = last = NULL;
      size = 0;
}

template<class T> TList<T>& TList<T>::operator= (const TList<T>& s)
// assignment overload
{
   if (this != &s)      // no need to assign to ourselves
   {
      Clear();

      // Now build the new list.
      Node<T> *lptr = s.first,
              *nptr;
      if (lptr == NULL)
      {    current = first = last = NULL; size = 0;}
      else
      {
         // Construct the first node in the list.
         nptr = new Node<T>;
         nptr->value = lptr->value;
         if (lptr == s.current)
            current = nptr;
         first = nptr;
         lptr = lptr->next;


         // Track through the remainder of the list,
         // copying nodes as we go.
         while (lptr)
         {
            nptr->next = new Node<T>;
            nptr = nptr->next;
            if (lptr == s.current)
               current = nptr;
            nptr->value = lptr->value;
            lptr = lptr->next;
         }
         nptr->next = NULL;
```

```
        last = nptr;
        size = s.size;
    }
  }
  return *this;
}
```

There are, as we have seen, two operations that insert a new element into a list. The basic idea behind both is simple enough in this implementation: We make a new node, place a value into the node, and link that node into the list in the appropriate location. The first two steps are trivial, and for insertion after the current position, the last step is almost as simple. Having built the new node and filled its *value* member datum, we first link the new cell to the node (if any) after the current position and complete the job by linking the current cell to the new one, as illustrated in Figure 2.8.

Notice that the order of operations is important here. You should convince yourself that the insertion operation wouldn't work if we performed the two statements in reverse order. It's easy to see that this operation runs in constant time, independent of the length of the list. This is a considerable im-

FIGURE 2.8

Inserting a new node
after the current
position

```
// (1) link new node into the list
nptr->next = current->next;
```

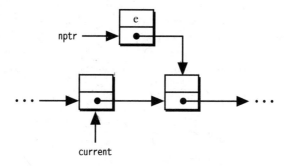

```
// (2) link the list to the new node
current->next = nptr;
```

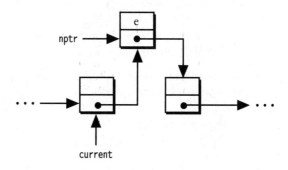

provement over the array version which, because we must shift all the array entries after the current position, could possibly take time proportional to the size of the list. As you read the definition of *InsertAfter*, notice that we have to treat insertion into an empty list as a separate case, and, of course, we have to remember to increment the *size* member datum to reflect the new list size.

```
template<class T> void TList<T>::InsertAfter(T e)
// Insert e after the current position.
{
    // Construct a new node and fill it
    // with the appropriate value.
    Node<T>* nptr = new Node<T>;
    nptr->value = e;

    if (size == 0)
    // Inserting into an empty list.
    {
        nptr->next = NULL;
        current = first = last = nptr;
    }
    else
    // Inserting into a nonempty list.
    {
        nptr->next = current->next;
        current->next = nptr;
        if (current == last)
            last = nptr;
        current = nptr;   // Move current to new node.
    }
    size++;
}
```

Guided by *InsertAfter,* it would seem that *InsertBefore* would require that we first find the position *prior* to the current position, thus taking the time necessary to traverse the entire list up to the position just before *current.* There is, however, a wonderfully clever and simple algorithm that eliminates the need for this traversal altogether. The trick here is to insert the new element *after* the current node and then swap the *value* data in the current node and the new node following *current,* leaving a list that looks exactly as if we had inserted *e* in a new location immediately before *current.* Pictorially, we have the steps shown in Figure 2.9.

```
template<class T> void TList<T>::InsertBefore(T e)
// Insert e at the current position.
{
    Node<T>* nptr = new Node<T>;
```

```
    if (size == 0)
    // Inserting into an empty list
    {
        nptr->value = e;
        nptr->next = NULL;
        current = first = last = nptr;
    }
    else
    // Inserting into a nonempty list
    {
        nptr->value = current->value;
        nptr->next = current->next;
        current->value = e;
        current->next = nptr;
        if (current == last)
            last = nptr;
    }
    size++;
}
```

FIGURE 2.9

Inserting a node be-
fore the current node

```
nptr->value = current->value; // copy current value
nptr->next = current->next;   // link new node to list
```

```
current->next = nptr;    // link list to new node
current->value = e;      // copy new value
```

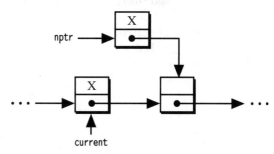

As clever as this algorithm is, it does incur a potentially large hidden cost. There are two data moves here: one to copy the current data into the new node and another to place the data to be inserted into the current node. Normally, this isn't a problem, but moving data around can be time-consuming if the list elements are very large (like gigantic arrays or structures).

Removing the node at the current position is a bit complicated, if only because we have several cases to consider. First, if the list is empty, we issue a warning to the operator and return from the function without doing anything else. If the list has a single element, we remove that node and set *current, first,* and *last* to be the NULL pointer. If the list has more than one element and we are removing the last element, life gets a bit tricky, because we have to update the *last* pointer as well as pointing around the last node in the list. Unfortunately, the only way to do that is to traverse the list until we point to the node immediately before the last one. This takes time proportional to the length of the list, but there's nothing else we can do.

The last case we need to consider is where we are deleting a node that is not the last one from a list of more than one node. To avoid having to traverse our way to the node before the one to be deleted, we adopt the data-moving trick we used in insertion: We save the value of the node *after* the current one, we delete the node after the current one, and we restore the saved data into the current node. Figure 2.10 shows how this works.

```
template<class T> void TList<T>::Remove()
// Delete the node at the current position.
{
    Node<T>* nptr;
    if (size == 0)
    {
        Warn(size > 0,
        "Attempt to Remove an element from an empty list");
        return;
    }
    else if (size == 1)
    // Removing the only node in the list
    {
        delete current;
        first = current = last = NULL;
    }
    else if (current == last)
    // Removing the last node of a list of > 1 nodes
    {
        nptr = first;
        // Find predecessor to current node.
        while (nptr->next != current)
            nptr = nptr->next;
```

```
      // Point around the last node,
      nptr->next = current->next;
      // and then delete it.
      delete current;
      current = last = nptr;
   }
   else
   // Removing a node that's not the last one
   {
      nptr = current->next;
      current->value = nptr->value;
      current->next = nptr->next;
      delete nptr;
   }
   size--;
}
```

FIGURE 2.10

Removing an element from a linked list

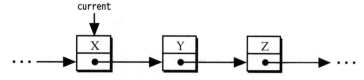

```
// (1) copy successor value into current node
nptr = current->next;
current->value = nptr->value;
```

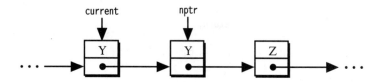

```
// (2) point around and delete
current->next = nptr->next;
delete nptr;
```

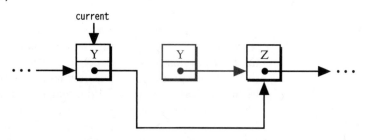

```
template<class T> TList<T>& TList<T>::operator++ (int)
// Move current location to next node.
// Do nothing if current is at the tail of the list.
{
    if (current != last)
        current = current->next;
    return *this;
}

template<class T> TList<T>& TList<T>::operator-- (int)
// Move current location to previous node.
// Do nothing if current is at the head of the list.
{
    if (current != first)
    {
        Node<T>* nptr = first;
        while (nptr->next != current)
            nptr = nptr->next;
        current = nptr;
    }
    return *this;
}

template<class T> T TList<T>::Retrieve() const
// Return the element at the current position.
{
    Assert(size > 0,
        "Cannot Retrieve an element from an empty list");
    return current->value;
}

template<class T> void TList<T>::Update(T e)
// Store e in current location.
{
    Warn(size > 0,
        "Cannot Update an element in an empty list");
    if (size > 0)
        current->value = e;
}
```

Testing for membership in this implementation uses the same linear search strategy we saw in the array version. The difference is that here we use the now-familiar statement ptr = ptr->next to traverse the list. We perform this statement repeatedly until either we run out of list elements (so *ptr* will be the NULL value, 0) or we find a match (so that we will have ptr->value == e). This means, then, that the condition for staying in the loop will be ptr && (ptr->value != e). Notice that we are making use of C++'s short-circuit evaluation in the loop condition: If *ptr* is zero, the condition will be false, so C++

will not need to perform the test ptr->value != e. This is a good thing, since looking for the contents of a nonexistent node would almost certainly give rise to a messy error.

```
template<class T> int TList<T>::Includes(T e)
// Returns 1 iff e is an element of the list.  If e is
// found, set current to the location of the first.
// instance of e.
// NOTE: This assumes the existence of operator != on T.
{
   Node<T>* ptr = first;
   while (ptr && (ptr->value != e))
      ptr = ptr->next;
   if (ptr)
      current = ptr;
   return (ptr != NULL);
}
```

2.3   COMPARING IMPLEMENTATIONS

You have just seen two entirely different ways of programming the *List* ADT. A bright but contentious apprentice might ask why we bothered to do the same thing in two different ways: "Why learn another way, since the first one worked just fine?" The glib answer to that would be "for the experience." A journeyman, though, might pose the better question, "You're evidently making me do the same job in two ways to teach me a lesson. What should I be learning here?" That question deserves a more complete answer, which is what we'll provide in this section. You have seen that there are always many ways of solving a programming problem; some are better in some respects and worse in other respects. It's worth considering the criteria we can use to compare different solutions to a problem.

Space

Our expressed motivation for considering a pointer-based implementation of the *List* ADT was that there were space considerations that gave a linked collection of many nodes an advantage over one large monolithic array. Recall that C++ arrays, like arrays in many other languages, must occupy adjacent locations in memory, whether they are allocated in free store or not. A request to set aside space for an array, as in the statement p = new int[10000], might fail even if there were 40,000 integer-sized locations available, simply because there was no single free block large enough to fill the request. On the other hand, a single node takes up very little space by comparison, and a collection of 10,000 such nodes, linked by pointers, can be scattered around in memory wherever there is room for them.

But there's more to the space issue than just avoiding asking for large chunks of memory. If our lists are large enough, we might need nearly the entire amount of available memory in our computer, regardless of implementation. In that case, we would be wise to consider the total amount of memory needed to store a list.

Suppose, for example, that we are going to use a computer/compiler combination in which pointers are 4 bytes long and integers are 2 bytes long and that the data type of the elements in the list requires d bytes (d might be 2 for lists of integers or perhaps 256 for a list of character strings). Let's compute the total amount of memory needed to store N entries of size d. The array implementation requires 6 bytes for the *size, max,* and *current* member data, plus d times the average size of the array. Because we double the size of the array when we run out of room to insert an element, we rather arbitrarily decide that the average size of an array holding N elements is $(3/2)N$. This means that the array implementation will require $6+(3/2)Nd$ bytes to store an N-element list, on the average. The linked list will require 14 bytes for the *first, current,* and *last* pointers and the *size* member datum, along with N nodes, each requiring d bytes for the element plus 4 for the pointer in each node. Therefore, the linked list implementation will use $14+N(d+4)$ bytes to store a list of N elements. This means that the array implementation will require less memory space as long as

$$6+\left(\frac{3}{2}\right)Nd < 14 + N(d+4)$$

which is equivalent to saying

$$\frac{d}{2}-4 < \frac{8}{N}$$

If you try some values for d, you'll see that the array implementation uses less memory, on average, if $d \leq 8$ and that the linked list implementation uses less space when $d \geq 24$. The behavior between $d=8$ and $d=24$ depends on N, but we can conclude, as a rule of thumb, that if space is our main criterion, we are better off using arrays if the list elements are small, and we should use linked lists if the elements are large.

Time

The choice of implementation not only affects the space needed to store an ADT object—it may also have a profound effect on the running times of the operations. Consider the *List* insertion operation, for instance. If we represent a list by an array, we must shift the list elements toward the tail of the list to make room for the new element. In the worst case, when we are inserting a new element at the head of the list, this could require us to shift the entire array element by element. The pointer version of list insertion runs in constant time in that the steps required to insert a new element are independent of the size of the list. Deletion behaves similarly. If we were writing a program that used a list, then, and we knew that the program would make a large number of insertions or deletions, we might well decide to choose a pointer implementation, even if it meant giving away some space in memory.

In a similar way, we can compare the rest of the *List* operations in terms of their running times. Table 2.1 shows that arrays have a time advantage for the destructor (unless the elements had their own destructors, in which case the time taken by the destructor would be proportional to the length of the list) and the -- operator, while linked lists have the edge in insertion and deletion.

Comprehensibility

Programs are written and maintained by people. Therefore, if we have several possible ways to write a program and there is no compelling space or time reasons for picking one implementation over the other, the smart choice would be to use the one that is easiest to understand and modify. For our *List* example, you would probably agree that the array version is the hands-down winner in terms of readability. Part of this preference comes from the fact that you've had far more experience with arrays than with linked structures. This choice will be much less compelling once you become comfortable with pointers, but even an experienced programmer would probably agree that the array implementation is the easiest to understand at first glance.

Comprehensibility is at least as important as the other two criteria. After all, there's no benefit to be gained from using a fast, small implementation if it is so complicated that it never gets successfully completed or is impossible to modify.

TABLE 2.1

Comparison of worst-case running times of *List* operations

Operation	Arrays	Linked
Default constructor	1	1
Copy constructor	n	n
Destructor	1	n
operator =	n	n
Insert	n	1
Remove	n	1 (n, if removing tail)
Head	1	1
Tail	1	1
operator ++	1	1
operator --	1	n
Retrieve	1	1
Update	1	1
Length	1	1

Trade-Offs

So which is the better implementation for the *List* ADT? The only answer to this question is perhaps another question: "What do you mean by 'best'?" The question of which way to solve a programming problem illustrates the engineering flavor of computer science.

We can look at computer science as the marriage of mathematics and engineering. (This twofold nature is reflected in its placement in the curriculum. At some schools, computer science is grouped with mathematics; at others, it finds itself in the School of Engineering.) The mathematical aspect is seen in questions like, How fast can we sort a list? and Is this algorithm correct?—questions where there is only one correct answer. Engineering, however, devotes considerable attention to choosing among alternate designs and basing the decision on a complex web of interdependent criteria. There are many ways to build a bridge, for instance. Deciding how to do the job depends on the factors that are considered important for the particular problem. If the only consideration is ease of maintenance, it might make sense to build the bridge out of gold, since gold never rusts or needs painting. However, gold is hideously expensive compared with steel and is much weaker and heavier.

To decide which *List* implementation we should use, then, we must answer questions like these: Is space important, or are we only going to be dealing with small lists? Are we going to be doing a lot of insertions into and deletions from large lists? Is our list package going to be maintained by novices or by experienced programmers? As is so often the case, there may not be any clear-cut preference. Instead, we are often faced with trade-offs, having to give up comprehensibility for a gain in speed, or picking an implementation that is space-efficient but not as fast as it could be.

 2.4 CS INTERLUDE: MEASURES OF EFFICIENCY

We can view the subject matter of computer science as the result of generalizing from specific problem-solving instances, which is to say that computer science seeks to find properties common to many instances of problem solving. Program design—the writing of programs to solve a problem—proceeds in the opposite direction: from a vague notion of what needs to be done, to the writing of a program in a specific language for a specific computer. The aim of program design is captured in the most appropriate title yet invented for a book on computer science, Nicholas Wirth's *Algorithms + Data Structures = Programs*. Wirth, the developer of the Pascal language, chose his title to point out the twofold nature of a computer program: an algorithm describing how to manipulate information with a computer, along with a data structure that provides a logical basis for organization of that information in the computer. These two aspects of a program are intimately intertwined: Making a decision about one of the aspects often profoundly affects the other.

Algorithms

An **algorithm** is a finite list of unambiguous instructions that can be performed on a computer in such a way that the process is guaranteed to halt in a finite amount of time. "Add up the integers from 1 to 100" could almost qualify as an algorithm except that the single instruction it uses does not provide sufficient detail for us to decide how to perform the required operation. The instruction does provide us with a useful starting point, however. Indeed, just getting to the point where we know what the problem is can often represent the major part of a programming task. Knowing the problem, we can now try to refine the problem into a suitable algorithm.

This simple addition problem occupies a hallowed place in mathematical folklore and will serve as a good example of a situation in which there is more than one algorithm to solve a given problem. Karl Friedrich Gauss was born in Germany in 1777 and grew up to be one of the best mathematicians who ever lived. The story goes that when Gauss was a boy in what would be the eighteenth-century German equivalent of present-day American elementary school, his teacher, J. G. Büttner, gave the class the problem of adding the numbers from 1 to 100 (presumably to give himself an extended break from lecturing). The students bent over their slates and in less than a minute young Gauss came to the teacher's desk, laid down his slate, and said "*Ligget se,*" which means, "There 'tis." Herr Büttner, incredulous, looked at Gauss's answer and found that it was indeed correct.*

Gauss's success came from what we would describe as a clever choice of algorithm. It is reasonable to guess that his classmates had all hit on a variant of the same algorithm, which we would describe in C++ terms as

```
int BusyWork(int n)
// Add the integers from 1 to n.
{
    int sum = 0;
    for (int i = 1; i <= n; i++)
        sum += i;
    return sum;
}
```

Gauss, on the other hand, is said to have argued as follows: "*Wenn ich die Summe im Geist ausschreibe, dann habe ich '1 + 2 + 3 + · · · + 98 + 99 + 100.' Nun, angenommen ich addiere diese Zahlen paarweise: 1 + 100 = 101,*

---

* This story is about as true as the tale of George Washington and the cherry tree and has survived for about the same reasons.

2+99=101 (*aha!*), 3+98=101, *und so weiter. Alle diese Paare ergeben eine Summe von* 101 *und es gibt* 50 *Paare, so muss die Summe* 50×101=5050 *sein. Ich bin fertig.*" You don't need to understand German to make sense of Gauss's argument; he mentally added the numbers in a different order, breaking them into 50 pairs, each of which summed to 101. In other words, Gauss's algorithm would take the form

```
int BetterSum(int n)
{
    return (1 + n) * n / 2;
}
```

Comparing the two algorithms, we see that not only is Gauss's algorithm more aesthetically pleasing, but it is also better in a way that we can measure. The obvious algorithm required 100 additions, along with the overhead inherent in the for statement, whereas Gauss's algorithm required only one addition, one multiplication, and one division. Although this would make no noticeable difference if the algorithms were run on modern computers, it would make a significant difference if the "computer" was a seven-year-old child. (We are actually cheating a little here, since multiplication and division take longer to compute than addition. We can explain this away, however, if we restrict our attention to numbers that are fairly small. In this case, multiplication and division typically take about 3 to 10 times as long as addition on most computers, so we still come out way ahead.) This provides a partial answer to one of the questions posed earlier: We can say that one algorithm to solve a problem is "better" than another if it requires less time to execute.

We don't need to stop here, though. It takes but a little thought to convince yourself that Gauss's algorithm would also be applicable to adding the numbers from 1 to 200 (quick, what's the answer?), so going from there to adding the numbers from 1 to *n*, for any $n \geq 1$, is not hard at all. Having done that, it is easy to convince yourself that the algorithm will work equally well to find the sum of the integers from *n* to *m*, for any $n \leq m$. In fact, the algorithm could be used to find the sum 3+11+19+27+35+43+51 or any **arithmetic series** of numbers in which the difference between any consecutive terms is the same (8, in the preceding sum, for instance). Finally, notice that we need not restrict ourselves to integers; Gauss's algorithm can be generalized to find the sum of any arithmetic series of real numbers. The moral of this little digression is that we should never try to solve a particular problem if we can solve a more general one with just a little more work. In this case, we have gone from an efficient algorithm for one problem to one that solves an infinite collection of related problems.

You have already seen several examples in which we considered the question of whether one data structure or algorithm was "better" than another. We saw that Gauss's summation algorithm was preferable to the obvious technique because it took less time to run, and the array implementation of a list was preferable to the linked version (for small data elements) because it took less space in memory. When we are faced with the problem of writing a program, we must be aware that we are dealing with two scarce resources: time and space. It is worthless to write a program that takes, say, 20 years of computer time to solve a problem, just as it makes no sense to choose a data structure that requires more memory than the computer has available. The study of the **computational complexity** of programs seeks to find general principles governing the use of these resources. This is a vast, fascinating, and as yet not completely explored aspect of computer science, one to which we will refer throughout this book.

For many programs, the running time depends largely on the size of the input: Multiplying two 10-digit numbers will likely take less time than multiplying 100 10-digit numbers (number of inputs) or two 100-digit numbers (length of inputs) with the same program. Because we can't guarantee what kind of computer or compiler we will use to run the program, it is customary to talk of the running time, $T(n)$, of a particular algorithm as a function just of n, the "size" of the input.

To use the example of multiplication, we might have a program that multiplies two n-digit numbers and find that it takes $117.65n^2$ milliseconds on a microcomputer but only $5.08n^2$ milliseconds on a fast mainframe computer. Rather than having to redo our timing estimates for every possible computer, we will simply say that the program we are investigating has a running time proportional to n^2, recognizing that the contributions from the particular machine/compiler combination only change the running time by a constant multiple, as a rule.

Furthermore, we will factor out as much of the contribution of the input as we can by restricting our estimates to a worst-case analysis. We recognize that not only is the size of the input significant in the running time, but so is the nature of the input; but we will choose to ignore all but those inputs for which the program takes the longest time possible. For example, it is not difficult to imagine that our unspecified multiplication program might take much longer to multiply 5,548,716,225 by 8,848,710,094 than it would take to multiply 5,000,000,000 by 8,000,000,000, but in estimating an upper bound for the time required, we will consider only the worst instances of problems of a given size.

Big-O

We are then in the position of trying to analyze a function $T(n)$ in such a manner that (1) we will not concern ourselves with constant multiples and (2) we will be concerned only with the largest (i.e., worst-case) estimates that are still "good" in some sense. This kind of analysis is sufficiently common that mathematicians have developed terminology to make our task easier as well as more precise.

Definition. If $f(n)$ and $g(n)$ are two functions of n whose values are always positive, we say that $f(n) = O(g(n))$, which is read "f of n is big-O of g of n," or simply "f is big-O of g," if there is some number c greater than zero for which $f(n) \leq c\, g(n)$ for all n greater than some fixed number N (i.e., for all n sufficiently large).

For instance, we can say that $n^2 + 4n = O(n^2)$ because $n^2 + 4n$ is less than or equal to $2n^2$ for all n greater than 4 (so in this case, c is 2 and N is 4). We can get some idea of the choice for c and N by arguing as follows. We first guess that $n^2 + 4n = O(n^2)$, and we see that the contribution of $4n$ will make $n^2 + 4n$ grow faster than $1n^2$, so we try $2n^2$, using the constant $c = 2$. We now try some values for n to see whether $2n^2$ eventually gets larger than $n^2 + 4n$.

n	$n^2 + 4n$	$2n^2$	
1	5	2	(smaller)
2	12	8	(smaller)
3	21	18	(smaller)
4	32	32	(equal)
5	45	50	(larger)
6	60	72	(larger)

The table seems to indicate that $n^2 + 4n \leq 2n^2$ for all $n > 4$, and indeed we could prove that with a little more algebraic manipulation. Thus, we see that $c = 2$ and $N = 4$ in the definition, and we have thus established the result $n^2 + 4n = O(n^2)$.

Notice how this choice of c effectively "cancels out" any constant multiples due to choice of machine, since we can say that both $117.65n^2$ and $5.08n^2$ are $O(n^2)$. Notice also that this notation allows us to consider just the worst-case situations, because if we had an algorithm that took n^2 time if n was evenly divisible by 10, and $2n$ time otherwise, we would still claim that the algorithm was $O(n^2)$ rather than $O(n)$.

Notice that this process of finding upper bounds on time complexity is only as good as our cleverness in evaluating time complexity. Suppose, for instance, we had an algorithm that, unknown to us, actually had timing function $T(n) = n^2 + 4n$. In this case, we would be correct if we said $T(n) = O(n^2)$ or $T(n) = O(n^{10})$. (Why?) Both estimates are correct, but clearly, the first is in some sense "more" correct than the second. Not uncommonly, the analysis of an algorithm is so complicated that we simply don't know whether the big-O estimate we've found is the best possible in the sense of providing the least upper bound on the running time.

As a brief digression, you might rightly ask why we concentrate on worst-case estimates. Might not the behavior of an algorithm be better expressed in terms of the average running times over all possible inputs? As it happens, we can do just that in some cases, but far more often than not, the average behavior is very difficult to calculate. Mathematicians and computer scientists, just like other folks, tend to shy away from the really hard stuff when there is a simpler way that is almost as good. Admittedly, there are instances when average-time estimates are very instructive; it's just that to do a proper job of average-case analysis would require an introduction to probability theory, which would take us too far afield at this time. On another subject, big-O notation provides what is probably your first exposure to industrial-strength jargon: If a function is constant or never gets beyond a fixed upper bound, you can refer to it as $O(1)$, so you can say of a particularly easy course that the homework assignments are always $O(1)$.

Big-O notation looks forbidding at first, but there is less here than meets the eye. It is easiest to think of the statement $f(n) = O(g(n))$ as saying, "f eventually grows no faster than (a multiple of) g." For example, **polynomials** like n^2 or n^{2000} are always beaten eventually by **exponential** functions like 2^n, no matter what the constants are. This is often a surprise the first time it is encountered. Comparing the values of n^{2000} with 2^n, for instance, we find that there is no contest at all, at least for small values of n. When $n = 3$, we have 3^{2000} (a number with 955 digits) for the polynomial, versus 8 (a number with 1 digit) for the exponential. Nevertheless, the exponential function eventually grows faster than the polynomial; in fact, if we try enough values for n, we discover that $n^{2000} < 2^n$ for all values of n greater than 29,718, so we can say that $n^{2000} = O(2^n)$. In a similar way, **logarithmic** functions are always eventually beaten by positive powers, so $\log n$ will eventually be less than, say, $n^{1/2000}$. Notice, too, that the relation "$= O(\ )$" among functions is not symmetric. Although it is true that $n^2 = O(n^{20})$, it is certainly not the case that $n^{20} = O(n^2)$.

Order Arithmetic

We would like to be able to develop a collection of rules for big-O that allow us to compute upper bounds of functions by combining big-O estimates of their parts. Throughout, we will keep to the assumption that we made earlier, namely, that all the functions we deal with have positive values. The first rule follows directly from the definition and tells us what we already know: that big-O ignores constant multiples.

Rule 1. For any k and any function f, $k\, f(n) = O(f(n))$.

The next thing to observe about big-O notation is that it is transitive.

Rule 2. If $f(n) = O(g(n))$ and $g(n) = O(h(n))$, then $f(n) = O(h(n))$.

To prove this, we first see that $f(n) = O(g(n))$ means that there are constants c_1 and N_1 such that $f(n) \le c_1 g(n)$ for all $n > N_1$, and similarly, $g(n) = O(h(n))$ means that there are constants c_2 and N_2 such that $g(n) \le c_2 h(n)$ for all $n > N_2$. Suppose we define N_3 to be the maximum of N_1 and N_2. For all $n > N_3$, we will have $f(n) \le c_1 g(n)$ and $g(n) \le c_2 h(n)$, and substituting for $g(n)$, we have $f(n) \le c_1(c_2 h(n))$. In other words, if we let $c_3 = c_1 c_2$, then for all $n > N_3$, we will have $f(n) \le c_3 h(n)$, which is just the definition that $f(n) = O(h(n))$.

We will frequently find ourselves in the position of knowing something like $f(n) = O(n^2)$ and $g(n) = O(n^3)$. What does this permit us to say about the function $f(n) + g(n)$? Well, since f is eventually dominated by some multiple of n^2, and a multiple of n^2 is certainly less than n^3 for n large enough, we know that $f(n)$ will eventually be no larger than n^3. This means that f and g together will eventually be bounded above by some multiple of n^3, so we can say $f(n) + g(n) = O(n^3)$. In fact, if we define $\max\{f(n), g(n)\}$ to be the function whose value at n is the larger of $f(n)$ and $g(n)$, then we can prove the following rule in much the same way as we proved Rule 2.

Rule 3. $f(n) + g(n) = O(\max\{f(n), g(n)\})$.

Since big-O changes addition to maximum, you might think that it has some unexpected action on multiplication. Not so, as you could see by using the techniques of the proof of Rule 2. We have as our last rule the following.

Rule 4.   If $f_1(n) = O(g_1(n))$ and $f_2(n) = O(g_2(n))$, then $f_1(n)f_2(n) = O(g_1(n)g_2(n))$.

We can now use these rules to compute big-O estimates without having to find explicit c and N values. For example, suppose we wished to find an estimate for the function $8n \log n + 4n^{3/2}$. We could argue as follows:

1. $\log n = O(n^{1/2})$, since logs are beaten by any positive powers (and we're thinking ahead a bit here).
2. $n \log n = O(n\, n^{1/2}) = O(n^{3/2})$ by Rule 4 (which is why we thought ahead in step 1).
3. $8n \log n = O(n^{3/2})$ by Rule 1.
4. $4n^{3/2} = O(n^{3/2})$, again by Rule 1.
5. $8n \log n + 4n^{3/2} = O(\max\{8n \log n, 4n^{3/2}\})$ by Rule 3.
6. $8n \log n + 4n^{3/2} = O(\max\{n^{3/2}, n^{3/2}\}) = O(n^{3/2})$ by Rule 2.

After you get a little practice doing order arithmetic, you'll see that such detailed analysis as we've just completed will become more or less unnecessary. The important idea is that big-O estimates can be made quickly by simply identifying the dominant (i.e., fastest-growing) term in the function being estimated. In the preceding example, for instance, we could immediately ignore the $8n \log n$ term, realizing that it will be dominated by the $n^{3/2}$ term. As we said before, there's less to big-O estimates than meets the eye.

You still might think that there is something vaguely unsatisfactory about ignoring constant multiples in our timing estimates, something mathematically not quite right. In a sense, such an objection is well founded. Suppose, for instance, that you had two programs to accomplish a given task, one that took $100n^2$ milliseconds to process an input of size n and another that took 2^n milliseconds. Which one is better? What we've seen so far would lead us to say that the $O(n^2)$ algorithm should certainly be preferred over the $O(2^n)$ one.

It turns out that we can't answer that question as stated. If you try some sample values for n, you'll see that 2^n is less than or equal to $100n^2$ as long as $n \leq 14$. So as long as you restrict yourself to running inputs of size 14 or less, the exponential algorithm beats the quadratic, even though in the long run the exponential one takes much more time. An old maxim among the people who employ computer scientists (though not necessarily among computer scientists themselves) runs, "Theory is fine, but there's nothing better than results." In fact, in many cases it is simply not worth the effort of developing and running a very complicated (though sophisticated) algorithm when there is a simple one already in the program library that is nearly as good or even better on the inputs you'll be using. Your choice will be dictated to a large extent by the reason for developing your program.

Timing Functions

Now that we have the machinery to analyze the running time of algorithms, it is time to see how this analysis works in practice. First, notice that we said "the running time of algorithms," not the running time of programs. Earlier in this section, we mentioned that the running time of a program depends not only on the size and the nature of the input, but also on such features as the computer the program runs on and the efficiency of the code produced by the compiler. The emphasis on big-O notation allows us to "factor out" the contributions that are beyond our control, such as the speed of the computer, and concentrate on the behavior of the algorithm behind the program. In general, an algorithm that has time complexity $O(n^2)$ will run as a program in time $O(n^2)$, no matter what language or machine is chosen for the implementation of the algorithm. Given an input of size n, whether the algorithm takes $117.65n^2$ milliseconds in BASIC on an IBM PC or $0.28n^2$ milliseconds in FORTRAN on a Cray X-MP is of little importance to us. What is important is that no matter how fast the computer chosen for the implementation, a program based on a $O(n^2)$ algorithm will, for large enough n, eventually run faster than an implementation of a $O(n^3)$ algorithm.

To analyze an algorithm, we make the simplifying assumption that each statement, except perhaps function calls, takes the same unit amount of time. This will not affect the timing analysis, because we are only interested in big-O estimates and so are ignoring constant multiples. For example, if multiplication takes five times as long as addition when implemented on a particular computer/compiler combination, we are off in our timing estimate by no more than a factor of five if we treat them as equal in the algorithm, and the multiple of five will be absorbed in our big-O estimate anyway.

The only statements in an algorithm that can result in a nonunit contribution to the running time are transfers of control, such as if statements, loops, and function calls. We will concentrate on simple transfers of control here and will defer detailed analysis of function calls until Chapter 5. If it were not for transfers of control, an algorithm would have time complexity equal to the number of statements in the algorithm and so would run in constant time, independent of the size of the input. It is only when some statements are to be executed more than once that we may have time complexity larger than $O(1)$.

There are two more simplifying assumptions we will make in the timing analysis of an algorithm:

1. Unless there is compelling reason to the contrary, we will always assume that an if statement takes time equal to the larger of its two branches (to obtain worst-case timing estimates).
2. Unless there is compelling reason to the contrary, we will always assume that the statements within a loop will be executed as many times as the maximum permitted by the loop control.

Example 1

Consider the following routine.

```
int LinearSearch(int n, int key,  NumberArray a)
// Searches an array with n elements for any element with
// value equal to key.  Returns the last location where key
// is found, or zero if not found.
{
   int where = 0;
   for (int index = 1; index <= n; index++)
      if { a[index] == key)
         where = index;
   return where;
}
```

In this algorithm, the loop is always executed *n* times. The body of the loop consists of a single if statement, which causes at most one statement to be executed each time it is encountered. To compute how long it takes for this algorithm to run, we consider the following **timing schematic:**

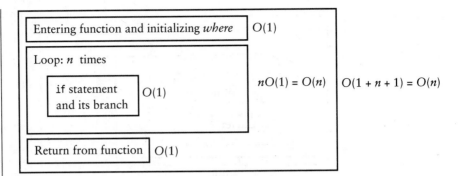

We have included timing for operations such as entering and leaving the procedure, which are not explicitly written as part of the routine. In the future, we will omit these from our timing analysis, since they contribute only a constant amount of additional time and so will not appear in the big-O estimate. Notice that we have made use of the rules for evaluating big-O expressions. ◁

Example 2

Now consider a routine with nested loops.

```
int SumProd(int n)
{
    int result = 0;
    for (int k = 1; k <= n; k++)
        for (int i = 1; i <= k; k++)
            result += k * i;
    return result;
}
```

To analyze the time complexity of this algorithm, we make use of assumption 2 and assume that the inner loop is executed the maximum number of times possible. Since the inner loop iterates k times each time it is entered, and k in the outer loop can be as large as n, we make the simplifying assumption that the inner loop iterates n times each time it is entered. You might well object that this overestimates the number of times the inner loop iterates, because there is only one instance when the inner loop actually iterates n times. You would be right, but we will show that this overestimate has no effect on the final timing estimate. Under our assumptions, we have the following timing schematic:

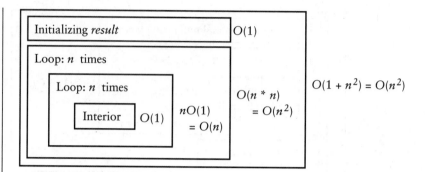

We mentioned the objection that we are overestimating the contribution of the inner loop, the one controlled by the index variable *i*. Suppose we took into account the fact that the first time the inner loop is encountered it iterates once, the second time it iterates twice, and so on. In that case, as *k* varies in the outer loop, it causes the inner loop to take time $O(k)$. Since *k* in the outer loop takes on the values 1, 2, . . . , *n*, the amount of time contributed by the outer and inner loops is proportional to $1+2+\cdots+n$. This, of course, is just the sum we saw in the discussion of Gauss's algorithm, and we can use Gauss's technique to evaluate it. The pairs of outer terms all sum to $n+1$, and there are $n/2$ such pairs, so the sum $1+2+\cdots+n$ is equal to $n(n+1)/2$, which is $O(n^2)$, the same result we obtained from our simplifying assumption that the inner loop is always iterated *n* times.   ◁

Whenever we are dealing with nested loops, as long as each inner loop is iterated a number of times that is a linear function of the number of times the next outer loop is iterated, we do not alter our big-O estimate by assuming that the inner loop iterates as often as the outer loop does. This result can be generalized to any depth of nesting. In fact, you may have seen generalizations of Gauss's identity for sums of powers other than the first power, some of which are given in Figure 2.11.

As an example of the use of these identities, consider the following segment:

FIGURE 2.11

Formulas for sums of powers

$$\sum_{i=1}^{n} i = \frac{n(n+1)}{2}$$

$$\sum_{i=1}^{n} i^2 = \frac{n(n+1)(2n+1)}{6}$$

$$\sum_{i=1}^{n} i^3 = \frac{n^2(n+1)^2}{4}$$

```
for (int i = 1; i <= n; i++)
    for (int j = 1; j <= i; j++)
        for (int k = 1; k <= i; k++)
            // something that is O(1);
```

Our simplifying assumption applies here, so we know that this segment of code will contribute $O(n \times n \times n) = O(n^3)$ to the timing. To be more precise (at the cost of slightly more involved calculations), we see that for each value of i in the outer loop, the two inner loops together will contribute i^2 to the timing. As i takes on the values $1, 2, \ldots, n$, then, the entire segment will contribute $1^2 + 2^2 + \cdots + n^2$, which is just the second sum in Figure 2.11. Thus, a more accurate timing estimate for this segment would be $T(n) = n(n+1)(2n+1)/6$, which is still $O(n^3)$.

Example 3

Finally, consider a program segment with a **multiplicative loop,** one whose iterations are not a linear function of the control variable of the outer loop. This is an instance of "compelling reasons to the contrary," where we will not be able to assume that the inner loop will iterate as often as the outer loop.

```
int m = 1;
for (int i = 1; i <= n; i++)
    m *= 2;
    for (int j = 1; i <= m; j++)
        // something that is O(1)
```

In this case, as the outer loop control takes on the values $1, 2, 3, \ldots$, the inner loop iterates $2, 4, 8, \ldots$ times, giving us a running time of $O(2 + 4 + \cdots + 2^n)$. This is a **geometric series,** in which each term is a constant multiple of the preceding one. It happens that for such a series with n terms, with first term s and constant multiple r (both of which are 2 in this case), the value of the series is

$$\sum_{i=0}^{n-1} sr^i = s\left(1 + r + r^2 + \ldots + r^{n-1}\right) = s\frac{r^n - 1}{r - 1}$$

so that we have a running time of $O(2(2^n - 1)/(2-1)) = O(2^{n+1})$ rather than the $O(n^2)$ that we would expect in a nonmultiplicative loop. ◁

2.5 APPLICATION: MEMORY MANAGEMENT

We mentioned earlier that there is an ecological aspect to computer science in that we must carefully manage the use of the finite amount of memory available in any machine. Much of that work is "transparent" to the programmer and is handled by the system programs that run in the background. For example, suppose that a computer must execute the C++ statement p = new T for a pointer *p*. The pointer itself can be handled in the same way as the rest of the program variables, such as integers, reals, and characters. But how does the computer find room in memory for what *p* points to without running the risk of overwriting already stored information? This **memory management** is at least partly handled by the compiler, which translates the statement p = new T into instructions to the **operating system**. Now, the operating system is itself a program, one that runs all the time and whose job is to manage all the resources of the computer, such as input/output, central processor access, file management, and—of particular interest to us here—memory management. Along with handling requests from a program for a new chunk of memory for a pointer to point to, the operating system may also have to deal with the similar problem of allocating space in memory for several programs in a multiuser environment. If a new user sits down at a terminal and wants to run a job of size 60K bytes, the operating system must find room in memory for the job without disturbing any job already in the system. In this section, we will explore some strategies for memory management.

We will use pointers as our model here, although much of what we discuss would apply equally well to (generally larger) program code segments. The two primary operations we will discuss are simple modifications of *new* and *delete*:

1. Pointer NewPtr(int size), a function that will return a pointer to a location in memory sufficiently large to hold *size* bytes.
2. void DisposePtr(Pointer p), which makes the location in memory pointed to by *p* available for later use.

In what follows, we will often refer to these two operations in more general terms of **allocating** and **deallocating** memory and will refer to the piece of memory allocated or deallocated as a **block.** These two operations should be thought of as operating system calls, so that, for instance, the statement p = new int would be translated into code that first looks up the size of an integer and then makes the operating system call *NewPtr* to allocate memory for the new object. Thinking of these two operations as system-level operations gives us a certain amount of freedom that we would not have if we worked exclusively at the source code level. In particular, we can free ourselves from having to worry about type compatibility between pointers and integers; that's a high-level convention, and we're operating at a level where we have no idea about the language of the program that makes the call. With this in mind, we will refer to **links**, rather than pointers, to emphasize that at this level there is no difference between pointers (which are, after all, just addresses of locations in memory) and integers (which can serve as indices to the array of bytes making up the memory).

In the model we are considering here, we are guided by three constraints:

1. The blocks we will deal with must be contiguous; if we must find space for a block of 300 bytes, it cannot be 120 bytes in one location, 80 in another, and 100 somewhere else.

2. The blocks, in general, will be of different sizes. This is not the case with memory allocation in LISP, where all the blocks are records with two identically sized fields, nor is it the case with many disk-based file systems, where all the blocks are the same size, often 512 bytes.

3. The blocks will have unknown contents; our memory manager will know only how large a requested block is, not what's in it. This will mean that, as we mentioned, we will treat memory as one very large array of bytes (or 2-byte words in some systems, although we'll just deal with bytes here). Some of the other consequences of this constraint are considered in the exercises.

By now, it should come as no surprise that we will make use of a **free list**, a list in which each cell consists of (1) a link to a **free block**, namely, one that is not currently being used, (2) a link to the next cell in the list, and (3) other information that we deem appropriate, such as the size of the free block referred to by the cell. Initially, we could imagine the free list consisting of a single cell linked to one large free block consisting of the entire memory available for dynamic storage. This memory is called the **heap** to distinguish it from the part of the memory reserved for program variables and system information. Where, then, would we put the free list itself? It shouldn't take you too long to hit on the idea of keeping the free list in the heap, along with all the other blocks. We will do this by reserving some space in each block for a block header, where we will keep all the information about that block, which means that we can dispense with the link to the block referred to by the cell. In Figure 2.12, we illustrate a typical heap consisting of five used blocks, shaded in the drawing, along with five free blocks of sizes 200, 50, 300, 75, and 100 bytes, each of which has a link to the next free block in the list. In Figure 2.13, we indicate the *link* and *size* fields of each free block.

FIGURE 2.12

A heap with five free blocks

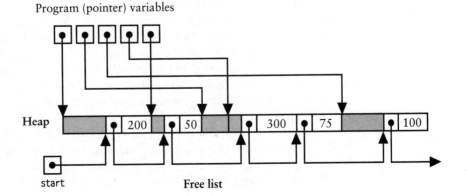

FIGURE 2.13

A free block before
and after allocation

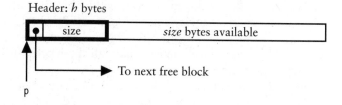

Header: h bytes

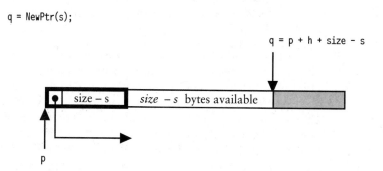

q = NewPtr(s);

Allocation

To allocate a block, what we do is find a block in the free list that is at least as large as the requested size and use all or part of that free block to fill the request. It seems simplest to allocate space for the used block from the right end of the original free block; then we don't have to move the location of the header for the free block, which means that we don't have to find and change any link to that block in the list. In Figure 2.13, we illustrate such an allocation.

We have to be careful about how we find the address (i.e., link) of the start of the newly allocated block. If a free block of size 200 began at byte p, and our request was for 90 bytes, we could not return the address $p+(200-90)$ for the start of the allocated block, since that would ignore the space occupied by the block header. Instead, if we are to allocate space of size s from a free block of $size$ bytes starting at p, the allocated block would begin at address $p+b+size-s$, where b is the size of the block header. In proper terms, we must be careful to distinguish between the **logical length** of a block, which is the number of bytes actually available, and the **physical length**, which is the total length of the block, including the header. In what follows, we will describe blocks in terms of their logical, rather than physical, lengths.

A problem arises when the request is for the whole free block. In that case, we must remove that free block from the free list entirely. Since the free list as described so far is a linked list, deletion will require that we know the prior cell in the linked list (along with the cell following, but that's simple). This isn't a problem if we know ahead of time that the free list will never be very long; but if we don't know that, we will have to decide how to delete, such as making the free list doubly linked (which then makes deletion run in constant time at the expense of making the block header larger) or using two links, one trailing the other, to find the cell prior to the one to be deleted. We will have more to say about this shortly, but first let's tackle the problem of how to find a free block of sufficient size to fill a given request.

Consider the situation of Figure 2.12 again. If we call *NewPtr(90)*, we have several options. The simplest strategy is known as **first fit**: To fill a request for a block, we start at the head of the free list and traverse the list until we come to the first block that is large enough to satisfy our request, in this case the block of size 200 at the head of the list. We would then use 90 of the 200 bytes of that block to satisfy the request, which would leave us with 110 bytes available. The block of size 90 would be added to the collection of used blocks, and the free block that used to be of size 200 would have its size field changed to 110. First fit would certainly be easy to implement and should be relatively fast, as well. We can't say too much about its speed without knowing the sizes of the blocks to be allocated, but it seems reasonable at this stage to guess that a block capable of satisfying our request should be found rather early in the free list. Or should it? One problem with the first-fit strategy is that in the long run, it will lead to a large number of small blocks at the start of the free list. In the exercises, we ask you to suggest a possible way to alleviate this problem.

Another allocation strategy is known as **best fit**. In this scheme, we traverse the entire free list and select the smallest free block that fills the request. In Figure 2.12, a request for 90 bytes would result in taking 90 bytes from the last free block, with 100 bytes available, leaving a tiny block of 10 bytes in its place. This tiny block is indicative of the nature of the best-fit strategy: It tends over the long run to produce many small and large blocks (the block of size 300, for instance, might very well be spared from any pruning for quite some time), but relatively few middle-sized blocks. In addition, best fit requires us to traverse the entire free list for each request, so it will certainly run slower, on average, than first fit.

Both of these allocation strategies have advantages and disadvantages; as we have remarked before, we must make an educated choice between them, based on such knowledge as the expected length of the free list and the distribution of request sizes. The consensus is that in most cases, the added time spent on a best-fit strategy simply isn't worth it, but your choice would, of course, be based on careful analysis of the system you have to implement.

One certain disadvantage of both strategies, and of almost any other based on free lists, is that they lead to **fragmentation**, the breaking of the total free memory into small blocks. In Figure 2.12, for example, there are 725 bytes of free memory, but the largest request that can be filled is for 300 bytes. In that case, what would we do if presented with a request for, say, 375 bytes or 500 bytes? The answer depends, in part, on what we have decided to do when a request comes to **deallocate** a used block and return it to the free list.

Deallocation

Deallocating a used block is easy. All we have to do is add that block to the free list. We can be a bit more sophisticated than that, however, by dealing with at least part of the fragmentation problem at the same time. A block to be deallocated might very well have adjacent blocks that are already free, so it would make sense to **coalesce** any newly freed block with its left and right free neighbors. In this way we avoid the situation of Figure 2.12, where we have two adjacent free blocks of sizes 300 and 75 bytes. In that situation, we really have a block of size 375 available, but we can't get at it because the operating system "thinks" it is divided into two smaller blocks.

But how should we perform the coalescing process? We must be able to find the left and right neighbors of the newly freed block and check whether they are free. Finding the right neighbor isn't too hard; we know that the present block starts at address p, that its logical size is *size*, and that h bytes are taken up by the block header. With that information, we know that the right neighbor must start at address $p+size+h$ (this is where the ability to do address arithmetic comes in handy). But checking whether the right neighbor is free is another matter. As we have set our data structure so far, the only way to check the right neighbor is to traverse the entire free list to see if the right neighbor is there. Things get even worse when we try to check the left neighbor. As things stand, we would have to traverse the free list and, for each block in the free list, perform the same address calculations as before, to find out whether the free block has the present block as its right neighbor. This is already a somewhat daunting task, and we haven't even considered how to perform the coalescing after we have found the free neighbors.

One way to simplify matters is to pay the price of using more space in the blocks to store information that would help us in coalescing. A common strategy is known as the **boundary tag** method. In this method, each block contains a left tag at the start of the block, which is 0 for free blocks and 1 for used blocks, along with a size field, and a right tag at the right end of the block, which contains the same value as the left tag. To facilitate moving through the free list, we will maintain it as a **doubly linked ring** (i.e., the last block in the list is linked to the first one), so that each free block will also contain two links, to the prior and next elements in the free list. Finally, to aid in finding left free blocks, each free block will also contain a **back link** to the start of the block, so that our blocks will take the form illustrated in Figure 2.14.

Notice that we have two distinct structures here: (1) the doubly linked ring of free blocks, which we will assume is accessed by a link, *free,* to some block in the free list (or has a flag value like 0 or −1 if the free list is empty), and (2) the heap itself, which may be regarded as linearly ordered by address. These two structures have nothing to do with each other. If free block A is prior to free block B in the free list, it is equally likely that A is before B in the heap or after B in the heap.

FIGURE 2.14
Boundary tag block
structures

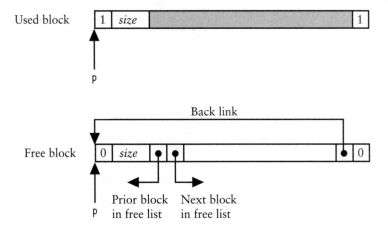

Now we can describe how coalescing would be accomplished. Because we are writing our routines at the system level, we will assume that the only heap operations available to us are Link GetVal(p), which returns the value stored in address *p* of memory, and void SetVal(p, n), which stores the value *n* in memory location *p*. It will be useful to keep some global constants: *SIZE_OFST, PRIOR_OFST, NEXT_OFST, BACK_OFST, FRTAG_OFST* (for FreeRightTAG OFfSeT), and *URTAG_OFST* (for UsedRightTAG OFfSeT), which are equal to the offsets from the start of a block of the *size, prior, next,* and *backlink* fields of the block and *rightTag* fields of free and used blocks. In a typical system, the tags would be 1 byte long, and sizes and links would require 4 bytes, so we would have *SIZE_OFST* = 1, *PRIOR_OFST* = 5, *NEXT_OFST* = 9, *BACK_OFST* = 13, *FRTAG_OFST* = 17, and URTAG_OFST = 5. Thus, for example, if we knew that a free block began at address *p,* then the *size* field would begin at address *p* + 1, the *next* field would begin at address *p* + 9, the back link would begin at *p* + *size* + 13, and the right neighboring block would begin at address *p* + *size* + 18.

To check whether the left neighboring block was free, then, we could use the function *LeftFree.*

```
const int HEAPSTART = 1;  // starting address of heap

int LeftFree(Link p)
// Returns true if and only if the left neighbor
// of the block at p is free.
{
    // Are we at the left end of the heap?
    if (p > HEAPSTART)
    {
        // If not, get the right tag of the left nbr,
        Link tag = GetVal(p - 1, tag);
```

```
        // and return true iff the tag is zero.
        return (tag == 0);
    }
    else
        return 0;
}
```

We could define *RightFree* in a similar fashion. Having done that, it is fairly simple to describe the coalescing routines. We show *CoalesceLeft* next.

```
const int
    BACK_LEFT_OFST = 5,  // distance of backlink field from
                         // right end of block
    TAGSIZE = 1,         // size of tag field in bytes
    LINKSIZE = 4;        // size of a link in bytes}


void CoalesceLeft(Link p)
// Merge the block at p with its free left neighbor to
// produce a large free block.
{
    // Find size of p block.
    Link uSize = GetVal(p + SIZE_OFST);
    // Set right tag of p block.
    SetVal(p + URTAG_OFST + uSize, 0);
    // Use backlink to find start of left neighbor.
    Link start = GetVal(p - BACK_LEFT_OFST);
    // Place backlink field into p block.
    SetVal(p + BACK_OFST + uSize, start);

    // Find logical size of left neighbor.
    Link fSize = GetVal(start + SIZE_OFST);
    // Set new size.
    SetVal(start + SIZE_OFST,
            uSize + fSize + 2*TAGSIZE + LINKSIZE)
}
```

The only part that might be tricky is the setting of the *size* field for the coalesced block. Figure 2.15 shows that when we coalesce a free and a formerly used block, the logical size of the new free block is equal to the sum of the logical size of the free block plus the total size of the old used block—that is, the old logical size plus the sizes of the left and right tags and the old size field.

We can now describe the routine *DisposePtr*. The skeleton is simple enough: We check the left and right neighbors and then coalesce as necessary. If no coalescing is needed, we just set the tag fields of the old used block to 0; modify the size field to make room for the prior, next, and back links; add in the back link; and add the newly freed block to the free list.

FIGURE 2.15

Before and after coalescing left

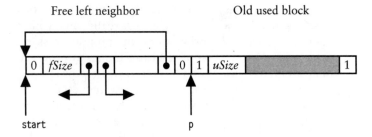

```
void AddToFreeList(Link p);
int LeftFree(Link p);
int RightFree(Link p);
void CoalesceRight(Link p);
void CoalesceLeft(Link p);
void CoalesceBoth(Link p);
void ConvertToFreeBlock(Link p);

void DisposePtr(Link p)
// Remove p block from used blocks,
// do coalescing as needed.
{
   if (LeftFree(p))
      if (RightFree(p))
         CoalesceBoth(p);
      else
         CoalesceLeft(p);
   else
      if (RightFree(p))  then
         CoalesceRight(p);
      else
      {
         ConvertToFreeBlock(p);
         AddToFreeList(p);
      }
}
```

Of course, we have omitted the definitions of some necessary functions, but if you want something you can really sink your teeth into, just take a look at the *HeapSim* program on the program disk accompanying this text, which provides the complete heap simulation program. The main function of that program consists of a loop in which the program generates a request for a new pointer at each iteration. These requests are for blocks of randomly chosen sizes, which have randomly chosen lifetimes. Each request that is successfully handled by *NewPtr* is placed on a waiting list of links to active blocks, along with the times when they will be deallocated. Each iteration, the waiting list is polled to see if there are any blocks whose time has expired. For every one of those blocks, a call is made to *DisposePtr*. Every so often, the simulation breaks off and prints statistics about the number of free blocks available, the number of used blocks currently in the heap, the number of requests for space that couldn't be filled, and the sizes of the present free blocks. If you have a computer with good graphics capabilities, it is well worth the effort to modify the sample program to produce a memory map of the free and used blocks in the heap, an example of which is given in Figure 2.16. In that map, the used blocks are indicated by shaded rectangles, and the free blocks are unshaded, with vertical tick marks separating the blocks. Typically, the low heap address is the top left corner, and the rest of the heap is arranged left to right and top to bottom on the page. If you redraw each block on the screen as its status changes, the display can provide many minutes of entertainment, as well as giving some genuine insights into the comparative behaviors of first-fit and best-fit selection algorithms.

Compaction

Even with the best selection and coalescing algorithms we can invent, fragmentation in the heap can still leave us in a situation where there is plenty of free space available to fill a request for memory, but no free block large enough for the request. What should our operating system do in such a situation?

Basically, we have two choices: We can either report failure or try to make room for the request. In some cases, reporting failure is an attractive alternative. It is certainly easy to implement, and we may be able to recover from such a failure. For example, if our system was responsible for handling

FIGURE 2.16

A typical memory map

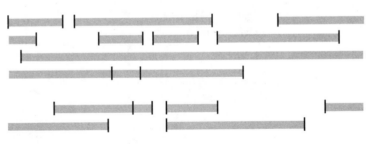

many programs using a single computer on a time-sharing basis, we might be able to swap out a job in the system (saving it on a disk, for instance), load the new job in the vacant space and run it for a while, and then swap that with the old job when it came time to run the old job. Even if there was no job large enough to swap out right away, we could still put the new job on a waiting list and load it when space became available. Done quickly enough, this process would be more or less invisible to the users, especially in light of the fact that in the time frame of the computer, the equivalent of days passes between the keystrokes entered by the vastly slower humans at the terminals. Of course, this would not work at all well for our example of allocating space for pointers. If one program was all that was resident on the computer, it would serve no useful purpose to tell the program to wait until space became available, since nothing would happen in the meantime to free any space.

The other option would be to make room for a request by moving the used blocks together, as in Figure 2.17, where the shaded blocks are used and the unshaded are free. It's not difficult to see how this compaction of memory would be implemented, but it is equally evident that this process could be very slow, since it would run in time proportional to the total number of bytes of used memory. As fast as a computer is, it could still take an unacceptably long time to move what may amount to megabytes of memory.

That's not the worst of our problems, however. Can you see why? The truly messy part of memory compaction is that the used blocks are referred to by pointers. If we move memory around without telling the resident program, that program is suddenly in the position of having most, if not all, of its pointers referring to locations in memory that no longer contain what the program expects them to contain. In other words, our operating system now has the responsibility of letting the resident program know that its pointers are no longer valid, and the resident program now must somehow update the values of its pointers to reflect the memory moves.

That's bad enough, but suppose the heap also contains pointers, as would be the case if some blocks contained pointers to other blocks. The resident program may not even have variables referring to these pointers and therefore wouldn't have a clue about what to update. This is enough of a

FIGURE 2.17

Compacting memory

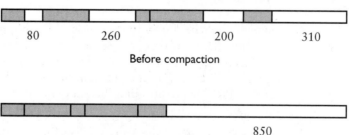

80   260   200   310

Before compaction

850

After compaction

mess that some operating systems don't do memory compaction at all. In the exercises, we ask you to explore some ways of dealing with these problems.

2.6 SUMMARY

The *List* ADT has as its structure a linearly ordered set of positions, with each position associated with a single list element. For every nonempty list, there is one position (which can be advanced or retreated in the list) where insertion, deletion, inspection, and modification of elements take place.

This chapter explored the two principal implementations of *List:* arrays and linked lists. The operations in the array implementation are conceptually simple, but suffer from the fact that the element array must be allocated as a contiguous block. Insertion and deletion within an array also suffer from the fact that they are not constant-time operations. With linked lists, these shortcomings no longer appear, but this benefit is bought at the cost of the relative complexity of pointer-based algorithms.

We often compare implementations of abstract data types by looking at the amount of space they require and the time the operations take to run. In both cases, we generally express our estimates by functions that measure space or time as a function of the size of the object. It is often sufficient to find worst-case upper bounds for the space and time functions; big-O notation allows us to find such estimates of the **asymptotic** (i.e., long-range) behavior of functions.

A natural use for lists is to maintain a free list of available blocks in a heap where memory is allocated and deallocated dynamically. We introduced the boundary tag method, which requires tag fields at both ends of each block, to facilitate the process of finding free neighbors of a block to be deallocated and coalescing adjacent free blocks. This is by no means the only way to handle memory management. In the exercises, we explore an alternative strategy.

2.7 EXERCISES

1. Pictures don't lie, but they can mislead. In the specification of the *List* operation *Remove*, there are several cases that are not covered by the accompanying figure (see p. 52). For instance, the figure shows a position preceding the current position, although that may not be true in general. Provide pictures that illustrate the action of *Remove* in all possible cases.

2. Suppose we changed the array implementation of *List* to include a special *T* value, *GONE,* so that deleting the element in position *i* from an

array is accomplished by replacing the element at that position by the *GONE* value. For example, in a list of positive integers, we might choose *GONE* to be −1. Discuss the advantages and disadvantages of such a scheme, particularly in terms of timing and the definition of the *List* operations.

3. In the array version of *InsertAfter,* what would happen if we shifted the array elements in reverse order, starting from the current position and working our way to the tail?

4. How many ways can you come up with to tell whether a list is empty in our linked implementation? How many ways are there to tell if a list has one element?

5. How would you solve the problem of aliasing that we mentioned in the discussion of the linked list version of the copy constructor? *Hint*: Consider modifying the type *T*.

6. This version of the linked list display operator << doesn't work.

```
template<class T> ostream& TList<T>:: operator<<(ostream& os, TList<T> l)
{
    Node<T> p = l.first;
    while (p)
    {
        os << p->value;
        p->next = p;
    }
    return os;
}
```

   a. Why doesn't it work?

   b. Are there any circumstances in which it will work?

7. In the linked list version of *Clear,* suppose we changed the loop to

```
while (current)
{
    delete nptr;
    current = current->next;
    nptr = current;
}
```

   Would this modified version still delete all nodes in a list? Draw pictures to support your claim.

8. The following statements are supposed to interchange the nodes immediately following the one pointed to by *p,* as in the accompanying diagram. The auxiliary pointer *q* is uninitialized at the start.

1. `p->next = q;`
2. `p->next->next = p->next->next->next;`
3. `q = p->next->next;`
4. `q->next = p->next;`

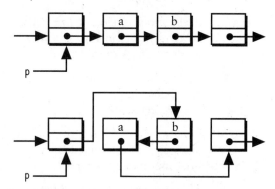

Unfortunately, the statements aren't in the right order. Which of the following orders is correct?

1, 3, 2, 4   2, 4, 1, 3   3, 2, 1, 4   3, 2, 4, 1   4, 1, 2, 3

Bonus: There are 24 ways to arrange these statements. Are there any correct orders in addition to the correct one in the preceding list?

9. The member function `Nth(int n)` sets the current position to the *n*th position in the list (assume that the list has at least *n* elements). Implement this function in both array and linked list forms, and give timing estimates for each.

10. The function *Reverse* reverses the order of elements in a list, so the list (a, b, c) would be changed to (c, b, a).

    a. Implement *Reverse* as an external function (i.e., using only the *List* operations that are publicly available).

    b. Implement *Reverse* as a member function for the array implementation.

    c. Implement *Reverse* as a member function for the linked list implementation.

    d. Compare the running times of the versions in parts (**b**) and (**c**).

11. There's a clever way to traverse a linked list in both directions, as long as you can perform bitwise logical operations on addresses. Suppose x and y are two binary digits; we can define the operation $\oplus$ (known as XOR, or "exclusive or") by $1 \oplus 1 = 0$, $0 \oplus 0 = 0$, $1 \oplus 0 = 1$, and $0 \oplus 1 = 1$, and for two binary numbers n and m, we define $n \oplus m$ to be the result of applying XOR to the corresponding bits of the numbers, so that

$010111 \oplus 111101 = 101010$. (Do you see why this operation is sometimes called "add without carry"?) To form a linked list in this scheme, each cell at address p has a single link field, *link(p)*, and the first and last cells in the list have a dummy prior cell at "address" 0. To traverse a list, starting at the cell at p, we use the following algorithm.

```
void Traverse(Pointer p)
{
   Pointer prior = 0;
   while (p !> 0)
   {
      // Visit the cell at p,
      // doing any necessary processing;
      Pointer save = p;
      p = prior ⊕ link(p);
      prior = save;
   }
}
```

a. Show that this works by tracing the action of *Traverse* in both directions on the list of cells at locations 19, 30, 28, 39, and 46 (in that order), where the link fields are defined by $link(19) = 30$, $link(30) = 15$, $link(28) = 57$, $link(39) = 50$, and $link(46) = 39$. Of course, you'll have to convert all these numbers to (6-bit) binary numbers.

b. What would the *link* values have to be for the linked list of cells at locations 40, 8, 6, 50, and 19 (in that order)?

c. Explain why this scheme would not be particularly good on lists that would be changed by insertions and deletions.

12. Suppose we overloaded the operator+to perform **concatenation** of lists, declared like this:

```
TList<T>& operator+ (TList<T> first, TList<T> second);
```

This operator takes as its argument two lists, *first* and *second,* and constructs a new list that consists of all the elements of *first,* followed by all the elements of *second.* For example, if *first* was (a, b, c) and *second* was (p, q, r, s), then the expression first + second would construct and return a reference to the list (a, b, c, p, q, r, s).

a. Implement this operator as a friend function for the array implementation.

b. Implement this operator as a friend function for the linked list implementation.

c. Compare the running times of the versions in parts (b) and (c).

13. The member function

    ```
    void Append(TList<T> second)
    ```

    acts like the concatenation operator given in Exercise 12, but instead of making a copy of the first and second lists, this routine joins the second list to the object itself (so changing *second* would also change this list). Implement *Append* for arrays and linked lists, and compare their running times.

    There's no reason why linked structures need to be restricted to one pointer per node. In Exercises 14 through 16, we'll consider some things that can be done with several pointers in each node.

14. In a **doubly linked list**, like the free list in the memory management example in the text, each node has two pointers, one (*next*) to the successor node and one (*prior*) to the predecessor, as shown here.

    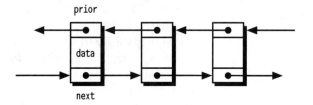

    a. Write *InsertAfter* for doubly linked lists.

    b. Write *Delete* for doubly linked lists.

    c. Is there a reason why we might want to use doubly linked lists, or are they just an invention to bedevil students?

15. In a **braid**, or **multilist**, each node contains two or more member data items and as many pointers. In the example that follows, we have a small telephone directory with name and number member data items. There are two sets of pointers, arranged so that one set (the upper one in the diagram) links the nodes in sorted order by name and the other set (the lower one) links the nodes in increasing order of numbers.

    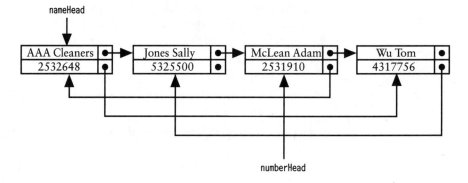

a. Discuss the advantages and disadvantages of such a structure.

b. Write a function that would delete a node in a two-braid like the one shown in the diagram.

c. Write a function that would insert a node in a two-braid. Assume that you have pointers to the cells that would be before the new cell in each of the two orders.

16. If we have a long linked list that doesn't require insertions and deletions, we could put an extra pointer in each node that points to the node twice as far along in the list. For example, the node in position 6 would have a pointer (which we might call the *step* pointer) to the node in position 7 and one (which we might call the *hop* pointer) to the node in position 12.

a. Draw a picture of such a structure with 16 nodes, and for each node indicate the least number of moves it would take to get there from the first node.

b. Find a way to describe how to get from the first node to the *n*th. In other words, given *n*, what should be the sequence of steps and hops to get there in the least amount of time?

c. Let $M(n)$ be a function that counts the least number of moves to get to the *n*th cell. What can you say about M? A suitable answer might be, "M never gets any larger than [some function of *n*]." Even better would be something exact, like, "$M(n)$ is equal to the number of digits in the binary expression of *n*, plus the number of 1s in the binary expression, minus 2."

d. Does this data structure make finding the *n*th node significantly faster than with a simple linked list?

e. *Bonus*: The *hop* pointers in the upper half of the list are never used. Can you think of a good use for them that would speed up access even further?

17. Prove the following identities by finding suitable values for *c* and *N* in the definition of big-O.

a. $n^3 + n^2 + n + 1 = O(n^3)$

b. $\dfrac{3n^3 + 9n^2 - 24}{n+1} = O(n^2)$

c. $\displaystyle\sum_{i=1}^{n} i^k = O\left(n^{k+1}\right)$

18. We could show that $\sqrt{8n^2 + 20} = O(n)$ by setting $c = 3$ in the definition of big-O. How large does *n* have to be before $\sqrt{8n^2 + 20} < 3n$?

19. Find the best big-O estimates you can for the following functions, without finding c and N.

    a. $f(n) = \dfrac{8n^5 - 25n^3 + 7n}{4n^2 - 1}$

    b. $g(n) = \begin{cases} 4n^2 + 1 & \text{if } n \text{ is even} \\ 3n - 5 & \text{if } n \text{ is odd} \end{cases}$

    c. $h(n) = 3^n - 2^{n+2}$

20. For two functions $f(n)$ and $g(n)$, we can define the relation $\leftarrow$ by saying $f(n) \leftarrow g(n)$ if $f(n) = O(g(n))$. Arrange the following functions in $\leftarrow$ order:

$$n^2, \; 2^n, \; \log n, \; n\log n, \; 3^n, \; (\log n)^2, \; n, \; \frac{n}{\log n}, \; n(\log n)^2$$

21. What, if anything, is wrong with the following statement?

Algorithm A and algorithm B both have the same result, but accomplish that result in different ways. Algorithm A runs in time $O(n^2)$, while algorithm B runs in time $O(2^n)$. If $n = 20$, $n^2 = 400$, and $2^n = 1{,}048{,}576$, for inputs of size 20, algorithm A will be approximately 2,621 times as fast as algorithm B.

22. Provide big-O timing estimates for the following algorithms.

    a.
```
int Mindex(IntegerArray a, int start)
// Returns the index of the smallest element
// in an array at or after position start.
{
    int smallest = a[start];
    for (int i = start + 1; i <= a.Upper(); i++)
        if (a[i] < smallest)
        {
            smallest = a[i];
            int index = i;
        }
    return index;
}
```

    b.
```
void SelectionSort(IntegerArray a)
// (Inefficiently) sorts a from smallest to largest.
{
    IntegerArray b = a;
    for (int i = a.Lower(); i <= a.Upper(); i++)
    {
        int small = Mindex(a, i);
        b[i] = a[small];
    }
```

```
        a = b;
    }
```

23. Consider the following two algorithms.
```
long Expo1(int x, int n)
```
```
// Returns x to the power n (n must be ≥ 0).
{
    long result = 1;
    for (int i = 1; i <= n; i++)
        result *= x;
    return result;
}
```

```
long Expo2(int x, int n)
// Does the same as Expo1.
{
    long result = 1;
    while (n)
    {
        if (n % 2) then
            result *= x;
        x = x * x;
        n = n / 2;
    }
    return result;
}
```

   a. Provide an example that *Expo2* does the same thing as *Expo1* by tracing the action of *Expo2*(2, 13).

   b. Find estimates of the running time of the two algorithms. Which is better?

24. Show that in Example 2, the function *SumProd* satisfies

$$SumProd(n) = \frac{n(n+1)(n+2)(2n+1)}{12}$$

25. Suppose S is a statement that takes time $O(1)$. We have seen that
```
for (int i = 1; i <= n; i++)
    S;
```
   takes time *n* and that
```
for (int i = 1; i <= n; i++)
    for (int j = 1; j <= i; j++)
        S;
```
   takes time $n(n+1)/2$.

   a. Find the best timing function you can (in the sense that an answer like $n(n+1)/2$ is to be preferred over $O(n^2)$) for the segment

```
for (int i = 1; i <= n; i++)
   for (int j = 1; j <= i; j++)
      for (int k = 1; k <= j; k++)
         S;
```

   b. (Difficult) Generalize your answer to part (a) for the case of k nested loops, as

```
for (int i₁ = 1; i₁ <= n; i₁++)
   for (int i₂ = 1; i₂ <= i₁; i₂++)
      for (int i₃ = 1; i₃ <= i₂; i₃++)
            .
            .
            .
         for (int iₖ = 1; iₖ <= iₖ₋₁; iₖ++)
            S;
```

26. Suppose that a heap contained free blocks of sizes 200, 50, and 100 bytes and that the blocks were arranged in that order in the free list, starting with the 200-byte block. Suppose also that requests for new blocks of sizes 100, 80, 50, and 70 bytes came in that order (i.e., first request for 100, second for 80, and so on). Describe the contents of the free list at each stage under

   a. The first-fit selection strategy

   b. The best-fit selection strategy

27. For the free list in Exercise 26, give a sequence of requests

   a. That can be satisfied using first fit, but not best fit

   b. That can be satisfied by best fit, but not first fit

28. We mentioned that a shortcoming of first fit is that over the long run, it tends to produce a large collection of tiny blocks at the start of the free list. How might you remedy this problem?

29. Discuss the advantages and disadvantages of keeping the free list sorted by address. Does such a choice allow you to dispense with any of the block fields?

30. Is memory management appreciably simpler if all requests are the same size? Explain by describing a data structure you would use and then implementing *NewPtr* and *DisposePtr* for your data structure.

31. Describe an implementation of memory management in which the heap contained 2^{20} (= 1,048,576) bytes and every request for a new block was either of size 2^8 (= 256) or 2^{16} (= 65,536) bytes. Try to make your implementations as efficient as possible in terms of both time and space.

32. Another common memory management scheme, the **buddy system,** is somewhat similar to Exercise 31. In this scheme, the heap consists of 2^m bytes, addressed from 0 to 2^m-1, and no matter what the size of the request, space is always allocated in blocks of physical size 2^k, for $k \leq m$. There are several free lists, one for each block size 2^k, and initially all free lists are empty, except for the one of size 2^m. Each block contains a used/free tag and a *size* field, containing the power of 2 that represents the size of the block, and free blocks contain the usual *prior* and *next* fields. One advantage of this scheme is that finding the start of a block is easy: Any block of size 2^k begins at address $p2^k$, for some integer p. Such a block can be split into two blocks of size 2^{k-1}, which are called left and right buddies, so that the left buddy begins at address $p2^k$, and the right buddy begins at address $p2^k + 2^{k-1}$.

   a. Show that under this scheme, a block of size 2^{k-1} that begins at address $p2^{k-1}$ is a left buddy (as a result of being split off earlier) if and only if p is even.

   b. If a block of size 16 begins at address 5024, is it a left or right buddy, and where does its buddy begin? What if the block is of size 1024?

   Allocation in this system is simple enough: If a request arrives, you compute the smallest block size 2^k that can fill the request, and then run up through the free lists of increasing size until you find an available block of size 2^j, with $j \geq k$. If $j > k$, remove that block from its free list, split that block into left and right buddies, add the right buddy to its free list, and continue the process, splitting the left buddy until the block size is 2^k, which can be used to fill the request.

   c. Show the results of filling requests for blocks of size 40, 300, 100, and 500 in a heap of size 4096.

   d. Write *NewPtr* for the buddy system.

   Deallocation frees a block and coalesces it with its free buddy (if it has one) into a larger block, which is also coalesced if it has a free buddy, and so on up.

   e. Suppose that after having allocated all the blocks in part (c), the blocks were then released in the order in which they were allocated. Describe what would take place at each deallocation. Do the same thing assuming that the blocks were released in opposite order.

   f. Write DisposePtr for the buddy system.

33. Write a compaction algorithm without worrying about how to deal with changing pointer references.

34. Do Exercise 33, worrying. One strategy you might consider is **double indirection,** in which a request for a new block is filled as usual, but the

address returned is not the address of the allocated block but rather the address of a **master pointer**, which always resides at a fixed location in memory and which actually contains the address of the allocated block, as in the following diagram. Relocatable blocks in the heap can be moved to compress memory, but master pointers never move.

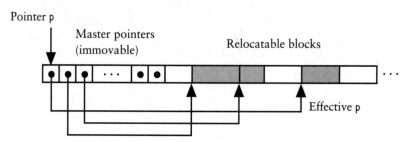

35. If, somehow, memory requests are known in advance, there is an elegant way to determine the best possible memory use. Suppose that we have n requests with sizes $r_1, \ldots, r_n$ and total available memory M. We will assume that $r_i \leq M$ for $i=1, \ldots, n$ (otherwise, there's no sense in even considering the request). We will consider the **knapsack problem**, finding the largest amount of memory that can be used by these requests without exceeding M. We first let a be a bit vector (an array whose elements are restricted to the values 0 and 1), indexed from 0 to M, with initial values $a[0]=1$ and $a[i]=0$ for $i=1, \ldots, M$, and then run the following algorithm:

```
for (int i = 1; i <= n; i++)
   for (int k = M; k >= r_i; k--)
      a[k] = a[k] || a[k - r_i];
```

Then the maximum amount of memory that can be used by any combination of requests is the highest index of the array that contains a 1.

a. Run this algorithm for $n=4$, $r_1=3$, $r_2=7$, $r_3=4$, $r_4=9$, $M=15$, and use this sample run to explain how the algorithm works.

b. Would the algorithm work if the inner loop went up from r_i to M, rather than down?

c. Modify the algorithm so that it tells you not only the maximum amount to be allocated, but also which requests could be used to obtain that amount.

d. How would you maximize the number of requests that could be filled, rather than the amount of memory used?

36. Go back to the *IntArray* class in Chapter 1, and rewrite it as a parametrized class.

37. Run the memory management program and discuss the effects of changing (a) the average sizes of requests and (b) the average duration of a block on the distribution of free blocks, and on the proportion of filled requests.

38. Change the memory management program to use a best-fit strategy, and repeat the tests of Exercise 37.

39. Change the memory management program to use a **worst-fit** strategy, where all requests are filled from the largest free block available, and compare its performance with those of the other two selection strategies.

40. Change the memory management program to use a buddy system. You'll have to modify the statistics routines.

41. If your computer has graphics capabilities, modify the memory management program to display a memory map like the one in Figure 2.16.

2.8 EXPLORATIONS

Sorted Lists

Often, there is an underlying linear order on the elements in a LIST structure, as well as the order on positions. It might be that the set of elements consisted of strings, with their associated dictionary order, if, for instance, we were writing a spelling checker that kept a dictionary of words in sorted order as a list. As another common example, the elements may not themselves have a natural order, but it might be the case that the atoms were records that could be sorted by one field, commonly called the **key** (as, for instance, if we kept a list of telephone book entries sorted by name but not by phone number). It would certainly be more difficult to maintain such a list than it would be if we didn't have to worry about how the elements were arranged, but there are times when the advantages would outweigh the added complications. Consider how much easier it is to find someone's phone number in a conventional phone book, given the person's name, than it is to find a person's name, given their phone number. Obviously, this is because the entries in a phone book are sorted by name, rather than by number. (Donald Knuth, in *The Art of Computer Programming,* suggests the nonalgorithmic technique of dialing the number and asking the person who answers what his or her name is.)

Sorted lists are structurally and functionally different enough from lists that they can be defined as an ADT on their own. When we do that, we see rather quickly that a sorted list is just a special case of *List,* with the added feature that the elements are arranged according to their underlying order. It then makes good sense to define *SortedList* as a derived class of *List,* so that it can inherit most of the *List* operations. There are just a few resulting differences we have to take care of. First, while we can remove an element from anywhere in a sorted list just as we did from a list, insertion of a new element can only be done in the location where the new element would properly belong. The ADT *SortedList* can be defined as follows.

▼

SortedList : List

Structure.   A List of elements of type T (which must be linearly ordered by some *key* member datum), where the elements are arranged so that their position in the list is compatible with the key order on the underlying type T.

Operations.   *SortedList* inherits all the *List* operations, with two modifications:

Insert(T e). Pre: No element in the list has the same key as *e*. Post: The list contains *e* where it should be, and the current position is changed to be the position of *e*. The *List* operations *InsertAfter* and *InsertBefore* must be overridden so that they do what *Insert* does.

Update(T e). Pre: The list is nonempty, and *e* has the same key as the current element. Post: The element at the current position has been replaced by *e*.

This specification reveals the ace we had up our sleeve when we declared the hidden members of *List* to be protected, rather than private. We knew that we were going to declare a derived class of *List* that had to have access to its member data (and its *Grow* function). There will be several times in the later pages of this text when you'll see that *List* is fundamental, at least in the sense that it will serve as a base class for several classes we will define.

To make sure that any insertions into a sorted list are done in such a way as to keep the resulting list sorted, we'll need a member function *Find(T e)*, which, given an object of type T (or that key of an element on which we will sort), will return the position after which that atom should be placed in the list to maintain the sorted order. The most obvious way to define *Find* is to traverse the list, starting at the head, until the proper location is found. Doing so, however, clearly could take $O(n)$ time on lists of length n. A much more efficient scheme takes advantage of the fact that the list is sorted. In a **binary search**, the element *e* is first compared with the value of the element in the middle of the list. If *e* has smaller value than the "middle" element, we know that it belongs somewhere in the first half of the list; otherwise, we know that *e* belongs in the last half of the list. We then repeat the process, comparing *e* with the middle atom in the half list where it is known to be and repeatedly halving the size of the list until the interval consists of a single position, which is where *e* must belong.

The only constraint on this search scheme is that it requires a data structure that allows direct access to a list element by specifying its numeric order in the list. In other words, binary searching will work with arrays, but not (or at least not efficiently) with pointers. With this in mind, it is easy to implement this function.

```
int Find(T e)
// Binary search of SortedList using array
// implementation.  Returns the location in the sorted
// list where e is, or where e would belong, if e is
// not in the list.
{
   int   low = 0,
         high = size;  // 1 larger than largest array index
   while (low < high)
   {
      int middle = (low + high) / 2;
      if (e <= a[middle])
         high = middle;
      else
         low = middle + 1;
   }
   return low;       // low = high when we exit
}
```

The function *Find* successively divides the interval *low . . . high* into halves (or as near to halves as possible) in such a way that the candidate element *e* always belongs in the half selected until the exit from the loop. Upon exit from the loop (and return from the function), the interval has been reduced to a single position. In that case, either *e* resides at that position (if *e* is in the list), or *e* is not in the list but could be inserted in the list at that position (shifting everything from that position on up one slot) and still maintain the sorted order of the list. (That's not entirely true: Notice that it is possible for *Find* to return an index larger than the last, indicating that *e* is not in the list but could be inserted after the last element in the list.)

Binary search is *very* fast. Since the interval is divided in two each time, the loop iterates only as many times as needed to chop the interval down to one position. In other words, if the list had n positions originally, the intervals would be of size $n/2$, $n/4$, $n/8$, $n/16$, and so on, until the kth iteration, when $2^k \geq n$. This, however, is just another way of saying that we stop as soon as $k \geq \log_2 n$, which allows us to say that binary search runs in time $O(\log n)$ on lists of length n. To give you an idea of how fast that is, 2^{30} is equal to 1,073,741,824, so to locate an atom in a sorted list of a billion elements would take no more than 30 **probes** into the list. For all practical purposes, then, a binary search runs in constant time, since 266 probes would allow you to locate anything in the universe (assuming that all of the estimated 10^{80} $(= 2^{266})$ atoms in the universe had been linearly ordered somehow; we leave the details to the reader).

42. Use *Find* to write *Insert(T e)*. How fast does *Insert* run? Discuss the running time in the context of our elevated expectations of the speed of *Find*.

43. Should *Find* be a public member function of *SortedList*, or should we hide it from the user of the class? There's no "right" answer to this question, so seek to demonstrate wisdom rather than intelligence.

44. Do some program verification to show that binary search works as it is supposed to. In particular, prove the following assertions.

    a. If *low* and *high* are integers with *low < high*, then if we set *middle = (low + high)/2*, we have *low ≤ middle < high*, with equality only if *low* and *high* were adjacent, that is, if *low = high − 1*.

    b. The difference *high − low* decreases at each loop iteration (so the interval always gets strictly smaller, guaranteeing that the loop will eventually terminate).

    c. The loop invariant property: Except for the last iteration (which results in *low* and *high* having the same value), it is always the case that *e* belongs in the interval from *low* to *high*.

45. a. How many probes would a binary search require to find an element in a list of 16 million elements?

    b. Trace the action of *Find*(70) on the sorted list

       (4, 6, 11, 17, 18, 26, 38, 40, 44, 51, 66, 78, 102, 141, 142, 166, 208)

46. Complete the definition of *SortedList* by implementing *Update*.

47. It's customary to assume that a sorted list will not have any two keys with the same value. Do duplicate keys cause any problems with either *Find* or *Insert*?

48. An **interpolation search** is somewhat like a binary search, except that the probe into a sublist is not always made at the middle element of the sublist. Instead, probes are made into the location where the element *e* is "expected" to be; for instance, if *e* was 2/3 of the way from *low* to *high*, then *middle* would be set to the location 2/3 of the way from *low* to *high*.

    a. Implement the interpolation search version of *Find*.

    b. Trace the action of this function by searching for 70 in the list (1, 2, 3, . . . , 1000) and in the list in Exercise 45b.

    c. Trace the action of this function by searching for 70 in the list (1, 2, 3, . . . , 70, 10,000,000).

    d. For what kinds of lists would interpolation searches be inefficient?

    e. Most of the time (whatever that means), interpolation search is blindingly fast. In fact, for lists other than the ones like you found in part (**d**), interpolation search uses about log(log n) probes. Using logarithms to the base 2, how big does n have to be before interpolation search requires 100 probes? Would it be worth it to use the Chapter 1 multiprecision package to compute your answer?

Self-Organizing Lists

Sometimes, we can improve the time it takes to find an element in a list without having to resort to keeping the list in sorted order. If we stipulate that we're going to use a linear search to find an element in a list, we can speed up the search process by moving a sought element toward the front of the list. That way, over time, the most frequently sought elements will tend to gravitate to the head of the list, where linear search takes less time to find them. In static form, this is just what some telephone directories do when they put the numbers of their business office and of federal, state, and local government in a special section. To modify the *List* ADT this way, all we have to do is change the *Includes* function so that after doing a search for an element, it moves that element toward the head of the list.

There are many ways to do this reorganization. We'll consider three variants that differ in how diligent they are about moving elements. Once we find an element, we might decide to do one of the following:

> *Strategy A.* Move it to the head of the list.
>
> *Strategy B.* Move it halfway from its present position to the head of the list.
>
> *Strategy C.* Move it one position nearer to the head of the list (by swapping it with its predecessor).

49. For each of the three preceding strategies, give the number of steps through the list (0, 1, 2, 3, . . . , 9) it takes to honor the requests for elements

    2, 6, 4, 7, 5, 2, 5, 1, 5, 2, 8, 5, 1, 1, 2, 5, 8, 5, 9, 5, 2, 2, 5, 8, 5, 3, 5, 2

50. Modify *Includes* according to the three strategies in the implementations for which they are best suited. For each of the three, provide a brief explanation of why you chose the implementation you did.

    Just how much these organization schemes contribute to the long-range efficiency of Includes depends in large part on the **distribution** (i.e., the relative likelihood) of requests to find an element. With a little effort, for instance, you should be able to convince yourself that if the requests for an element are **uniformly distributed** (each as likely as the next—see Appendix B for a detailed explanation), there is no particular advantage to any of the strategies; the time it takes to find an element isn't affected by the organization strategy. On the other end of the spectrum, if one element is sought 100% of the time, strategy A results in the best long-term performance, followed closely by strategy B, followed somewhat belatedly by strategy C.

51. Write *Includes* for each of the three strategies. Include a counter that records the number of steps through the list that the operation took to find an element. Assume for simplicity that the list to be used consists of the integers 1 to *n,* initially arranged in random order. Suitably measure the efficiency of your routines (in terms of how much of the list has to be inspected) on a sequence of requests for elements under the following distributions (again, see Appendix B for help).

    a. An **exponential distribution,** where element 1 is sought 1/2 of the time, element 2 is sought 1/4 of the time, . . . , element k is sought 2^{-k} of the time, and so on.

    b. The **Zipf distribution,** where element 1 is sought 1/2 of the time, element 2 is sought 1/3 of the time, . . . , element k is sought $1/(k+1)$ of the time, and so on. In both this and the exponential distributions, the individual probabilities should be multiplied by a scale factor so that they all sum to 1.

52. Repeat Exercise 51 for a strategy of your own.

3

STRINGS

A **string** is a collection of characters written in order, as, for example, "Alan Turing". In all programming languages in which strings are defined, the underlying set of characters contains not only the letters of the alphabet, but also nonalphabetic characters, such as '7' and '+'. We will follow the C++ notation by enclosing strings in double quotes; for example, we can write the strings "AARDVARK" and "%*blort!!". Notice that we said that the order of characters was important: Although "TEACHER" and "CHEATER" contain the same characters, your authors, in particular, would consider them to be unequal (from several points of view). Consider also the string "1667": Although it looks like an integer, it is a different animal entirely; it is a string consisting of the four characters '1', '6', '6', and '7', and as a string has no more numeric meaning than "AARDVARK".

Structurally, there's no difference between the *String* ADT and an array of char. The difference between the two ADTs, then, lies entirely in their operations. When we deal with arrays, we are most interested in accessing and modifying single elements, whereas strings tend to be manipulated in "chunks" of adjacent elements, and this difference is reflected in our choice of operations for the *String* ADT.

3.1 ADT: *STRING*

As was the case when we designed the *IntegerArray* class, we find ourselves in the position of designing a class that is very similar to an existing C++ data

117

structure. C++ strings are arrays of characters, so to make our *String* class as transparent and predictable as possible for the user, we want to design our class so that it includes features, such as access by subscript, that are already in C++ strings. Of course, we want to include other operations as well, such as a "deep" assignment that copies elements, rather than simply copying the pointer to the array of elements, but we should try as much as possible to make our *String* class behave as if it is an *extension* of C++ strings.

(S)trings, (s)trings, and Arrays

Our Strings (with a capital S), like C++ strings (with a lowercase s), will be **zero-terminated** arrays of characters; that is, the last character in the array will be the character with numeric code equal to zero, which in C and C++ is written '\ 0'. This will imply that a string with seven "visible" characters will in fact consist of an array of *eight* characters: the seven visible ones, followed by '\ 0', as illustrated in Figure 3.1.

Figure 3.1 points out the relation between string length, array size, and subscripts. In that example, the length of the string is 7, because we measure the length without including the zero terminator. Since we will begin our indices with zero, a string s of length n will be stored in array locations $s[0], \ldots,$ $s[n-1]$, and the zero terminator will always be stored in $s[n]$. Even if it weren't already part of C++ strings, we'd probably still opt for including a zero terminator, since it makes some of the string operations simpler, providing (like the NULL pointer in a linked list) an easy way to find out where the string ends.*

Because Strings are just a special case of arrays of characters, with some extra operations, it makes good programming sense to build on work we've already done and define *String* as derived from the ADT *Array<char>*. The class corresponding to the ADT *Array<char>* is the parametrized version of the *IntegerArray* class we described in Chapter 1, with char for the type parameter *T*. This class has a number of operations that *String* can call with little or no further ado, like

1. A default constructor
2. A constructor that makes a copy of an array of chars
3. A copy constructor
4. A destructor
5. A deep assignment operator
6. A subscript operator

---

* Another way to find the end of a string is the way Pascal does it, by starting the string at index 1 and storing the length in the 0th array position. Since characters are often represented by a 1-byte numeric code, though, this limits the length of such strings to 255, since 255 is the largest value that can be stored in a byte of 8 binary digits.

FIGURE 3.1

A String storing the value "Eclipse"

0	1	2	3	4	5	6	7
'E'	'c'	'l'	'i'	'p'	's'	'e'	'\0'

String: Array<char>

Structure. A *String* object is an array of characters. Each String contains one and only one zero character, '\0', which is always in the last position in the array.

Operations. All the operations available to users of the *Array<char>* class, except for *SetBounds*. Beyond the inherited operations, *String* includes the following.

1. Constructors:

   String(char* a). Pre: *a* is a zero-terminated array of char. Post: This String is constructed elementwise from the C++ string *a*.

   String(char[] a, int sz). Pre: true. Post: This String is constructed from an array that is not necessarily zero terminated.

   String(int len). Pre: true. Post: This String has length *len*; the characters in this String are undefined, except that the zero character is in position *len*.

2. Assignment:

   String& operator+= (const String& str). Pre: true. Post: This String is the concatenation of itself and *str*. A reference to this String is returned.

3. Access:

   int operator== (const String& str1, const String& str2). Pre: true. Post: *str1* and *str2* are unchanged, and 1 is returned if and only if the Strings are equal, which is to say that they have the same length and the same characters in each position.

   int operator!= (const String& str1, const String& str2). Pre: true. Post: *str1* and *str2* are unchanged, and 1 is returned if and only if the Strings are not equal, as previously defined.

   int operator< (const String& str1, const String& str2). Pre: true. Post: *str1* and *str2* are unchanged, and 1 is returned if and only if *str1* is less than *str2* in lexicographic order, as defined shortly.

   int operator<= (const String& str1, const String& str2). Pre: true. Post: *str1* and *str2* are unchanged, and 1 is returned if and only if *str1* is less than *str2* in lexicographic order or *str1* and *str2* are equal.

   int operator> (const String& str1, const String& str2). Pre: true. Post: *str1* and *str2* are unchanged, and 1 is returned if and only if *str1* is greater than *str2* in lexicographic order.

`int operator>= (const String& str1, const String& str2)`. Pre: true. Post: *str1* and *str2* are unchanged, and 1 is returned if and only if *str1* is greater than *str2* in lexicographic order or *str1* and *str2* are equal.

`unsigned int Length(const String& str)`. Pre: true. Post: *str* is unchanged, and the number of characters (not counting the zero terminating character) in str is returned.

4. Input/output:

`ostream& operator<< (ostream& os, const String& str)`. Pre: true. Post: *str* is unchanged, the nonzero characters of *str* are inserted in *os*, and a reference to *os* is returned.

`istream& operator>> (istream& is, String& str)`. Pre: true. Post: Characters are extracted in order from *is*, up to the first newline character (which is discarded from *is* and not placed in *str*) or until some internal maximum number of characters have been extracted. The extracted characters are placed in *str*, starting in position 0, and are terminated by a zero character. Finally, a reference to *is* is returned.

5. Manipulation (see Figure 3.2):

`String operator+ (const String& str1, const String& str2)`. Pre: true. Post: *str1* and *str2* are unchanged, and a newly created String is returned. The new String has all the nonzero characters of *str1*, in order, followed by all the nonzero characters of *str2*, in order, followed by a zero character.

`String Substring(unsigned int start, unsigned int size)`. Pre: start$\geq$0. Post: This String is unchanged; returns a copy of a String of length *size*, which consists of the characters from this String with indices *start, start*+1, . . . , *start*+*size*−1. If *start* is greater than or equal to the length of this String, the empty String is returned. If *start* is less than the length of this String but *start*+*size* is greater than or equal to the length of this String, the returned String will consist of the tail of this String, beginning with position *start*.

`String Insert(const String& inner, unsigned int start)`. Pre: *start*$\geq$0. Post: *inner* is unchanged, and this String has a copy of *inner* inserted, in order, starting at position *start*. The characters in this String from positions *start* to the end of this string are shifted so that they occur immediately after the newly inserted characters. If *start* is greater than or equal to the original length of this String, *inner* is appended to the end.

> `String Remove(unsigned int start, unsigned int size)`. The pre- and postconditions of this function are the same as those of *Substring*, except that instead of returning a copy of the indicated substring, that substring is removed from this String and a copy of the result is returned.

We included the concatenate and concatenate-assign operators, + and +=, for the user's convenience, although they can be defined in terms of the other *String* operations. For example, the expression st += right does the same thing to *st* as the less concise (and less comprehensible) expression `st.Insert(right, Length(st))`.

Lexicographic Order

The String comparison operators <, <=, >, and >= rely on a linear order on Strings. This order is based on a machine-dependent order on the underlying character set. In C++ and most other languages, characters are represented internally by numeric codes, so the character 'A' might be represented by the number 65, for instance. These codes, then, give a natural order on characters, so that it makes sense to say that some character is "before" or "less than" another. In particular, the order for sets of characters is almost always taken to be an extension of alphabetic order. This order for characters de-

FIGURE 3.2

String manipulation functions

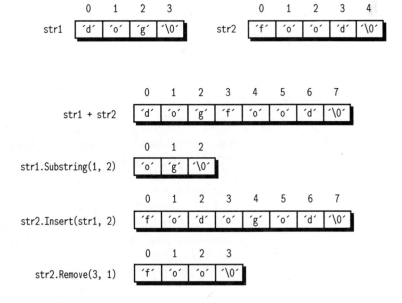

pends on the machine on which a program is run, and it differs from manu-facturer to manufacturer. The most common orders for printable characters (i.e., excluding characters that represent line feeds, carriage returns, bells, tabs, and the like) are:

ASCII (American Standard Code for Information Interchange) order: (space) ! " # $ % ' ( ) * + , - . / 0 1 2 3 4 5 6 7 8 9 : ; < = > ? @ A B C D E F G H I J K L M N O P Q R S T U V W X Y Z [\ ] ^ _ ` a b c d e f g h i j k l m n o p q r s t u v w x y z { | } ~

EBCDIC (Extended Binary Coded Decimal Interchange Code) order: (space) ¢ . < (+ | & ! $ *) ; ¬ - / ^ , % _ > ? : # @ ' = " a b c d e f g h i j k l m n o p q r s t u v w x y z \ { } [ ] A B C D E F G H I J K L M N O P Q R S T U V W X Y Z 0 1 2 3 4 5 6 7 8 9

Because the underlying characters can be ordered (so we can say, for in-stance, that the character '+' is "less than" the character 'A' in either of the preceding orders), it is possible to extend this to an ordering on character strings. This **lexicographic order** is similar to that used in dictionaries and telephone books: We define the lexicographic order < on strings as an exten-sion of the order on characters as follows:

1. The empty string is less than any nonempty string.

2. If $S = $ "$c_0 c_1 \ldots c_n$" and $T = $ "$d_0 d_1 \ldots d_m$", then $S < T$ if

    a. There is a number p, with $0 \leq p \leq \min(n, m)$, such that $c_i = d_i$ for all $0 \leq i \leq p$ (so the first p characters of S and T match).

    b. Either $c_{p+1} < d_{p+1}$ (the first nonmatching character of S is "less than" the corresponding character of T) or $p = n$ (i.e., S complete-ly matches the first n characters of T, but T is longer than S).

For example, using either the ASCII or EBCDIC orders for characters, we see that "A" < "Z", "BRAINS" < "BRAWN", and "HOT" < "HOTTENTOT".

Declaring Strings

The declaration file for the *String* class reflects the specification of the ADT. There are three design decisions we made here that deserve mention, because they exemplify common issues that arise when we go from a specification of an ADT to an implementation of the ADT as a C++ class.

First, notice that quite a few of the operations are defined as friends rather than as member functions. The comparison operators and the concate-nation operator were declared as friends because they do not modify the String object and take two arguments, neither of which is modified. Declaring them as friends allows the declaration to reflect the way they will be called. We could, for example, have declared the equality operator as a member function, but the implicit first argument of member functions would have made the declaration look like

```
int operator== (const String& str) const;
```

which, you'll agree, doesn't express its call form (str1 == str2, in both versions) nearly as well as the friend version. We had a similar reason for declaring the function *Length* as a friend. Making it a member function would require us to call it as *st.Length*( ), rather than the much more natural *Length(st)*.

Another decision we made was the choice of return types in the manipulation functions *Insert* and *Remove*. These member functions modify the object itself (which is why we made them member functions), so they could have been declared to have void return types. The extra work of returning a copy String was justified, we thought, by the observation that these functions might be combined in complicated expressions like a.Insert(b.Remove(3, 4), 1).

Finally, we had to modify some of the functions *String* inherits from *Array<char>*. We already mentioned that we didn't want the user of the *String* class to be able to set the bounds of the array of characters, but we also have to write our own versions of the two constructors Array(int len) and Array(char* a, int sz) so that they would append the zero character to the end of the arrays they construct. Constructors aren't inherited, you may recall (nor are friends), but our definitions will call the appropriate *Array<char>* constructors in their initialization lists.

```
//==================== Strings.h ====================
#ifndef STRINGS_H
#define STRINGS_H

#include <iostream.h>
#include "Arrays.h"

class String : public Array<char>
{
    // Comparison operators
    friend int operator== (const String& str1, const String& str2);
    friend int operator!= (const String& str1, const String& str2);
    friend int operator<  (const String& str1, const String& str2);
    friend int operator<= (const String& str1, const String& str2);
    friend int operator>  (const String& str1, const String& str2);
    friend int operator>= (const String& str1, const String& str2);

    // Return the length of a String.
    friend unsigned int Length(const String& str)
        {  return (str.Size() - 1);} ;
```

```
    // Concatenate two Strings.
    friend String operator+ (const String& str1, const String& str2);

    // I/O overloads
    friend ostream& operator<< (ostream& os, const String& str);
    friend istream& operator>> (istream& is, String& str);

public:
    String(char* a);
    String(char a[], int sz);              // override

    void SetBounds(int up, int low = 0);  // override
    String& operator+= (const String& str);

    String Substring(unsigned int start, unsigned int size) const;
    String Insert(const String& inner, unsigned int start);
    String Remove(unsigned int start, unsigned int size);

private:
    String(int len);                       //override
};
#endif
```

3.2   IMPLEMENTATION

Most of the implementation details in the *String* class are little more than further practice in array manipulation, since we inherit all the data members from *Array<char>*.

To compare two strings for equality, we first eliminate the case where the strings have different lengths. Having done that, we then scan past the characters that are equal in the two strings, using the loop

```
while ((i < len1) && (str1[i] == str2[i]))
    i++;
```

The exit condition of this loop is satisfied when either (1) i is equal to the length of the strings or (2) we find a pair of mismatched characters. Condition (1) is true if and only if we've run out of characters before finding a mismatch, so the strings are equal if and only if condition (1) is true, which makes it a perfect choice for the return value. The inequality operator is defined in terms of ==, and we leave it as an exercise.

```
int operator== (const String& str1, const String& str2)
{
    int   len1 = Length(str1),
          len2 = Length(str2);
    if (len1 != len2)    // Unequal-length strings cannot be equal.
        return 0;

    // Strings are equal length, so compare chars.
    int   i = 0;
    while ((i < len1) && (str1[i] == str2[i]))
        i++;
    return (i = len1);
}
```

Comparing two strings in lexicographic order is complicated, as you would expect from the complexity of the definition. The function definition, though, is a straightforward implementation of the definition of lexicographic order.

```
int operator< (const String& str1, const String& str2)
// Returns 1 if and only if str1 is less than str2
// in lexicographic order.
{
    if (Length(str1) == 0)  // empty string (rule 1)
        return 1;

    int min;                    // last index of shorter of str1, str2
    // First, find the smaller last index.
    int m1 = Length(str1) - 1,
        m2 = Length(str2) - 1;
    if (m1 < m2)
        min = m1;
    else
        min = m2;

    // Then, skip past the characters that are equal.
    int i = 0;
    while ((i <= min) && (str1[i] == str2[i]))
        i++;

    // Now we either have a mismatch or we've
    // run out of characters in one string.
    if (i > m1)
        return 1;   // run out of chars in str1 (rule 2b)

    if (i > m2)
        return 0;   // run out of chars in str2 (rule 2b)
```

```
        return (str1[i] < str2[i]);  // return match (rule 2a)
}
```

All the hard work of comparison is done by <. The rest of the comparison functions have one-line definitions using <, and we leave them as exercises.

Concatenation consists of constructing a return String of the appropriate size and filling it, first with characters from *str1* and then with characters from *str2*. Having defined concatenation, the concatenate-assign operator is easy to define, and we again leave it for you.

```
String operator+ (const String& str1, const String& str2)
// Returns a String that is the concatenation of str1 and str2.
{
    int len1 = Length(str1),
        len2 = Length(str2),
        i;
    String r(len1 + len2);        // Construct return string.

    for (i = 0; i < len1; i++)    // Fill from str1.
        r[i] = str1[i];
    for (i = 0; i < len2; i++)    // Fill from str2.
        r[i + len1] = str2[i];
    return r;
}
```

To get characters from an istream and make a String from them would be easy except for the fact that we have to read the characters before we know how much space to allocate for them. This means that we must first read the characters into a temporary storage *buffer* array and then use that array of characters to construct the String. We don't have to put in the zero terminator explicitly; remember, that's done for us by the String(char*) constructor. The insertion operator whose definition follows is, as usual, far simpler than the extraction operator.

```
istream& operator>> (istream& is, String& str)
// Get a String from the input stream is.
// Reads at most MAX chars and stops at the first
// newline.
{
    const int MAX = 256;    // the most chars we'll read
    char buffer[MAX];       // temporary storage for chars

    int i = 0;
    is.get(buffer[0]);
    while ((i < MAX - 1) && (buffer[i] != '\ n'))
        is.get(buffer[++i]);
```

```
    str = String(buffer);
    return is;
}

ostream& operator<< (ostream& os, const String& str)
// Send a String to the output stream os.
{
    for (int i = 0; i < Length(str); i++)
        os << str[i];
    return os;
}
```

We define three constructors for our class, one new one and two overrides of base class constructors. In the first, we construct a String from a C++ string *a* by iterating through the characters of *a* until we come to the zero terminator. Once we know the size of the string *a* (which is what the utility function *Last* is for), we call the inherited constructor that uses *a* and its size to build our String. The two overrides that follow just call constructors from *Array<char>* and then insert the zero terminator.

```
int Last(char* a)
// Utility function: Returns the index of '\ 0' in a.
// Called in String(char *).
{
    int i = 0;
    while (a[i])
        i++;
    return i;
}


String::String(char* a) : Array<char>(a, Last(a) + 1)
// Construct a String from a C++ string a.
{
}


String::String(char a[], int sz) : Array<char>(a, sz + 1)
// Override.  We need to modify this to put in the
// zero terminator.
{
    (*this)[sz] = '\ 0';
}


String::String(int len) : Array<char>(len)
// PRIVATE override: Create an uninitialized String
// of length len.
{
    (*this)[len] = '\ 0';   // Put in zero terminator.
}
```

The only reason we need to override the inherited *SetBounds* function is to see to it that the user of the *String* class can't use it.

```
void String::SetBounds(int up, int low)
// Override: We just warn the user that this function
// is unavailable.
{
    cerr << "*** SetBounds is not available in String.\ n";
}
```

The function that returns a substring from this String has a somewhat complicated collection of pre- and postconditions, which we illustrate in Figure 3.3. Let *thisLength* represent the length of the source string; we then have three cases that could apply:

1. *start≥thisLength*. Pre: The starting index is beyond the end of the source string. Post: Returns the empty String.
2. *start<thisLength* and *start+size−1≥thisLength*. Pre: The requested substring is longer than the tail of the source String. Post: Returns the String consisting of the characters from *start* to *thisLength−1*.
3. *start<thisLength* and *start+size−1<thisLength*. Pre: The requested substring lies wholly within the source string. Post: Returns the String consisting of the characters from *start* to *start+size−1*.

FIGURE 3.3

Substring(7, 2),
Substring(4, 5),
Substring(3, 4)

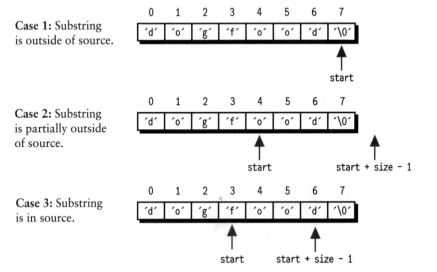

```
String String::Substring( unsigned int start,
                          unsigned int size) const
// Returns a String that is equal to that part of this
// String starting in position start and having length
// size.
```

```
{
    int thisLength = Length(*this);
    if (start >= thisLength)          // Case 1
    {
        String r(0);
        r[0] = '\ 0';
        return r;
    }

    int lastIndex = start + size - 1;
    if (lastIndex >= thisLength)      // Case 2 or Case 3
        lastIndex = thisLength - 1;   // Case 2

    // Construct a String to return.
    String r(lastIndex - start + 1);

    // Fill the return String.
    for (int i = 0; i <= lastIndex - start; i++)
        r[i] = (*this)[start + i];

    return r;
}
```

Inserting a String into this String is easier than finding a substring because there are only two possible cases: *start* is within this String, in which case we insert as requested, or *start* is beyond this String, in which case we append the inserted String to the end of this String. The heart of the algorithm is to construct a return String, *r*, and then into *r* we (1) copy the characters from positions 0 to *start*−1, (2) copy the characters of *inner*, and finally (3) copy the characters (if any) from positions *start* to the end of this String. After we've made *r*, we finish the job by copying all of *r* into this String.

```
String String::Insert(const String& inner,
                        unsigned int start)
// Returns a string that results from inserting inner
// into this string, starting at position start.
{
    int   thisLength = Length(*this),
          inLength = Length(inner),
          i;
    if (start > thisLength)
        start = thisLength;
```

```
    String r(thisLength + inLength);

    // Copy the chars up to start.
    for (i = 0; i < start; i++)
        r[i] = (*this)[i];

    // Then copy the chars of inner.
    for (i = 0; i < inLength; i++)
        r[start + i] = inner[i];

    // Finally, copy the remaining chars in this.
    for (i = start; i < thisLength; i++)
        r[start + inLength + i] = (*this)[i];

    *this = r;
    return r;
}
```

We leave the definition of *Remove* as an exercise. Its pre- and postconditions are similar to those of *Substring*, and it uses the same sort of copying into a return String that we saw in *Insert*.

Efficiency

Whenever we define a function, whether it's a member function or friend of a class or a free function that's not part of a class, one of our concerns should be how efficiently the function works. For instance, we generally will want at least a rough estimate of the big-O running time of our algorithms. Getting exact estimates is complicated in C++ because the language includes a fair amount of work that goes on behind the scenes. Consider what happens, for example, when we execute the expression s = "Test" for some String s. It appears that things are pretty simple. Look what really happens, though. The train of calls looks like this:

```
String::String(char *)                          O(1)
    Last(char *)                                O(n)
    Array<char>::Array(char [], int)            O(n)
        Assert(int, char *)                     O(1)
        Assert(int, char *)                     O(1)
Array<char>::operator= (const Array<char>& )    O(n)
String::~String()                               O(1)
```

There are *seven* function calls hidden in one apparently simple expression! Fortunately, only three of the calls contribute anything other than a constant amount of time to the time of execution of the expression, and it was clear that the expression was going to take time $O(n)$ anyway on strings of size n.

If you look at the *String* operations, you can see that they all run in time proportional to the length of the String (or the sum of the lengths of the

Strings in cases like +, +=, and *Insert,* where two Strings are involved), with the exception of the constant-time constructor *String(int)* and the access function *Length( )*. It should come as no surprise that most of these operations run in linear time; after all, most of these could, in the worst case, require us to inspect or otherwise manipulate all the characters in the String. The good news is that none of the *String* operations take any longer than $O(n)$—at least, none that we've discussed so far.

Consider, though, a reasonable *String* operation that we haven't mentioned yet. We might find it useful to find a substring in a given String. If we wanted to use our *String* class to implement a word processor, for example, such an operation would come in very handy for such things as global search-and-replace to correct consistent misspellings. The function we might call *Find* is the "deepest" of the *String* operations in that we can see almost immediately how we could describe algorithms for all the other operations; but we have to think a bit before we see how to attack the definition of *Find*. An algorithm that would probably occur first to most people would be to search the source string character by character to find matches for the characters in the target string, using a somewhat informal description.

```
int Find(const String& source, const String& target)
// Returns the position in source of the first
// occurrence of substring target, and returns -1
// if target is not part of source.
{
    if  ((source or target is empty)
        return -1;              // no match possible

    int current = 0;           // possible location in this
                               // of the start of a match
    while  (complete match not found && any characters left in source)
        if  (current character in source != first target character)
            current++;
        else                   // Found a partial match.
        {
            do
                Step through source and target together
            while  (chars left to compare && still have a match);

            if  ((no more target characters to inspect)
                return current;  // Found a full match.
            else
                current++;       // Keep looking.
        }
    return -1;                   // No match found anywhere.
}
```

For example, if *source* was "ACTCTAGA", and *target* was "CTA", this algorithm would make the following steps, where the characters presently being compared are highlighted. While you read through this example and the ones to follow, bear in mind that we are not actually moving *target*; we are incrementing the *index* to characters in *target*. The apparent shifts of *target* in the examples are only to make the process easier to read.

1. C T A
   A C T C T A G A   No match, advance *target*.

2. C T A
   A C T C T A G A   Match, look at subsequent characters.

3. C T A
   A C T C T A G A   Still matches, pass to next position.

4. C T A
   A C T C T A G A   Failed to match, advance *target*.

5.   C T A
   A C T C T A G A   Failed to match, advance *target* again.

6.   C T A
   A C T C T A G A   Match, look at subsequent characters.

7.   C T A
   A C T C T A G A   Still matches, pass to next position.

8.   C T A
   A C T C T A G A   Still matches, search complete.

This search required eight comparisons to find *target* in *source*. It is clear that if *source* had length *s*, *target* had length *t*, and the first occurrence of *target* in *source* was at position $p \geq 1$, it would require at least $p+t-1$ comparisons to complete the search, since all the first *p* characters of *source* would have to be inspected, as well as the remaining $t-1$ characters of *target*. Similarly, an unsuccessful search would require at least *s* comparisons. In fact, the number of comparisons might not even be a linear function of the lengths of the strings involved, because some of the characters in *source* are inspected more than once, when the algorithm backs up after an initial match followed by a failure, as happened in steps 3 and 4 in the preceding example. This is not a very efficient way to perform string searches: It is not difficult to show that if *source* has length *n* and *target* has length *m*, it is possible for *Find* to require as many as $O(nm)$ steps. In the next section, we will show how to improve this algorithm.

3.3 APPLICATION: STRING MATCHING

We didn't just pick the characters in the preceding example out of a hat. The letters A, C, G, and T are common abbreviations for the nucleotides adenine, cytosine, guanine, and thymine that make up DNA, the fundamental building block of genetic structure. A molecule of DNA may be seen as an immensely long "ladder," where the "rungs" are comprised of complementary pairs of nucleotides, A with T and G with C. The molecule actually has a spiral shape, as if someone had grabbed the ends of a rubber ladder and twisted them, but that—and the complementary pairing—won't be important in our discussion. To simplify the problem immensely, let's describe the DNA fragment as the string of nucleotides on one rail of the ladder, like ACCTAG ATGTCTTTGCA . . . , where the sequence could be hundreds or thousands of characters long.

One problem with finding the sequence that defines a DNA molecule is that in the chemical analysis, the DNA sample may get broken into a number of separate strands, so the original sample may become a soup of fragments, such as ACCTAGA or TAGATGT. We can see that these two fragments have the substring TAGA in common and that they would together form the first part, ACCTAGATGT, of our molecule. This was a fairly easy problem to solve by inspection, but even ignoring such difficulties as order (ACCT could equally well be TCCA) and complementarity (ACCT could be the other rail of TGGA), you can see that if the strings were thousands of characters long, a $O(n^2)$ matching algorithm could take so much time that it would be infeasible to attack, even on the fastest computer we could find.

The "obvious" algorithm we presented examined the characters in *source* one by one, moving from left to right, until a match was found for the first character in *target*. Once a match was found for the first character of *target*, the remaining characters of *target* were tested until either all were matched or a mismatch was discovered. If a mismatch was found, the algorithm "backed up," advancing *target* by one position, and continued the search.

A much faster algorithm for string searching was published in 1977 by Robert S. Boyer and J. Strother Moore. Their algorithm is decidedly nonobvious in that it examines the characters of *target* from right to left, while still moving from left to right in *source*. The important difference between the obvious algorithm and the Boyer-Moore algorithm is that the Boyer-Moore algorithm preprocesses *target* to make two auxiliary tables, which are then used to make large jumps through *source*, rather than inspecting each character in turn. The Boyer-Moore algorithm not only runs in time $O(s+t)$, but also executes fewer than $s+t$ statements when t, the length of *target*, is large enough. In other words, quite unlike the obvious algorithm, the Boyer-Moore algorithm is more efficient the longer *target* is.

Before we explain the algorithm in detail and discuss the two tables made in the preprocessing stage, let us consider an example, due to Boyer and Moore, in which *source* is the string "WHICH_FINALLY_HALTS. _ _ AT_THAT_POINT" and *target* is "AT_THAT".

1. We begin, as in the obvious algorithm, with *target* aligned to the left of *source*, but we inspect characters from right to left in *target*.

```
A T _ T H A T
W H I C H _ F I N A L L Y _ H A L T S . _ _ A T _ T H A T _ P O I N T
```

2. The character 'F' does not occur at all in *target,* so we can, in effect, shift *target* completely beyond the 'F' without looking at any of the intervening characters. (As we did in the example for the obvious version of Find, we remark that we are not actually moving *target*: We are really only shifting our reference to the characters in the two strings.)

```
A T _ T H A T
W H I C H _ F I N A L L Y _ H A L T S . _ _ A T _ T H A T _ P O I N T
```

3. Now we don't have a match, but the character '_' does occur in *target,* so we can shift *target* four places to the right, to line up the rightmost instance of '_' in *target* with the '_' in *source.* We then begin comparisons anew at the right end of *target.*

```
A T _ T H A T
W H I C H _ F I N A L L Y _ H A L T S . _ _ A T _ T H A T _ P O I N T
```

4. We have a match, so we "back up" to inspect the previous character.

```
A T _ T H A T
W H I C H _ F I N A L L Y _ H A L T S . _ _ A T _ T H A T _ P O I N T
```

5. Again, as in step 2, the character 'L' is known not to be in *target,* so we can shift *target* beyond the position of 'L'.

```
A T _ T H A T
W H I C H _ F I N A L L Y _ H A L T S . _ _ A T _ T H A T _ P O I N T
```

6, 7. Since we have a match of the character 'T', we back up twice until we again come to a failure to match.

```
A T _ T H A T
W H I C H _ F I N A L L Y _ H A L T S . _ _ A T _ T H A T _ P O I N T
```

8. The present character, '_', of *source* fails to match the corresponding 'H' in *target.* We could appeal to the reasoning used in step 3 and slide *target* to the right to align the '_' characters, but we can do even better. If we recognize that we have already seen "AT" in *source* and that "AT" occurs earlier in *target,* then we may slide *target* to align the two instances of "AT". In such cases, we always may choose the larger of the two distances, arguing that if we aligned the '_' characters, there could not then be a possible match for the characters 'AT', which we have already seen.

```
A T _ T H A T
W H I C H _ F I N A L L Y _ H A L T S . _ _ A T _ T H A T _ P O I N T
```

9–14. Having found a match, we again back up, and this time we inspect all the characters of *target* and find the required location for *target* in *source*.

This algorithm, which we will define in detail shortly, required only 14 comparisons, whereas the obvious algorithm would have required 31 comparisons. In steps 1, 2, 3, and 5, we relied on knowledge of the locations of the rightmost instances of the characters of *target*. We build in this knowledge as part of our preprocessing of *target*. Prior to starting the string search, we construct a table, *delta1*, which is defined for every character in the underlying character set, as follows:

$$delta1[ch] = \begin{cases} \text{The distance from the right end of } \textit{target} \text{ of the} \\ \text{rightmost occurrence of } \textit{ch} \text{ in } \textit{target}, \text{ if any} \\ \\ \textit{Length}(\textit{target}), \text{ if } \textit{ch} \text{ is not in } \textit{target} \end{cases}$$

For example, if *target* = "AT_THAT", then we have *delta1*['T'] = 0, *delta1*['A'] = 1, *delta1*['H'] = 2, *delta1*['_'] = 4, and *delta1*[*ch*] = 7 for all other characters. In simple terms, if we fail to match *ch* at position *p* in *source*, then we can move to the position *p* + *delta1*[*ch*] in *source*, align the right end of *target* to that position, and continue the search. What we have done is to ensure that the character *ch* in both *source* and *target* are aligned. Notice that this does not say that we will slide *target* to the right by *delta1*[*ch*]; in step 5 of the preceding example, we failed to find a match for 'L' in position 16, found that *delta1*['L'] = 7 (since 'L' was not in *target*), and aligned the right end of *target* to position 7 + 16 = 23 in *source*, a move that slid *target* only six places, since the current position was one place to the left of the end of *target*.

The other part of the preprocessing involves the construction of a table *delta2*, defined for each position in *target*, which defines the amount that the current position in *source* can be moved, based on the characters so far seen in *target*. This table reflects, for instance, the choice we made in step 8 in the previous example. Let $t = Length(target) - 1$ (the last position in *target*), and define *delta2*[*t*] = 1. For all other values, let *p* be a position in *target*, with $1 \leq p < t$, and define *delta2*[*p*] = *length* + *offset*, where *length* is the length of the suffix of *target* that begins in position *p* + 1 (so *length* is just $t - p$), and *offset* is the least amount that that suffix must be moved to the left to match another occurrence in *target* without matching the character in position *p*.

Got it? We thought not. Such a complicated definition begs for examples, so consider the following.

1. Let *target* = "AT_THAT" and *p* = 5. The suffix starting in position 5 + 1 is the string 'T', of length 1. The least distance we need to move to the left to find a match for 'T' is 3, and this is allowed, since the

character preceding the suffix, 'A', does not match the character preceding the 'T' in position 3. Graphically, we could write:

```
position:   0 1 2 3 4 5 6
target:     A T _ T H A T
match:            T
```

so $delta2[5] = length + offset = 1 + (6-3) = 4$.

2. Again, let target = "AT_THAT", but this time let $p = 3$. We are attempting to match the suffix "HAT", and, as before, we have

```
position:   -1 0 1 2 3 4 5 6
target:         A T _ T H A T
match:       H A T
```

In this case, we imagine *target* to be padded on the left with dummy characters that match everything in the suffix but do not match the character before the suffix. We have $delta2[3] = length + offset = 3 + (4-(-1)) = 8$.

3. Finally, let *target* = "BAHAMA_MAMMA" and $p = 10$. The rightmost occurrence of the suffix 'A' is in position 8, but we cannot use that one because the 'M' in position 7 matches the character immediately before the suffix. In fact, we must pass by the 'A' in position 8, as well as the one in position 5, before we come to a match for the suffix that is not preceded by an 'M'.

```
position:   0 1 2 3 4 5 6 7 8 9 10 11
target:     B A H A M A _ M A M M  A
match:            A
```

So, in this case, $delta2[10] = 1 + (11-3) = 9$.

4. By now you should be able to verify the following table

p:	0	1	2	3	4	5	6	7	8	9	10	11
target[p]:	B	A	H	A	M	A	_	M	A	M	M	A
delta2[p]:	23	22	21	20	19	18	17	16	15	5	9	1

If we return to the second example in the list, we can see exactly what happens when we use *delta2* to guide our choice of how much to slide *target*. We looked for a rightmost plausible reoccurrence of the suffix "HAT" in the *target* string. We saw that an offset of 5 to the left allowed us to match the suffix with an earlier occurrence in *target*. What this means is that if we had seen "HAT" in *source*, but had failed to match the 'T' preceding the suffix, then it would be possible to slide *target* to the right to align the rightmost plausible reoccurrence of "HAT" (or at least part of it) with the instance of "HAT" in *source*. In other words, the construction used to generate *delta2* is mirrored in the reverse direction when we come to a situation where we use the *delta2* table. For instance, if we had come to the following situation prior to looking up the value delta2[3]:

> *target*:   A T _ T H A T
> *source*:   ? ? ? C H A T ? ? ? ? ?

we would then have the following snapshot after having moved the current position, that is, the position where the unmatched 'C' was in *source*, to the right by *delta2*[4]=8 places.

> *target*:   A T _ T H A T
> *source*:   C H A T ? ? ? ? ? ? ?

We are now in a position to describe the Boyer-Moore algorithm. We will denote the position of the characters presently being inspected in *source* and *target* by *i* and *j*, respectively.

```
int Boyer_Moore_Find(source, target)
// Improved string search algorithm.  Returns starting
// position of leftmost occurrence of target in source, // and returns -1 if no
                                                    match found.
{
```

Preprocess *target* to produce tables *delta1* and *delta2*;

```
    int   i = Length(target) - 1;
    while (i < Length(source)
    {
        int j = Length(target) - 1;
        while ((j >= 0) && (source[i] = target[j]))
        {
            // Back up through source and target.
            i--;
            j--;
        }
        if (j == -1)
            return i + 1;      // Found complete match.
        else
        // Here is where big jumps take place.
            i += max(delta1[source[i]], delta2[j]);
    }
    // Can only get here if we didn't find any match.
    return -1;
}
```

Although we leave the details of coding this algorithm as an exercise, some points bear noting. First, the function we've sketched here isn't quite as nice and simple as it appears; for ease of explanation, we described *delta1* as an array indexed by the characters in the underlying character set. Of course, C++ converts characters to their internal integer representation, but we have to bear that in mind when we're writing the actual function.

Another point concerns an objection you might have made in thinking this algorithm through. "Hey," you might say, "I'm willing to be convinced by the example that this is a fast algorithm, once you've done the preprocessing to make the two tables. That's not worth much, though, if the preprocessing takes, say, $O(t^2)$ time for *target* strings of length t." That's a good objection, but you'll have to take our word that there is a way to produce both *delta1* (which is easy to figure out) and *delta2* (which is not) in time $O(t)$. If you would like to see how to do the preprocessing efficiently, we refer you to the Boyer and Moore article mentioned in the Summary.

While we are on the subject of preprocessing, note that it probably wouldn't be too efficient to include the preprocessing routine within the definition of *Find*. To do so would force us to preprocess *target* each time we made a call to *Find*, which would be inefficient in the common case where repeated *Find*s were called on the same *target* string, as would happen if we wanted to find all instances of a misspelled word. In fact, if we were writing *Find* for a word processor, it might be preferable to rewrite the function so that a call would look like Find(p, source, target), which would return the position of the first instance of *target* that occurred at or after position p in *source* and would return −1 if no match was found.

Finally, we have said that the Boyer-Moore algorithm is more efficient than the obvious algorithm, but haven't included details about how much more efficient it is. It is clear that the execution time for both algorithms is driven primarily by the number of comparisons of characters that need to be made. The obvious algorithm inspects each character in *source* until *target* is found and sometimes has to back up if partial matches are discovered along the way. We mentioned that in the exercises you are asked to show that there are situations in which as many as $O(st)$ comparisons are needed, where s is the length of *source* and t is the length of *target*. Furthermore, although the calculations are too cumbersome to deal with here, it is possible to show that for a successful search by the obvious algorithm, the number of *source* characters inspected (not counting the ones where *target* is found) divided by the number of characters passed before the function returns should have an average value of approximately $1/(1-r)$, where r is 1 divided by the size of the underlying character set. For example, for a character set consisting of the letters 'A' through 'Z', we have $r = 1/26 = 0.03846$ (approximately), and $1/(1-r)$ for this value is 1.04. This means that in dealing with randomly chosen strings, the obvious algorithm must inspect each character in turn and must back up about 4% of the time.

We can perform similar calculations on the average efficiency of the Boyer-Moore algorithm, but the calculations in that case are really gruesome, as you might imagine. However, it is possible to get some empirical results about the average efficiency without too much work. We can write the Boyer-Moore algorithm, run it on a number of randomly chosen sample strings, for each sample compute the number of comparisons before a complete match divided by the number of characters passed, and average the results. If we do this for enough sample cases, we see that the ratio averages very close to $1/t$, where t is the length of *target*. This is a considerable improvement over the obvious algorithm, as illustrated in Figure 3.4.

In essence, the "efficiency" of $1/t$ in the Boyer-Moore algorithm stems from the fact that it is usually possible to skip ahead in *source* by an amount equal to the length of the entire *target* string. This means that no matter how many instructions it takes to do each comparison and move, eventually, for long enough *target* strings, less than one instruction is performed for each character passed in *source*, effectively making the Boyer-Moore algorithm run in *less than* constant time.

 ## 3.4 SUMMARY

A string is an array of characters, with the same access by subscript that exists with any array. The *String* ADT has, in addition to the array operations, a number of its own operations, primarily concerned with substring-level manipulations like copying a substring and inserting a String into an existing String. As with any ADT, we have a certain amount of freedom in deciding what operations to include in *String*. As usual, we based our decision on our perception of what the user of this ADT might expect.

We chose to declare our implementation of the *String* class as a derived class of *Array<char>*, with the added requirement that our Strings, like C++ strings, would be terminated by a zero character. In the implementation we presented, almost all of the operations run in time $O(n)$, where n is the length

FIGURE 3.4

Average efficiency of string search algorithms

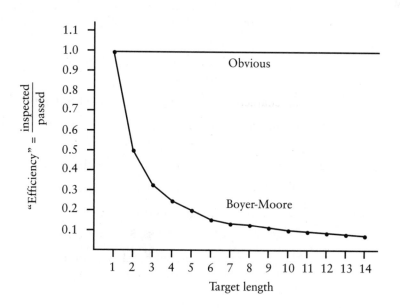

of the string (or strings) involved in the operation. We mentioned that C++, more so than many other languages, imposes a hidden cost on many operations, mainly because an apparently simple C++ statement might generate a number of function calls implicitly.

String searching is a common application of the *String* ADT. Of the many algorithms that exist for this problem, we discussed two in the text. The obvious algorithm inspects, on the average, slightly more than one character for each character passed, and for some strings may require much more than linear time. The Boyer-Moore algorithm requires an extra routine to preprocess the target string, but then performs much better than the obvious algorithm. If you're intrigued by the Boyer-Moore algorithm, you might want to read the original paper by R. S. Boyer and J. S. Moore: "A Fast String Search Algorithm," *Communications of the ACM* 20 (October 1977): 762–772.

3.5   EXERCISES

1. In Section 3.1, we showed that we could define += in terms of *Insert* and *Length*. Do the problem in reverse, defining *Insert* in terms of +, *Substring*, and *Length*.

2. We decided to use a zero terminator for our Strings because C++ strings are zero-terminated and so the user of our class would expect that from us. Aside from that consideration, how much use do we make of the zero terminator? Specifically, find every function in *String* where lack of a zero terminator would cause the function to malfunction.

3. In ASCII order and EBCDIC order, what expression could you use to test whether the char variable *ch* was

   a. An uppercase letter
   b. An alphabetic character (i.e., 'A' through 'Z' or 'a' through 'z')
   c. A digit ('0' through '9')
   d. An **alphanumeric** character (a letter or digit)

4. Complete the definitions of the String comparison operators by giving definitions for !=, <=, >, and >=.

5. Write the definition of the String member function *Remove*.

6. Write the definition of the String concatenate-assign operator +=.

7. Write a friend function for the *String* class

   ```
   friend String Difference(const String& str1, const String& str2);
   ```

   that will compare *str1* and *str2* and will return the tail of *str1*, starting at the first character where *str1* and *str2* don't match. For example, if we had *str1* = "unintelligent" and *str2* = "under" (or "un"), then the function would return "intelligent". If all of *str1* matches the start of *str2*, the function should return the empty string.

8. Consider the function *Reverse* that reverses the characters in a String, changing "alligator" to "rotagilla", for instance. Write this function as

   a. A *String* member function:

      `void Reverse().`

   b. A member operator overload:

      `void operator- ().`

   c. A friend of the *String* class:

      `friend String Reverse(const String& st).`

   d. A free function, defined outside the class:

      `String Reverse(const String& st).`

   e. Comment on the relative merits of these versions in terms of ease of writing and ease of use.

9. Write

   `friend String operator- (const String& str1, const String& str2)`

   that returns the String that would result from removing every instance of *str2* from *str1*, so `"This String"` - `"i"` would return `"Ths Strng"`.

10. If we represented integers as strings of characters (so "–44591" would represent the integer –44,591), would the String operator < give rise to the same order as the operator < that is defined on integers?

11. Any one-argument constructor can be regarded as a type conversion operation. For example, the constructor `String(int len)` takes in an `int` and makes a String (zero-terminated, with '\ 0' in position *len*), so we could "convert" the integer 10 into a String *s* by writing s = `String(10)`.

    a. Write the definition of a different version of `String(int n)` that converts an integer into a String that represents the characters we would use to write the number. For example, *String*(-44591) would construct the string "–44591".

    b. C++ provides us with a way to do this sort of type conversion in reverse, namely, from a user-defined class object (like a String) to a predefined type (like `int`). A member function whose name is a type name is known as a **conversion operator**. For example, we could provide a way to change a String into an `int` by declaring the *String* member function

       `operator int();`

       and writing the definition

```
String::operator int()
{
   ...
   return i;   // where i had been computed above
}
```

(Conversion operators are declared somewhat like destructors in that they may not take arguments and have no return values specified.) Suppose we had a class, *NumString,* with underlying character set { '+', '–", '0', . . . , '9'} , that represented integers as Strings in the expected way. Write the definition of `NumString::operator int()` in such a way that `int("-44591")` would return the int –44591.

 c. Modify the conversion operator of part (b) so that it extracts a number from an arbitrary String, discarding all nonnumeric characters (including '+', and '–', to make your task easier), so that `int("x3yx4")` would return the int 34.

12. Here's a first-class example of excessive C++ trickiness. What does this function do when given zero-terminated C++ strings *p* and *q*?

```
void Mystery(char* p, const char* q)
{    while (*p++ = *q++); }
```

Hint: Recall that * and ++ have the same precedence and group from the right and that we're using the postincrement form of ++. If you code this and try to run it, you may get a warning from the compiler, but it's righteous C++ code.

13. How would you use the *String* class to write a word processor? Consider such problems as what extra variables or operations you would need, whether it would be better to store the entire document as one long string or as a list of words, how to recognize a word (leading and trailing spaces aren't enough), and how to deal with such things as different typefaces or styles (such as boldface).

14. Fill in the missing parts of the definition of the obvious version of *Find.* In other words, write a correct C++ version of the one given in the text.

15. Modify the obvious version of *Find* as suggested in the text. Specifically, write the function

```
FindFrom(int p, const String& source, const String& target)
```

that returns the starting position of the first instance of *target* in *source* at or after position *p*. As in *Find,* this function should return –1 if no match is found.

16. Show that the obvious definition of *Find* could require $O(st)$ steps, where *s* is the length of *source* and *t* is the length of *target*. *Hint*: Suppose *source* and *target* were of the form "AA . . . AB".

17. Compute the tables *delta1* and *delta2* for the following target strings.
    a. "ABCD"
    b. "DERIDE"
    c. "GOOD_DOGGO"

18. a. Find a string for which *delta2* has the values 7, 6, 5, 3, 1.
    b. Show that there is no string for which *delta2* has the values 9, 8, 4, 3, 1.

19. For target strings of length n, what are the largest and smallest possible values of *delta2*[j], for $j = 0, 1, \ldots, n-1$?

20. Trace the actions of the obvious and the Boyer-Moore algorithms on the following *source* and *target* strings, and count the number of comparisons made by each algorithm.
    a. *source* = "ABNORMALCABDRIVERS", *target* = "ABD"
    b. *source* = "AAAAAAAAB", *target* = "AAAB"

21. Write preprocessing algorithms that produce the tables *delta1* and *delta2* in the Boyer-Moore algorithm. Find timing estimates for your algorithms.

22. Fill in the missing parts of the definition of the Boyer-Moore version of *Find*. In other words, write a correct C++ version of the one given in the text.

23. (Lengthy) Write a line-based word processor. The word processor accepts commands of the form "command-code number [optional-number] [optional-string] [optional-string]" of the following forms:

    A n st,   Adds the String *st* into the document between lines *n* and $n+1$, with the understanding that if $n < 0$, a new first line will be added.

    D n m,   Deletes *n* lines from the document, starting at line *m*.

    P n m,   Prints *n* lines of the document, starting with line *m*.

    I n m st,   Inserts String *st* into line *n* , starting in position *m*.

    R n st1 st2,   Replaces every instance of *st1* in line *n* with *st2*.

    L n st,   Prints the line number and the contents of each line at or after line *n*, which contains String *st*.

24. (Time-consuming) Write a program that compares the obvious version and the Boyer-Moore version of *Find*, and include in each version statements that count the number of comparisons made. Try enough test cases to demonstrate the relative efficiencies of the two algorithms for *target* strings of varying lengths.

3.6 EXPLORATIONS

Advanced Pattern Matching

The SNOBOL language was designed to provide support for pattern matching and replacement in character strings.* One of SNOBOL's fundamental operations is replacing all instances of a *pattern* string in a *subject* string with an *object* string. In C++ terms, we would have a function

```
void Replace(String& subject,const String& pattern, const String& object)
```

For example, if we had *sub* = "mississippi", then after the call

```
Replace(sub, "ipp", "lipper")
```

we would have *sub* = "mississlipperi". Notice, by the way, that the only substrings that are replaced are those of the original subject; in particular, the "ipp" in "lipper" is not replaced. In the exercises that follow, perform matching and replacement from left to right.

25. Write *Replace*. You might find it handy to assume that you already have available the function *FindFrom*, described in Exercise 15.

26. Explain why we restricted replacement to only those strings in *subject* by showing the catastrophe that would result in our example if we did not.

27. **a.** Extend your definition of *Replace* to allow *pattern* to have a special character '.' (which we assume will never appear in *subject*) that matches any character. In our earlier example, *Replace(sub, "i.", "o")* would result in *sub* = "mososopi".

    b. Using the information from part (a), show why the left-to-right matching direction is important by producing a *subject* string for which *Replace(sub, "i.", "o")* gives different answers, depending on the direction of search.

28. Extend *Replace* to allow *pattern* to contain the character '#', which matches any substring, trying to match the longest possible string it can. In our example, the string "i#s" will match "is", "iss", "issis", and "ississ" and when used in *Replace* will cause replacement of "ississ".

29. Further extend *Replace* so that it accepts another special character '|', which, when placed between two strings in *pattern*, matches either substring. For example, *Replace(sub, "i|s|p", "")* will eliminate any instance

---

* A similar feature is available in the unix operating system, under the name grep (which stands for "g/regular-expression/p" if you're really curious). In this exploration, we will freely mix SNOBOL and grep features.

of 'i', 's', or 'p' in *sub*. This is trickier than it appears. You'll have to decide what to do with situations like *pattern*="is|i". The SNOBOL rule is to match alternative strings left to right, so at any point in *subject*, it would try to match "is" before it tried to match "i".

30. Here are some more special *pattern* characters. Include them in *Replace*.

    a. '*', which matches zero or more instances of the character before it, so "yx*" will match the "y" "yx", "yxx", "yxxx", and so on. As with '#', when used in *Replace*, this will match the longest substring it can.

    b. '+', which acts like '*' except that it doesn't match zero instances of the character before it.

    c. (Hard) The pair '(' and ')', which serve to group patterns, so the string "(a|e|i|o|u)#" will match any string that begins with a lower-case vowel.

31. Using the conventions of Exercises 25 through 30, describe the strings that would be matched by the following patterns.

    a. ".e."

    b. "T#"

    c. "bo*"

    d. "a.|e.|i.|o.|u."

    e. "x*|y*"

    f. ".#."

    g. ".#*"

    h. "(x|y+)#x*"

    i. "(x.x)|(y.y)|(xx|yy)|(x|y)"

4

OTHER LINEAR STRUCTURES

> *And the rule for building shall be this: that no stone be placed but atop another and that no stone be removed but that it be the topmost.*
>
> Egyptian mason's instructions
> (c. 1230 B.C.)

Often, when writing programs, we find that the information used by the program has a natural linear form, but the application is such that we do not need the full set of *List* operations. In particular, it is frequently the case that inspection, modification, insertion, and deletion need only be performed at one or two locations in the list, typically at the head and the tail. Such restricted list structures occur often enough that they warrant consideration as separate ADTs. In this chapter, we will discuss two such structures in detail: stacks and queues.

4.1 ADT: *STACK*

A **stack** is nothing more than a list for which insertion, deletion, and inspection all take place at one end of the list. The standard metaphor of a stack is a plate holder of the kind commonly found in cafeterias: Plates are stored in a well with a spring at the bottom, so that when the top plate is removed, the spring pushes the entire pile up just enough to allow the next plate to be accessed; and when a new plate (a clean one, supposedly) is added, its weight compresses the spring just enough so that it (and it alone) is accessible at the top. Like all metaphors, this is an approximation of the truth: Don't be misled into thinking that the data move, as the plates do. There is no reason that the data elements must be advanced in memory: All we need to do is shift our *reference* to the top element. The metaphor does, however, enforce the idea that with a stack, the only directly accessible location is at the top.

In computer applications, stacks are commonly used as intermediate storage, and many computers have stacks wired in as part of their hardware to provide fast and efficient stack manipulation. Consider, for example, what a computer must do when a function is called. When the function is invoked, the computer must save information such as the location in the program where the call was made, the contents of any variables used in the calling routine, and the arguments used in the call (which is one reason that function calls can be time-consuming). Of course, the function may itself call another function, necessitating additional saving of information, and so on. One way to deal with all this storage of what are known as **activation records** is to store each record on a stack; then, when a function call is complete, the contents of the top of the stack are available to provide orderly return to the location of the call, after which the activation record at the top of the stack is removed.

For example, suppose we had the following program skeleton:

```
      void A()
      {
(4)       B();
(5)   }

      void B()
      {    // do something }

      void C()
      {    // do something else }

(1)   void main()
      {
(2)       C();
(3)       A();
(6)   }
```

When *main* begins execution (1), the first thing to be done is (2) a call to function C. The computer must store on the stack of activation records the present location in the *main* function, among other things, to know where to go when C is finished. Function C then does whatever it does, and control is passed back to *main*, using the information stored in the activation stack. Upon reaching the call (3) to A, the new *main* function information must again be saved to guarantee a safe return. In A, however, there is another call, this time (4) to B, so the present location in A must be saved on the stack, along with the values of any of A's local variables. B runs to completion and returns control (5) to A, using the information on the top of the stack, which is no longer needed and so is removed from the stack. *A* then returns control (6) to *main,* using the information on top of the stack, and the program halts. This sequence of stack operations is shown in the following diagram:

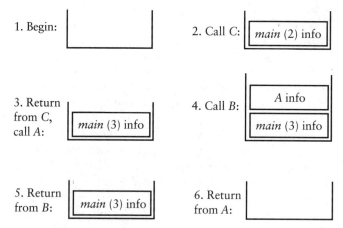

A stack is useful in this case because the last activation record placed on the stack is the first one to be used and discarded when control passes from the subroutine back to the calling routine. Because the last element added to a stack is the first one to be removed, stacks are called **last-in–first-out** (**LIFO**) structures.

The *Stack* abstract data type has a particularly simple specification. We will consider a stack to be a subtype of the *List* ADT, with the same linear structure and five operations of its own.

Stack : List

Structure. A *Stack* is a special case of a *List* of elements of type *T,* where all operations are performed at one end of the list, called the **top** of the stack.

Operations. With the exception of assignment, none of the *List* operations are directly available to users of the *Stack* ADT. *Stack* has five operations:

Stack(). Pre: true. Post: The stack is empty.

void Push(T e). Pre: true. Post: The element *e* is at the top of the stack and the other elements (if any) are in their original order.

void Pop(). Pre: The stack is not empty. Post: The element that was at the top position has been removed. The remaining elements are in their original order and the element that was adjacent to the original top is now in the top position.

> T Top() const. Pre: The stack is not empty. Post: The stack is unchanged, and a copy of the top element is returned.
>
> int IsEmpty() const. Pre: true. Post: The stack is unchanged, and the function returns 1 if and only if the stack is empty.

An alert is in order here. There is a roughly even split among computer scientists about how to define the *Stack* operations. Those who do not prefer the operations given here would combine *Pop* and *Top* into one operation that returns the value of the top element in the stack and also deletes that element from the stack. We have noted that computer science frequently involves choices based on informed personal assessment, and this is a good example. Combining the two operations into one has the advantage of simplicity, but it obscures the fact that there are two distinct operations possible. In fact, it makes no real difference which definition we choose, since the combined operation could be defined in terms of *Pop* and *Top,* both of which could be defined in terms of the combined operation. The only thing that should concern you is that not all authors use *Pop* the way we do here, so you need to be careful when reading other books.

Notice that we didn't specify *which* end of the underlying list should be the top of the stack. That's an implementation issue, and we'll discuss it when we get there.

The declaration of the *Stack* class is almost trivial. We declare a stack of elements of parametrized type, *TStack<T>*, and we use *TList<T>* as a private base class, since we're only interested in using the *List* operations and don't want the user of our *Stack* class to be able to do things like inserting a new element in the middle of a stack.

```
template<class T>
class TStack : private TList<T>
// Declaration of a parametrized stack class.
{
public:
   TStack();
   void Push(T e);
   void Pop();
   T Top() const;
   int IsEmpty() const
} ;
```

Notice that we didn't include a copy constructor or an assignment operator. For completeness, it would be easy enough to define them in terms of the corresponding *List* members; we omitted them because a program using stacks generally uses only one stack and so would never need these two operations.

As with any ADT, we can write other functions in terms of the *Stack* member functions. For instance, we could define a function *Over* to make a copy of the second element in a stack and place the copy on top of the stack. Thus, if a stack *stk* contained the elements . . . *a b* (reading from bottom to top), then *Over(stk)* would result in *stk* being changed to . . . *a b a*. The definition could take the following form.

```
void Over(Stack& stk)
{
   if (stk.IsEmpty())
   {
      cerr << "Stack too small for Over" << endl;
      return;
   }


   // Save and then remove top element
   // so we can get to the next-to-top element.
   T saveTop = stk.Top();
   stk.Pop();


   if (stk.IsEmpty())
   // Oops! Only one element in the stack, so restore
   // it to its original state and bail out.
   {
      cerr << "Stack too small for Over" << endl;
      stk.Push(saveTop);
      return;
   }


   // Now restore old top element and put a
   // copy of the second element on top.
   T saveSecond = stk.Top();
   stk.Push(saveTop);
   stk.Push(saveSecond);
}
```

It might appear that the abstract data type *Stack* is too simple to do anything but provide intermediate storage of the kind we mentioned earlier. To conclude this, however, would be to confuse elegance with triviality. As a matter of fact, there is a language, called FORTH, that uses the stack as its primary organizing structure. We take no stand on the comparative merits of FORTH and, say, C++, except to note that there are many FORTH adherents out there. Some of the exercises explore this language in more detail.

IMPLEMENTATIONS OF *STACK*

We indicated that we will consider *Stack* a subtype of the *List* ADT. When it comes to turning our specification into a C++ class, though, we have to remember that we have two different *List* implementations, one using arrays and the other using linked lists. Of course, from the point of view of declaring and defining the *Stack* class, it makes no difference: The *List* functions have exactly the same names, arguments, and return types in both implementations. Is there any good reason, then, to choose one of these implementations over the other, or should we just flip a coin? In fact, there *are* reasons to prefer one implementation of *List* over another, but the choice depends, as is so often the case, on the intended use of our *Stack* class.

Efficiency Issues

In Chapter 2, we saw that in terms of memory usage, the array version of *List* was better than the linked list when the data elements were small, and linked lists were more space-efficient when dealing with lists of big elements. An array may not always be completely full, leading to some wasted space, but a linked list always has the overhead of one extra pointer for each data element.

When we consider the running times of the *Stack* operations, we first observe that the constructor and the functions *Top* and *IsEmpty* all run in time $O(1)$, regardless of the size of the list, so we can disregard them and just look at *Push* and *Pop*. If you remember, the *Stack* specification deliberately avoided any decision about which end of the underlying list should be used for the top of the stack. Defining the *Stack* operations in terms of those of *List*, then, gives us two options:

1. If the head of the list is the top of the stack, we can define *Push* and *Pop* as

```
void Push(T e)              void Pop()
{                          {
   Head();                    Head();
   InsertBefore(e);           Remove();
}                          }
```

2. If the tail of the list is the top of the stack, we have

```
void Push(T e)              void Pop()
{                          {
   Tail();                    Tail();
   InsertAfter(e);            Remove();
}                          }
```

If you think about how insertion and deletion work in arrays, you can see that insertion and deletion at the head take time $O(n)$, since the subsequent n elements must be shifted to make room for the new element or to close the space left by the deleted element, while insertion and deletion at the tail both take time $O(1)$, since no shifting is needed. For the array version of *List,* then, there's no choice: We pick option 2, where the top of the stack is defined to be the tail position in the list.

For linked lists, insertion and deletion work in time $O(1)$, *except* that deletion of the tail element requires a $O(n)$ list traversal to find the position just before the tail position. Our conclusion here is just the opposite of the array one: For the linked version of *List,* we pick option 1 and consider the head of the list to be our stack top.

Stacks as a Derived Class

Because we don't know the intended use of our *Stack* class, we have no compelling reason for illustrating one implementation over another, so we tossed a coin and chose to illustrate how stacks could be written as a derived class of the linked version of *List.*

```
//============== TStacks.cpp ==============

#include "TStacks.h"

template<class T> TStack<T>::TStack() : TList<T>()
{
}

template<class T> void TStack<T>::Push(T e)
{
    InsertBefore(e);
}

template<class T> void TStack<T>::Pop()
{
    Remove();
}

template<T> T TStack<T>::Top() const
{
    return Retrieve();
}

template<class T> int TStack<T>::IsEmpty() const
{    return (Length() == 0); }
```

If you compare these definitions with option 1, you'll notice that we omitted any calls to *Head*. If you go back to Chapter 2 and look at the specification of *List*, you'll see why; *Retrieve* and *Length* never modify the list at all, and if the current position is the head of the list (or undefined, for empty lists), the functions *InsertBefore* and *Remove* leave the current position at the head. In program verification terms, *current=head* is an invariant for all of our stack operations.

Stacks from Scratch

There is a hidden disadvantage to writing our *Stack* class as a derived class of *List*: The *Stack* operations are, obviously, defined in terms of functions from *List*. You have seen that function calls require pushing activation records on a stack, and this data movement necessarily takes time. Simply said, function calls and returns take time. That's not a terrible problem here, since there's only one function call involved with each of the *Stack* member functions, and when they happen, there's not very much information that has to get passed through the activation records. Still, it's often useful to circumvent the overhead of inheritance by defining a class so that it stands on its own, so to speak.

Suppose we decided to implement *Stack* with a simple array: We will build the stack upward from the zero index of the member array *s*, keeping a member datum, *topIndex*, to mark the current top of the stack. Then when time comes to push an element, all we have to do is increment *topIndex* and place the new element in the required location. Take a look at how easy our stack operations are to write now.

```
template<class T> void TStack<T>::Push(T e)
{
    s[++topIndex] = e;
}

template<class T> void TStack<T>::Pop()
{
    topIndex--;
}

template<T> T TStack<T>::Top() const
{
    return s[topIndex];
}

template<class T> int TStack<T>::IsEmpty() const
{    return (topIndex == -1); }
```

We have left out some details, like the hidden parts of the declaration and what value we should initially assign to *topIndex*, but the message should be clear enough. Incidentally, we'll see a similar implementation when we investigate the *Queue* class.

 ## 4.3 APPLICATION: POSTFIX ARITHMETIC

We all learned early in our educational careers how to write and evaluate arithmetic expressions. Presumably, most of us would have little difficulty in evaluating an expression like $4+8*(9-6)$. The answer (which you should be able to compute in less time than it takes to read this parenthetical comment) is 28. Most people could even describe the steps necessary to arrive at the answer, saying something like, "Subtract six from nine to get three, multiply that three by eight to get twenty-four, and add that to four to get twenty-eight." Things get a little more difficult, however, if we try to explain *why* we performed the operations in the order we did. A typical explanation might be, "We did the subtraction first because it was inside the parentheses, then we did the multiplication before the addition because . . . well, because that's the way it's supposed to be done." With a little more thought and effort, however, we might eventually come up with a set of rules, a sort of quasi algorithm, that would run something like, "Evaluate from the most deeply buried parentheses outward, and in case there are no parentheses to guide you, do multiplication and division before doing any additions and subtractions."

Well, this is probably a good enough description for human beings, despite the fact that it leaves out some details (like how to treat negation, such as the – in front of –7, which is not quite the same as the – in the middle of 9–6, and what to do with exponents). Realizing that this book is about computer science, you have probably guessed that the next question will be, "How do we specify our expertise, gained through years of experience and intuition, in a form precise enough for a computer?" We could do it, given enough time, but it would be complicated and tricky, as you might imagine. (How, for instance, do you tell the computer to find the most deeply nested parentheses?)

Interestingly enough, the difficulty stems entirely from the fact that we are burdened with a historical accident. For as long as people have been writing about arithmetic (and that's a *long* time—nearly 4,000 years), arithmetic expressions, almost without exception, have been written in **infix notation**, in which the symbols for operations occur between the objects on which they operate. Nothing, however, except millennia of inertia, says that that is the only way to write and do arithmetic. It is quite possible to write our expressions in **postfix notation**, where the operators occur immediately *after* the objects on which they operate. In postfix notation (also called **reverse Polish notation**, or **RPN**, after the Polish logician Jan Lukasiewicz), the preceding expression would be written 4 8 9 6 – * +. We would read this expression from left to right until we came to an operator, in this case the subtraction symbol. Since each symbol operates on the numbers immediately preceding it, we would subtract 6 from 9 and replace 9 6 – by the result, 3. Our expression would then be 4 8 3 * +, and we would evaluate the next operator, replacing 8 3 * by its result to yield the new expression 4 24 +, which evaluates to 28. Seeing no more operators, we would know we were done. To do a longer problem is no more difficult.

Example 1

The infix expression (3 + 4 / 2) * (5 * 3 – 6) – 8 would be written in postfix form as 3 4 2 / + 5 3 * 6 – * 8 – (you can take that on faith for the time being) and would be evaluated as follows, where the subexpression being evaluated is highlighted:

```
3   4   2   /   +   5   3   *   6   –   *   8   –
        3   2   +   5   3   *   6   –   *   8   –
                5   5   3   *   6   –   *   8   –
                    5  15   6   –   *   8   –
                        5   9   *   8   –
                           45   8   –
                               37          ◁
```

It might take a little getting used to, but bear in mind that you have had years of practice with infix arithmetic and almost no practice with postfix (unless you own a calculator that is designed to use postfix notation). We did not introduce postfix notation just to provide a recondite example. There is a genuine benefit to be gained here. It is not difficult to show that *a correctly formed postfix expression is completely unambiguous.* Not only do we never need parentheses in a postfix expression, but we can completely dispense with the precedence rules that tell us that the infix expression 4 + 8 * 3 evaluates to 28 rather than the 36 that we would get if we added first and then multiplied. There is only one rule with postfix expressions: *Perform the operations from left to right, replacing as you go.* This is sufficiently simple that we can easily mechanize it. Suppose that *post* is a list of **tokens**, which are objects that are either numbers or operators. The algorithm that follows will evaluate the postfix expression using a stack, *eval*, to store numeric tokens awaiting operators.

```
long Evaluate_Postfix(TList<Token> post)
// Evaluates a postfix expression represented as a
// list of tokens.
{
    TStack<Token> eval;
    while (any tokens remain in post)
    {
        Token t;

        Remove a token, t, from the head of post;
```

```
      if (t is a number token)
        eval.Push(t);
      else
      // t is an operator token.
      {
          long topNum = eval.Top();  // Get one operand.
          eval.Pop();
          long nextNum = eval.Top(); // Get the other.
          eval.Pop();

          Evaluate answer = nextNum t topNum;

          eval.Push(answer);              // Push the result.
      }
  }
  return eval.Top();
}
```

This is certainly simple, as the next example demonstrates, but it doesn't bring us appreciably closer to solving the problem of mechanizing the evaluation of infix expressions. What we need is a translation routine that would take an infix expression and return the equivalent postfix expression, which we could then evaluate by the algorithm we have just seen. That is exactly what we will do—after we introduce another abstract data type in the next section.

Example 2

We will trace the postfix evaluation routine on the expression given in the last example.

Unused Postfix Tokens	**eval stack (bottom → top)**		
3 4 2 + 5 3 * 6 − * 8 −	(empty)		
4 2 / + 5 3 * 6 − * 8 −	3		
2 / + 5 3 * 6 − * 8 −	3	4	
/ + 5 3 * 6 − * 8 −	3	4	2
+ 5 3 * 6 − * 8 −	3	2	
5 3 * 6 − * 8 −	5		
3 * 6 − * 8 −	5	5	
* 6 − * 8 −	5	5	3
6 − * 8 −	5	15	
− * 8 −	5	15	6
* 8 −	5	9	
8 −	45		
−	45	8	
(empty)	37		

◁

4.4   ADT: *QUEUE*

A **queue** is a linear data structure for which insertions are made at one end and deletions and inspections at the other end. Queues are frequently used to model real-world situations. A typical modeling use would be to simulate the action of a car wash, in which cars enter the driveway from one end, move up in turn to the wash bay, are serviced, and leave. The owner of the car wash might be interested in how long a driveway to construct, given that, on the one hand, pavement is expensive, but on the other hand, turning cars away because of lack of room is not good for business. If we could obtain data on how frequently cars arrive and how these arrival times are distributed (perhaps by watching a competitor's business for a few weeks), we could use this information to construct a computer model of the car wash, the output of which might help the owner to decide how long the driveway should be. Such models are commonly employed when it would be impractical or expensive to use the real activity as a test (the owner might very well go broke in the time it would take to use the car wash itself to provide statistics).

In a queue, the first element to arrive is the first one to leave, and for this reason a queue is sometimes referred to as a **first-in–first-out** (**FIFO**) structure. Airplanes lined up to use a runway, people waiting for tickets to a theater, and potato chips on a grocery shelf are all examples of queues.*

▼

Queue : List

Structure.   A *Queue* is a special case of a *List* of elements of type *T*, where all insertions are performed at one end of the list (called the **rear**) and all deletions and inspections are performed at the other end (called the **front**).

Operations.   Except for assignment, none of the *List* operations are directly available to users of the *Queue* ADT. *Queue* has five operations of its own:

Queue(). Pre: true. Post: The queue is empty.

void Enqueue(T e). Pre: true. Post: The element *e* is at the rear of the queue and the other elements (if any) are in their original order.

---

* Potato chips are an example of a queue because it is a good idea to sell the oldest chips first, before they have a chance to get too stale, thereby making it necessary to add new bags behind the old ones. (Now you know how to pick the freshest bags.) As a matter of fact, a dirty trick sometimes played by unscrupulous potato chip distributors is to reverse the order of bags in their competitors' displays, placing the scrungy stale chips at the back.

> void Dequeue(). Pre: The queue is not empty. Post: The element that was at the front position has been removed. The remaining elements are in their original order, and the element that was adjacent to the original front is now in the front position.
>
> T Front() const. Pre: The queue is not empty. Post: The queue is unchanged, and a copy of the top element is returned.
>
> int IsEmpty() const. Pre: true. Post: The queue is unchanged, and the function returns 1 if and only if the queue is empty.

You can see that the *Queue* ADT is in many ways quite similar to *Stack*. *Enqueue* is like *Push*, *Dequeue* is like *Pop*, and *Front* is like *Top*. In fact, you'll see that the same sort of criteria apply to our choice of implementation as when we implemented *Stack*, with a few important differences. In the declaration of the *Queue* class that follows, you can see that we use a parametrized list as a private base class, as we did with *Stack*.

```
template<class T>
class TQueue : private TList<T>
// Declaration of a parametrized stack class.
{
public:
    void Enqueue(T e);
    void Dequeue();
    T Front() const;
    int IsEmpty() const;
} ;
```

4.5 IMPLEMENTATIONS OF *QUEUE*

Recall what we said in our discussion of the run time efficiency of arrays and linked lists: Array insertion and deletion are fast at the tail of a list and slow at the head, while linked list insertion is fast at either end and deletion is fast at the head and slow at the tail. That makes for an easy choice if we're using the linked version of *List*: The front, where deletion takes place, will be the head of the list. This choice will make all the *Queue* operations run in constant time.

Since a queue, considered a special case of *List*, requires insertion at one end and deletion at the other, we can see that arrays lose no matter which end we choose for the front: No matter which we pick, one of the array operations will have to be done at the head, thereby eliminating any chance that all operations will run in constant time. Obviously, the best choice is to implement *Queue* as a derived class of the linked version of *List*.

In fact, that's not true at all, as you'll see. We will indeed do the linked version, but we'll scoot through it quickly so that we can discuss the array version, where the real cleverness of this section resides.

Queues as Linked Lists

The implementation of our *Queue* class is so similar to that of *Stack* that we'll simply list it here, with no explication beyond that provided in the definition file itself.

```
//=============== TQueues.cpp ===============

#include "LinkedLists.h"
#include "TQueues.h"

// In this implementation, the front of the queue
// is the tail of the inherited list and the rear
// of the queue is the head of the list.

template<class T> void TQueue<T>::Enqueue(T e)
// Put e at the rear of the queue.
{
   Tail();
   InsertAfter(e);
}


template<class T> void TQueue<T>::Dequeue()
// Delete the element at the front of the queue.
{
   Head();
   Remove();
}


template<T> T TQueue<T>::Front() const
// Return the element at the front of the queue.
{
   Head();
   return Retrieve();
}


template<class T> int TQueue<T>::IsEmpty() const
// Return true if and only if the queue is empty.
{    return (Length() == 0); }
```

Circular Arrays and Queues

The inefficiency of the array implementation of *Queue* has nothing to do with any inherent limitation of arrays. Instead, it's entirely due to our insistence on using the array *List* operations. All is not lost, though, if we're willing to implement *Queue* from scratch, as we did with *Stack*. The fact that, abstractly, a queue is "a kind of" list may help us think about queues and their properties, but there is no reason why this abstract inheritance should blind us to the possibility that there is a much better implementation of this ADT.

The simplest way to implement *Queue* by arrays would be to maintain two indices, *frontIndex* and *rearIndex,* with, say, *frontIndex≤rearIndex* (the other order would be equally as good). Then, to enqueue an element, we would increment *rearIndex* and place the new element at the *rearIndex* position of the array. To dequeue, we would simply increase *frontIndex* by 1, as in Figure 4.1.

The problem is that each *Enqueue* causes the queue to grow to the right in the array, eventually leading to a situation in which the next *Enqueue* will cause the queue to "fall off" the right end of the array, even though there may be plenty of space available at the left end. It would not be too difficult to deal with such a situation. All we would have to do is watch the

FIGURE 4.1

An array implementation of *Queue*

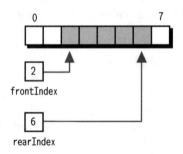

Original *Queue*

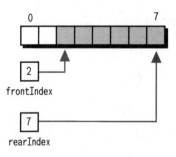

After *Enqueue*

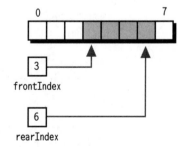

After *Dequeue*

rearIndex, and as soon as an *Enqueue* operation would cause the *rearIndex* cursor to exceed the maximum size of the array, we would shift the entire queue so that it would be aligned as far to the left as possible.* This would make *Enqueue* and *Dequeue* O(1) operations most of the time, but occasionally would introduce a factor of O(n) for *Enqueue,* where n is the size of the array. In fact, although it is beyond the scope of this book to prove, such a scheme is not all that bad in practice. If we assume that there is a long random sequence of *Enqueue*s and *Dequeue*s, where each operation is equally likely to be chosen, then the average time for *Enqueue* is only O(log n) on arrays of size n. In other words, *Enqueue* will not require shifts too frequently, and when it does, the number of elements to be shifted will be relatively small. Still, such a scheme does complicate the programming job a little, and it would be nice to find a way to avoid shifting entirely.

Instead of thinking of an array as a snake laid out on the ground with its head at one end and its tail at the other, suppose we forced the snake to bite its own tail, so that its head and tail were adjacent. In such a **circular array,** we would never have to deal with the possibility that *Enqueue* would force us to shift the queue elements. As long as it didn't grow to fill the entire array, the queue would continue to migrate around the circle, as in Figure 4.2.

Notice that we have departed slightly from the convention we made earlier that both *frontIndex* and *rearIndex* refer to occupied cells. Instead, *frontIndex* refers to the location of the front element in the queue, and *rearIndex* refers to the location *after* the rear element in the queue, so that *frontIndex* and *rearIndex* point to locations at which dequeueing and enqueueing, respectively, will take place. We can tell the size of the queue easily enough by a computation involving the difference between the two indices, with one exception: We will need a variable that tells us whether the queue is empty or full, because in both cases, *frontIndex* and *rearIndex* refer to the same location. With these facts in mind, it is easy to provide the necessary declarations and definitions.

---

* We could also grow the array, but that would lead to increasingly large chunks of unused elements on the lower end.

FIGURE 4.2

Circular array implementation of *Queue*

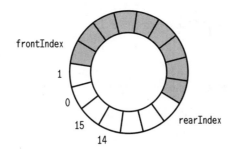

```
template<class T>
class TQueue
// Circular array implementation of Queue.
{
public:
   TQueue(int sz = 10);
   void Enqueue(T e);
   void Dequeue();
   T Front() const;
   int IsEmpty() const{  return empty;} ;
private:
   Array<T> data;
   int size,          // size of the array
        frontIndex,   // where we inspect and remove
        rearIndex,    // where we insert
        empty;        // 1 = empty, 0 = not empty
} ;

template<class T> TQueue::TQueue(int sz)
: data(sz - 1),
   size(sz),
   frontIndex(0),
   rearIndex(0),
   empty(1)
{
}

template<class T> void TQueue::Enqueue(T e)
{
   if ((frontIndex == rearIndex) && (!empty))
   {
      cerr << "Queue full, cannot Enqueue" << endl;
      return;
   }
   data[rearIndex] = e;
   rearIndex = (1 + rearIndex) % size;
   empty = 0;
}

template<class T> void TQueue::Dequeue()
{
   if (empty)
   {
      cerr << "Queue empty, cannot Dequeue" << endl;
      return;
   }
```

```
        frontIndex = (1 + frontIndex) % size;
        if (frontIndex == rearIndex)
            empty = 1;
}

template<class T> T TQueue::Front()
{
    if (empty)
    {
        cerr << "Queue empty, cannot inspect Front" << endl;
        exit(1);
    }
    return data[frontIndex];
}
```

It is easy to see that all the *Queue* operations run in constant time in this implementation. The only part of these definitions that need explanation is the increment used in *Enqueue* and *Dequeue*. We imagine the array as wrapped around so that the indices visited in order would be 0, 1, 2, . . . , $(size-1)$, 0, 1, 2, ... For all indices i, except $i=size-1$, we can increment i by setting i to $i+1$. In the case $i=size-1$, we want the increment to set i to 0. If we observe that for $0 \le i < size-1$ we have $i+1 = (i+1)$ % $size$ and that $(i+1)$ % $size = 0$ when $i=size$, we see that the expression i = (i + 1) % size will serve to increment i correctly in all cases. In the jargon, we're performing **modular arithmetic,** taking the remainder upon division by $size$ to limit our expressions to the range 0, . . . , $size-1$.

4.6 APPLICATION (CONTINUED): INFIX TO POSTFIX CONVERSION

We promised earlier that we would not only provide a means to evaluate postfix expressions, but also give a method to provide input for that evaluation algorithm, namely, a way to convert a token list representing an infix expression into a token list representing the corresponding postfix expression. Frankly, the only reason you had to wait this long for the conversion techniques is that it is convenient to use a queue as output from the conversion routine (and as input to the evaluation routine).

For reasons that will become clear shortly, we use a stack, *opStack*, to store the pending operator tokens (those for which we have not yet seen both arguments) and a queue, *postQ*, to store the postfix expression as it is being constructed. Each operator in the infix expression will be assigned an integer precedence with multiplication and division having the highest precedence, and addition and subtraction having the next highest precedence. We will artificially assign to the left parenthesis, (, the lowest precedence, to make the algorithm simpler to design. We will describe the algorithm, give an example of how it works, and then provide some justification that it does indeed do what it is claimed to do.

```
void Transfer(Stack<Token> s, Queue<Token> q)
// Utility: Transfers top of stack s to tail of queue q.
{
   q.Enqueue(s.Top());
   s.Pop();
}
```

```
Queue<Token> Convert_To_Postfix(List<Token> infix)
      var  OpStack : STACK;
{
   Stack<Token> opStack;
   Queue<Token> postQ;
   while  (any tokens remain on Infix)
   {
```
Remove a token, *t*, from the head of *infix*;
```
      if  (t is a number token)               // (1)
         postQ.Enqueue(t);
      else if (opStack.IsEmpty())             // (2)
         opStack.Push(t);
      else if  (t is the left parenthesis token)   // (3)
         opStack.Push(t);
      else if  (t is the right parenthesis token)  // (4)
      {
         while (opStack.Top()   is not a left parenthesis)
            Transfer(opStack, postQ);
         opStack.Pop();  // discard a left paren from stack
      }
      else                                    // (5)
      {
         while ((!opStack.IsEmpty)&&
         (precedence of t≤precedence of  opStack.Top()))
            Transfer(opStack, postQ);
         opStack.Push(t);
      }
   }
   // Now there are no tokens left in infix, so just
   // transfer all remaining operators.
      while (!opStack.IsEmpty());  // (6)
         Transfer(opStack, postQ)
}
```

Example 3

We'll trace the action of this routine on $7 - (2 * 3 + 5) * (8 - 4 / 2)$. In the table describing the action of the algorithm, *opStack* is written bottom → top and *postQ* is written rear → front, so that you can imagine elements moving across the page, from left to right. In the description of the rule used to produce each line, 5* indicates a transfer of higher or equal precedence operator(s) from *opStack* to *postQ*.

Unused Infix Tokens	opStack	postQ	Rule
$7 - (2 * 3 + 5) * (8 - 4 / 2)$	Empty	Empty	
$- (2 * 3 + 5) * (8 - 4 / 2)$	Empty	7	1
$(2 * 3 + 5) * (8 - 4 / 2)$	−	7	2
$2 * 3 + 5) * (8 - 4 / 2)$	− (	7	3
$* 3 + 5) * (8 - 4 / 2)$	− (	2 7	1
$3 + 5) * (8 - 4 / 2)$	− (*	2 7	5
$+ 5) * (8 - 4 / 2)$	− (*	3 2 7	1
$5) * (8 - 4 / 2)$	− (+	* 3 2 7	5*
$) * (8 - 4 / 2)$	− (+	5 * 3 2 7	1
$* (8 - 4 / 2)$	−	+ 5 * 3 2 7	4
$(8 - 4 / 2)$	− *	+ 5 * 3 2 7	5
$8 - 4 / 2)$	− * (	+ 5 * 3 2 7	3
$- 4 / 2)$	− * (	8 + 5 * 3 2 7	1
$4 / 2)$	− * (−	8 + 5 * 3 2 7	5
$/ 2)$	− * (−	4 8 + 5 * 3 2 7	1
$2)$	− * (− /	4 8 + 5 * 3 2 7	5
$)$	− * (− /	2 4 8 + 5 * 3 2 7	1
Empty	− *	− / 2 4 8 + 5 * 3 2 7	4
Empty	Empty	− * − / 2 4 8 + 5 * 3 2 7	6

◁

As this example indicates, the infix expression $7 - (2 * 3 + 5) * (8 - 4 / 2)$ is converted to its postfix equivalent, which we would write as $7\ 2\ 3 * 5 + 8\ 4\ 2 / - * -$. Comparing the two, we notice that the number tokens in each expression are in the same order, as will always be the case in this algorithm. That the postfix expression stored in *postQ* is written "backward" is due only to the way in which we decided to represent the queue. Transfers from *opStack* to *postQ* are made to the left (rear) end of *postQ*, so in the preceding table, you can imagine the tokens migrating from the top of *opStack* (the right end) to the tail of *postQ* (its left end). Now you should be able to see why we used a queue for the output of this algorithm: Since the output will be used as the input of the evaluation algorithm, the evaluation algorithm will repeatedly dequeue tokens from *postQ*, starting with 7, then 2, then 3, then *, and so on. In fact, it is not difficult to see that we could combine the two algorithms into one, using another stack for evaluation and eliminating *postQ* entirely.

This is only a small part of what a compiler or interpreter must do to translate a program from a language like C++ to machine language. Even so, we have left out a number of details, such as how the compiler "recognizes" tokens in an input string (i.e., the source code of the program), how it keeps track of where a number ends and an operator begins, and how it decides what is a variable and what is a constant.

Verification

We can show that the conversion algorithm works correctly by using an **induction proof**. We describe induction in more detail in Appendix B, but the essential idea is to show that if the conversion algorithm works for any infix expression with fewer than n tokens, then it must work for any infix expression with n tokens. Doing this will allow us to prove that the conversion algorithm must work for all possible infix expressions.

The major part of the proof goes roughly as follows: Let I be an infix expression with n operators. Then it must be that $I = I_1 \; op \; I_2$, where I_1 and I_2 are infix expressions. Since I has n operators, I_1 and I_2 must each have fewer than n operators. We would choose the operation to be the last one to be performed if we were evaluating I, so if $I = (22 / 7 + 4) * (6 \; 2)$, we would have $I_1 = (22 / 7 + 4)$ and $I_2 = (6 - 2)$.

Since both I_1 and I_2 have fewer than n operators, we assume that they can be correctly converted to postfix expressions P_1 and P_2, which in the example we are using would be 22 7 / + and 6 2 –, respectively. We would then show that since the conversion of both I_1 and I_2 left nothing on *opStack*, we could "glue" these two constructions together to form the construction for I so that after having seen all the tokens in I, the conversion routine would have only *op* on the *opStack* and $P_1 \; P_2$ as the contents of *postQ*. Then the last step in the conversion algorithm would transfer the contents of *opStack* to *postQ*, giving the desired result $P_1 \; P_2 \; op$. In our example, then, the postfix equivalent would be 22 7 / + 6 2 – *.

 SUMMARY

Both the *Stack* and *Queue* abstract data types are linear structures. They differ (and they differ from *List*) in their operators. The *Stack* operators are defined so that insertion, inspection, and deletion all take place at one end in the linear order, whereas for *Queue*, insertion is done at one end of the structure, inspection and deletion at the other.

We investigated an implementation of *Stack* that treated it as derived from *List*. Stacks are most useful in instances where the most recently saved information will be accessed first (LIFO, or last-in–first-out) and so are valuable for storing activation records of procedure calls. In fact, this application is used so often that many computers have stacks wired in as part of their hardware, for fast stack operations. We saw that the *Stack* ADT is a natural choice for evaluation of postfix expressions.

Queues, on the other hand, arise frequently in models of real-world processes, where the most recently saved information will be the last to be accessed (FIFO). Queues can be implemented by arrays, circular arrays, and linked lists. The array implementation of *Queue* requires us to circumvent direct inheritance from *List* to get $O(1)$ running time for all operations. The straightforward array implementation of *Queue* requires an occasional reorganization of the elements in the array, a shortcoming that is eliminated by using circular arrays.

4.8 EXERCISES

1. Suppose that the function T PopTop() was defined to combine the action of *Pop* and *Top,* so that it returned the top element on the stack and then removed that element from the stack.

   a. Write *PopTop* as a *Stack* member function.

   b. Show that both *Pop* and *Top* can be defined in terms of *Push, Empty,* and *PopTop.*

2. A **recursive** function is one whose definition includes one or more calls to itself. We'll have lots more to say about recursion in the next chapter. Consider the function

   ```
   void X(unsigned int n)
   {
      if (n > 0)
      {
         X(n / 2);
         cout << (n % 2);
      }
   }
   ```

   a. Show the successive states of the stack of activation records when the call $X(13)$ is made. To keep things straight, put the current value of n in each activation record.

   b. What does this function do?

   c. What would the function do if we reversed the order of the statements in the if block?

3. In the language FORTH, almost all operations are performed on a predefined stack. Commands are entered from the keyboard and are executed in the order entered as soon as the <return> key is pressed. If a number is seen, it is pushed on the stack, so the input sequence 2 3 8

<return> would cause the numbers 2, 3, 8 to be pushed on the stack in that order (so that 8 would be the new top element on the stack). An arithmetic operator causes the top two elements of the stack to be inspected and removed, the operation to be performed, and the result to be pushed onto the stack, so the sequence consisting of 8 4 / <return> would leave the stack with 2 on top (the 8 and 4 having been popped by the operator). In FORTH, it is possible to define complex operations by name, prefacing the name with : and following the name with the stack operations to be performed, so that the operator EXAMPLE defined by

```
: EXAMPLE  2  *  +
```

would take a stack . . . a b (from bottom to top, as usual) and perform the operations "push 2," "multiply the top two elements," and "add the new top elements," thus changing the stack to . . . $2b+a$, with the old top elements a and b having been popped by the operations * and + in the definition.

a. Assuming that the stack contained . . . a b c before the calls, what would be the effect of the following operations?

```
: OP1  3  *  -  *
: OP2  -  2  *  -
```

b. Show that one of the reasons FORTH contains the operation OVER, which we described in the text, is that it makes it possible to define operations like : OP3 OVER + *, which, when performed on a stack of the form . . . a b, allows the computation of $a*(a+b)$.

c. Show that, using what we know so far, it is impossible to define an operation that takes a stack of the form . . . c a b and computes $(a-b)/c$, and show that such an operation is possible if we have another operation, SWAP, that interchanges the top two elements of the stack.

d. Define SWAP in terms of the *Stack* operations.

4. Show how you would use a stack of characters to reverse a string by writing a stack-based definition of the function void Reverse(String& st).

5. In a C++ program, every instance of } must be matched by a previously unmatched {.

a. Show how you would use a stack to make sure that the block delimiters { and } are properly matched.

b. How would you check the balance of three pairs of symbols, like { and }, (and), and [and]?

6. Find a way to represent two stacks in a single array, and tell how *Push* and *Pop* would have to be modified for your data structure. Your im-

plementation should be written so that it will allow *Push* to succeed as long as there is any space at all left in the array.

7. Not all sequences of *Push* and *Pop* can be performed without error, starting with an empty stack. For example, the sequence *Push, Pop, Pop, Push* will lead to a "pop empty stack" error at the second *Pop*.

    a. Find a simple rule to describe all "legal" sequences of *Push* and *Pop* that can be performed starting with an empty stack.

    b. Relate your rule to a rule describing all sequences of **balanced parentheses,** such as (()(()())).

8. **Dijkstra's railroad:** One way to look at a stack is as a railroad siding with two tracks leading to it—an input track, from which cars are pushed onto the siding, and an output track, from which cars are removed (popped) from the siding.

Out   In

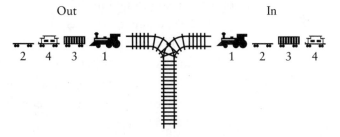

2   4   3   1   1   2   3   4

The diagram indicates the result of applying the sequence *Push, Push, Pop, Push, Push, Pop, Pop, Pop:* If the cars were originally in order 1, 2, 3, 4, then that sequence results in the permuted order 2, 4, 3, 1.

    a. Show that it is not possible to obtain all possible permutations by this scheme by showing that 5, 4, 1, 3, 2 cannot be obtained from input 1, 2, 3, 4, 5.

    b. Find a rule that describes which permutations cannot be obtained from the input $1, 2, \ldots, n$.

    c. Describe the railroad equivalent of queues, and show that as a generator of permutations, queues are trivial.

9. Implement the function int Length() for *Queue,*

    a. Implemented as a derived class of *List.*

    b. Implemented using circular arrays.

10. A **double-ended list** (or **deque,** pronounced "deck") is a special case of *List,* where insertions, deletions, and inspection of elements are only done at the head and tail ends of the underlying linear structure.

    a. Write a declaration for this class.

    b. Write definitions of the member functions and friends you decided to use.

    c. Show how we could derive *Stack* and *Queue* from *Double-Ended List*.

11. **Automata theory** is devoted to the study of abstract machines, languages, and the sorts of computations that can be performed on those machines. A **language** is just a set of strings over some fixed alphabet of characters, so the set $P = \{a, ab, aabb, aaabbb, \ldots\}$ could be described informally as the language consisting of all strings of $n \geq 1$ a's followed by n b's. A **machine** M is said to recognize a language L if it can be programmed to halt and print "yes" for every input consisting of a string from L, and halt and print "no" for every input string that is not in L. The input is read from left to right, one character at a time, and typically the machine M is allowed to have a program consisting of a sequence of such simple operations as

    READ [an input character] and store it [somewhere]

    GOTO [some instruction]

    IF [some variable] equals [some value], then [do some instruction]

    SET [this variable] to be [some value]

    STORE [this variable] at [some specified location]

    WRITE_YES and halt

    WRITE_NO and halt

The operations are the same in all the abstract machines (and do not include such things as arithmetic), but different machines are distinguished by the data structures used for storage.

For instance, a **finite automaton** has as its only data structure a fixed finite number of variables (of a fixed finite size), $v_1, v_2, \ldots, v_n$.

    a. Show that a finite automaton can recognize $L = \{b\$, ab\$, aab\$, aaab\$, aaaab\$, \ldots\}$ by writing a program for such a machine using only the seven instructions given previously (the $\$$ characters are there only to let your program know the end of the input and will be assumed to be part of subsequent examples). The collection of languages recognized by finite automata are called **regular languages**.

    b. Argue informally that no finite automaton can recognize the language P given earlier—that is, that P isn't a regular language. *Hint:* You're not allowed to change the number or size of variables to suit the input, because you don't know the input size ahead of time.

    c. A **pushdown automaton** (**PDA**) is an enhancement of a finite automaton in that it has a finite number of variables, along with a single stack and the usual stack operations. Find a program for a PDA that recognizes P. Languages recognized by PDAs are called **con-**

text-free languages (CFLs) and are important because they are both large enough to be interesting (many computer languages are CFLs, or very close to being so) and small enough to be recognized easily.

d. Show that the language L = {abb, aabbbb, aaabbbbbb, . . .} is a CFL.

e. Argue informally that L = {abc, aabbcc, aaabbbccc, . . .} is not a CFL.

f. A **two-stack PDA** has, as its name implies, two stacks rather than one. Are two-stack PDAs more powerful than PDAs in the sense that there are languages recognized by two-stack PDAs that are not CFLs?

12. Evaluate the following postfix expressions.

a. 3 4 8 + 2 * 5 1 - * +

b. 3 4 8 2 5 1 + * - * +

13. The description of postfix expressions is incomplete, because it fails to include (among other things) unary negation, which we will denote by ~. With this notation, the expression 2 4 ~ * would be equivalent to the infix expression 2 * (–4). Modify the postfix evaluation algorithm to include treatment of unary negation.

14. a. How many operator tokens must a correctly formed postfix expression have if it has n number tokens? *Hint*: This is a trick question, having something to do with a previous question.

b. Give a rule that describes all correctly formed postfix expressions, so that you can show that 3 4 5 + 6 * – * 7 8 9 + – is not correctly formed, even though it has the correct number of operators and numeric tokens.

15. Both the postfix evaluation function and the infix-to-postfix conversion function used a data type, Token, that we didn't specify. Remedy this by designing a *Token* class and showing how it would be used.

16. Modify the infix-to-postfix algorithm to include unary negation, as mentioned in Exercise 13.

17. Design a postfix calculator that reads a correctly formed postfix expression from standard input and displays the result.

18. Extend the program of Exercise 17 so that it handles incorrectly formed postfix expressions. As one example of error handling, when given the incorrectly formed input 3 2 + * 4, the program might report

3 2 + * ...   Too few operands for this operation

19. Trace the infix-to-postfix algorithm on the following expressions.

a. 1 + 2 * (1 + 2 * (1 + 2))

b. 3 – 8 / 4 + 5 * 6 * 7 – 2 * 9

c. (((3 + 5) * 2) – 4)

20. (Challenging) Design a postfix-to-infix conversion algorithm.

21. In a **priority queue**, each element to be inserted comes with a number, called its **priority**, and *Front* and *Dequeue* deal only with the element of highest priority on the queue at the time they were called. Implement a priority queue, and compare the running times of its operations with those of an ordinary queue.

22. The **problem of Josephus** is usually stated in the following rather grisly form: You are part of a group of people who are captured by blood-thirsty pirates and told that only one of your number will survive. Your group is made to stand in a circle, and a number *n* is chosen. Starting at some person, the pirates count off every *n*th person, remove that person from the circle, toss the unlucky individual overboard into shark-infested waters, and continue until only one person remains, who is then declared the captain and given all the booty the pirates have collected. Write a program that, given *n* and the number of people in your group, tells you how far to stand from the starting person.

23. Write an infix evaluator that, when given a string of characters like 34 * (8 − 21), prints the value of the expression. You may wish to include such refinements as (in approximate order of increasing difficulty) checking for run time errors such as division by zero, including unary negation and exponents, checking whether the original infix expression was correctly formed, indicating where in the infix expression the first indication of incorrect form was observed, and trying to recover from incorrect form errors by making an educated guess as to what was intended.

For the remaining exercises, it would be a good idea to read Appendix C on random numbers and simulation.

24. In discussing array implementations of queues, we mentioned that it was possible to maintain a queue as a linear, rather than circular, array by shifting the entire contents of the array as far left as possible whenever an *Enqueue* operation would cause the queue to overflow the right end of the array. We said that the average cost of such a scheme was $O(\log n)$ for arrays of size *n*. Implement *Queue* as a linear array, and include in your implementation counters for the number of steps performed (so *Dequeue* always adds 1 to the count, and *Enqueue* adds 1 to the count except for those times when the array needs to be shifted, in which case the count is increased by the number of elements that were shifted). For various values of *n*, the size of the array, find the average number of steps (i.e., the count divided by the number of operations) required by a long sequence of randomly chosen *Enqueue* and *Dequeue* operations.

25. Simulate the action of a car wash. Assume at first that the car wash consists of one wash bay and a driveway long enough to hold four cars.

Suppose it takes 10 minutes to wash a car, and that cars arrive at random in such a way that the average **interarrival time** (that is, the average time between arrivals of cars) is also 10 minutes. Write your program to simulate the activity of an 8-hour workday, keeping track of the average wait time for each car (from entering the driveway to entering the wash bay) and the number of cars that had to be turned away because the driveway was full. Investigate the effects of changing the capacity of the driveway and changing the interarrival time on the average wait time and number of cars turned away. (Incidentally, in many such situations, the interarrival times are not **uniformly distributed** (see Appendix C) but rather are **exponentially distributed.** You might want to investigate what difference, if any, this makes.)

4.9 EXPLORATIONS

The Electronic Labyrinth

As we have seen, a stack may be the data structure of choice if we find ourselves in a situation where we need to provide intermediate storage, especially if the intermediate storage is such that the item most recently stored will be the first item to be inspected or removed from storage. Suppose, for instance, that we wanted to write a program that would find a way out of a maze. Perhaps the most obvious strategy would be to mark the rooms visited (think of dropping bread crumbs, as Hansel and Gretel did) and also to keep track of the rooms visited so far in the order in which they were visited. If we come to a room with no adjacent unvisited rooms, we would then "backtrack" to the previously visited room and check whether there were any adjacent unvisited rooms. We would then continue as before, either going to an unvisited room or backtracking again.

The example we will use consists of a maze with eight rooms, connected as shown in Figure 4.3, where we start in room number 1 and wish to finish in room number 8.

FIGURE 4.3

A maze

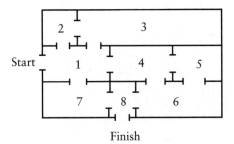

Finish

To write our maze-tracing algorithm, we will use a bit vector *visited*[*i*], where $0 < i \leq N$, and N is equal to the number of rooms, to keep track of the rooms already visited. The entry *visited*[*k*] will be 1 if room *k* has been visited and 0 otherwise. We will also maintain a stack, *soFar*, consisting of the number of rooms visited so far, in order, which we will use in case it becomes necessary to backtrack. Upon a successful completion, it will turn out that *rooms* will contain a path, without duplication of rooms, from *start* to *finish*.

One way to conceptualize such a process is to use a **solution tree**, which not only describes all possible paths, but also gives the relations between the paths. For our example, the solution tree would take the form diagrammed in Figure 4.4. In this tree, each node represents a partial solution, that is, a path from room 1 to another room without any duplication of rooms. The boxes with heavy borders, like the one representing the path (1, 4, 6, 8), denote complete solutions—paths from room 1 to room 8. In the solution tree, any node representing a partial solution is linked to nodes below it that represent solutions that may be reached from that partial solution. For example, the node (1, 4, 6) leads to the further paths (1, 4, 6, 5) and (1, 4, 6, 8).

26.   Give the solution tree for the maze-tracing example if a doorway was made between rooms 3 and 5.

Not only does the solution tree provide a systematic means of describing all three complete solutions, but it also allows us to describe the maze-tracing algorithm. For instance, beginning at node (1), we might then move to room 2, which would be described by the node (1, 2). Notice that in this example, the labels of the nodes also describe the contents of the stack of rooms visited

FIGURE 4.4

The solution tree of
the maze of Figure 4.3

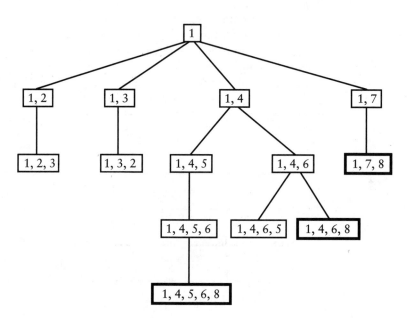

in each path. From node (1, 2) there is only one possible "legal" move, namely, to room 3, giving us the partial solution (1, 2, 3). From that node, there are no legal moves, so it is necessary for us to backtrack from room 3 to room 2. In stack terms, we would pop the stack, eliminating room 3 from our solution path. We find that there are no legal moves from room 2, since from node (1, 2) the only other solution is (1, 2, 3), which we have already discovered is a dead end. We then have to backtrack once more, pop the stack again, and start fresh from node (1).

It is easy to see that our maze-tracing algorithm will eventually produce a solution, if there is any at all. In technical terms, our algorithm represents a **depth-first search** through the solution tree. In a depth-first search (about which we will say much more in Chapter 8), we begin at the top of the tree and go as far down as we can. If we find a solution, fine, we stop there; but if we fail to find a solution, we back up the tree until we come to the first unused branch, then take that branch and again go down as far as possible, continuing the process of descent and backtracking until we either reach a solution or have visited every node in the tree. Having done the preliminary work, it is now easy to describe the maze-tracing algorithm.

```
void MazeTraverse(int start, int finish)
// Depth-first search for a path from start to finish
// in a maze with N rooms.
{
    //----------- Initialization
    Stack<int> soFar;      // current path
    int   current = start; // current room number

    Array<int> visited(N, 1);
    for (int i = 1; i <= N; i++)
        visited[i] = 0;
    visited[current] = 1;
    soFar.Push(now);

    //----------- Main traversal loop
    // Keeps following a path until a dead end.
    // If a dead end is reached, backtrack until there
    // is an unvisited adjacent room.
    // Leave the loop if we find a solution or exhaust
    // all possible paths.

    while (current != finish)
    {
        Set next to be an unvisited room adjacent to current, or to 0,
        if there are no adjacent unvisited rooms;

        if (next == 0) // dead end: backtrack if possible
        {
            soFar.Pop();
```

```
            if (soFar.IsEmpty())      // can't backtrack
            {
               cout << "There is no path from " << start
                  << " to " << finish << endl;
               return;
            }
            else
               current = soFar.Top();  // backtrack
         }

         else                          // go onwards
         {
            current = next;
            soFar.Push(current)
         }
      }
   cout << "Found the following solution:" << endl;
   while (!(soFar.IsEmpty()))
   {
      cout << soFar.Top() << '\ t';
      soFar.Pop();
   }
}
```

Notice that we haven't mentioned how we will find a room adjacent to the room we are now in. In Chapter 8, when we discuss the *Graph* ADT, we'll discuss solutions to this problem, but for now we'll just consider one possibility, the **adjacency matrix**. Such a structure is a two-dimensional array, a, where the entry $a[i][j]$ is 1 if rooms i and j are adjacent (i.e., have a connecting door) and 0 otherwise. Our example maze, then, has the following adjacency matrix:

	1	2	3	4	5	6	7	8
1	1	1	1	1	0	0	1	0
2	1	1	1	0	0	0	0	0
3	1	1	1	0	0	0	0	0
4	1	0	0	1	1	1	0	0
5	0	0	0	1	1	1	0	0
6	0	0	0	1	1	1	0	1
7	1	0	0	0	0	0	1	1
8	0	0	0	0	0	1	1	1

27. Implement the maze-tracing function, using an adjacency matrix.

When picking an unvisited adjacent room, we have a certain amount of freedom. In our examples, we've chosen the lowest-numbered possibility: We would start at room 1, go to room 2, then to room 3, backtrack through rooms 2 and 1, continue to room 4, then to room 5, then to room 6, and finally arrive in room 8, the exit. In the solution tree, then, we would visit the following nodes: (1), (1, 2), (1, 2, 3), (1, 2), (1), (1, 4), (1, 4, 5), (1, 4, 5, 6), and (1, 4, 5, 6, 8). This solution requires us to visit eight rooms, counting backtracks, before we come to the exit. In this case, and in many others, this backtracking technique is not very efficient. When we return to this problem, it will be in a context in which we will be able to find a far better solution.

Notice, also, that this algorithm may not necessarily find the best (i.e., the shortest) path from *start* to *finish*. Choosing to visit the lowest-numbered unvisited room, as we did, gave the path (1, 4, 5, 6, 8), which is much longer than the best path (1, 7, 8). This is a deficiency that we will also remedy later.

28. Assume, as in the maze-tracing example, that the lowest-numbered unvisited adjacent room was the one visited next at each step. Assume also that in the maze given in the text, there was a door between rooms 3 and 5, but no door between rooms 6 and 8.

    a. What solution would the algorithm find?

    b. How many rooms would the algorithm visit, counting backtracks, before finding the exit?

29. Draw a picture of the maze with the following adjacency matrix, and find a path from 1 to 10, again choosing the lowest-numbered adjacent room.

	1	2	3	4	5	6	7	8	9	10
1	1	1	0	1	0	1	0	0	0	0
2	1	1	1	0	0	0	0	0	0	0
3	0	1	1	0	0	0	0	0	0	0
4	1	0	0	1	1	0	1	0	0	0
5	0	0	0	1	1	0	0	1	0	0
6	1	0	0	0	0	1	0	0	1	0
7	0	0	0	1	0	0	1	0	0	1
8	0	0	0	0	1	0	0	1	0	0
9	0	0	0	0	0	1	0	0	1	0
10	0	0	0	0	0	0	1	0	0	1

30. Another, very simple, maze-tracing algorithm is the **left-hand rule**: Walk through the maze by keeping your left hand on a wall at all times. For the example in the text, this would lead to the path (1, 2, 3, 1, 4, 5, 6, 8).

    a. Given a solution path from the left-hand rule, describe an algorithm to eliminate duplications of rooms, so that the cycle (1, 2, 3, 1) would be eliminated, leading to the shorter solution (1, 4, 5, 6, 8).

    b. Find a maze for which the left-hand rule will fail to find the exit.

Operating System Simulation

A common means of providing permanent storage of information in a computer system is to use a magnetic disk, such as the floppy disks you use to save your programs. Such a disk is a circular piece of plastic that is coated with a magnetic material similar to that used on audio- or videotapes. Typically, such a disk is organized into concentric *tracks,* much like the bands on a phonograph record. The disk rotates at high speed, usually between 300 to 4000 rpm, and information is read from or written to a particular track by a moving **read-write head,** which, like the tone arm on a phonograph, can be moved from one track to another.

Disk access is slow compared to access to the memory of a computer, largely because of the need to move the read-write head. In general, it takes a lot more time to move a large physical object like the read-write head than it does to shuffle the electrons through the computer's memory. Consider, for instance, a typical 20-megabyte hard disk. Such a disk might be divided into 512 tracks, each capable of storing 40K bytes of data. The **data transfer rate** (i.e., the rate of reading or writing information) might be 512K bytes per second, which is pretty fast compared to the time necessary to move the read-write head, typically about 0.3 millisecond per track (1000 milliseconds equals 1 second). For example, if the head was at track 1 and a request came in to read 512 bytes of data from track 400, it would take $0.3 * (400-1) = 119.7$ milliseconds to move the head into the proper position, but then would take only 1 millisecond to read the data, not counting the time it would take for the disk to spin into the proper location on the track where the data was located (that's called the **latency time** and would be 8 milliseconds, on average, for a disk spinning at 3750 rpm).

Because the comparatively long seek time to move the read-write head is what determines the efficiency of disk access, many disk drives are controlled by a small disk driver program that keeps track of disk requests and schedules them in some efficient fashion. Three common scheduling algorithms are **first-come–first-served (FCFS), shortest seek time (SST),** and **sweep/shortest seek time (sweep/SST).** To illustrate these algorithms, suppose that requests are pending for tracks 50, 420, 100, 300, and 190 and that the head is presently on track 250.

> **FCFS** processes disk requests in the order in which they arrive. Thus, the seek time would be
>
> $$0.3 * \left(\left|250-50\right| + \left|50-420\right| + \left|420-100\right| + \left|100-300\right| + \left|300-190\right| \right)$$
> $$= 0.3 * \left(200 + 370 + 320 + 200 + 110 \right) = 360 \text{ milliseconds}$$
>
> for an average seek time of $360/5 = 72$ milliseconds per request.
>
> **SST** processes the requests in order of least distance to the present head position. For this example, the requests would be processed in the order 300, 190, 100, 50, 420 for a seek time of

$$0.3 * \left(|250 - 300| + |300 - 190| + |190 - 100| + |100 - 50| + |50 - 420| \right)$$
$$= 0.3 * \left(50 + 110 + 90 + 50 + 370 \right) = 201 \text{ milliseconds}$$

for an average seek time of 201/5=40.2 milliseconds, which is only 56% of the time required by FCFS. The problem with SST is that in the unlikely event that requests come in alternate clusters, some of the clusters may take a very long time to process. If, for instance, the requests were for tracks 5, 405, 6, 406, 4, 404, . . . , SST may spend all of its time processing the 400-series tracks and never get to the low track requests at all. A way to alleviate this problem is to modify SST.

Sweep/SST services requests by "sweeping" the head from one end of the disk to the other and serving the closest request in the direction of the sweep. In our example, if the initial sweep direction was toward the smaller tracks, the requests would be processed in order 190, 100, 50, and then the sweep direction would be reversed and the remaining requests would be processed in order 300, 420 for a seek time of

$$0.3 * \left(|250 - 190| + |190 - 100| + |100 - 50| + |50 - 300| + |300 - 420| \right)$$
$$= 0.3 * \left(60 + 90 + 50 + 250 + 120 \right) = 171 \text{ milliseconds}$$

which is over twice as fast as FCFS.

31. Show the action of the three scheduling algorithms on the requests for the following tracks (in the order that they arrived): 269, 8, 404, 173, 128, 480, 119, 382, 10, 133, 381, 57. Assume that the read-write head is initially at track 1 and the initial sweep direction is upward. Which is the most efficient algorithm?

32. Previously, we have assumed that we had all the requests ahead of time. Of course, in a real system, requests would arrive as we were processing. For the case given in Exercise 31, assume that you begin with the requests 269, 8, 404, 173, 128 and that each remaining request arrives (unrealistically) as soon as you've finished processing an existing one. How does that change your results in Exercise 31?

33. Describe the data structures you would use for the efficient implementation of each of the three algorithms.

34. Implement and test the three algorithms, using the DiskSim program shell we have provided.

NONLINEAR STRUCTURES

5

RECURSION

A **recursive** definition is one that refers to the object it is defining as part of its definition. There's more to recursion than that, however, since we wish to avoid definitions like "A rose is a rose," which, poetic insights notwithstanding, does not give us much hard information on the nature of roses. The important feature of recursive definitions is that they always provide a means of "bailing out" of the definition, of avoiding circularity. The notion of recursion is exemplified by a definition like "A bouquet of roses is either (1) a single rose or (2) a single rose, along with a smaller bouquet of roses." In this example, condition 1 serves as the **exit case**, providing a way out of the definition, and condition 2, the **recursive case**, guarantees that we will always eventually reach the exit case. Recursive definitions are characterized by their elegance and simplicity (contrast the foregoing definition with the **iterative** version "A bouquet of roses consists of either one rose, or two roses, or three roses, ...") and are a valuable tool in the computer scientist's collection. In this chapter, we will investigate recursive definitions of both algorithms and data structures.

5.1 RECURSIVE ALGORITHMS

An algorithm is said to be recursive if its definition includes at least one call to itself, either directly (**direct recursion**) or indirectly, through a sequence of calls to routines that eventually result in a call to the routine itself (**indirect** recursion). Consider, for instance, the function int Factorial(int n), which is also written $n!$. We could make an iterative definition of $n!$ by asserting

$$0! = 1$$
$$n! = 1 \times 2 \times ... \times n \quad \text{for } n > 0$$

This would lead to the iterative definition

```
int Factorial(int n)
{
   if (n <= 1)
      return 1;
   else
   {
      int product = 1;
      for (int i = 1; i <= n; i++)
         product *= i;
      return product;
   }
}
```

That is, however, not the only possible way to define *Factorial*. We can get a recursive definition if we can answer the fundamental question, "Can I solve this problem, *assuming that I could solve a smaller instance of the problem?*" In this case, of course, it is easy to see how to compute $n!$, assuming that we could compute the factorial of smaller numbers. We could write the following recursive definition:

$$0! = 1 \quad \text{(the exit case)}$$
$$n! = n \times (n-1)! \quad \text{for } n > 0 \quad \text{(the recursive case)}$$

This definition translates directly to the recursive declaration

```
int RecursiveFactorial(int n)
{
   if (n <= 1)
      return 1;
   else
      return (n * RecursiveFactorial(n - 1));
}
```

Although *RecursiveFactorial* is certainly simpler to write than the iterative version, it is not necessarily any easier to understand, nor, as we will see shortly, is it any faster. It is, however, more compact and in some sense more elegant. Although any recursive definition can be written without recursion, we frequently find ourselves in situations where recursive definitions are the most natural ones to employ. The nicest thing about recursion is that it permits us to define algorithms seemingly out of thin air. Nowhere in the definition of *RecursiveFactorial* does there appear any obvious description of how

$n!$ is computed, except as a leap of faith asserting, "Assuming I know how to find $(n-1)!$, I'll find that and multiply by n to get $n!$."

To see how the recursive definition of $n!$ works, consider the call *RecursiveFactorial*(3). Since $3 > 1$, the function will multiply 3 by the result obtained by calling *RecursiveFactorial*(2), which will itself require another call, to *RecursiveFactorial*(1), which will return 1. After all three calls, we will have the following situation:

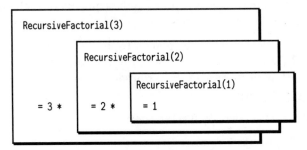

The calls to the outer functions cannot be completed until *RecursiveFactorial*(1) is evaluated. At that point, the values are repeatedly passed back to the calling routines, as follows:

```
RecursiveFactorial(3)

        RecursiveFactorial(2)

   = 3 *     = 2 * 1
```

```
RecursiveFactorial(3)


   = 3 * 2 * 1
```

In all these recursive algorithms, we are letting the computer keep track of pending results by pushing them on the stack of activation records that results from successive function calls. The first call, with $n=3$, is pushed on the stack and is followed by another push when *RecursiveFactorial* is called with $n=2$, which is followed by another push of activation records for the call with $n=1$. This value can be computed, and the result, 1, is passed back when the top activation record (for $n=1$) is popped. Then *RecursiveFactorial*(2) can be completed, so its activation record is popped, and control is passed to *RecursiveFactorial*(3), along with the value 2 for the previous call. This value, in turn, is used to compute *RecursiveFactorial*(3), after which control passes to the main program (or whichever routine made the original call to *Recursive-Factorial*(3)).

We do not have to restrict our attention to numeric calculations, however. Suppose that we had a linked list of nodes, each of which had a *data* member containing some information and a *next* member pointing to the succeeding cell. Suppose also that the last cell in the list had a NULL *next* field and that we were given a pointer to the first node in the list. We could traverse the list recursively, printing the contents of each *data* field, if we broke the problem into two parts:

1. We exit when the pointer to the current cell is NULL.
2. In every other case, we print the contents of the current cell and then perform the traversal routine beginning at the next cell after the current cell.

The traversal algorithm is then easy to write.

```
void Traverse(NodePtr p)
{
   if (p)
   {
      cout << p->data;
      Traverse(p->next);
   }
}
```

Notice that in this algorithm, the exit condition is implicit: When we come to the end of the list, the current pointer is zero, so we exit from the function without taking any action at all. The nicest feature of this algorithm is not its brevity but rather the fact that if we interchanged the two statements in the body of the `if` statement, we would have a routine that printed the contents of the list in *reverse order,* without our having to worry about how to traverse a one-way linked list in a direction opposite to that of the pointers. Do you see why? The algorithm for reverse traversal would then be described as follows: "To traverse the list, traverse the smaller list that begins after the current position, and when you're completely done, write out the value at the current position," so that the value at position *p* would be printed only after all the values following *p* had already been printed, thus traversing the list in reverse order. As with the recursive factorial algorithm, we let the computer keep track of the pending results in the stack of activation records. We could do explicitly what the computer does implicitly by keeping our own stack, simulating the pending procedure calls. An example of this technique of eliminating recursion is shown in the following iterative version of the routine to traverse a linked list in opposite order.

```
void ReverseTraversal(NodePtr p);
{
   Stack<NodePtr> s;
```

```
// Fill stack with pending pointers,
// simulating pending function calls.
while (p)
{
    s.Push(p);
    p = p->next;
}

// Now retrieve the pending pointers.
while (!(s.IsEmpty()))
{
    p = s.Top();
    cout << p->data;
    s.Pop();
}
}
```

An entirely reasonable question at this point is, Why would we want to eliminate recursion, especially since the iterative version of the reverse traversal routine requires twice as many lines as the recursive version? The answer is that the number of lines in a program is not necessarily a reflection of how long the program will take to run. It is not difficult to imagine that function calls take a considerable amount of time, saving all the local variables, addresses, and such, and pushing them on the stack of activation records. Although we have made the simplifying assumption that all statements take equal amounts of time (indeed, this assumption does not affect the big-O timing estimates), in practice, when we are writing programs to run on real machines and compilers, we may need to be more careful about the kind of statements our programs contain.

To give an example of the time difference between iterative and recursive versions of the same algorithm, we coded and ran both versions of the factorial algorithms given here on the same computer with the same compiler. To be completely honest, that's not exactly what we did: $n!$ grows so rapidly that the answers would quickly overflow the available size for integers on most computers, so we changed each algorithm so that instead of multiplying by n (or i, as the case might be), we actually multiplied by 1 in each step. At any rate, the timing results are graphed in Figure 5.1.

The time difference is quite apparent. The observed timing function, $T_i(n)$, for the iterative factorial algorithm, is approximately $T_i(n) = 0.0018n + 0.0033$, whereas the timing function for the recursive algorithm is approximately $T_r(n) = 0.0056n + 0.017$. In other words, although both algorithms run in $O(n)$ time, the recursive algorithm is about four times slower than the iterative version.

Although a recursive version of a program may well be slower than the equivalent iterative version, and any recursive routine can be changed into an

FIGURE 5.1

Timing of recursive
and iterative factorial
routines

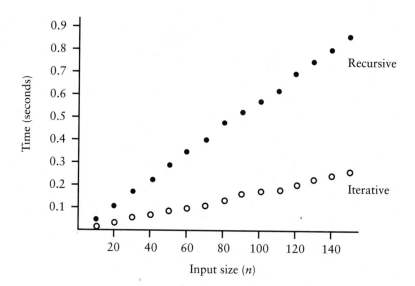

iterative one, we should not give up on recursion entirely. Very often, thinking recursively may give us an insight into a problem that we simply wouldn't have gotten otherwise. Having gotten the idea, we could always eliminate the recursion if doing so turned out to make the solution program run more efficiently.

A further, and much more important, caution about recursion is that, unbeknownst to us, a recursive routine may be written in such a way as to be hideously inefficient. A common example of the inefficient use of recursive functions is the calculation of the **Fibonacci numbers**, a sequence that appears in all sorts of unexpected places in computer science and mathematics, and in the real world as well (as, for instance, in the description of the scales on a pineapple). This is a sequence of numbers beginning with 1, 1, 2, 3, 5, 8, . . . , which has the property that, except for the first two numbers, each number is formed by adding the two preceding numbers. In other words, the Fibonacci numbers may be described by the recursive definition

$$Fib(0) = Fib(1) = 1$$
$$Fib(n) = Fib(n-1) + Fib(n-2) \quad \text{for } n > 1$$

It is easy to turn this recursive definition into a function that evaluates Fibonacci numbers.

```
long Fib(int n)
{
    if (n <= 1)
        return 1;
    else
        return (Fib(n - 1) + Fib(n - 2));
}
```

It would be a useful exercise for you to stop now, find a computer, code this routine, and test it for various values of n. It happens that the Fibonacci sequence grows fairly rapidly. If we look at *Fib* as a function, we can show that $Fib(n) = O(1.62^n)$. To give you a little help if you decide to write and test the algorithm, you can check that $Fib(31) = 2,178,309$. If you do try the function, it would be more instructive if you did it before you went on to the next paragraph. Go ahead, we'll wait.

*   *   *

If you did code the Fibonacci function, you probably noticed that it ran *very* slowly once you got beyond fairly small values for n. On many computers, for $n = 31$, you would probably have time to go out for coffee while the program was running, and for $n = 100$, you would probably have time to go to Colombia and pick the beans, assuming that the program would even run to completion without an error. The reason for this terrible running time is that this recursive definition does a great many duplicate function calls, each of which is pretty fast by itself, but which together take a noticeable amount of time. Consider what happens even in a simple case, when we call $Fib(4)$. In Figure 5.2, we have indicated each function call by a box, with the parameter value in a small box in the upper left-hand corner.

The original call to $Fib(4)$, for instance, resulted in two further calls, to $Fib(3)$ and $Fib(2)$. Since each box represents a function call, we can count boxes to find that just to compute $Fib(4)$ required nine function calls, most of

FIGURE 5.2

Function calls needed to calculate *Fib*(4)

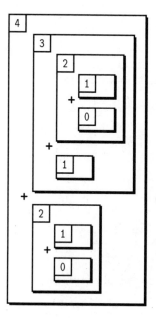

which were duplicates of other calls (*Fib*(0) was called twice, for instance, and *Fib*(1) was called three times). We will soon be able to show that the number of function calls required by this algorithm to compute *Fib*(*n*) is larger than *Fib*(*n*) itself and hence the running time is at least a multiple of 1.62^n, so that if it took, say, 5 minutes to compute *Fib*(20), it would take at least $5 \times 1.62 = 8.1$ minutes just to compute *Fib*(21), and $8.1 \times 1.62 = 13.12$ minutes to compute *Fib*(22). The moral is clear: Elegance and simplicity are not always sufficient justification for choosing to write an algorithm recursively.

Induction and Recursion

Recursion and induction are two sides of the same coin. In a recursive definition, we have an exit case to allow us to leave the definition, as well as a recursive case to allow us to reach the exit case. In a proof by induction, we have a base case that permits us to start the chain of arguments, and an inductive case that permits us to continue the chain from the base case. If you are not familiar with induction proofs, it would be a good idea to look over the material in Appendix B before going much further. We will demonstrate the connection between induction and recursion by proving a property of the Fibonacci numbers. Once the mathematical machinery has been developed, it is not too hard to show that $Fib(n) = O(1.62^n)$, but to do so would take us too far afield for inclusion in this book. Instead, we will show a simpler result, namely, that $Fib(n) > (3/2)^n$, for $n \geq 5$.

Let $P(n)$ be the statement $Fib(n) > (3/2)^n$. We seek to show that $P(n)$ is true for all $n \geq 5$.

1. **Base case.** We show that $P(5)$ and $P(6)$ are true by observing that $Fib(5) = 8 > 7.59375 = (3/2)^5$ and $Fib(6) = 13 > 11.390625 = (3/2)^6$.

2. **Induction case.** Now we would like to build the chain from the base case by showing that if we assume that $P(j)$ is true for all $5 \leq j < n$, then $P(n)$ is true. Let n be any integer larger than 6; we wish to show that $P(n)$ is true—that is, that $Fib(n) > (3/2)^n$. We know that

$$Fib(n) = Fib(n-1) + Fib(n-2)$$

and the induction hypothesis allows us to assume that $Fib(n-1) > (3/2)^{n-1}$ and $Fib(n-2) > (3/2)^{n-2}$ (since we assume that $P(n-1)$ and $P(n-2)$ are true), so we can conclude that

$$Fib(n) > \left(\frac{3}{2}\right)^{n-1} + \left(\frac{3}{2}\right)^{n-2}$$

$$= \left(\frac{3}{2}\right)^{n-2}\left(\frac{3}{2}+1\right) = \left(\frac{3}{2}\right)^{n-2}\left(\frac{5}{2}\right)$$

But $5/2 > 9/4 = (3/2)^2$, so we can replace 5/2 in the preceding line to yield

$$Fib(n) > \left(\frac{3}{2}\right)^{n-2}\left(\frac{5}{2}\right) > \left(\frac{3}{2}\right)^{n-2}\left(\frac{3}{2}\right)^2 = \left(\frac{3}{2}\right)^n$$

which is nothing but a statement of $P(n)$, which was what we wanted.

5.2 TIMING RECURSIVE ALGORITHMS

In Chapter 2, we saw that we could find big-O timing estimates of a nonrecursive algorithm by counting the number of statements executed by the algorithm. That, in turn, led us to the rule of thumb that the running time of such an algorithm was driven largely by the depth of nesting of loops in the algorithm. But what are we to do in a case where the algorithm calls itself? Consider, for example, the algorithm for factorials that we saw earlier.

```
int RecursiveFactorial(int n)
{
    if (n <= 1)
        return 1;
    else
        return (n * RecursiveFactorial(n - 1));
}
```

First, we will suppose that there is a timing function, $T(n)$, that expresses the amount of time the algorithm takes on input n. Then we will try to find an expression involving that timing function. Finally, we will use that expression to find $T(n)$. In this example, we note that if n is 0 or 1, then the algorithm terminates without any further ado, so there is some number A for which $T(0) = T(1) = A$. This accounts for the time taken by the function call, the if statement, and the return from the function. If $n > 1$, we still have all the overhead we did in the $n = 1$ case, but we also have a function call to *RecursiveFactorial*$(n-1)$ and a multiplication by n. Now, we may assume that the multiplication takes time B (which is not really the case, since multiplication takes time proportional to at least the number of digits of the factors being multiplied, but let us assume in the interest of efficiency that multiplication takes constant time), but we do not know how long the function call will take, except that we may write it as $T(n-1)$. Therefore, the time to perform *RecursiveFactorial*(n) will be given by a function $T(n)$ that satisfies

$$T(0) = T(1) = A$$
$$T(n) = A + B + T(n-1) \quad \text{for } n > 1$$

or, writing $C = A + B$ to make our life a little easier, we are faced with the problem of finding a function $T(n)$ that satisfies the recursive definition

$$T(0) = T(1) = A$$
$$T(n) = T(n-1) + C \quad \text{for } n > 1$$

One way to help guess a solution for a function defined in this fashion is to use what is known as **iterative expansion**. Remember, the definition says that $T(n) = T(n-1) + C$ no matter what we put in place of n (as long as it is more than 1), so $T(8) = T(7) + C$, $T(x) = T(x-1) + C$, and so on. In particular, we see that $T(n-1) = T(n-2) + C$ (putting $n-1$ in place of every n in the definition). Thus, we see that

$$
\begin{aligned}
T(n) &= T(n-1) + C \\
&= (T(n-2) + C) + C \\
&= T(n-2) + 2C \\
&= (T(n-3) + C) + 2C \\
&= T(n-3) + 3C
\end{aligned}
$$

and so on. The pattern is clear enough: $T(n) = T(n-k) + kC$, for all $k = 1, 2, \ldots$, until we come to $T(n) = T(1) + (n-1)C$ (i.e., when $k = n-1$). But we know that $T(1) = A$, so (assuming that our guess about the pattern is correct) we can conclude that *RecursiveFactorial* has timing function

$$T(0) = T(1) = A$$
$$T(n) = A + (n-1)C \quad \text{for } n > 1$$

In other words, $T(n) = O(n)$, so we have good reason to believe what the timing analysis in the graph of Figure 5.1 led us to suspect, namely, that *RecursiveFactorial* runs in linear time, which makes it about as efficient as we could wish.

Another example of the timing of recursive algorithms comes from a sorting algorithm that is probably more efficient than any you have seen so far. Exercise 22b in Chapter 2 contained an algorithm, *SelectionSort*, to sort a list (of numbers, say) from smallest to largest. This algorithm took time $O(n^2)$, which means that it is unsuitable, on most computers, for lists larger than a few thousand elements. We can produce a better algorithm if we employ a technique called **divide and conquer**—taking a problem and dividing it into smaller problems. If we can solve the smaller problems, and if the solutions of the smaller problems can be efficiently combined into a solution to the large problem, we may then be better off than if we had attacked the large problem directly.

Suppose, for instance, that we had two small sorted lists. We could **merge** them together to form a large sorted list in a very natural fashion by working from left to right in each list, selecting the smaller element from the present two elements, copying that element to the end of the output list, moving to the element immediately after the one selected, and continuing the process until one of the two lists was empty, whereupon we would copy the leftover elements onto the tail of the output list and be done. An example of such a merge follows, where the elements being compared are highlighted.

List 1	List 2	Output
102 151 204 283	87 91 113 200	
102 151 204 283	87 **91** 113 200	87
102 151 204 283	87 91 **113** 200	87 91
102 **151** 204 283	87 91 **113** 200	87 91 102
102 **151** 204 283	87 91 113 **200**	87 91 102 113
102 151 **204** 283	87 91 113 **200**	87 91 102 113 151
102 151 **204** 283	87 91 113 200	87 91 102 113 151 200

At this stage, since there is nothing left in list 2, no further comparisons are needed, so the remaining two elements in list 1 are simply appended, in order, to the end of the output list. It is an easy exercise to write a procedure to accomplish this merging, using the *List* operations, for instance. The important thing about merging is that it takes no more than time proportional to the sum of the lengths of the two lists. Every comparison results in an element added to the output list, so there can be no more comparisons than the eventual size of the merged list. Thus, merging of two lists of size $n/2$ can be accomplished in time $O(n)$.

We can use this technique to write a very simple recursive sorting program that takes the following form.

```
void Mergesort(List& ls, int low, int high)
// Sorts a sublist in positions low ... high.
{
    if (low < high)
    {
        int mid = (low + high + 1) / 2; // Find middle.
        Mergesort(ls, low, mid - 1);    // Sort low half.
        Mergesort(ls, mid, high);       // Sort high half.

        Merge the two sublists to form ls;

    }
}
```

The idea behind this program is a direct application of the divide-and-conquer paradigm: If the list has more than one element in it (otherwise it's already sorted), split the list in two nearly equal pieces, sort them (recursively), and merge the results. The nature of divide-and-conquer routines make them natural choices for recursive programs.

At this point, it should be by no means obvious what the timing of *Mergesort* is at all, let alone whether it is an improvement over something like *SelectionSort*. But certainly it is not unreasonable to assume that the worst time to run *Mergesort* on a list of size n should be no greater than some function, $T(n)$, of the length of the list to be sorted. Assume, then, that *Mergesort* on a list of n elements takes no more than time $T(n)$. We will see if we can get an upper estimate for $T(n)$. If $n=1$, the function returns directly, so in this case we see that $T(1)=A$, for some number A, which takes care of the overhead caused by the test in the if statement and the return from the function call. If $n>1$, *Mergesort* calls itself twice on the smaller lists and calls *Merge* on the result. Each call to *Mergesort* on the lists of size $n/2$ takes time no greater than $T(n/2)$ by our previous assumption, and *Merge* takes time Bn, for some fixed constant B, since we have seen that *Merge* runs in linear time on the two smaller lists. What we have, then, is a function T for which

$$T(1) = A$$

$$T(n) \le 2T\left(\frac{n}{2}\right) + Bn \quad \text{for } n > 1$$

Our mission now is to try to find a function T that satisfies this recursive definition. Notice that T, as written, is defined only for even values of n and so, by the recursive nature of the definition, is actually defined only for values that are powers of 2. In almost all situations encountered in practice, this presents no problem, since the function T that is found by considering only those n that are powers of 2 serves as a good upper bound for all values of n.

Consider, then, the definition for $n=2^k$.

$$T(2^k) \le 2T\left(\frac{2^k}{2}\right) + B2^k \tag{5.1}$$

$$= 2T(2^{k-1}) + B2^k$$

Since inequality 5.1 is assumed to hold for all powers of 2, it certainly must be true in the case $n=2^{k-1}$, so we can rewrite it with $n=2^{k-1}$ to yield

$$T(2^{k-1}) \le 2T\left(2^{k-2}\right) + B2^{k-1} \tag{5.2}$$

Substituting inequality 5.2 into inequality 5.1 yields

$$T\left(2^k\right) \le 2\left(2T\left(2^{k-2}\right) + B2^{k-1}\right) + B2^k$$

$$= 2^2 T\left(2^{k-2}\right) + 2B2^{k-1} + B2^k$$

$$= 2^2 T\left(2^{k-2}\right) + 2B2^k$$

Repeating the foregoing steps, we find that

$$T\left(2^k\right) \le 2^3 T\left(2^{k-3}\right) + 3B2^k$$

$$\le 2^4 T\left(2^{k-4}\right) + 4B2^k$$

$$\vdots$$

$$\le 2^k T\left(2^0\right) + kB2^k = 2^k T(1) + kB2^k = 2^k A + kB2^k$$

and since $n = 2^k$, we can write the preceding inequality as

$$T(n) \le An + (\log_2 n)Bn = O(n \log n)$$

Thus, *Mergesort* allows us to sort a list of n elements in time $O(n \log n)$, whereas *SelectionSort* took time $O(n^2)$. To get a feel for the difference this makes, let us ignore any multiplicative constants in the big-O estimates and consider just the functions n^2 and $n \log_2 n$. If $n = 65,536$, n^2 is equal to 4,294,967,296, while $n \log_2 n$ is only 1,048,576, a reduction by a factor of over 4000.

We should emphasize that in neither of the preceding examples have we actually *proved* that the timing functions we found satisfied the recursive definitions. Iterative expansion is very close to being a rigorous proof, except that we relied on our intuition to guess the general pattern for the timing function. To be strictly correct, we should treat the function found through iterative expansion as a guess until we have proved (almost invariably by induction on n) that the timing function satisfies its recursive definition.

We now list the solutions to some common recurrence relations.

Case 1. $T(1) = 1$; $T(n) = p\, T(n/q) + n^d$, for $n > 1$.

$$T(q^k) = \begin{cases} (k+1)p^k & \text{if } q^d = p \\[2ex] \dfrac{p^{k+1} - (q^d)^{k+1}}{p - q^d} & \text{if } q^d \neq p \end{cases}$$

so we have

$$T(n) = \begin{cases} O(n^d) & \text{if } q^d > p \\[1ex] O(n^d \log n) & \text{if } q^d = p \\[1ex] O(n^{\log_q p}) & \text{if } q^d < p \end{cases}$$

Case 2. $T(1) = 1$; $T(n) = p\, T(n/q) + \log n$, for $n > 1$.

$$T(q^k) = \begin{cases} 1 + (\log q)\dfrac{k(k+1)}{2} & \text{if } p = 1 \\[2ex] p^k + (\log q)\dfrac{k(1-p) - p}{(1-p)^2} & \text{if } p \neq 1 \end{cases}$$

so we have

$$T(n) = \begin{cases} O(\log^2 n) & \text{if } p = 1 \\[1ex] O(n^{\log_q p}) & \text{if } p \neq 1 \end{cases}$$

Example 1

Consider an algorithm with a timing function given by

$$T(1) = 1 \text{ (or any other constant, as it happens)}$$

$$T(n) = 3T\left(\frac{n}{2}\right) + n \quad \text{for } n > 1$$

Such a timing function arises from a fast multiplication algorithm and expresses the time needed to multiply two n-digit numbers by that algorithm. This function is an example of case 1, with $p = 3$, $q = 2$, and $d = 1$. Since $q^d < p$, we see that the timing function must satisfy

$$T(n) = O\left(n^{\log_2 3}\right) = O\left(n^{1.59}\right)$$

◁

Example 2

Suppose that we have an algorithm with a timing function, $T(n)$, that satisfies

$$T(1) = 1$$

$$T(n) = T\left(\frac{n}{4}\right) + \log n$$

Because of the log n term, we find ourselves in case 2, with $p = 1$ (and the value of q immaterial in this case), so we have $T(n) = O(\log^2 n)$. ◁

5.3 COMPUTER SCIENCE INTERLUDE: DESIGN OF ALGORITHMS

The analysis of *Mergesort* and *SelectionSort* has provided us with evidence that there's more than one approach to solving a problem. Often the first algorithm we come up with is by no means the most efficient way to solve the problem. We have seen another example of this in the difference in running times of the obvious and the Boyer-Moore algorithms for pattern matching with strings.

Creating an efficient algorithm to perform a task is somewhat like designing an efficient data structure: While they both require a degree of creativity, there are some general principles that may make the design process easier. For instance, one of the organizing themes of this book is that categorizing possible organizations of data into linear, hierarchical, and network abstract data types allows us to ignore the superficial differences between problems and concentrate on the essential features that lead to efficient implementations. A similar level of abstraction for the design of algorithms provides us with **design paradigms**: a collection of commonly used techniques, such as divide and conquer, that are applicable to a wide variety of seemingly different algorithms. In this section, we will explore some of these paradigms and see how they may be used to produce algorithms for the computation of the Fibonacci numbers.

We have already seen one algorithm for computing Fibonacci numbers, a recursive algorithm that is so simple to state yet so inefficient that it serves as a classic example of when *not* to use recursion. Here is a simple example of a divide-and-conquer algorithm: We compute *Fib(n)* by breaking the problem into two smaller pieces, namely, computation of *Fib(n−1)* and *Fib(n−2)*, and then combining the smaller solutions (by adding them, in this case) into a solution of the original problem. Although we do not do it here, it is not difficult to show that the timing function, $T(n)$ for this algorithm, is proportional to *Fib(n)* itself, and hence we could show that $T(n) = O(1.62^n)$. Of course, any exponential time algorithm is so time-consuming, even for small problems, that we should try to avoid it if at all possible. What we will do is explore some other ways of attacking this problem, and learn a little about algorithm design in the bargain.

The problem with the divide-and-conquer version of *Fib* is, as we mentioned, that it makes so many duplicate function calls. A divide-and-conquer algorithm typically works from the top down, with each successive function call requiring the solution of a smaller instance of the problem. We might eliminate the effects of the duplicate function calls if we use a technique known as **dynamic programming,** in which we work from the bottom up rather than from the top down. With dynamic programming, we first solve and save the small instances of the problem and then combine these as we go to produce solutions for successively larger instances, until we come to the solution we originally required. For our example, we know that $Fib(0) = Fib(1) = 1$, so we can use these to find *Fib(2)*, and we can use *Fib(1)* and *Fib(2)* to find *Fib(3)*, and so on. This is a particularly nice instance of dynamic programming in that we need to save only the two most recently computed values of *Fib*, so the amount of memory required is constant (which is not the case with many other dynamic programming instances, occasionally leading to real trouble).

Having provided the background, it is now quite easy to write a dynamic programming version for *Fib*.

```
long IterativeFib(int n)
{
    long    prior = 1,
            old = 0,
            recent;
    for (int i = 1; i <= n; i++)
    {
        old = prior;
        prior = recent;
        recent = prior + old;
    }
    return recent;
}
```

If we look at the time this takes to run, it is clear that we have a considerable improvement here over the original exponential version. The time required by this algorithm is driven by the for loop, which is repeated n times. We thus have an algorithm with $O(n)$ running time.

We have improved the time needed to compute $Fib(n)$ from exponential to linear. This in itself is no mean feat, but a natural question is whether we can do even better. As it happens, we can, and by a considerable margin. In fact, we can find another algorithm that is, in a sense, as much of an improvement over linear time as linear time was over exponential. Such an improvement, however, depends on how clever we can be and is not gained just by considering another design paradigm. In other words, having an arsenal of abstract notions can be helpful, but it is not always a substitute for plain old good thinking.

If we play with the Fibonacci numbers enough, or search the (copious) literature on the subject, we may be lucky enough to discover the identities

$$Fib(2k) = \left(Fib(k)\right)^2 + \left(Fib(k-1)\right)^2$$

$$Fib(2k+1) = \left(Fib(k)\right)^2 + 2Fib(k)Fib(k-1)$$

which hold for all $k \geq 1$. These identities immediately suggest our first try: a divide-and-conquer scheme, one in which the smaller problems to be solved are *half* the size of the original, rather than just 1 or 2 less than the original, as was the case with our first algorithm. The implementation of this algorithm follows immediately from the definition.

```
long BetterDCFib(int n)
{
   if (n <= 1)
      return 1;
   else
   {
      long half = BetterDCFib(n / 2);
      long halfLess1 = BetterDCFib(n / 2 - 1);
      if (n % 2 == 1)
         return (half * (half + 2 * halfLess1));
      else
         return (half * half + halfLess1 * halfLess1);
   }
}
```

We see that the timing function for this algorithm satisfies

$$T(1) = A$$

$$T(n) = 2T\left(\frac{n}{2}\right) + B$$

for some constants A and B, where we have assumed that multiplication requires constant time.* If we use the tables given previously for the solution of recurrence relations with $p=2$, $q=2$, and $d=0$, we see that the timing function $T(n)=O(n)$, so we have a divide-and-conquer algorithm that is a great improvement over the original exponential divide-and-conquer version, but which, to our chagrin, is no better than the dynamic programming version we just invented and is far less obvious in the bargain.

We may still be able to find a better Fibonacci algorithm, however, if we apply dynamic programming to the halving identity we gave before. For example, if we need to compute $Fib(61)$, the halving identity tells us that

$$Fib(61) = Fib(30)^2 + 2Fib(30)Fib(29)$$

$Fib(30)$ and $Fib(29)$, in turn, may be computed from $Fib(15)$, $Fib(14)$, and $Fib(13)$, and so on, as Figure 5.3 indicates.

The bottom row of Figure 5.3 contains the numbers that we will use to begin the algorithm. It turns out that the halving identities are valid for these numbers if we interpret the bottom row to be $Fib(1)$, $Fib(0)$, and $Fib(-1)$. This algorithm has the nice property that the original dynamic programming version also had, namely, that at each stage we need only generate and store

FIGURE 5.3

Computation tower for $Fib(61)$

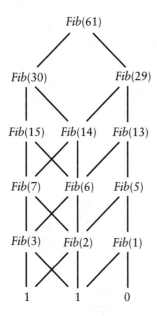

---

* As it happens, it makes no difference here even if we assume that multiplication runs in time proportional to the square of the number of digits in the numbers to be multiplied, as it does in the elementary school multiplication algorithm. The timing estimate will be the same, although it is a trifle tricky to calculate.

a constant number of intermediate values (three, in this case). The algorithm is implemented as follows.

```
long BetterItFib(int n)
{
  // First, set values for the left column of
  // the computation tower.
  Array<int> v(100, 1);
  v[1] = n;
  int k = 1;
  while (v[k] > 1)
  {
    k++;
    v[k] := v[k - 1] / 2;
  }
  // Fill in the bottom row of the tower.
  long    recent = 1,
          prior = 1,
          oldest = 0;
  // Fill in the rest of the rows from bottom to top
  for (int i = k - 1; i >= 1; i--).
  {
    long  s = recent * recent,
          t = prior * prior,
          u = prior * oldest;
    if (v[i] % 2)                 // Right-hand value is odd.
    {
      recent = s + 2 * recent * prior;
      prior = s + t;
    }
    else                          // Right-hand value is even.
    {
      recent = s + t;
      prior = t + 2 * u;
    }
    oldest = recent - prior;
  }
  return recent;
}
```

Now we do have an improvement over the two prior linear algorithms. The timing of this algorithm is obviously driven by the number of iterations of the while and for loops, and each of these loops iterates not more than k times, where k is the number of times n can be divided by 2 before becoming less than or equal to 1. In the preceding example , for instance, we successively divided 61 by 2, obtaining 30, 15, 7, 3, and 1. It took only five divisions to complete, and in general we will have k equal to the integer part of $\log_2 n$, just as we saw with the binary search algorithm. In other words, we have obtained an algorithm to compute $Fib(n)$ that runs in time $O(\log n)$, which is a considerable improvement over the linear algorithms we obtained earlier.

To show just how much of an improvement this is, the following table lists the running time, in seconds, of the last three Fibonacci algorithms when coded and run on a computer. We have omitted the first version, which takes exponential time, because even for $n = 500$, that algorithm takes so long that we would probably still be sitting around waiting for the routine to finish by the time this book reached your hands. We also cheated here as we did with the factorial timing figures, doing dummy calculations rather than computing actual values, which would have quickly overrun the available integer size on the computer being used.

n	Iterative (linear)	Divide-and-Conquer (linear)	Better Iterative (logarithmic)
500	2.18	4.93	0.25
1000	4.35	9.85	0.28
1500	6.53	14.73	0.32
2000	8.72	19.68	0.35
2500	10.90	24.70	0.42

Notice that for $n = 2500$, the logarithmic version runs nearly 26 times faster than the best of the two linear algorithms. Not only is this a considerable gain in speed, but we should also note that the factor of improvement gets steadily better as n continues to increase. It would be a shame to have this zippy algorithm and not try it out, so we combined the logarithmic Fibonacci algorithm with the multiprecision arithmetic package from Chapter 1 to compute $Fib(2500)$. Here are the results:

21310 97222 36481 72589 63242 99517 04797 43181 82053 63701
26875 36286 82558 35307 75962 65908 63125 48730 00201 26214
96898 63548 93376 81055 89937 52038 31678 59730 52343 74709
69374 68058 04846 42829 49473 92542 08489 07002 68999 40079
55245 76061 32292 71988 13891 46345 17152 25018 97283 38958
65782 03918 75946 09662 37273 83020 86808 97754 80618 27768
74273 19326 52665 55633 51096 37048 85724 90223 86306 65583
32769 19447 11144 05709 16925 03000 91519 44351 33550 74402
82898 89121 17721 50743 92607 24419 66483 49939 23257 78345
04373 01079 83191 48002 43767 65760 08087 84351 53403 30624
11236 40660 84217 04602 501

If you're thinking, "Why would anyone have the slightest interest in finding all 523 digits of a number that itself has no apparent use?"—then shame on you. We spent several pages pursuing this topic mainly because it is intellectually stimulating. It is a reflection of the human drive to explore—to go higher, farther, deeper, or faster than we have gone before—and this alone is enough for us to consider our time well spent. There are some purely practical benefits as well, some of them immediate and others only potential. You have had the barest introduction to algorithm design, a topic that is the subject of entire textbooks and that might just come in handy when you find yourself with the task of designing a program of your own. In addition, we can rarely tell ahead of time where a particular line of inquiry might lead us. Just because a problem like this has no apparent applicability doesn't mean that it has no application. We may just not have discovered it—yet.

We haven't finished off this problem. You might want to consider whether there is an even faster algorithm lurking out there. We haven't proved that O(log n) is the best we can do when computing Fibonacci numbers; all we have done is to put it aside for a while so that we can go on to other material.

5.4   RECURSIVE DATA STRUCTURES

We could define the structure of the abstract data type *List* by giving the following recursive definition.

> **Definition.**   The abstract data type *List* consists of a set, *Atom*, of elements and a set of objects, called lists, such that each list consists of either (1) nothing at all (which is conventionally denoted by NIL) or (2) an atom, followed by a list.

In this definition, the linear order of the structure is implicit in the phrase "followed by," and the definition allows us to show that an element is a list by repeatedly building a list from atoms. For instance, the object (x, y), where x and y are members of *Atom,* is a list because, first, (y) is a list (since it consists of an atom, y, followed by the empty list), so (x, y) is a list, because it consists of the atom x followed by the list (y), as we illustrate in Figure 5.4. We could generalize this argument by induction on the number of elements in

FIGURE 5.4

Recursive definition
of *List*

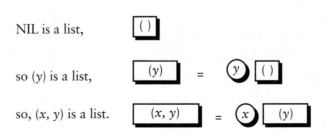

a list to provide the iterative definition that $(a_1, a_2, \ldots, a_n)$ is a list if all the a_i's are atoms.

We have seen all along that decisions of form (the structure of an ADT) may imply decisions of function (those operations that can be performed on the data structure). With this recursive definition of *List*, for instance, we think of a list as either empty or having an atom at the head and a sublist at the tail, so it would be quite natural to have operations like the following:

Atom Header(List ls) returns the atom at the start of the list *ls,* assuming *ls* is not NIL (i.e., is not empty).

List Trailer(List ls) returns the sublist of *ls* consisting of everything except for the first atom, assuming *l* is not NIL.

List Insert(Atom a, List ls) returns the list that has *a* as its first atom and *ls* as its trailer.

One reason that we did not choose to define the *List* ADT in this fashion originally (apart from the pedagogical reason that no one would have understood it so early in the game) is that the uses we had in mind for *List* frequently made explicit reference to positions in the list, and positions are not directly available in the recursive definition. For instance, recall that *Update,* the operation that replaced the atom in the current position with the atom *a,* ran in constant time in both of the implementations we gave. In the recursive form of *List,* however, we do not have direct access to any position except the first, so we would be forced to make a definition like the following—assuming, to make life easy, that we refer to positions in the list by integers.

```
void Update(Atom a, int p, List& ls)
// Changes the atom in the p-th position of ls to be a,
// assuming, for simplicity, that ls has at least p
// elements.
{
    //-------- Exit case -------
    if (p = 1)
        // It's easy to update the first element.
        ls = Insert(a, Trailer(ls));

    //----- Recursive case -----
    else
    {
        // (1) Get the trailer of ls.
        List m = Trailer(ls);
        // (2) Recursively, put a where it belongs in
        // the shorter list.
        Update(a, p - 1, m);
        // (3) Once a's where it should be, rebuild
        // the list by putting the header element back.
        ls = Insert(Header(ls), m);
    }
}
```

You can see that the definition of *Update* is not much longer for the recursively defined *List* than it was for the iterative version in Chapter 2, but if you trace the action of this algorithm, you'll see that it runs in time $O(n)$, rather than in constant time. It is also likely that you would have had a more difficult time writing the definition of *Update*, at least until you had had a bit more practice with recursive algorithms. With this definition, *Header, Trailer,* and *Insert* are easy to describe, but we have no direct way of even *defining* what the *p*th position was. One advantage that we do gain, however, is that a recursively defined data structure may make us aware of elegant recursive forms of algorithms on that data structure. Suppose, for instance, that *Atom* consisted of integers. Then we could find the sum of the atoms in a list by adding the head atom to the result obtained by summing the tail of the list.

```
int SumList(List ls)
{
   if (1 == NIL)
      return 0;
   else
      return (Header(ls) + SumList(Trailer(ls)));
}
```

The point is not that this is the only (or even necessarily the best) way to perform this operation, but rather that recursively defined data structures may point out good solutions that might escape us at first glance.

General Lists and LISP

If we make a seemingly small change in the recursive definition of *List,* we find ourselves in possession of an ADT of surprising complexity, one that is used as the primary structure of the language LISP, and which provides us with our first example of a data structure that is not inherently linear in nature.

Definition. The *GenList* abstract data type consists of a set, *Atom,* and a set of elements, called **general lists**, each of which consists of either

    1. Nothing at all (which we will also denote by NIL), or

    2. Two parts:

        a. A header part (called the CAR of the list), which is an atom or a general list, and

        b. A trailer part (called the CDR of the list), which is itself a general list.

Notice that the only difference between this definition and the recursive definition of a list is that we allow the head to be a list here. The names CAR (pronounced as it is written) and CDR (pronounced "cudder") seem to have little to do with the head and the tail of a list, but they have been firmly en-sconced in the jargon for nearly three decades and are kept, at least in part, because they provide that heady sense of power that comes from knowing arcane names for simple things. (This completes the standard disclaimer that appears the first time anyone is exposed to CAR and CDR; some authors delve even more deeply and mention that CAR was derived from the expression "contents of the address register," and CDR originally stood for "contents of the decrement register," but we wouldn't dream of going into that much detail.*) A general list, then, may be referred to simply by what is known as a CONS cell (for "CONStruction"), which just contains pointers to the CAR part and the CDR part of the general list, as shown in Figure 5.5.

From the definition of *GenList,* we see that anything that is a list under our old definition is also a general list (since a list is nothing but a special case of a general list), so (d) is a general list (consisting of the atom *d* followed by NIL), and for the same reason, (b c) is a general list (consisting of the atom *b* followed by the general list (c)); hence, ((b c) d) is also a general list (consisting of the general list (b c) followed by the general list (d)), so (a (b c) d) is also a general list, which we illustrate in Figure 5.6.

This list contains three elements, in order: the atom *a,* the list (b c), and the atom *d.* We can count the number of elements of a list in a CONS cell picture by counting the number of cells in the top row, and we can tell what sort of objects these elements are by referring to the CAR portions of each of the top-level CONS cells. For this list, the CAR part is the atom *a,* while the CDR part is the list ((b c) d), which itself has CAR part (b c) and CDR part (d).

A careful look at the definition should convince you that NIL itself is a list, which we would write (), and which is different from the list (NIL), which we would write (()). The former list has no elements, while the latter has a single element, the empty list. In Figure 5.7, we show the CONS cell representations of these lists, along with a more complicated example. If you can understand that Figure 5.7c denotes the list (()(())), consider yourself well on the path to enlightenment.

FIGURE 5.5

Recursive picture of general lists

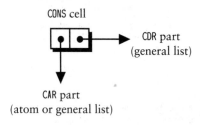

CONS cell

CDR part
(general list)

CAR part
(atom or general list)

FIGURE 5.6

The general list
(a (b c) d)

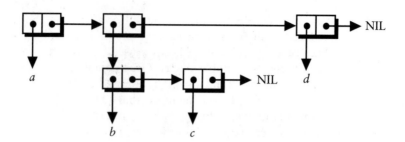

We could implement *GenList* by making the CONS cells the fundamental structures and using pointers to link the cells together. Because the CAR pointer can point to an atom or a CONS cell, we will derive the classes *Atom* and *Cons-Cell* from an abstract class *AbstractCell*. The only thing in *AbstractCell* is a **pure virtual function** (distinguished by the "= 0" part of its declaration) *IsAtom*, whose sole purpose is to be overridden in the two derived classes. With a virtual function, we leave to C++ the task of taking a function call ptr->IsAtom(), and applying the correct function, depending on whether *ptr* points to an atom or a CONS cell.

```
class AbstractCell
{
public:
   virtual int IsAtom() const = 0;
} ;
```

An *Atom* object is a data holder, pure and simple. In our example (which is a considerable simplification of what really goes on in LISP), all that *Atom* does is respond correctly to *IsAtom* and return the value of its data.

FIGURE 5.7

Some lists with no atoms

a.   ()

    NIL

b.   (())

c.   (() (()))

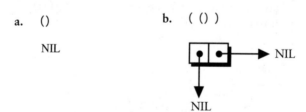

```
class Atom : public AbstractCell
{
public:
   Atom(int a);    // Construct an atom with data = a.
   int IsAtom() const
       { return 1;} ;
   int Value() const
       { return data;} ;
private:
   int data;
} ;
```

The *ConsCell* class is also fairly simple. It keeps two pointers: *carPtr* to either an atom or a CONS cell and *cdrPtr*, which, as we've seen, must be a pointer to another CONS cell. Like *Atom,* the member functions are very simple. We'll discuss the two friend functions in a moment.

```
class ConsCell : public AbstractCell
{
   friend ConsCell* Cons(AbstractCell* xp, ConsCell* lp);
   friend ConsCell* Append(ConsCell* c1p, ConsCell* c2p);
public:
   // Construct a cell with NULL pointers.
   ConsCell();
   // Construct a cell with car ptr to the Atom a.
   ConsCell(int a);
   // Construct a cell with given pointers.
   ConsCell(AbstractCell* ca, ConsCell* cd);
   int IsAtom() const
       { return 0;} ;
   AbstractCell* Car() const
       { return carPtr;} ;
   ConsCell* Cdr() const
       { return cdrPtr;} ;
private:
   AbstractCell*   carPtr;
   ConsCell*       cdrPtr;
} ;
```

We will represent the *GenList* type by a pointer to a CONS cell, so all we have to do is conclude our declaration file with

```
typedef ConsCell* GenList;
```

LISP, which we are modeling here, is a **functional language:** Every statement is a function. This takes some getting used to, especially if you are familiar only with languages like C++, in which the statements generally describe actions to be taken. The difference is exemplified by noting that the if statement in C++ describes a transfer of control to another location in the program, whereas the corresponding statement in LISP,

```
(IF condition list1 list2)
```

is a list that is thought of as a function that returns the value of *list1* if the condition evaluates to any non-NIL value (which is interpreted to mean *true*) and returns the value of *list2* if the condition evaluates to NIL. LISP attempts to evaluate every list it sees by applying the CAR part of a list to its CDR part, so the list (+ 3 4 5 6) would evaluate to the list (18), and the list (EQUAL 3 8) evaluates to NIL (which, remember, is understood to denote *false*). In other words, with very few exceptions, every statement in LISP is itself a list, one that is treated as a function that takes lists or atoms as arguments and returns a list as its result. One implication of all this is that arithmetic expressions in LISP are parenthesized versions of **prefix notation**, in which an operator precedes the arguments it operates on, so that the expression we would write as $(3+4) * (8+6)$ would be written in LISP as (* (+ 3 4) (+ 8 6)).

One of the LISP primitives provides a means of making new lists by inserting a new element at the head of a list. If *L* is a list and *x* is either a list or an atom, the action of (CONS x L) is to return a list with CAR part equal to *x* and CDR part equal to *L* (which is why CONS is named after "construct"). LISP does this in the easiest way possible, namely, by creating a new CONS cell, for which the CAR part points to *x* and the CDR part to *L,* as shown in Figure 5.8.

We encountered a similar construction back in Chapter 2, when we defined the copy constructor for linked lists (see Figure 2.7, for instance). At that time we said that such a shallow clone was not a good idea, since it led to the problem of aliasing; that is, any subsequent change to *L* would be reflected (invisibly) in the value of the copied list. LISP avoids the problem of aliasing in part by the way in which variables are assigned to values. In Figure 5.8, for instance, it would not be difficult to change *L,* but it would be

FIGURE 5.8
The LISP operation CONS

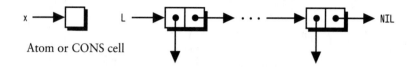
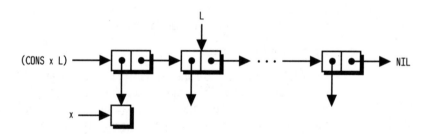

difficult in LISP to change L accidentally in such a way as to make a change in the list pointed to by the arrow labeled (CONS x L).

LISP allows us to assign a variable to a value by the expression SETQ, so that (SETQ variable object) in our conceptualization would result in the variable being assigned a pointer to the object. In other words, we could change L in Figure 5.8 by, say, calling (SETQ L (CDR L)), where CDR returns the tail portion of the list; but all that would accomplish would be to move the L pointer one cell to the right, leaving all the cells connected as they were before. In simple terms, "what CONS hath joined together, LISP cannot (easily) tear apart." We could write the implementation of one version of this function as follows.

```
ConsCell* Cons(AbstractCell* xp, ConsCell* lp)
// Creates and returns the list (x l).
// This is a shallow clone.
{
    return new ConsCell(xp, lp);
}
```

Another common LISP expression also builds a list from pieces, but in this case the pieces must both be lists. If $L1$ was the list $(a\ b\ c)$ and $L2$ was the list $(c\ d)$, then (APPEND L1 L2) would return the list $(a\ b\ c\ c\ d)$, consisting of the elements of the original lists concatenated together. Notice the difference between CONS and APPEND: (CONS L1 L2) constructs a new list with $L1$ as its first element, so that the result of (CONS L1 L2) would be $((a\ b\ c)\ c\ d)$. The elements of a list, you'll recall, do not need to be atoms, so if $L3$ was the list $(x\ (y\ z)\ w)$, then evaluating the list (APPEND L3 L1) would return the list $(x\ (y\ z)\ w\ a\ b\ c)$. We could define (APPEND L1 L2) by making the last cell of $L1$ have its CDR pointer point to the first cell of $L2$, as we indicate in Figure 5.9. The problem with this definition is that it changes $L1$. Since a list consists of all

FIGURE 5.9

Incorrect definition of APPEND

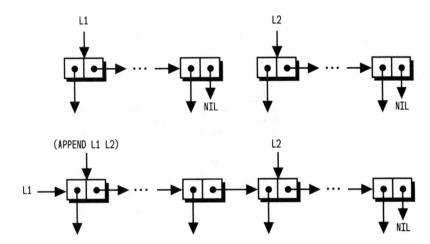

the cells linked by CDR pointers, APPENDing *L1* to *L2* destroys the original *L1* and makes it equal to the concatenation of *L1* and *L2*. So as not to introduce this side effect into the definition of APPEND, we must first copy the contents of *L1* to a temporary list *T* and then concatenate *T* to *L2*, as we do in Figure 5.10.

The "incorrect" definition of APPEND, by the way, is available in some dialects of LISP under the name NCONC. A recursive definition of APPEND for our implementation is nice and short, although it takes a bit of careful thought to understand. We copy *L1* as we go, following the CDR pointers (in the jargon, we "CDR our way down through *L1*") and CONSing new cells onto the copy of *L1*. All the calls to CONS are pending until we reach the end of the copied list, at which time we just link the last cell of the copy to the first cell of *L2*.

```
ConsCell* Append(ConsCell* cp1, ConsCell* cp2)
// Concatenates two lists.  We might call this a
// "semishallow clone."
{
    if (cp1 == 0)
        return cp2;
    else
        return Cons(cp1->Car(), Append(cp1->Cdr(), cp2));
}
```

As a final example, consider the function FLATLIST, which takes a general list and returns an ordinary list consisting of the atoms in the original list. For instance, FLATLIST applied to the list

(a (b a (c b a)) (((d a) c) d (a))

would return the result

(a b a c b a d a c d a)

FIGURE 5.10

Correct definition of APPEND

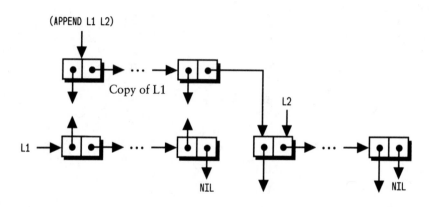

We could write a recursive definition by observing that the bailout condition is to return the zero pointer if the list was empty; otherwise, the recursive step would be to return the list that resulted from applying FLATLIST to the CAR part and the CDR part and concatenating the results. In the following function, the only part that might trip you up is that FLATLIST expects a pointer to a CONS cell, so when we apply FLATLIST to the CAR part of a cell, we have to make an explicit type cast: (ConsCell*)(cp->Car()).

```
ConsCell* FlatList(ConsCell* cp)
{
    if (cp == 0)
        return 0;
    else if (cp->Car()->IsAtom())
        return Cons(cp->Car(), FlatList(cp->Cdr()));
    else
        return Append(FlatList((ConsCell*)(cp->Car())),
                      FlatList(cp->Cdr()));
}
```

For those interested in the arcana of LISP, a LISP definition of FLATLIST is

```
(DEFUN FLATLIST (L)
    (IF (NULL L)
        NIL
        (IF (ATOM (CAR L))
            (CONS (CAR L) (FLATLIST (CDR L)))
            (APPEND (FLATLIST (CAR L)) (FLATLIST (CDR L)))
        )
    )
)
```

Some people say that LISP stands for "Lots of Incredibly Stupid Parentheses," though that could also be said of C++; count the parentheses in these two examples.

5.5 SUMMARY

A recursive definition is one that refers to the object it is defining in such a way as to avoid unending loops. Recursive definitions are frequently more elegant than iterative definitions and can sometimes provide insights lacking from iterative definitions, especially in situations where it is natural to define something in terms of a smaller instance of itself.

Recursively defined algorithms should be part of every computer scientist's vocabulary, because there are times when an algorithm would be much more difficult to define iteratively. We should always be careful, however, since recursive algorithms usually take longer to run than the equivalent iterative versions, and the simplicity of recursion can mask serious inefficiencies.

In spite of these cautions, we saw that recursive definitions can aid us in the process of designing very efficient algorithms, as was the case when we began with an exponential time algorithm to compute Fibonacci numbers, improved upon that with two linear time algorithms, and then further improved upon these alogorithms with a logarithmic time algorithm.

This chapter serves as a transition from linear to nonlinear data structures. We saw that we could define lists recursively by saying that a list either was empty or consisted of an atom followed by a list. A slight generalization of the recursive definition of a list led to general lists, each of which is either empty or consists of an atom or a general list, followed by a general list. Such a structure does not have the linear structure of a list and is the basis of the LISP language. Keep general lists in mind as you read the next chapters. General lists are really nothing but special cases of the nonlinear *Tree* data type.

5.6 EXERCISES

1. Since $n! = (n+1)!/(n+1)$, why couldn't we compute factorials by the following algorithm?

    ```
    int UpFact(int n)
    {
        if (n <= 1)
            return 1;
        else
            return (UpFact(n + 1) / (n + 1));
    }
    ```

2. We mentioned that with the original recursive Fibonacci algorithm, *Fib*(100) might not run to completion on a real computer. Why?

3. The standard nonnumeric example problem for recursion is the **Towers of Hanoi**. The folktale that goes with the problem tells of a certain monastery where the monks are charged with the task of completing a puzzle, after which the world will end. The pieces of the puzzle consist of 3 posts and 64 disks of graduated sizes, each of which has a hole in the center so it will fit on the posts. (In the long version of the tale, the posts are made of diamonds and the disks are made of gold.) The following diagram shows a 5-disk version of the puzzle.

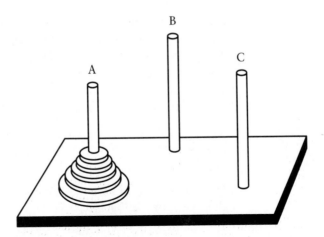

The object of the puzzle is to begin with all the disks stacked on one post in descending order of size and to transfer all the disks to another post, again in descending order of size. The disks are moved one at a time, and at no time may a disk be placed atop one that is smaller. For example, to move two disks from post A to post C, we could use the sequence A → B (top disk to B), A → C (second disk to C), B → C (old top disk to C, done).

a. Find the shortest sequence of moves to transfer three disks.

b. How many moves would you guess are required to transfer n disks?

The preceding sequence could be described as "Move 2 from A to C using B." Having done that, we could define "Move 3 from x to y using z" by

```
void Move 3 from x to y using z
{
    // Move top two disks to holding post.
    Move 2 from x to z using y;
    // Move remaining disk to destination post.
    Move 1 from x to y using z;
    // Move disks from holding post to destination.
    Move 2 from z to y using x;
}
```

c. Write a recursive definition for "Move n from x to y using z," and trace its execution when $n = 3$.

d. Using timing functions for your algorithm, how many disk moves are required to transfer n disks?

e. At one move per second, how long will it take for the world to end? Should we be worried about the imminent demise of everything?

4. Let the expression $K(n)$ denote the number of function calls made during the execution of the inefficient algorithm for $Fib(n)$. We saw that $K(4)=9$, and it is clear that $K(0)=K(1)=1$, since we must call Fib once just to get started.

    a. Compute $K(n)$ for $n=0, 1, 2, \ldots, 8$, and compare with $Fib(n)$.

    b. Show that $K(n)=2Fib(n)-1$ (preferably by induction).

5. Observe that $Fib(4)=5=2+3$ and that during execution of $Fib(4)$, there were two calls to $Fib(0)$ and three calls to $Fib(1)$. Show that this property can be generalized.

6. The numbers $C(n, k)$ are called **binomial coefficients** and are defined for all $n, k \geq 0$, by the following rules:

$$C(n, 0) = 1 \quad \text{for } n \geq 0$$
$$C(n, k) = 0 \quad \text{for } k > n$$
$$C(n, k) = C(n-1, k) + C(n-1, k-1) \quad \text{for } n \geq k > 0$$

    a. Compute $C(3, 0)$, $C(3, 1)$, $C(3, 2)$, and $C(3, 3)$.

    b. Write a recursive definition of a function that computes $C(n, k)$.

    c. The number $C(n, k)$ counts the number of different subsets of size k that can be made from a set of n elements. Prove this fact using the recursive definition of $C(n, k)$. *Hint*: Select any particular element from the set, then count the number of k-element subsets that do contain that element and those that do not.

    d. Prove that $C(n, k)$ can also be defined by $C(n, k) = n!/(k!(n-k)!)$.

7. Write recursive routines for the following operations.

    a. `int Intlog(int n)`, which is defined to be the highest power of 2 that is less than or equal to n, so `Intlog(8)` $=3$, and `Intlog(40)` $=5$.

    b. `int Find(T e, List<T> ls)`, which returns the position in ls of the first instance of e, or -1 if e is not in ls. You may want to write this so that it consists of a main routine to get started and a recursive subroutine to track through the list.

    c. `int Member(T e, List<T> ls)`, for ordinary lists, which returns 1 if and only if e is in the list ls.

    d. `Purge(List& ls)`, which removes any duplicate elements from ls. In other words, `Purge` applied to the list (a, b, a, c, b, c, d, a) might result in the list (b, c, d, a). You might want to use `Member` here.

    e. `T Max(List<T> ls)`, which returns the largest element in a list (assuming that the underlying set of atoms is linearly ordered).

8. Write a function that computes x^n in time $O(\log n)$, assuming that multiplication takes constant time. *Hint*: Use a divide-and-conquer algorithm that halves n and squares the product.

9. Describe as simply as possible what the following algorithms do. (In other words, do not just parrot the definition of the algorithm.)

    a.
    ```
    int What(int p, int q)
    // Pre: p, q > 0.
    {
        int r = p % q;
        if (r == 0)
            return q;
        else
            return What(q, r);
    }
    ```

    b.
    ```
    void Change(Stack<T>& s)
    {
        if (!(s.IsEmpty()))
        {
            T x = s.Top();
            s.Pop(S);
            if (!(s.IsEmpty()))
                s.Pop();
            Change(S);
            s.Push(x)
        }
    }
    ```

10. The following function takes an array, *a*, of characters and returns 1 if and only if the array segment *a*[*start*], *a*[*start*+1], . . . , *a*[*end*] is a palindrome, that is, if it reads the same from left to right as it does from right to left (like "NOON" or "STATS").

    ```
    int IsPalindrome(Array<char> a, int start, int end)
    {
        if (start >= end)
            return 1
        else
            return ((a[start] == a[end]) &&
                IsPalindrome(a, start + 1, end - 1));
    }
    ```

    Use a stack to eliminate recursion from *IsPalindrome,* as was done in the text for *ReverseTraversal.*

11. The following recursively defined functions have interesting properties. Try some sample values of the arguments and explore their properties. It would be valuable for you to code and run these functions.

    a.
    ```
    int Ulam(int n)
    // It is not known whether this function always halts.
    {
        if (x == 1)
    ```

```
            return 1;
         else if (n % 2)
            return Ulam(3 * x + 1);
            // Dangerous? We're going up here, not down.
         else
            return Ulam(n / 2);
      end;
```

b. int Ackermann(int x, int y)
   // This gets large *very* rapidly, as x
   // and y increase.
```
   {
      if (x == 0)
         return y + 1;
      else if (y == 0)
         return Ackermann(x - 1, 1);
      else
         return Ackermann(x - 1, Ackermann(x, y - 1));
   }
```

c. int Takeuchi(int x, int y, int z)
   // This uses a *lot* of calls to find the result.
```
   {
      if (x <= y)
         return z;
      else
         return   (Takeuchi(Takeuchi(x-1, y, z),
                   Takeuchi(y-1, z, x),
                   Takeuchi(z-1, x, y)));
   }
```

12. How long do the following functions take on input n?

a. int P(int n)
```
   {
      if (n <= 1)
         return 1;
      else
         return (3 * P(n / 2));
   }
```

b. int Q(int n)
```
   {
      if (n == 1)
         return 1;
      else
      {
         int t = 1;
         for (int i = 1; i < n; i++)
            t += Q(i);
         return t;
      }
   }
```

c.
```
int S(int n)
{
    if (n == 1)
        return 1;
    else
        return (n + S(n - 1));
}

int R(int n)
{
    if (n == 1)
        return 2;
    else
        return (R(n - 1) + S(n));
}
```

13. Consider the timing function $T(n)$ defined by

$$T(1) = 1$$

$$T(n) = pT\left(\frac{n}{3}\right) + f(n) \quad \text{if } n > 1$$

There are nine combinations of functions that can be made by letting $p=2$, 3, 4 and $f(n)=\log_2 n$, n, n^2. Find big-O estimates for each of the timing functions that result.

14. Diagram with nested boxes the procedure calls used to compute *Better-DCFib*(4), and compare your diagram with that of the original *Fib*(4) given in the text.

15. Trace the action of *BetterItFib*(29).

16. a. (Math) What do you notice about the powers A, A^2, A^3, A^4, A^5 of the following matrix?

$$A = \begin{bmatrix} 1 & 1 \\ 1 & 0 \end{bmatrix}$$

   b. Using the fast exponentiation algorithm of Exercise 8, describe another way to compute *Fib*(n) in logarithmic time, assuming that matrix multiplication can be done in constant time.

   c. What matrix would you use in place of A to help you compute the values of the function defined by $f(0) = 1$, $f(1) = 1$, $f(n) = 3f(n-1)-f(n-2)$, for $n>2$?

17. Show that if you restrict yourself to the arithmetic operations +, −, *, and /, then it is impossible to compute *Fib*(n) by any algorithm in fewer than $c\log n$ steps, for some positive constant c. *Hint*: Count digits. How large is *Fib*(n), and how fast can you get there?

18. If L is a nonempty list, what is (CONS (CAR L) (CDR L))?

19. What are the results of (CONS x NIL) and (APPEND x NIL) if

   a. x is an atom?

   b. x is a list?

20. In the definition of our version of APPEND, why did we call it a "semishallow clone?"

21. Suppose we write APPEND as the symbol • in infix notation, so that (APPEND L1 L2) and L1 • L2 would be understood to refer to the same operation.

   a. Provide an example to demonstrate that • is **associative**; that is, L1 • (L2 • L3) = (L1 • L2) • L3, for lists L1, L2, L3.

   b. Provide an example to demonstrate that NIL is the **identity element** for •; that is, L • NIL = NIL • L = L, for a list L.

   c. Is NIL the identity element for CONS?

22. Write functions to perform the following operations on general lists, using the implementation of *GenList* described in the text.

   a. int AtCount(GenList l), which counts the number of atoms in a general list; for example, AtCount of (a (b c) d) is 4, and AtCount of (a (a) ((a))) is 3.

   b. int ConsCount(GenList ls), which counts the number of CONS cells in the internal representation of *ls,* so that ConsCount of (a (b c) d) is 5, and ConsCount of (a (a) ((a))) is 6. (This, by the way, can be found from the written representation by counting the atoms plus the left parentheses and subtracting 1.)

   c. GenList TotalReverse(GenList ls), which returns *ls* with every sublist reversed, so that TotalReverse of (a (b c) d) is (d (c b) a).

   d. void PrintList(GenList ls), which causes the list *ls* to be printed with parentheses, as we would normally write it. You may assume existence of a Print function that prints atoms. This is a bit tricky.

23. Write a program that will print the moves in an n-disk Towers of Hanoi solution.

24. a. Write a program that will print binary numbers from 0 to $2^n - 1$ in increasing order. The algorithm should not perform any decimal-to-binary conversion. *Hint*: It goes without saying, we hope, that your solution will be recursive. Try thinking about printing all the numbers that begin with 0, followed by all the numbers that begin with 1.

   b. Using part (a) as a guide, write a program that will list all subsets of a set of n objects.

25. Combine the multiprecision arithmetic package of Chapter 1 with either of the factorial algorithms given in the text, and test your program by

computing 200! and comparing your answer with those of your class-mates.

26. Verify, by whatever means you wish, the value for *Fib*(2500) given in the text.

27. If your version of C++ has an internal timer or (even better) a profiler, use it to compare the running times of the four Fibonacci algorithms given in the text.

5.7 EXPLORATIONS

Quicksort

The divide-and-conquer nature of *Mergesort* makes it a very time-efficient algorithm, one that runs in time proportional to *n*log*n* on lists of *n* elements. With certain restrictions, that's as fast as we can sort. In fact, it's not frightfully difficult (once you see the trick) to show that *any sorting algorithm that relies solely on comparisons and data moves must take time at least n log n.* Unfortunately, *Mergesort* isn't very space-efficient. Where, for instance, do we put the list that *Merge* constructs? The easiest way is to have *Merge* build a separate list, which we then use to replace the sublist we are sorting, but that requires room to store *n* extra list elements.

28. (Tricky) Show that it is possible to design *Mergesort* in such a way that it sorts **in place**, which is to say that it uses only a fixed amount of auxiliary storage whose size is independent to the size of the list being sorted. *Hint*: Use a linked list.

We can, though, invent a time-efficient in-place sorting routine. Suppose that we have a list of numbers that we wish to sort, and suppose we are willing to settle for a "partial" sorting with the following property: After the partial sorting, the list will be divided into a left and right sublist in such a way that every element in the left sublist will be less than or equal to every element in the right sublist. For example, starting with the list (4, 5, 2, 1, 3), we might be content to wind up with the arrangement (3, 1, 2; 5, 4). In this arrangement, every element in the left sublist (3, 1, 2) is less than or equal to every element in the right sublist (5, 4). Does this lead to anything useful? It sure does.

Notice that each sublist is in its correct position. The elements of the left sublist aren't where they should be, but the sublist itself is. The same, of course, holds for the right sublist. Here's the clever part: What happens if we apply the same partial sort, *recursively,* to the left and right sublists? Nothing we do to either sublist alters the fact that the lists are where they should be, and every time we apply the partial sort to a sublist, we'll wind up with two smaller sublists, each of which is now in its correct position. For example, the sublist (3, 1, 2) might wind up as (2, 1), (3), and the right sublist must necessarily become the two smaller lists (4), (5). Now our entire list looks like (2, 1), (3), (4), (5). That's almost perfectly sorted and indeed becomes perfectly sorted as soon as we do a partial sort on the sublist (2, 1). This algorithm is called *Quicksort* (see Figure 5.11).

FIGURE 5.11

Quicksort in action

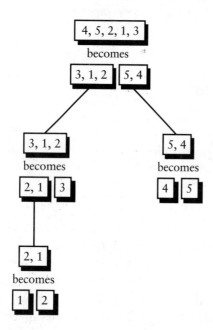

Quicksort is almost too good to be true. Because the elements in every sublist are no farther from their correct, sorted, positions than the size of the sublist, then as long as we can guarantee that at every stage a sublist will be split into nonempty sub-sublists, we will eventually wind up with a collection of lists of size 1, each of which consists of a single element in its correct position. *Quicksort*, like *Mergesort*, is basically a function that makes three function calls: one to split the list and two recursive calls to sort the sublists. The major difference between the two algorithms is that *Mergesort* does the two recursive calls first, while *Quicksort* does its two recursive calls last. *Quicksort* looks like this.

```
void Quicksort(Array<T>& a, int start, int finish)
// Sorts part of an array in place, from position
// start to position finish.
{
    if (start < finish)   // Don't sort a 1-element list.
    {
        // Rearrange a in such a way that every element
        // in { start .. split]  is less than or equal to
```

```
// every element in [split + 1 .. finish].
int split = Partition(a, start, finish);
// Sort the left sublist.
Quicksort(a, start, split);
// Sort the right sublist.
Quicksort(a, split + 1, finish);
}
}
```

Can this be correct? Based on our understanding of recursion, it seems like it has to work. *Quicksort* clearly works correctly on lists with a single element (that's our exit case), and if it sorts lists of size smaller than *n*, it will certainly work on lists of size *n* (that's the recursive part, after we invoke *Partition* to produce the two sublists).

Of course, all the real work of *Quicksort* is done by the helper function *Partition*. The idea behind *Partition* is also rather clever: We work our way inward from *start* and *finish*, and every time we find a pair of elements that are in the wrong sublists, we just swap them. Here are the steps to follow:

1. Pick an array value, *pivot*. We'll rearrange the list by putting on the left all values ≤ *pivot* and on the right all values ≥ *pivot*.

2. Use two indices, *left* and *right*. We'll walk these indices toward each other, using them to swap array elements as we go.

    a. Begin with *left* = *start* − 1 and *right* = *finish* + 1.

    b. As long as *left* < *right*, do the following:

        i.   Keep increasing *left* until we come to an element $a[left] ≥ pivot$.

        ii. Keep decreasing *right* until we come to an element $a[right] ≤ pivot$.

        iii. Swap $a[left]$ and $a[right]$.

    c. Do one last swap of $a[left]$ and $a[right]$.

3. Return *right*.

29. Show how *Partition* works on the list (4, 5, 2, 1, 3). One way to choose *pivot* is to let it be the first element in the sublist, namely $a[start]$.

30. What's the purpose of the last swap, in step 2c of the *Partition* algorithm?

31. Show that *Partition* runs in time $O(n)$ on sublists of size n.

32. Write *Partition*.

33. Write and test *Quicksort*. A good idea would be to include (global) counters to keep track of the number of comparisons and swaps.

Quicksort is certainly simple to write, but it suffers from one disadvantage that *Mergesort* doesn't: It runs in time $O(n \log n)$ on most lists, but there are some lists for which *Quicksort* runs far slower.

34. Find big-O timing estimates for *Quicksort* in the following cases.

    a. *Partition* splits its sublist in half each time it is called.

    b. (Challenging) *Partition* splits its sublist of size n into lists of size $n/10$ and $9n/10$ each time.

    c. *Partition* splits its sublist of size n into lists of size 1 and $n-1$ each time.

    d. *Partition* splits its sublist of size n into lists of size 2 and $n-2$ each time.

35. Cases like (c) and (d) in Exercise 34 are ones that get us into trouble.

    a. What arrangements of the original list will cause case (c) to apply?

    b. Our version of *Partition* chose *pivot* to be the first element in the sublist. How could you change the choice of *pivot* so that the arrangements you found in part (a) will not necessarily cause trouble?

6

TREES

The monkey's survival can only be understood by comprehending the inherent connectedness of the forest with its branches linked for fast escape.

Gilda Needles
Life in the Trees

We began this text by discussing arrays, lists, and strings. By removing many of the operations that define the *List* abstract data type, we were able to define two new ADTs, stacks and queues. In each case, however, the underlying structure was the same: a linear structure with a unique first position, immediately followed by a unique second position, immediately followed by a unique third position, and so on, until the unique last position. This linear structure is important because there are so many cases in which information has a "natural" linear order. Of course, "so many" does not mean *all*: There are numerous instances in which information does not have a natural linear structure. You will see that once we remove the requirement that our data types have a linear structure, we will have easy access to a treasure trove of applications, such as representation of arithmetic expressions, improved sorting and searching, and codes for data compression. In this chapter and throughout the rest of the text, we will continue our program of gradually relaxing the restrictions on an ADT to produce new and more general abstract data types.

One obvious structural requirement we might consider dropping is that an element have at most one successor. The **hierarchical structure** that we then obtain is common among cataloging schemes for published work. For example, *Computing Reviews,* published by the Association for Computing Machinery, has adopted a classification scheme for computer science literature that, in part, has the following form:

    A. General Literature
        A.0 General
        A.1 Introductory and Survey

In this classification, each major topic has several subsidiary topics, each of which may itself be broken down into several subtopics, and so on. Although this scheme could be viewed as a linear arrangement (indeed, such an organization is suggested by the linear arrangement from top to bottom), the indentation we used suggests that there is more to the structure than a simple linear arrangement. This behavior is typical; in fact, the fewer restrictions we place on the structure of an ADT, the more conceptually complex the instances of the ADT become.

6.1 THE STRUCTURE OF TREES

A hierarchical data structure—one for which an element may have at most one predecessor but many successors—is called a **tree.** As usual, the underlying set of atoms may be any set we wish, and the structure of the positions is defined by three simple rules. An element of the *Tree* abstract data type is, as usual, defined by a collection, P, of positions (where elements reside), satisfying

1. There is a unique position, $r \in P$, called the **root,** that has no predecessor.
2. Every position in P except the root has exactly one predecessor.
3. Every position in P except the root has the root as a (perhaps not immediate) predecessor.

Customarily, the positions in a tree are referred to as **nodes** in computer science (they're called **vertices** in mathematics), and the structural relation predecessor is called "the **parent**." We frequently wish to extend the definition of the "parent" relation. We say that a node n is the **ancestor** of a node m if either

1. $n=m$ (if this does not happen, we say that n is a **proper ancestor** of m)
2. n is the parent of an ancestor of m

In other words, n is an ancestor of m if n and m are the same node or if there is a "parent of" chain from m to n. Using this notation, we then may define a tree as a set of nodes, one of which we distinguish by calling it the **root**, along with a parent relation such that (1) the root has no parent, (2) every node except the root has a parent, and (3) the root is the ancestor of every node. In Figure 6.1, we show several examples of trees and nontrees, using arrows between nodes to indicate a parent-child relationship and indicating the root by a filled circle.

In Figure 6.1, (d) is not a tree because there are two possible roots, that is, nodes with no parents, and also because there is a node with two parents; (e) is not a tree because it is not **connected**, which is to say it fails condition (3), and likewise has two candidates for roots; and (f) is not a tree because it has no node that could be the root. Incidentally, we should not dismiss (e) out of hand; it is the disconnected union of several trees and, as such, is called (to no one's surprise) a **forest**. We will see forests later in this chapter and again in Chapter 9.

It is customary when drawing trees to eliminate the arrows and link the nodes with simple edges instead. To eliminate confusion, we adopt the convention that any node will be drawn lower on the page than its parent. This

FIGURE 6.1

Three trees and three nontrees

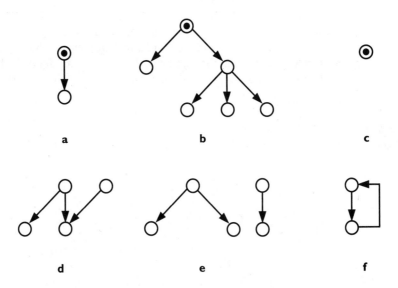

is consistent with the way family trees are generally drawn, but it has the disadvantage that the root appears on the top of the picture so that, as is said about the African baobab tree, the tree grows down from its root.

Because trees are structurally more complicated than lists or the other linear structures, we need a number of terms to describe the nodes of a tree and the relationships between those nodes.

Definition.   Let T be a tree, and let n and m be nodes of T. We say that

1. n and m are **siblings** if they have the same parent.
2. m is a **descendant** of n if n is an ancestor of m.
3. A node is a **leaf** of T if it has no children.
4. A node is an **internal node** if it is not a leaf.
5. An **edge** of T connects two nodes, one of which is the parent of the other.
6. A **path** in T is the collection of edges that join two nodes, one of which is the ancestor of the other, and the **length** of a path consists of the number of edges in the path.
7. The **height** of a node is the length of the longest path from that node to a leaf.
8. The **depth** of a node is the length of the (unique) path from that node to the root.
9. The height (or depth) of a tree is the height of the root, namely, the length of the longest path from the root to a leaf.
10. A **subtree**, S, of T **rooted at** n is a tree that is made from T by considering n to be the root of S and including in S all descendants of n.

In the tree in Figure 6.2, we see that a and b are siblings; that h is a descendant of b; that the nodes e, f, g, and h are leaves; that r, a, b, c, and d are internal nodes; that the height of b is 2 and its depth is 1; that the tree has height 3; and that the subtree rooted at node b consists of nodes b, d, e, f,

FIGURE 6.2

A sample tree

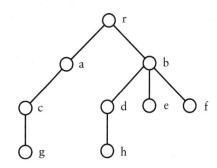

and h, along with all the edges connecting those nodes. Notice that we have adopted the convention of drawing children below parents, so r must be the root of this tree.

We will define a **k-ary tree** to be a tree for which each node has at most k children, so that the tree in Figure 6.2 would be a 3-ary tree. In what will follow, it will be useful for us to know how many nodes a k-ary tree of depth d could have. We will do this by looking at the maximum and minimum number of nodes possible at each depth. At depth 0 there is only the root, which could have at most k children at depth 1. Each of these children could have k children at depth 2, for a maximum of k^2 children possible at depth 2, and it is clear that we could continue this process to show that at depth d, there could be at most k^d nodes. Therefore, the maximum possible number of nodes in a tree of depth d is

$$n \leq 1 + k + k^2 + \cdots + k^d = \frac{k^{d+1} - 1}{k - 1} < k^{d+1} - 1 < k^{d+1}$$

and since there could be as few as one node at each depth from 0 to d, we see that

a k-ary tree of depth d can have n nodes, with $d < n < k^{d+1}$

If we look at this from another point of view, taking logs of both sides of the inequality $n < k^{d+1}$, we could equally well say that

a k-ary tree with n nodes could have depth d, with $\log_k n < d < n$.

Computer scientists, however, rarely make use of such general trees as we have defined here. It is customary to impose an additional linear order on each set of siblings, so we would say that if the tree in Figure 6.2 was considered an **ordered tree**, then node d would be the **left child** of b, node e would be the **right sibling** of d, and node f would be the right sibling of e. In other words, the objects in Figure 6.3 would be equivalent as trees, but would be different as ordered trees. If the reason for this distinction escapes you, think of the left child as the eldest child and imagine siblings ordered by age. In many historical novels and plays (not to mention many contemporary families), one's position in age order makes a significant contribution to the part one plays.

Before we leave general trees entirely, it is worth mentioning that there is a natural recursive definition for trees, one that generalizes slightly the definition we have already made. We may define a tree by stipulating that a tree consists of either (1) nothing at all, which we will call the **empty tree**, or (2) a

FIGURE 6.3

Order matters in ordered trees

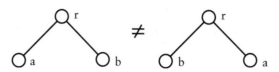

node, along with a (possibly empty) collection $\{T_1, T_2, \ldots, T_n\}$ of subtrees, each of which is itself a tree. We could modify this definition to refer to ordered trees by insisting that the subtrees be in linear order rather than an unordered set.

6.2 ADT: *BINARYTREE*

In many applications, we need only be concerned with trees (usually ordered) for which each node has at most two children—that is, 2-ary ordered trees. Because "2-ary ordered trees" is such a cumbersome locution, we call such trees **binary trees**. Not only do they permit simpler implementations (since we always know the maximum number of children any node can have), but they are also all we really need to represent any kind of ordered tree whatsoever, as we shall see shortly. The recursive definition of binary trees is particularly simple.

> *Definition.*   A binary tree is made up of nodes, which are elements of some set. A binary tree consists of either (1) nothing at all (the empty tree) or (2) a node, called the root of the binary tree, along with a **left subtree** and a **right subtree**, both of which are binary trees.

To see this definition in action, consider Figure 6.4. This object might be a binary tree, because it has a node, *a,* and we can demonstrate that it is by showing that the left and right subtrees are binary trees. The left subtree is a binary tree because it consists of a node, *b,* along with two subtrees, both of which happen to be empty. In a similar way, we can show that the right subtree is also a binary tree because it consists of a node, *c,* along with an empty left subtree and a right subtree that is itself a binary tree because it consists of a node, *d,* along with two subtrees, both of which are empty.

Although the recursive definition of binary trees is certainly elegant, proving that an object is a binary tree by this definition seems to involve a lot

FIGURE 6.4

A binary tree

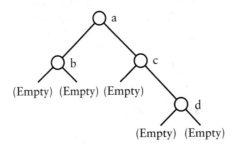

(Empty) (Empty) (Empty)

(Empty) (Empty)

of work. You may have also noticed that so far we have made no mention of the operations that define the *BinaryTree* abstract data type (or any of the other tree ADTs, for that matter). Rest assured, we will remedy these deficiencies, but before we do, a word is in order about the hint we dropped earlier that binary trees were all we really needed. What we meant was that any ordered tree could be represented as a binary tree in such a way as to preserve all the information about the original ordered tree. This might seem impossible, because a general ordered tree seems to have a much more complicated structure than a binary tree, but the transformation becomes clear if we realize that the structure of an ordered tree is captured by two relations: leftmost child and right sibling. Fortunately, we have in binary trees two places where this information might be kept, namely, the left and right subtrees. Given any ordered tree, we can convert it to a binary tree by the following correspondence:

1. The binary tree will have the same nodes as the ordered tree.
2. If *n* is the leftmost child of *m* in the ordered tree, then *n* will be the left child of *m* in the binary tree.
3. If *n* is the right sibling of *m* in the ordered tree, then *n* will be the right child of *m* in the binary tree.

In most dealings with trees (and graphs, which we will introduce later), pictures speak more eloquently than words. Let's look at Figure 6.5 to see how this conversion process would work on the ordered tree in Figure 6.2. The edges of the original tree are now dotted, and the edges of the binary tree are solid, with single arrows for left children and double arrows for right children. All we need do now is to grab the resulting binary tree by the root and give it a shake, so that it falls into the familiar form of Figure 6.6. It is not difficult to convince yourself that the original tree would be easy to reconstruct from the resulting binary tree.

Now that we understand the structure of trees, we can complete the definition of the *BinaryTree* abstract data type by defining the operations we may perform on the ADT. If you look at the literature, you will find that there is less agreement about the operations on binary trees than about the operations on the linear structures. For our purposes, we will consider here nine

FIGURE 6.5

Representing an ordered tree as a binary tree

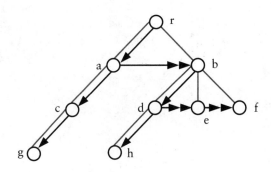

FIGURE 6.6

After shaking out the
tree of Figure 6.5

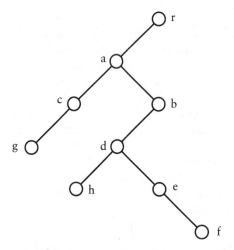

"primitive" operations and will discuss some nonprimitive operations later. Of our nine primitives, eight deal with the structure of the binary tree, and one, the overload of the () operator, is concerned with the atoms that "reside" in the positions in the tree.

BinaryTree

Structure: An arbitrarily large (finite) collection of positions (called **nodes**), arranged in an order such that each position has at most two successors, called *left* and *right*. If the set of positions is not empty, there is a unique distinguished position, called the **root**, which has no predecessor and which is the eventual predecessor of every other position.

Operations

BinaryTree(). Pre: true. Post: This tree is empty.

BinaryTree(T rootValue). Pre: true. Post: This tree has a single node in the root position, and that node contains *rootValue*.

BinaryTree(T rootValue, const BinaryTree& left, const BinaryTree& right). Pre: true. Post: The root node of this tree contains *rootValue,* and the left and right subtrees of the root are *left* and *right,* respectively. Notice that this function does not make a copy of the two subtrees; some authors call this operation a **merge** of two trees.

void Clear(). Pre: true. Post: This tree is empty.

BinaryTree Left() const. Pre: This tree is not empty. Post: This tree is unchanged. Returns the binary tree rooted at the left child of this tree's root.

> BinaryTree Right() const. Pre: This tree is not empty. Post: This tree is
> unchanged. Returns the binary tree rooted at the right child of this
> tree's root.
>
> int IsEmpty() const. Pre: true. Post: This tree is unchanged. 1 is returned
> if this tree has no nodes; otherwise, 0 is returned.
>
> T& operator() const. Pre: This tree is not empty. Post: This tree is un-
> changed, and a reference to the value contained in the root node is
> returned.
>
> BinaryTree& operator= (const BinaryTree& b). Pre: true. Post: This tree is a
> copy of b; that is, it has the same structure as b and has the same
> values in the corresponding nodes. Returns a reference to the newly
> constructed copy.

As we have mentioned before, this specification (and any other) should be regarded more as a suggestion than as an unalterable requirement. For instance, some authors add a *current* position in the tree, as we did when we defined the *List* ADT, and others include operations we have omitted here, such as inserting a new node, deleting a node and its successors, and *Find*, which locates the node where a particular element resides.

6.3 BINARY TREE TRAVERSALS

If we think for a minute about the operation *Find,* we see that there is a lot more to trees than might appear at first. When we implemented *Find* for lists, the task was made simpler by the fact that the linear structure of *List* made it possible to start at the head and inspect each element in turn until we found the atom we wanted or reached the end of the list without success. Clearly, we can't do that in general for trees, because there is no obvious "next" node to inspect. One possibility would be to do a **depth-first search**, searching as far down from the root as we can, then backing up to the first node with a child we haven't seen, searching the descendants of that child as far as we can, backing up again, and so on. This is a perfectly respectable scheme, but it seems to require a considerable amount of care to remember or find the nodes to which we have to return in backtracking. Another possibility would be to do a **breadth-first search**, searching all the nodes at depth 1, then all the nodes at depth 2, and so forth; but that also appears to require that we remember the positions of the nodes at level n while we are looking at the nodes at level $n+1$. Indeed, we will discuss these search schemes in Chapter 8, but the comparatively simple structure of binary trees, coupled with the recursive nature of the tree data structures, permits three similar traversal techniques, which are defined recursively and for which the need to "remember" where to backtrack is met automatically by the computer as it keeps track of nested function calls.

If we keep in mind that (1) a nonempty binary tree consists of a root node and left and right subtrees of that node and (2) every subtree of a binary tree is a binary tree, then we can inspect every node of a binary tree by inspecting the root, then the left subtree, and finally the right subtree. All we need to do to inspect the subtrees is to apply the inspection routine recursively to those parts, which leads to the following algorithm, known as a **preorder traversal.**

```
void Preorder()
{
   if (!IsEmpty())
   {

      Do whatever processing is needed at the root;

      Left().Preorder();  // Inspect left subtree.
      Right().Preorder(); // Inspect right subtree.
   }
}
```

That's all there is to it. Simple, eh? We need only call *t.Preorder*( ) to visit every node of *t*. Recall that we did just this sort of algorithm when we defined a recursive list traversal: Look at the head of the sublist, then look (recursively) at the list that follows the head—or, in LISP terminology, inspect the CAR, then call the inspection routine on the CDR.

Consider the binary tree in Figure 6.4, which we reproduce here with all its nonempty subtrees indicated.

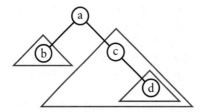

If we called *Preorder* on the root, *a*, we would have the following sequence of function calls and inspections:

> *a.Preorder*( )
>> Inspect *a*
>> *b.Preorder*( )
>>> Inspect *b*
>>> NULL.*Preorder* ( )—the left subtree of *b* is empty
>>> NULL.*Preorder* ( )—the right subtree of *b* is empty

> *c.Preorder*( )
> Inspect *c*
> NULL.*Preorder* ( )—the left subtree of *c* is empty
> *d.Preorder*( )
>   Inspect *d*
>   NULL.*Preorder* ( )—the left subtree of *d* is empty
>   NULL.*Preorder* ( )—the right subtree of *d* is empty

All the nodes would be visited, in the order *a, b, c, d.* Of course, there is nothing sacred about visiting the root of each subtree first. You may recall that when we looked at recursive list traversal and tried visiting the head of the sublist *after* having visited the tail of the list, we saw that the resulting algorithm also produced a traversal, from back to front of the list. An analogous situation holds for binary trees, yielding two other traversals, the **inorder** and **postorder.**

```
void Inorder()
{
   if (!IsEmpty())
   {
      Left().Inorder();

      Do whatever processing is needed at the root;

      Right().Inorder();
   }
}

void Postorder()
{
   if (!IsEmpty())
   {
      Left().Postorder();
      Right().Postorder();

      Do whatever processing is needed at the root;

   }
}
```

This is a good time to test your ability to trace recursive routines by verifying that for the foregoing tree, the traversals would be, inorder, *b, a, c, d,* and postorder, *b, d, c, a.* Take your time; we'll wait.

*   *   *

Your experience in doing these traversals was probably typical. Tracing the recursive routines required a fair amount of care, enough so that you would be reluctant to perform these traversals on any but the smallest binary trees.

Fortunately, there is an equivalent algorithm that is much better suited to humans than to computers. Given a binary tree to traverse, first draw a triangle for each node, then "shrink-wrap" the tree by drawing the smallest closed curve that encloses all the edges and nodes of the tree, as illustrated here.

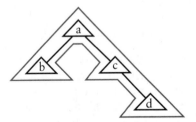

Then make a complete circuit around the curve, starting at the left side of the root triangle and moving in a counterclockwise direction. To perform a preorder traversal, mark a node as visited each time the path follows the *left* side of the node triangle, in this case *a, b, c, d*. To perform inorder and postorder traversals, do the same thing, but mark a node as visited each time the path follows the *bottom* or *right* side, respectively.

When we do this "manual" traversal, we're mimicking what goes on in any of the three traversals; the only difference is when we decide to "visit" a node. The patterns for the three traversals are the same; we simply repeat the following steps until every node has been seen three times: (1) follow left children as far as possible, (2) back up until you can go right, and (3) go right. As a matter of fact, these three rules can be used in a general-purpose traversal routine that does not use recursion. To be able to back up the tree, we keep a stack of node pointers, and we repeat the three preceding steps until the stack is empty.

Here's the traversal function.

```
template<class T> void BinaryTree<T>::IterativeTraversal()
// Non-recursive traversal routine
{
    TStack<TreeNode<T>*> s;
    TreeNode<T>* p = root;
    do
    {
        // Rule (1)--go left as far as you can
        while (p)
        {
            s.Push(p);
            // PREORDER: Seen p for the first time, inspect s.Top()
            p = p->leftPtr;
        }
        // Rule (2)--back up the branch
        while ((!s.IsEmpty()) && (s.Top() == NULL))
```

```
    {
        s.Pop();
        // POSTORDER: Seen p for the last time, inspect s.Top()
        s.Pop();
    }
    // Rule (3)--step off the branch by going right
    if (!s.IsEmpty())
    {
        p = s.Top()->rightPtr;
        // INORDER: Seen p for the second time, inspect s.Top()
        s.Push(NULL);
    }
  } while (!s.IsEmpty());
}
```

The only tricky part comes in step 3: We need to indicate that we have gone right from a node, but we don't want to remove that pointer from the stack until the last time we visit it, in step 2. We do this marking by pushing a NULL pointer on the stack, so that a NULL pointer on the top of the stack indicates that we have inspected the right child of the node pointed to by the pointer immediately below the top. The following table provides a trace of this function on our example tree.

Iteration	Stack	Step	PRE	IN	POST
1:	a	1	a		
	$a\,b$	1	b		
	$a\,b\,0$	3		b	
2:	a	2			b
3:	$a\,0$	3		a	
4:	$a\,0\,c$	1	c		
	$a\,0\,c\,0$	3		c	
5:	$a\,0\,c\,0\,d$	1	d		
	$a\,0\,c\,0\,d\,0$	3		d	
6:	$a\,0\,c\,0$	2			d
	$a\,0$	2			c
		2			a

The left-right structure of trees allows us to define a linear order on the nodes of a tree. This linear order, we will see, is closely connected to tree traversals. Let T be a binary tree (although we could easily extend the definition to any ordered tree), and let n and m be nodes of T. We say that n is **left of** m if one of the following conditions is met:

1. $n=m$.
2. There is a node, p, of T such that n is in the left subtree of p and m is in the right subtree of p.

3. *n* is in the left subtree of *m*.
4. *m* is in the right subtree of *n*.

For example, in the binary tree in Figure 6.7, the left-right order of the nodes is *h, e, i, b, a, f, c, j, k, g.* The entire subtree rooted at *b* is to the left of the root *a*, since it is the left subtree of *a*, and we can see that *b* is to the left of itself and *a, c, f, g, j,* and *k*. We have drawn the tree to emphasize the left-right order, in that any node that is left of another is left of that node in the figure; but be aware that the leftmost node of a subtree may not appear as the leftmost node in a picture.

The interesting part of this linear order is that it is exactly the order we obtain by an inorder traversal. A bit of thought should convince you that this must be the case. In left-right order, any left subtree must be to the left of its parent and also would be visited before its parent in an inorder traversal, whereas any right subtree must be to the right of its parent and would be visited after its parent in an inorder traversal.

6.4   IMPLEMENTATION OF *BINARYTREE*

There are a number of implementations of *BinaryTree*, but they all can be divided into two classes: those that are inherently linear in nature and those that more closely reflect the nonlinear structure of trees. We will discuss the most obvious implementation here and will mention another in Chapter 9.

The pointer implementation of the *List* was perhaps not the most obvious choice at the time. Part of that deficiency might have been due to your unfamiliarity with pointers back then, but mostly it was because we had available a natural predefined data type with a linear structure, namely, arrays. Now that we are more comfortable with pointers, however, the pictures of binary trees should suggest a simple implementation immediately. All we need to do is create a linked collection of nodes, each of which contains a

FIGURE 6.7

A binary tree drawn to illustrate left-right order

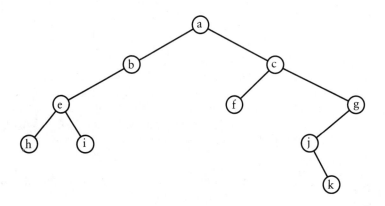

FIGURE 6.8

Pointer implementation of the tree in Figure 6.4

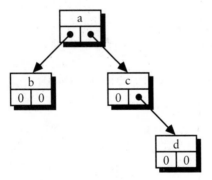

field for an atom and *two* pointer fields: to the left and right children of the nodes. In Figure 6.8, we show a typical binary tree in this implementation.

In this implementation, we will have two classes, just as we did with *List*: a *TreeNode* class for the nodes and the *BinaryTree* class itself, which accesses the node structure by means of a pointer to the root node.

```
template<class T>
class TreeNode
{
public:
   TreeNode(T e)
     : data(e), leftPtr(NULL), rightPtr(NULL) { } ;
   TreeNode(T e, TreeNode<T>* left, TreeNode<T>* right)
     : data(e), leftPtr(left), rightPtr(right) { } ;

   T data;                    // information stored in node
   TreeNode<T>    *leftPtr,   // ptr to left child
                  *rightPtr;  // ptr to right child
} ;


template<class T>
class BinaryTree
{
public:
   BinaryTree() : root(NULL) { } ;
   BinaryTree(T rootValue);
   BinaryTree(T rootValue,
              const BinaryTree<T>& left,
              const BinaryTree<T>& right);
   ~BinaryTree() { Clear();} ;
   void Clear();
   BinaryTree<T> Left() const;
   BinaryTree<T> Right() const;
```

```
    int IsEmpty() const
        {  return (root == NULL);} ;
    T operator() () const;

    BinaryTree<T>& operator= (const BinaryTree<T>& b);

    void Preorder();
    void Inorder();
    void Postorder();

protected:
    TreeNode<T>* root;
} ;
```

Notice the advantage we gain in this implementation by knowing that we are dealing with binary trees: We know that there will never be more than two children per node, so we don't have to worry about defining an arbitrary number of child pointers in each node cell. The definitions of the member functions are, for the most part, simple in this implementation. We will show some of the definitions, leave some for exercises, and save some until a later section.

The constructor that merges two trees makes a new root node and relies on the *TreeNode* constructor that sets the *data, leftPtr,* and *rightPtr* member data of the node.

```
template<class T>
BinaryTree<T>::BinaryTree(T rootValue,
                          const BinaryTree<T>& left,
                          const BinaryTree<T>& right)
{
    root = new TreeNode<T>(rootValue, left.root, right.root);
}
```

To dispose of all the nodes in a tree, we use a postorder traversal, first clearing all the nodes in the left subtree of the root, then clearing out the right subtree, and finally disposing of the root node. You might want to consider whether this function would work equally well if we had used an inorder or a preorder traversal instead.

```
template<class T> void BinaryTree<T>::Clear()
{
    if (!IsEmpty())  // No need to clear a tree that's already empty.
    {
        Left().Clear();
        Right().Clear();
        delete root;
        root = NULL;
    }
}
```

It's easy to get the left subtree of a tree: We check whether the tree is empty, and if it isn't, we construct a new tree whose root is the left child of the root of this tree. It's even easier to get the root value.

```
template<class T> BinaryTree<T> BinaryTree<T>::Left() const
// Shallow copy of the left subtree of this tree.
{
    Assert(!IsEmpty(), "Can't get the left child of an empty tree");

    BinaryTree<T> l;
    l.root = root->leftPtr;
    return l;
}


template<class T> T& BinaryTree<T>::operator() () const
{
    Assert(!IsEmpty(), "Can't get the root value of an empty tree");

    return root->data;
}
```

The only tricky member function is the overload of the assignment operator. We make a copy of a binary tree by first clearing the nodes in this tree. Then we recursively copy the left and right subtrees of the argument tree and use the *TreeNode* constructor to make a new node whose left and right subtrees are copies of the left and right subtrees of the argument tree. Finally, we return a reference to the new tree we built.

```
template<class T>
BinaryTree<T>& BinaryTree<T>::operator= (const BinaryTree<T>& b)
{
    if (this != &b)  // No need to assign to self.
    {
        Clear();
        if (b.root)
        {
            BinaryTree<T>      leftCopy,
                               rightCopy;
            // These are the two recursive calls.
            leftCopy = b.Left();
            rightCopy = b.Right();

            root = new TreeNode<T>(b(), leftCopy.root, rightCopy.root);
        }
        else
            root = NULL;
    }
    return *this;
}
```

6.5 **COMPUTER SCIENCE INTERLUDE: PARSE TREES**

In ages past, when the authors of this book were in elementary school, the accepted wisdom was that the best way to teach English syntax was to require the students to diagram sentences, a mind-numbing exercise that required identifying the subject, verb, and object and then splitting these into noun phrases and verb phrases, which were further divided into nouns, adjectives, adverbs, pronouns, auxiliary verbs, articles, and so on. Later, linguists, who had presumably had the same training in their early years, attempted the much grander project of trying to determine whether there were inherent "deep structures" that underlay the structure of all languages, a project that met with limited success (partly because meaning does not reside wholly in syntax; consider, for instance, the two interpretations of "The clams are ready to eat").

Later still, computer scientists successfully used this notion of hierarchy to provide a framework by which the syntax of programming languages could be represented by compilers and interpreters, to translate languages such as C++ and FORTRAN into **machine language**, the language of the statements that could actually be executed by computers. The problem of program translation is a fascinating one, about which mountains of words have been written. But the essential question is this: How do we write a program that will take a collection of **source code** in one language and produce the equivalent **object code** in another? For our purposes, the interesting part of that question is, What data structures can we use to make the translation process as efficient as possible?

Consider, for instance, the very small subproblem of how to store the "sense" of arithmetic expressions, such as a + b * c. Because arithmetic is inherently hierarchical—requiring evaluation of small parts, which are then combined into large parts, which are further combined into larger parts—trees (known as **parse trees**) are the data structure of choice. The technique is best illustrated by examples, like the two in Figure 6.9.

We adopt the convention that these parse trees represent expressions that would be evaluated from bottom up, so that in the simpler example, the subexpression b * c would be evaluated, and then that result would be added to a to produce the result. With this convention, then, the parse tree contains all the information in the original expression in a form that permits easy implementation in the translator program. That by itself is worth noting, but the truly appealing part of these parse trees lies in their traversals. An inorder traversal of the simpler tree yields a + b * c, which is exactly the infix representation of the expression, while the complicated tree has inorder traversal 1 + 2 - x * y / x + y, which is what we would obtain if we stripped the parentheses from the infix expression, which we would write 1 + (2 - x * y) / (x + y). If inorder traversal yields an infix expression, what do you think

FIGURE 6.9

Two parse trees of algebraic expressions

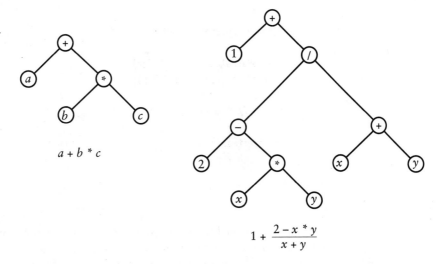

$a + b * c$

$$1 + \frac{2 - x * y}{x + y}$$

would happen if we traversed these two trees in *post*order? Try it before continuing.

*   *   *

Well, well, well. The postorder traversal of the small tree is a b c * +, and the postorder traversal of the large tree is 1 2 x y * - x y + / +, both of which are precisely the postfix equivalents of the original expressions. Thus, not only does the parse tree of an arithmetic expression contain all the information needed to reconstruct the expression, it also allows us to reconstruct the expression in any of three different notations!

Constructing a parse tree from a source code input string is a fascinating (and very large) subject, one on which whole books have been written. If you continue to study computer science, you will almost certainly see this topic again in a compiler design course. We'll give you a taste of the subject by constructing a parse tree for an arithmetic expression from the postfix form of that expression. Here's the algorithm.

```
void BuildParseTree(TreeNode*& np)
// Constructs a parse tree rooted at np corresponding to
// a postfix expression.
{
    Token t;
    GetToken(t);    // Get the next token in right-left order.
    if (there are any more tokens)
    {
```

Build a new node pointed to by *np*;

Place *t* in the new node;

```
    if (t is an operator token)
    {
        BuildParseTree(np->rightPtr);
        BuildParseTree(np->leftPtr);
    }
    else     // Nonoperators are always leaves.
    {
        np->leftPtr = NULL;
        np->rightPtr = NULL;
    }
    }
}
```

This function builds the parse tree from the top down by reading the postfix expression from right to left. The construction algorithm proceeds from the (recursive) observation that a correctly formed postfix expression always consists of (1) a single identifier (a variable or constant) or (2) two correctly formed postfix expressions followed by an operator. In case 1, the parse tree will consist of just the identifier, and in case 2, the parse tree will have the operator as the root and the trees of the preceding expressions as the subtrees of the operator, which is the root. This is the heart of our parsing algorithm: If, for example, the input string is "abc*+,", we first see the "+" operator, so we know that the parse tree will have "+" as its root token, with the postfix expressions "bc*" and "a" as subtrees of the root. Now, parsing "bc*" gives us a subtree with "*" as root and "b" and "c" as subtrees, and we have completed the parse tree. For the input string "abc*+," Figure 6.10 shows the steps of the parsing algorithm.

Of course, if we were designing an industrial-strength compiler, we would use more sophisticated techniques than to begin with the postfix expression. But even for our purposes, it is not hard to imagine how we would construct the parse tree within the infix-to-postfix algorithm. We mention in passing that these parse trees were easy to produce and amenable to traversal because the common arithmetic operations are at worst binary, which is to say that they require no more than two arguments. A similar technique can be used to store the syntax of an entire program as a large parse tree, but the task is made slightly more complicated by the fact that the resulting parse tree is not necessarily a binary tree. For instance, a parse tree for a C++ class specification might look in part like the tree in Figure 6.11.

 ## 6.6 DATA-ORDERED BINARY TREES

In Explorations in Chapter 2, we saw that it was much faster to find an element in a list if the data contained a key field on which we could define a lin-

FIGURE 6.10
Constructing a parse
tree from a postfix
expression

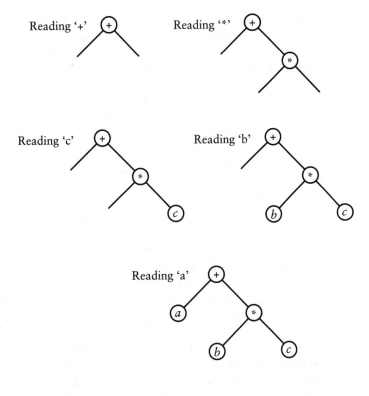

FIGURE 6.11
Sample parse tree
for a C++ class
specification

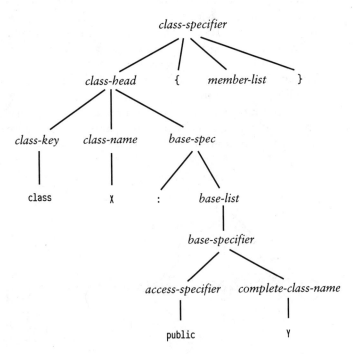

ear order. If the list were maintained so that it was always sorted by the key field, *Find* could be made to run in O(log *n*) time using a binary or interpolation search. The good news, then, was that when inserting an element into a sorted list, it took very little time to find where the element should go. The bad news, you'll recall, was that the speed of *Find* was completely wasted, because binary and interpolation searches had to be defined on arrays, and insertion into arrays takes linear time. Insertion into linked lists takes constant time, but with a linked list we have no way to find the middle of a sublist. Trees to the rescue!

Binary Search Trees

In a binary tree, we do have a way of finding the "middle" element: The root node of a subtree is to the right of its left subtree and to the left of its right subtree. We will arrange our data in the tree so that this order is maintained on the key fields. We say that a **binary search tree (BST)** is a binary tree with the property that the value of the key field of a node is larger than the value of the key field of any node in its left subtree and smaller than that of any node in its right subtree. In Figure 6.12, we present a typical binary search tree.

It is easy to show that the tree in Figure 6.12 has the binary search tree property. For instance, every element (4, 8, and 11) in the left subtree of the root has value less than the value of the root, and every element (26, 27, 31) in the right subtree of the root has value larger than the value of the root element. You can check that this property holds for every subtree of the tree. But be careful in reading the picture; the node containing 11 is to the left of the root, even though it may not appear to be. Notice that the left-right order of the nodes is exactly numeric order: 4, 8, 11, 17, 26, 27, 31. You should be able to convince yourself that this is not a fluke, but is a property that holds for all BSTs.

Because we have imposed additional structure on BSTs, and because the operations are slightly different from those of binary trees, BSTs rate a definition as a separate ADT.

FIGURE 6.12

A binary search tree

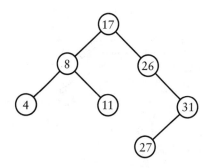

▼

> ### BinarySearchTree: BinaryTree
>
> **Structure.** A *BinarySearchTree* has the structure of a *BinaryTree*. In addition, there must be a linear order defined on the underlying set of atoms, and the atoms stored in the BST must obey the property that the atom in each node is greater than the atoms in the left subtree of the node and less than the atoms in the right subtree.
>
> **Operations.** All the operations of *BinaryTree*, except the merge-constructor. In addition, a BST has the following operations.
>
> BST(). Pre: true. Post: This tree is empty.
>
> void Insert(T e). Pre: true. Post: This tree is a BST and contains the nodes it did before, along with a new node with value *e*.
>
> void Delete(T e). Pre: true. Post: If this tree did not have a node with value *e*, it is unchanged; if *e* was in this tree before, it has been removed in such a way that the new tree is still a binary search tree.
>
> int Contains(T e). Pre: true. Post: This tree is unchanged. Returns 1 if *e* is in this tree; otherwise, returns 0.

We will implement binary search trees as a derived class of *BinaryTree*, and we will take the time to define the entire package of types and algorithms here. In the declarations, notice that all the real work is accomplished by means of private member functions *Find, Insert, Delete,* and *DeleteMin*. These functions are kept private because they access nodes in the tree and so should be kept out of the hands of the user of this class.

```
//================== BST.h ==================
#ifndef BST_H
#define BST_H
#include "BinaryTrees.h"

template<class T>
class BST : public BinaryTree<T>
{
public:
    BST() : BinaryTree<T>() { } ;

    void Insert(T e) { Insert(e, root);} ;
    void Delete(T e) { Delete(e, root);} ;
    int Contains(T e) const { return (Find(e, root) != NULL);} ;

private:
    TreeNode<T>* Find(T e, TreeNode<T>* np) const;
    void Insert(int e, TreeNode<T>*& np);
```

```
        void Delete(int e, TreeNode<T>*& np);
        T DeleteMin(TreeNode<T>*& np);
} ;
#endif
```

In *Find,* we use the BST property to guide us through the tree. If the element we are seeking has a value less than that of the node we are currently inspecting, we know that the element we seek can only lie in the left subtree of the current node, so we recursively continue the search there. We act in a similar way if the key is greater than that of the current node. The exit conditions are either successfully finding the key or running out of nodes to search. In addition to using *Find* to define *Contains, Find*'s main use would be in an application where the data elements stored in the nodes were complex structures indexed by some key field, like employee IDs. In that case, we could define the function *Update* with the header

```
template<class T> void BST<T>::Update(T e)
```

whose action would be to replace the atom with a given key value with a different atom with the same key (as would happen if we needed to modify the marital status of an employee without changing his or her ID, for instance). To do that, we would invoke *Find* to locate the correct node and then replace that node's *data* member by the new value *e.* Since the key value wasn't changed, the tree would still satisfy the binary search tree property.

```
template<class T>
TreeNode<T>* BST<T>::Find(T e, TreeNode<T>* np) const
// Returns a pointer to the node containing e, in the subtree
// pointed to by np.  If e isn't in the subtree, returns NULL.
{
    if ((np == NULL) || (np->data == e))
        return np;
    else if (e < np->data)
        return Find(e, np->leftPtr);
    else
        return Find(e, np->rightPtr);
}
```

To insert an element into a BST, we track our way through the tree, guided by the BST property, until a vacant subtree is found. If we had to insert a node with key value 9 into the BST of Figure 6.13, we would first compare 9 with the root key, 17. Since 9 is less than 17, we move to the left subtree and compare 9 with the root key, 8, of that subtree. Since 9 is greater than 8, we move to the right subtree. Since 9 is less than 11, we move to the left subtree, which is empty, and that's where we place the new node, as illustrated in Figure 6.13.

FIGURE 6.13

Insertion into a binary
search tree

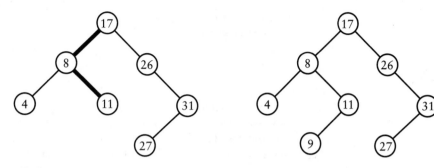

Original BST with search path darkened   After inserting 9

```
template<class T> void BST<T>::Insert(T e, TreeNode<T>*& np)
// Insert the element e into the subtree pointed to by np.
{
    if (np == NULL)
        np = new TreeNode<T>(e);
    else if (e < np->data)
        Insert(e, np->leftPtr);
    else
        Insert(e, np->rightPtr);
}
```

Take particular note of the argument to this function:

```
TreeNode<T>*& np.
```

We need a reference argument because we are actually modifying the value of
the (NULL) pointer we eventually find, changing it to point to the new node
where the inserted element will go. You'll see the same argument in the deletion routines.

Deleting the node with the smallest key from a BST is easy. We know
that the smallest key must be in the leftmost node, so all we do is travel along
left edges until we can go no farther, copy the data in that node, and then remove the node. We need to exercise a modicum of care, however, because we
do not want any right subtree of that node to be cut off when we delete the
node. What we must do is point around the leftmost node, so that its right
subtree becomes the left subtree of the parent of the leftmost node.

```
template<class T> T BST<T>::DeleteMin(TreeNode<T>*& np)
{
    Assert(np != NULL, "Can't delete from an empty tree");
    if (np->leftPtr)
        return DeleteMin(np->leftPtr);
    else
    {
        T returnValue = np->data;
```

```
        TreeNode<T>* temp = np;
        np = np->rightPtr;
        delete temp;
        return returnValue;
    }
}
```

Now we must decide how to delete a node from a BST in such a way that the resulting tree is still a BST. If the node to be deleted has no children, we can simply remove that node. Things are almost as simple if the node to be removed has a single child; in this case, we point around the node, so that the child "moves up" to the position occupied by the deleted node, as shown in Figure 6.14.

The only real difficulty comes in deciding what to do in case the node to be deleted has two children. We cannot just remove the node, of course, because that would leave the subtrees of that nodes as orphans, having no connection to the tree. We cannot move the left or right subtree up to the deleted position either, because that could destroy the binary search tree property. (Imagine what would happen in the right tree of Figure 6.14 if we were to delete the root by moving node 8 to the root position.)

If we keep in mind the need to preserve the left-right order (which, of course, is nothing but the BST property), it should be clear that we can delete a node with two children by replacing it with its nearest right neighbor, just as we would delete an element from a list. We know just where the nearest right neighbor is, too: It's the leftmost element in the right subtree of the node. In other words, to delete a node with two children, we find the leftmost node in the right subtree, delete that node, and place its data in the node we intended to delete. But that's the same thing as performing *DeleteMin* on the right subtree of the node to be deleted, which is the reason we defined *DeleteMin* in the first place. Figure 6.15 shows this deletion in action. Notice, too, that we could perform the deletion in a mirror-image fashion by replacing the node to be deleted by the rightmost child of its left subtree, but then

FIGURE 6.14

Deleting a node with a single child

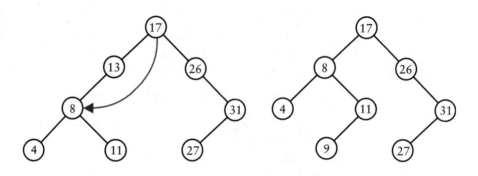

About to delete 13   After deletion

FIGURE 6.15

Deleting node 14, when leftmost node of right subtree is 19

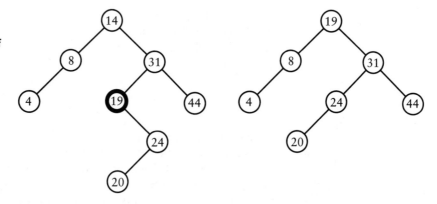

we would need to define the mirror image *DeleteMax* (not that that would be difficult).

```
template<class T> void BST<T>::Delete(T e, TreeNode<T>*& np)
// Delete the node containing e from the subtree
// of this tree pointed to by np.
{
    if (np)
    {
        if (e < np->data)
            Delete(e, np->leftPtr);
        else if (e > np->data)
            Delete(e, np->rightPtr);

        // Now we know that np points to the node
        // we will delete.
        else if ((np->leftPtr) && (np->rightPtr))
        {
            // Has left and right children
            T min = DeleteMin(np->rightPtr);
            np->data = min;
        }
        else
        {
            TreeNode<T>* temp = np;
            // Has no children
            if ((np->leftPtr == NULL) && (np->rightPtr == NULL))
                np = NULL;
            // Has only a right child
            else if (np->leftPtr == NULL)
                np = np->rightPtr;
```

```
        // Has only a left child
        else if (np->rightPtr == NULL)
            np = np->leftPtr;
        delete temp;
    }
  }
}
```

Now, where are we? We are in possession of a data type that permits, in most cases, exceptionally efficient access to its elements. We can locate objects, insert new objects, and delete or modify existing objects quite rapidly. All we require is that the objects have keys that can be linearly ordered, like numbers, characters, or strings. But what exactly do we mean by "exceptionally efficient"? Notice that so far we have not mentioned the timing of any of the BST algorithms. The reason is that it is not all that easy to get good timing estimates for these algorithms.

Consider *Find*, for example. In one sense, we can analyze this algorithm easily. The length of time it will take to find a given key in a BST is certainly no worse than proportional to the depth of the tree, since we find a key by stepping down the tree, starting from the root, so *Find*—and all the other operations except for the constructor, for that matter—run in time $O(d)$, where d is the length of the longest path in the tree. However, we would like to have a timing function that is a function of n, the number of nodes in the tree, and there's where the canker gnaws. There simply is no way to tell the exact depth of a binary search tree if all we know is the number of nodes in the tree; all we know is that a binary tree of height h has between $h+1$ and $2^{h+1}-1$ nodes. See Figure 6.16, for example, where we illustrate two binary search trees of size 7, the worst and best cases for height with this many nodes.

FIGURE 6.16

Two binary search trees of the same size

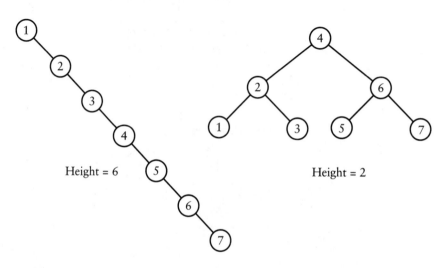

Height = 6

Height = 2

We see immediately that a BST with n nodes could have height equal to $n-1$, a dreadful state of affairs, since that would make all of our operations except the constructor run in linear time. We would be better off in this case to chuck it all and keep our data in an array, sorted by keys. In the best case, however, where all the internal nodes have two children (except perhaps those at the lowest level), the tree is very shallow indeed, being logarithmic in the number of nodes.

At this point, it would seem that all we can say is that with the exception of the constructor, all the BST operations run in log time at best, but could run in linear time if the tree was very unbalanced. Now comes the part where the authors pull the rabbit out of the *deus ex machina*. One fact and one observation come to our rescue:

> **Fact.** Although the mathematics is too delicate for us to go into here, it turns out that under certain simplifying assumptions, it is possible to prove that, on average, a "random" binary search tree with n nodes has depth proportional to $\log n$. In other words, most binary search trees "should be" very shallow.

> **Observation.** Because it is risky to extrapolate from theoretical results to actual figures (what do we mean, for instance, by a "random" BST?), some researchers have gone in the opposite direction, looking at the statistics on BST depth from practical situations. Here, too, the evidence is in our favor. Most of the data indicate that in practice, where binary search trees are made by long sequences of mixed insertions and deletions, most of the trees have a depth that is not too much worse than a fixed multiple of $\log n$.

This is good news indeed. In real-world terms, this means that if you had to maintain a database that had, on average, a million elements in it (sometimes more, sometimes less, depending on insertions and deletions), you should expect that most of the time, all the operations should take no more than some fixed multiple of 20 steps through the tree, since 2^{20} is approximately 1 million. (Of course, you would live in a terror of expectation that the tree might wind up looking like the worst case, a linked list with a million elements in it, whereupon your boss would ask you to explain why it takes three days to retrieve an element from your database.)

Application: *Treesort*

Binary search trees give us, almost for free, a simple and (usually) efficient sorting algorithm. To sort a collection of data, we need only feed the data into a BST. As new data come in, *Insert* places the data in their proper location in the tree in left-right order. What algorithm do we use to retrieve the data in the sorted order? Think about it.

* * *

Got it? Inorder! Remember, the inorder traversal of a binary tree visits the nodes in exactly their left-right order, and that's exactly the sorted order of the nodes. How long should such a sort take? Let's assume that we're always in the "nice" case, where insertion into a tree with n nodes takes $O(\log n)$ time. We place the first element at the root, since it has no other place to go, and after that we're inserting the nth element into a BST with $n-1$ nodes, a process that we assume takes $O(\log(n-1))$ time. The total time to build the tree, then, is $O(\log 1) + O(\log 2) + O(\log 3) + \cdots + O(\log(n-1))$, a quantity that is certainly no larger than $O(n \log n)$. Getting the data back by *Inorder* takes $O(n)$, which would be absorbed by the larger $O(n \log n)$ term, giving us a sorting algorithm that is asymptotically as good as any we've seen.

This sorting algorithm, known as **treesort,** has certain other advantages, as well. Unlike *Mergesort* and *Quicksort,* the other $O(n \log n)$ algorithms we've seen, we don't need to have all the data in place at once. As the data dribble in, we just insert them into the tree, where they can be retrieved in sorted order at any time.

6.7 SUMMARY

We have covered a lot of material in this chapter, reflecting the importance of trees. Lists are very useful, but there are many instances in which the information to be represented has a hierarchical, rather than linear, structure.

Binary trees are fundamental hierarchical structures in the sense that any tree can be represented as a binary tree, with a possible increase in depth. The depth of a tree is an important parameter because many of the tree algorithms run in time proportional to the depth of the tree.

Because trees have a natural recursive definition, it is not surprising that there is a simple recursive technique for tree traversal. In fact, if we permute the statements in the tree traversal algorithm, we can derive three different ways to traverse a tree. (There are actually six different permutations, but we restrict our attention only to those that visit the left subtree of a node before the right subtree.) The traversal routines lend themselves very readily to translating arithmetic expressions stored in parse trees, as well as to sorting routines, such as *Treesort.*

In cases where the set of atoms has a linear order, we can structure binary trees in such a way as to make insertion, deletion, and membership testing quite simple, and usually fast as well. Binary search trees have the property that each node has a value greater than any value in its left subtree and less than any value in its right subtree. The operations on binary search trees usually run in time that is logarithmic in the size of the tree, but in the worst cases the running time may be only linear.

6.8 EXERCISES

1. Is there anything in the definition of a tree that prohibits a node from being its own parent? In other words, can the structural relation of a tree have any reflexivity?

2. If a tree has n nodes, how many edges can it have? Prove your assertion. (*Hint*: Try induction on n.)

3. Answer the following questions for the following tree.
   a. What are the siblings of e?
   b. What are the descendants of d?
   c. Which nodes are leaves?
   d. What are the height and depth of g?
   e. What is the height of the tree?

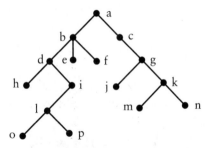

4. Convert the tree shown in Exercise 3 from a 3-ary ordered tree into a binary tree, using the algorithm in the text.

5. Describe the operations you would include in the specification of *OrderedTree*. You should consider which of the operations in *BinaryTree* to include, which would need to be modified, which would be inappropriate, and what other operations should be added.

6. Eliminate node e from the tree shown in Exercise 3, thus making the tree a binary tree. Answer these questions about the resulting tree.
   a. Which nodes are to the left of f?
   b. What is the rightmost node?
   c. Which nodes are to the right of b and to the left of k?
   d. What is the rightmost node of the left subtree of b?

7. In a **breadth-first traversal**, we repeatedly visit a node, then all its children, all the children of the children, and so on. For example, in the tree shown in Exercise 3, a breadth-first traversal would visit the nodes in

order a, b, c, d, e, f, h, i, l, o, p, g, j, k, m, n. Write a breadth-first traversal routine. *Hint*: Use a queue.

8. For binary trees, which of our three traversal orders is the same as a depth-first traversal?

9. Produce a binary tree with nodes a, b, c, d, e, f such that b is second in inorder and fifth in postorder.

10. In the mathematical literature, a **reconstruction problem** is one in which you are given some information about an object and are required to use that information to produce the object.

   a. Show that you cannot reconstruct a binary tree given only its inorder traversal, by producing two different binary trees that both have inorder traversal a, b, c.

   b. Show that you do not need all three traversal orders to reconstruct a binary tree, by showing that some two of the three traversals provide enough information to reconstruct the tree. (That is, produce an algorithm that will build a binary tree from some two traversals.)

11. What can you say about the order in which the leaves of a binary tree are visited by each of the three traversals?

12. Give an algorithm that would take a parse tree of an arithmetic expression and produce a correctly parenthesized infix expression from the tree.

13. (You need to know calculus for this.) Parse trees of algebraic expressions are useful in problems of **symbolic algebra,** in which algebraic expressions are manipulated by the computer. We could, for instance, write a program to find factors of polynomials or perform the sort of integration so near and dear to the hearts of calculus students. In fact, programs already exist that can do integration well enough to handle most of the problems on a first-semester calculus final exam. An easier problem in symbolic algebra is to write a program that differentiates. Given a parse tree of an expression in one variable (for simplicity, assume it's a polynomial in one variable), describe the rules that would be used to transform that parse tree into the parse tree of the derivative of the original expression. Your rules will be most easily expressed in recursive form.

14. In the definition of *Clear,* we disposed of a subtree using a postorder traversal of the subtree. What would happen if we used a different traversal?

15. a. If node n is an ancestor of node m, can we guarantee that n will appear before m in either preorder, inorder, or postorder?

b. If n is to the left of m, can we guarantee that n will appear before m in either preorder, inorder, or postorder?

16. Show that if we are given a preorder traversal of a binary tree, along with the information about whether each node has a left or a right child, then we can reconstruct the tree. (*Hint*: Consider the information obtained about what the next node in preorder is in each of the four possible cases for existence or nonexistence of children. You may find a stack helpful.)

17. Show all possible binary search trees on the keys 1, 2, 3, 4. If you are ambitious, try to find a formula that expresses the number of BSTs on the keys $1, \ldots, n$.

18. If we delete a node from a BST and then insert that node again, is the resulting BST necessarily the same as before?

19. If we delete two nodes from a BST, does the resulting BST ever depend on which of the nodes was deleted first?

20. Show the BST that results from inserting the keys 8, 13, 10, 12, 6, 9, 5, 2, in that order (8 first, then 13, and so on). Quick, give an inorder traversal of the tree.

21. Under what conditions on a list of keys does inserting the list into a BST lead to a single path with no branching, that is, a BST that looks like a linked list?

22. In the specification of binary search trees, the BST property guaranteed that a BST would never have two nodes with the same key value. Is this a necessary restriction? In other words, what changes, if any, do we have to make to the BST operations if we allow duplicate keys?

23. Write a function that, given a pointer to the root of a binary tree, returns the height of the tree. *Hint*: There is a simple recursive definition.

24. (Hard) Do Exercise 12 in reverse, by producing a program that will take as input an infix expression and produce a parse tree for that expression.

25. Write a program that will take an algebraic expression in a single variable and produce its derivative.

26. Consider the problem of constructing a BST by inserting the integers 1 to n in random order.

    a. If $n = 3$, there are six possible insertion orders: (1, 2, 3), (1, 3, 2), (2, 1, 3), (2, 3, 1), (3, 2, 1), (3, 1, 2). Show the BST that results from each of these six insertion orders.

    b. Over all six trees, what is the average depth of a node?

   c.   If $n=4$, there are 24 possible insertion orders. Show that the average depth of a node over all possible insertion orders is $29/24=1.208$.

   d.   (Hard) Show that for n elements, the average depth of all nodes is $O(\log n)$.

27.   Write a program that will take an integer, n, insert n randomly chosen integers into a binary search tree, and measure the height of the resulting tree. The fact and observation we mentioned in the section on BSTs indicate that the height should be approximately $K\log n$, on average. Run enough test cases to determine whether this appears to be true, and if it is, find K.

28.   Sometimes we need to deal with a **static** data structure, one that supports *Find* and *Retrieve,* but not *Insert* or *Delete,* except at the very beginning, while the structure is being built. If, for instance, we were to build a static binary search tree, it would make sense to put the frequently sought elements near the root to make *Find* as fast as possible. The only problem is that we may not know ahead of time which elements would be sought more frequently than others. One way to deal with this problem is to use a **self-organizing binary search tree (SOBST)**, which has the property that each time a nonroot node is found, that node is promoted one level up the tree by a **rotation**. In the following figure, we show a **left rotation**, used when the node sought (*y*, in this case) is a right child, and we define a right rotation similarly.

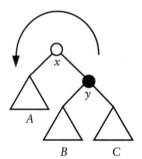 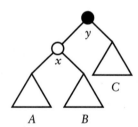

Notice that this rotation preserves the left-right order of the nodes and their subtrees—*A, x, B, y,* and *C*—and hence must preserve the binary search tree property. Write *Find* for SOBSTs. If you are comfortable with simulations, it would be worth investigating whether SOBSTs produce a significant saving of time over purely static binary search trees and what the average depth of the nodes are over a long run of repeated *Find*s.

29.   Run *Treesort* on several lists of randomly chosen numbers. See if it does indeed have running time bounded above by $Kn \log n$, and find K.

6.9 EXPLORATIONS

Threaded Trees

The very observant reader may object that we have omitted the definition of a fairly obvious operation: *Parent*. The action of *Parent* is simple enough, but how do we find the parent of a node, given only a pointer to the node itself? It may be a wise child who knows its parent, but our nodes just don't have that wisdom. We find ourselves in a situation similar to that of trying to implement the decrement operator, --, for linked lists: Movement *down* the tree is trivial, but movement *up* the tree is impossible, so all we can do is start at the root and perform a traversal until we find the node we wish, complicated by the fact that we need to remember the current node and its parent at every stage.

30. Write the function TreeNode* Parent(TreeNode* np) that returns the parent of the node pointed to by *np*, if any, and returns NULL if *np* points to the root of a binary tree.

Fortunately, the need to find the parent of a given node seldom arises in practice, but when it does, it is often better to adopt the stratagem, familiar by now, of modifying the data structure rather than relying on a complicated algorithm.

The most obvious choice would be to imitate what we did with two-way linked lists, namely, to include one more pointer in each node, pointing to the parent of that node. If the *data* field of the nodes was fairly large, the marginal increase in memory needed would be minimal, and the other operations would be only slightly more complicated, if at all.

31. What changes would we have to make to the *BinaryTree* operations if we modified *TreeNode* to include a pointer to the parent node?

Another possibility (one that is often used for general trees as well) would be to realize that every node that has fewer than two children has a pointer or two left over that is not pointing to anything useful except the flag value NULL. The most common use to which these leftover pointers is put is to have them point to nodes in the tree that would precede or follow the pointers in some traversal order. For example, we may decide to have unused right pointers point to the next node in an inorder traversal, and unused left pointers point to the previous node in an inorder traversal. Of course, since we are "overloading" the pointers, we need to include some sort of tag to indicate whether a pointer is an edge of the tree or a **thread**, a nonedge that is there to help us point through the tree in nonedge order. The implementation of such a **fully threaded tree** (a threaded tree with both left and right threads) would have the following member data in the nodes.

```
T data;                      // the data stored in the node

int   leftThread,            // = 1 if this node has a left thread
      rightThread;           // = 1 if this node has a right thread

TreeNode<T>   *leftPtr,      // pointer to the left child of this node
              *rightPtr;     // pointer to the right child of this node
```

In Figure 6.17, we draw the tree of Figure 6.7 with left and right threads indicated by dashed lines. Recall that the inorder traversal of the tree is *h, e, i, b, a, f, c, j, k, g,* so the left thread of node *i* points to node *e,* its predecessor in inorder, and the right thread of *i* points to *b,* its successor in the inorder traversal. Notice that the leftmost node of each right subtree has a thread that points to the parent of that tree, as does the rightmost node of each left subtree. Notice also that in the full tree, the leftmost node must always have a NULL left thread, and the rightmost node always has a NULL right thread.

FIGURE 6.17

A fully threaded tree

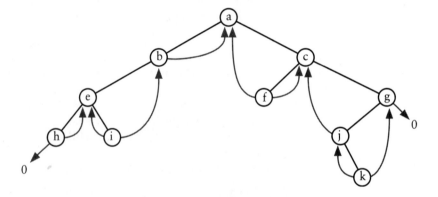

The first advantage we gain by this implementation is that it provides us with another means of inorder traversal without recursion. To make sense of the traversal algorithm that follows, bear in mind that in an inorder traversal, the first node to be visited in a subtree is always the leftmost node of that subtree. After that node has been visited, the next one to be visited is always its parent, which in our threaded tree is always reached by the right thread from that node. Once the parent has been visited, the process is repeated with the right subtree, and it continues until the rightmost node of the entire tree is visited, which we can recognize by realizing that the rightmost node is the only one with a NULL right thread. Compare this with the other iterative traversal routine we introduced earlier. Notice that they both have the same "go left as far as you can; back up; go one step right" form.

```
void IterativeInorder(TreeNode* np);
// Perform an inorder traversal of a threaded BST,
// starting at the node pointed to by np.}
```

```
{
    // Loop until rightmost thread has been visited.
    while (np)
    {
        // Move as far left along edges as possible.
        while ((!(np->leftThread) && (np->leftPtr))
            np = np->leftPtr;

        Inspect np;

        // Move up the tree in inorder.
        while (np->rightThread)
        {
            np = np->rightPtr;
            Inspect np;
        }

        // Move down to right subtree.
        np = np->rightPtr;
    }
}
```

32. Trace the action of this routine on the threaded tree of Figure 6.17. You should find it easier going than tracing the recursive version of *Inorder*.

33. Show that it is now possible to begin a traversal at any node of the tree we wish. Could we do this with the recursive or original iterative version?

  Most of the operations of this implementation of *BinaryTree* are almost identical to those of the original pointer implementation. The only difference is that we need to take care of the threads when inserting or deleting a subtree.

34. Write *Insert* for fully threaded trees.

35. Write *Delete* for fully threaded trees.

  We'll close this exploration where we started. We were motivated to use threaded trees by considering how to find the parent of a node. Can we solve this problem if we have threaded trees available? We certainly can.

36. Show how to find the parent of a node pointed to by *np* in a fully threaded tree.

Preamble: Tree Applications

The next two explorations are related in a number of ways: (1) they both deal with characters and strings, (2) they both are concerned with representing information in a space-efficient fashion, and (3) they both use trees. We begin with a puzzle: Look at the tree in Figure 6.18, and see if you can notice any significant properties it has and if you can determine the rule used to generate the tree.

Finding properties is easy: The tree is a binary tree; it's as shallow as it can be for the number of nodes it has; it contains all 26 letters in the English alphabet; and it is arranged so that the commonly used letters tend to be near the top of the tree. It's a safe bet that unless you had seen this tree before, you wouldn't guess how it was built, so we'll tell you. It turns out that this tree is a decoder for Morse code. You may know that Morse code consists of three types of symbols—dots, dashes, and spaces—and was originally invented for transferring information over telegraph wires. The dot was a short pulse of current (which would be transformed into a short sound at the receiver's end), the dash was a longer pulse (long sound), and the space was no current (used as a separator between letters and words). To use this tree as a decoder, we built it so that each left edge represented a dot, and each right edge represented a dash. Thus, to decode "··−" we begin at the root, follow the left edge corresponding to the first dot, take the left edge from there for the second dot, and take the right edge for the dash, which leaves us at node U, the letter corresponding to "··−".

Samuel F. B. Morse was not the first person to come up with the idea of sending characters by encoding them as pulses of current, but the code associated with his name has the advantage that the letters that are most often sent have short codes. This is important when the code is being sent by human telegraphers, since more than 10 or so dots and dashes per second would be difficult to send, as well as to interpret. To speed up transmission, we must try to make the codes as short as possible, on average. In the first application, we will explore the problem of producing codes that have the least average length.

Another nice feature of the decoding tree is that much of the code information is represented in the tree in such a way that it serves several purposes at once. The left branch from the root represents the initial dot for the letters

FIGURE 6.18

A mystery tree

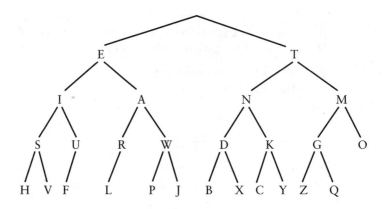

E, I, A, S, U, R, W, H, V, F, L, P, and J. The fact that the codes for all these letters begin with a dot is implicit in the fact that all these letters are in the left subtree of the root and does not need to be mentioned explicitly in our data structure. The second application will explore this representation by position in more detail.

Huffman Codes

Usually, we don't have to concern ourselves with the details of how characters are represented in memory. Generally, a character is stored as a number that represents that character by an agreed-on coding scheme, such as ASCII. The standard character codes are **fixed-length codes** in that the number of bits in the code is the same for each character. Commonly, a byte is enough to store the code for a character, since an 8-bit byte provides 256 possible codes, more than enough for most character sets. In fact, it's more than we need, and that's the point of our discussion.

Consider a simple example of an alphabet of five letters: 'a', 'b', 'c', 'd', 'e'. Three bits give us eight possible code sequences, which is more than enough to encode five different characters, so we might represent these letters with a fixed-length code, as follows:

Letter	Code
a	000
b	001
c	010
d	011
e	100

In this case, the **average code length**—the expected length of the code of each letter—is 3. Suppose we knew that in a typical message in our alphabet, the letter 'a' appeared 35% of the time, 'b', 20% of the time, 'c', 20%, 'd', 15%, and 'e' 10% of the time. With this knowledge, we might decide to use a **variable-length code**, like Morse code, representing the common letters by short codes:

Letter	Frequency	Code
a	0.35	0
b	0.20	1
c	0.20	00
d	0.15	01
e	0.10	10

We can find the average code length for this code by adding, for all letters, the code length times the probability that the letter will appear. In our example, the average code length is just $1(0.35) + 1(0.20) + 2(0.20) + 2(0.15) + 2(0.10) = 1.45$, which is less than half the average code length for the fixed-length code we started with. In other words, a message of 200 letters should require about $200(1.45) = 290$ bits. Unfortunately, it won't work. For example, what are we to do with the message 0010? That could be interpreted as "aaba", or "aae", or "ada", or "cba", or "ce". We must have some way of determining where a code group ends.

Morse code deals with this problem by sending a blank, but we would like to restrict ourselves to just two symbols. One possibility would be to decide that each code will begin with 11 and that 11 would not appear anywhere else in any code (effectively encoding a space by 11). Now our code would look like this:

Letter	Frequency	Code
a	0.35	110
b	0.20	111
c	0.20	1100
d	0.15	1101
e	0.10	1110

This code has average length 3.45. We would be better off with the original fixed-length code.

Another possibility would be to insist that our code have the **prefix property**, whereby no code sequence can be the prefix of any other. For example, if one sequence was 110, no other sequence could begin with 110, and we could not have 1 or 11 as another code sequence. Here is an example of a code with the prefix property:

Letter	Frequency	Code
a	0.35	00
b	0.20	10
c	0.20	010
d	0.15	011
e	0.10	111

This code has average length 2.45 and so is better than the fixed-length code. It has the further advantage that there is one and only one way to interpret any code sequence. But is this the best we can do? No, not in this case. The following algorithm, by D. A. Huffman, can be shown to produce minimal-length prefix codes, and we will illustrate it on our alphabet of five letters.

Begin with a **forest** of trees, each consisting of a single node and corresponding to a single letter in the alphabet. Throughout the algorithm, each tree in the forest will have a **weight** assigned to it; at the start, the weight of each tree is just the probability of occurrence of the corresponding letter. Repeat the following process until the forest consists of a single tree: Find the two trees of smallest weight, merge them together by making them the left and right children of a new root, and make the weight of the new tree equal to the sum of the weights of the two subtrees. We illustrate this process in Figure 6.19.

Having constructed the tree, assign to each left edge the value 0 and to each right edge the value 1, and read the codes for the letters by tracking down the tree, as we did with the Morse decoder tree. We have the following code with average length 2.25—as good as we can do with this distribution.

Letter	Frequency	Code
a	0.35	10
b	0.20	00
c	0.20	01
d	0.15	110
e	0.10	111

37. Produce a Huffman code for the alphabet a, b, c, d, where the letters have respective frequencies 0.35, 0.35, 0.20, 0.10.

FIGURE 6.19

Constructing Huffman codes

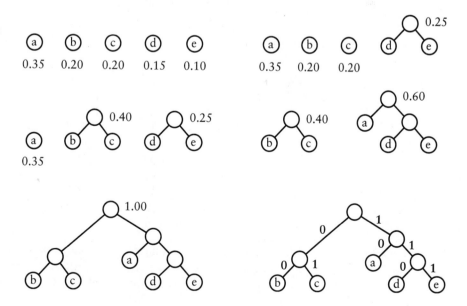

38. Write a program that, when given a list of letters and their frequencies, produces a Huffman code for that alphabet and computes the average length of the code. This is a bit trickier than it appears, because you have to find a way of merging the subtrees. Usually, what is done is to provide an extra *link* field in each node and to use that field to keep the roots in a linked list.

39. a. There is no Huffman code on four letters with code lengths 3, 2, 2, 2. Why?

    b. Show that a tree with leaves at depths $d_1, d_2, \ldots, d_n$ can be a Huffman tree if and only if

    $$\sum_{i=1}^{n} 2^{-d_i} = 1$$

    so that, for example, a tree with four nodes at depths 3, 3, 2, 1 could be a Huffman tree, since $1/8 + 1/8 + 1/4 + 1/2 = 1$. *Hint*: Every Huffman tree with more than one node is made by merging two smaller Huffman trees.

40. The frequency of occurrence of letters in English is found by taking a large, representative sample of English text (like the Sunday *New York Times*) and counting letters. There is therefore minor disagreement about the numbers to assign to the frequencies, but most studies have nearly identical numbers. In the following table, we provide such a frequency list, taken from the text of Chapters 5 and 6 of this book.

Letter	Frequency	Letter	Frequency
E	0.1311	U	0.0259
T	0.1076	M	0.0219
I	0.0796	W	0.0211
O	0.0742	P	0.0202
A	0.0720	G	0.0165
N	0.0704	B	0.0162
S	0.0640	Y	0.0137
R	0.0626	V	0.0094
H	0.0518	K	0.0038
L	0.0421	X	0.0028
D	0.0324	Q	0.0017
C	0.0312	J	0.0008
F	0.0265	Z	0.0005

a. Use the table to produce a Huffman code for English. To make all answers consistent, perform the merging so that the subtree of lower weight always appears at the zero branch. If you do your work correctly, there shouldn't be any ties—that is, subtrees of equal weight—to mess things up.

b. Find the average length of your code.

c. A message with 97 bits should contain about how many letters?

d. Here's a message of length 97. Decode it. The fact that it is broken into groups of 5 bits is not significant. We do that only to make the message easy to read.

00110 00111 11111 11010 00111 01001 01110 00110 01101 11101
00111 11000 10111 01011 01101 01010 11110 10111 00001 00

e. The order of the entries in our table differs slightly from the agreed-on order of frequency of letters in English. Not only are there more E's and T's in Chapters 5 and 6 than there are in "typical" English, but also the order usually given is E, T, A, O, I, N, S, R, H, L, D, C, U, ... How might you account for these differences?

Tries

In the two examples we have seen so far, information has been represented implicitly in a tree by its position in the tree. We can use this idea to store a dictionary of strings, representing words, for example. Such a structure is a tree in which each node represents the prefix of a word and has as its children nodes representing strings that have the parent as their prefix. Because there is a considerable overlap of prefixes in most natural languages, such as English, this storage scheme can be quite efficient in terms of space. Such a structure is called a **trie** (pronounced "try" despite the fact that it is derived from "retrieval"). We could, of course, store a dictionary in a number of other ways, such as with a binary search tree. One of the nice properties of a trie is that it allows us to perform partial lookups—for instance, of all the words that begin with CA. This would be difficult to do with another data structure and would be useful if, say, we wanted to automate a crossword puzzle dictionary.

In Figure 6.20, we show a typical trie, which stores the words ALL, ALP, AN, ANT, ANY, ARC, ARCH, ARM, ARMY, ART, CAD, CAN, CAR, CARD, and CARP. The darkened nodes in the figure represent full words, rather than just prefixes of words, so we know that both AN and ANT are stored in the trie, but that A is not. A trie supports the usual constructors, destructor, and assignment, along with *Member, Insert,* and *Delete,* where *Member* is a function that returns 1 if and only if a given string is in the trie. We will also be able to provide a traversal of the tree, despite the fact that a trie is not usually a binary tree. In fact, we could have as many as 26 children for any node in the trie, although that does not happen as a rule. (How many children would a node have if the edge going into it was a Q edge, for instance?)

FIGURE 6.20

A trie

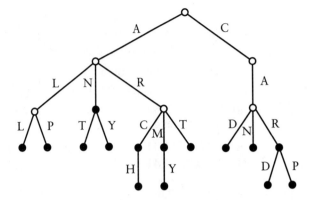

41. The most obvious implementation of a trie is with pointers. Each node will contain a Boolean flag indicating whether the node represents a word or just a prefix, along with an array of 26 pointers for all the possible children of that node. Write the declaration of the *TrieNode* class.

42. Write the function int Member(char* st, TrieNode* np) that returns 1 if and only if the string *st* is represented in the trie rooted at the node pointed to by *np*.

43. Write the function void Insert(char* st, TrieNode*& np) that inserts the string *st* into the trie rooted at the node pointed to by *np*.

44. a. Show that *Member* and *Insert*, defined in Exercise 42 and 43, can be implemented to run in time proportional to the length of *st*.

     b. Suppose we wanted to implement a dictionary for a word processor. Assume that we had 50,000 words in our dictionary and that the average length of a word was five characters. Compare the running times that would result if our dictionary was represented as (1) a binary search tree and (2) a trie.

45. Another way to implement a trie node is as a pointer to a linked list of pointers to other nodes, as shown in the following diagram.

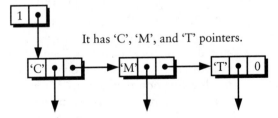

Discuss the advantages and disadvantages of this approach, compared to the array of pointers used in Exercise 41.

46. (Challenging) Get a large text file and use it to create a trie-based dictionary.

7

SPECIALIZED TREES

Binary search trees are very efficient data structures—most of the time. They support a wide range of operations, and these operations run in logarithmic time—most of the time. The problem with BSTs, as you know by now, is that the timing for the operations may degrade to linear if the tree happens to become very badly unbalanced, with all or most of its nodes linked in a long linear chain. If you think about this problem in the right way, though, you can see that this is really an implementation issue and not an inherent flaw in the ADT itself. We took the time to specify the *BinarySearchTree* ADT for two reasons. First, there was a historical precedent: Binary search trees have been around for a long time (well, a long time for the discipline of computer science; they date to the 1950s), and it's right that we do them homage in a text devoted to data structures. Second, binary search trees are simple and efficient, and the BST property would be worth studying even if the algorithms were less elegant than they are. If you look at the specification of *BinarySearchTree*, though, you'll see that the operations make no mention of the fact that we're dealing with a tree. Were it not for the reasons we just gave, we could have equally well specified a *SearchStructure* ADT, where the goal was to support the operations *Insert, Delete,* and *Contains* as efficiently as possible.

We will discuss here two improved implementations of binary search trees. Both have the left-right order property that BSTs have, so we do not have to give up easy finding of elements, and both avoid the possibility of runaway inflation of the tree height, so the operations always run in log time. The price we pay for these improvements is a moderate gain in the amount of programming detail. But the concepts behind these two improvements are fairly simple, and the programming complexity of the algorithms is evidently not sufficient to keep at least one of these data structures from being very widely employed out there in the real world.

7.1 BALANCED TREES

One way of ensuring that a binary tree does not have runaway branches is to insist that the tree be **balanced;** that is, at every node, the heights of the left and right subtrees must not differ by more than 1. Clearly, we can't do better than that and insist that the heights of the left and right subtrees always be equal, because that can happen only when the tree is **complete,** that is, when every internal node has exactly two children. In Figure 7.1, tree (a) is complete (hence balanced); tree (b) is balanced but not complete; and tree (c) is not balanced, because at the root the left subtree has height 3, while the right subtree has height 1. To be consistent, we say that the height of a tree with one node is 0, and the height of an empty tree is −1.

If we are going to deal with balanced trees, and if the efficiency of our algorithms depends on the depth of the tree, we had better be able to find an upper bound on the depth of a balanced binary tree of n nodes. As it happens, it's easier to answer the question in reverse: What is the least number of nodes in a balanced tree of height h? Let $S(h)$ denote the least size (i.e., the number of nodes) in any balanced tree of height h. Obviously, we must have $S(0)=1$ and $S(1)=2$, since a tree of height 0 must have at least one node, and a tree of height 1 must have at least 2 nodes. We can make a tree of height h by merging two subtrees of heights $h-1$ and $h-2$: Their heights differ by 1, and we can make the new tree have the smallest size by using minimal trees for the subtrees. If we denote such minimal-size balanced trees of height h by F_h, then the construction is that of Figure 7.2.

These minimal balanced binary trees are called **Fibonacci trees,** for the following reason: If we start with F_0 and F_1, trees consisting of a single node and two nodes linked by an edge, respectively, and note that $S(h)$ is just the number of nodes in F_h, then we see from the construction of Figure 7.2 that $S(h)=S(h-1)+S(h-2)+1$, because the number of nodes in the new tree is

FIGURE 7.1

Balanced and unbalanced trees

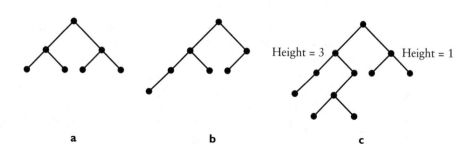

a   b   c

FIGURE 7.2

Merging balanced
trees

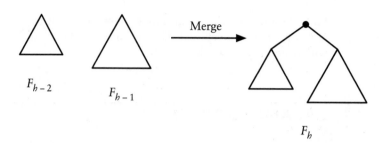

F_{h-2}

F_{h-1}

Merge

F_h

equal to the number of nodes in the subtrees plus 1 for the new root used to merge the subtrees. The first few values of $S(h)$ are 1, 2, 4, 7, 12, 20, and 33, and it is not hard to prove by induction that $S(h) = Fib(h+2) - 1$. Now, the Fibonacci numbers grow quite rapidly; in Chapter 5, we proved that $Fib(h) > (3/2)^h$ for all $h > 4$. Therefore, we must have $S(h) > (3/2)^{h+2}$, so if we let n be the number of nodes in a balanced tree of height h, we have $n > (3/2)^{h+2}$, and taking logs of both sides yields

$$\log n > \log \frac{3}{2}^{h+2} = (h+2)\log \frac{3}{2}$$

Solving for h, we find

$$\frac{\log n}{\log \frac{3}{2}} > h + 2$$

so we have, finally,

$$h < \frac{\log n}{\log \frac{3}{2}} - 2 < K \log n$$

Well, this is just the sort of behavior we wanted: The height of a balanced tree with n nodes is always less than some multiple of $\log n$, since every balanced tree of height h must have at least as many nodes as F_h. In Figure 7.3, we illustrate the first few Fibonacci trees.

AVL Trees

A consistent theme of this book has been that the operations on a data structure be structure preserving: All the list operations maintained the linear structure of the lists upon which they operated, and all the operations on binary search trees preserved the binary search tree property of left-right order. We want to do the same thing with balanced trees: to define the BST operations in such a way that the trees stay balanced at all times, while at the same time preserving the binary search tree property. The algorithms we will pre-

FIGURE 7.3

Some Fibonacci trees

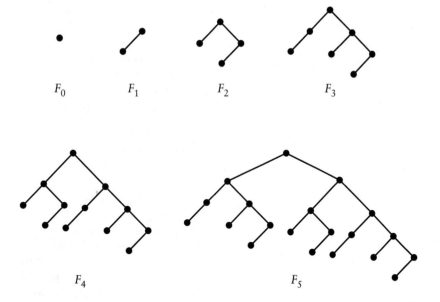

F_0 F_1 F_2 F_3

F_4 F_5

sent were published in 1962 by G. M. Adel'son-Velskii and Y. M. Landis, and in their honor, the elements of this data structure are called **AVL trees**.

The essential parts of the insertion and deletion algorithms for AVL trees will be exactly the same as for binary search trees. However, insertion or deletion could cause a previously balanced tree to become unbalanced, as would happen in the following tree if we inserted 25 or deleted 9. Should that happen, we will call a "fire-fighting" algorithm to rebalance the tree.

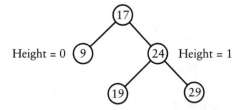

To facilitate the balancing algorithm, we will implement AVL trees in almost exactly the same way we implemented binary search trees, with the exception that each node will contain an additional member datum that stores the height of the subtree rooted at that node.

```
template<class T>
class TreeNode
{
public:
    TreeNode(T e)
        : data(e), leftPtr(NULL), rightPtr(NULL) { } ;
```

```
TreeNode(T e, TreeNode<T>* left, TreeNode<T>* right)
  : data(e), leftPtr(left), rightPtr(right) { } ;

T data;                 // information stored in node
int height;             // height of the tree rooted here
TreeNode<T> *leftPtr,   // ptr to left child
            *rightPtr;  // ptr to right child
} ;
```

We will restore the balance of an AVL tree by **rotations** of the tree at or below the node where the imbalance was detected. There are two possible cases with which we must deal, and they both come in two flavors, each a mirror image of the other. In describing the two cases, we will assume that one flavor of the imbalance was caused by the right subtree of a node x being too high, either by an insertion to the right of x or a deletion to the left of x. We will denote the root of the right subtree of x by y throughout this discussion. The other flavor, in which the imbalance was caused by the left subtree of x being too high, is dealt with in an analogous fashion, interchanging "left" and "right" in all of the subsequent discussions.

Case 1 Suppose that the right subtree of y has height larger than that of the left subtree of y, as in Figure 7.4, caused by deletion of a node from subtree A or insertion into subtree C. We see that a left rotation preserves the left-right order A, x, B, y, C, so that the binary search tree property is preserved by left rotations, and that the left rotation in this case has restored the balance at node x.

```
void RotateLeft(TreeNode<T>*& x)
// Rotate nodes pointed to by x and x->rightPtr.
{
   if ((x) && (x->rightPtr))
   {
      TreeNode<T>* y = x->rightPtr;
      // Make the left subtree of y the right subtree of x.
      x->rightPtr = y->leftPtr;
      // x becomes left child of y.
      y->leftPtr = x;
      // y becomes new root of whole subtree.
      x = y;
   }
}
```

If we had been in the mirror-image situation to that of Figure 7.4a, we would restore balance by a right rotation. (As we mentioned, we would define *RotateRight* by interchanging the words "left" and "right" everywhere in the foregoing definition.) Of course, by restoring balance at x, we may have changed the height of the subtree rooted at x, so we may have to continue the balanc-

FIGURE 7.4

Restoring right imbalance by left rotation

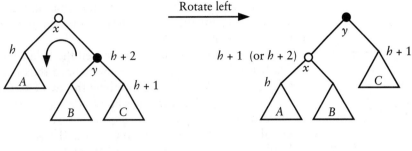

(a)   Unbalanced   **(b)**   Balance restored

ing process at the parent of *x,* and so on, up to the root of the AVL tree, but that won't cause any serious difficulties, as you'll see.

Case 2 Suppose now that the imbalance at *x* is caused by the left subtree of *y* being too high, as in Figure 7.5. You should be able to convince yourself that in this case a simple rotation will not be sufficient to restore balance at *x.* We must perform two rotations, and to do this we must begin one level farther down the tree.

In Figure 7.6, we have expanded subtree *B* into its root and subtrees *B′* and *B″*, one of which must have height *h* in this case, and show the result of the first rotation, at the right child of *x.* Of course, the tree is still not bal-

FIGURE 7.5

Left child of right child too high

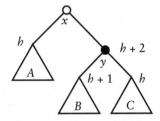

FIGURE 7.6

Case 2, first step in restoring balance

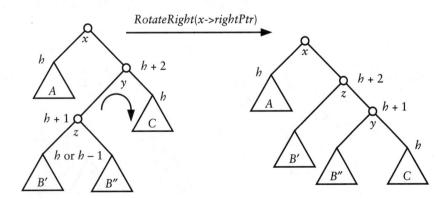

anced, and it looks as if we have done the rotation for nothing. However, the stage is now set for the second step, a rotation at *x*, which will restore the balance we sought (see Figure 7.7).

Notice that not only have we restored the balance (at least of the subtree originally rooted at *x*), but we have maintained the original left-right order *A*, *x*, *B′*, *z*, *B″*, *y*, *C*. We can now combine the two balancing procedures into a single procedure, *BalanceRight*. For both *BalanceRight* and *BalanceLeft*, which is defined similarly, we require an auxiliary function, *Difference*, which takes a node pointer as argument and returns the difference between the heights of the left and right subtrees of the argument node.

```
int Difference(TreeNode<T>* n)
// Returns the height difference between the left and right
// subtrees of the node pointed to by n.
{
    if (n == NULL)
        return 0;

    int leftHeight;
    if (n->leftPtr == NULL)
        leftHeight = -1;
    else
        leftHeight = n->left->height;

    int rightHeight;
    if (n->rightPtr == NULL)
        rightHeight = -1;
    else
        rightHeight = n->right->height;

    return (leftHeight - rightHeight);
}
```

We may now define *BalanceRight*. When reading the definition, notice that we adjust the heights of the nodes after balancing. In this regard, Figures

FIGURE 7.7

Case 2, second step in restoring balance

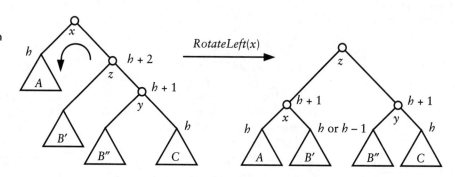

7.4 through 7.7 are slightly misleading in that they show nodes x, y, and z as labeled, although strictly speaking, the nodes are accessed by pointers, so that, for instance, in the single rotation in Figure 7.4, the pointer *n* in *BalanceRight* points to the old root, *x*, prior to the function's execution, and to the new root, *y*, after the function's return. In other words, before *BalanceRight* in Figure 7.4a, *n* points to *x*, and *n–>rightPtr* points to *y*, while in Figure 7.4b, *n* points to *y*, and *n–>leftPtr* points to *x*.

```
void BalanceRight(TreeNode<T>*& n)
// Restores balance at n, assuming that the right subtree of n
// is too high.
{
    if (Difference(n->right) == 0)
    {
    // Case 1(a): both subtrees of right child of n have same height.
        RotateLeft(n);
        n->height = n->height - 1;
        n->leftPtr->height = n->leftPtr->height + 1;
    }
    else if (Difference(n->right) < 0) // (Use '>' in BalanceLeft.)
    {
    // Case 1(b): right subtree of right child of n is higher.
        RotateLeft(n);
        n->leftPtr->height = n->leftPtr->height - 2;
    }
    else
    {
    // Case 2: left subtree of right child of n is higher.
        RotateRight(n->rightPtr);
        RotateLeft(n);
        n->height = n->height + 1;
        n->leftPtr->height = n->leftPtr->height - 2;
        n->rightPtr->height = n->rightPtr->height - 1;
    }
}
```

Although we have not defined *RotateRight* or *BalanceLeft*, we may do so easily by interchanging "left" and "right" in the definitions of *RotateLeft* and *BalanceRight*, respectively.

At last, we can define *Insert* for AVL trees. If you compare the following definition with the definition of *Insert* for BSTs, you'll see that the only difference is that here we test for imbalance upon the return from the recursive call to *Insert* and do whatever balancing is necessary. When reading the algorithm, remember that the precondition for *Insert(n)* is that the subtree rooted at *n* is balanced and that after *Insert(n)*, the subtree is again balanced. Note also that we make use of an auxiliary routine, *FixHeight*, which corrects the height of a node after insertion into one of its subtrees.

```
void FixHeight(TreeNode<T>* n)
// Sets the correct height for node pointed to by n.
// Used after insertion or deletion.
{
   int leftHt;
   if (n->leftPtr == NULL)
      leftHt = -1;
   else
      leftHt = n->leftPtr->height;

   int rightHt;
   if (n->rightPtr == NULL)
      rightHt = -1;
   else
      rightHt = n->rightPtr->height;

   if (leftHt > rightHt)
      n->height = leftHt + 1;
   else
      n->height = rightHt + 1;
}


procedure Insert(T a, TreeNode<T>*& p)
// Inserts a in the subtree rooted at p.
{
   if (p == NULL)  // Found where a  belongs, build a new node.
   {
      TreeNode<T>* p = new TreeNode<T>(a);
      p->height = 0;
   }
   else
   {
      if (a < p->data)            // a belongs in left subtree of p.
         Insert(a, p->leftPtr)
      else if (a > p->data)       // a belongs in right subtree of p.
         Insert(a, p->rightPtr);
      FixHeight(p);               // Adjust height if subtree grew.

      if (Difference(p) > 1)    // Left subtree is too high.
         BalanceLeft(p)
      else if (Difference(p) < -1)
         BalanceRight(p)
   }
}
```

Using *Insert* as a guide, it should not be difficult to define *DeleteMin* and *Delete* for AVL trees. We leave these definitions as exercises, and simply observe that all that is necessary is to balance the tree, if necessary, after each recursive call has returned.

Efficiency and Verification

Has all this work been worth it? By using *BalanceRight* and *BalanceLeft* after every recursive call to *Insert* or *Delete,* we have guaranteed that a tree with *n* nodes will always have height $O(\log n)$, so the insertion, deletion, and *Find* operations will make no more than a logarithmic number of recursive calls. It would appear that we've done what we set out to, but we have to be a bit careful. Two things could mess us up: The balancing functions could take longer than constant time, or they might be called more than $O(\log n)$ times. It is easy to see that the balancing algorithms run in constant time; after all, they consist of nothing but straight-line code, with no loops or recursive calls.

If you look at the definition of *Insert,* you'll see that the balancing functions are called at most once for each recursive call to *Insert.* That's all we need; the balancing functions contribute a constant amount of time for each of the (no more than logarithmic) times they're called.

Finally, we mentioned that a balance operation at a node will restore balance at that node, but might change the height of that node in such a way as to require a balancing of the node's parent. Fortunately, that's taken care of by the nature of calls in *Insert.* Notice that *Insert* builds a stack of pending function calls as it walks its way down the tree to find where the new element belongs. Once the new node has been built and inserted, the pending calls are popped from the stack, effectively retracing the path used to find where the new node belonged. Look at where the balancing functions are called: just before the end of each call. That means that as *Insert* backs its way up the tree, it calls the balancing functions to restore balance from bottom up, exactly as required.

7.2   B-TREES

By now you should be completely comfortable with the principle that the timing of the search tree operations is driven by the height of the tree. As long as we can keep our tree broad and shallow, we can be sure that all our tree operations will be fast, which is to say logarithmic. With AVL trees, we kept the tree shallow by forcing the heights of the subtrees of any node to be nearly equal, using rotations to restore balance each time we inserted or deleted an element. The best case, the one in which the tree had the maximum number of elements for a given height, is clearly obtained with a complete binary tree, and we saw in Chapter 6 that the height of a complete binary tree with n nodes is always less than $\log_2 n$. It would seem that we can't do any better than that, but in this section we will show a tree data structure that does indeed have less depth than $\log_2 n$ for n nodes, and we will explore the reasons that this data structure has become the standard in many applications.

k-ary Trees, Again

Up to now, we have concentrated almost entirely on binary trees, on the grounds that (1) they are easy to implement, (2) there are many good applications using binary trees, and (3) any tree can be mapped to a binary tree, anyway, with leftmost children becoming left children and right siblings becoming right children. The problem with this mapping is that we usually wind up with a binary tree that is higher than the original. Since we are interested in keeping the height of the tree as small as possible, it might be worth exploring these trees in more depth (pun intended).

Recall that a k-ary tree (also called a **multiway tree** of order k) is just a tree in which every node may have as many as k children, for some integer k. In Figure 7.8, we show a 4-ary search tree. Notice that each node has at most four children, and each node has one less data element in it than it has children. Notice also that this tree generalizes the binary search tree property, in that the pointers between data elements in each node point to subtrees, each of which has all its data values strictly between the values that bracket the pointer. For instance, suppose we are searching for the element 71 in the tree. We begin at the root and find (perhaps by a sequential search) that 71 lies between the elements 34 and 80. We then take the pointer to the subtree whose values lie between 34 and 80 and repeat the process. We find that 71 is larger than the last element, 68, in that node, so we follow the pointer to the subtree whose values are all larger than 68 (and necessarily less than 80). We repeat the search at the leaf node and find 71 among the values in that leaf node, so the search is successful. If we were seeking 70, we would attempt to take the leftmost pointer in the 71

FIGURE 7.8

A 4-ary search tree, showing the search path for 71

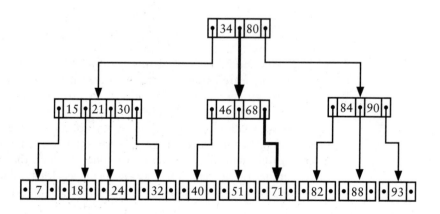

node, find that it was NULL, and report failure, since there is no subtree that could possibly contain 70.

In the tree of Figure 7.8, notice that all the leaves are at the same level. This is certainly a stronger condition than we had for AVL trees. This will be one of the properties of the data structure we will introduce in this section; and it, along with a condition we will require on the sizes of the nodes, will enable us to get a good estimate on the height of such trees if we know the number of nodes in the tree. For now, we will just note that because of the higher **fanout**—that is, the number of pointers out of the nodes—we can pack much more information in a multiway tree than we could in a binary tree of the same height. For instance, Figure 7.8 shows 19 data elements in a tree of height 2, whereas a binary tree would need to be at least twice that height to store the same amount of information.

B-Trees Explained

We define a **B-tree of order** d to have as its structure a $(2d+1)$-ary tree with the following properties:

1. The data elements (or at least the key fields) in each node are assumed to be linearly ordered. If the data elements are records consisting of several fields, then one field of the record is a key field, with values taken from a linearly ordered set.
2. Each internal node has one more child than it does data elements (and leaves, of course, have no children).
3. The root contains between 1 and $2d$ data elements.
4. Each node except for the root contains between d and $2d$ data elements.
5. All leaves are at the same depth in the tree.
6. The tree has the **extended search tree property:** If the keys in a node n are arranged in their linear order, $k_1, k_2, \ldots, k_m$, then there is an associated linear order among the subtrees, $S_0, S_1, \ldots, S_m$, of that node such that (a) every key in S_0 is less than k_1, (b) every key in S_m is greater than k_m, and (c) for $1 \leq i < m$, every key in S_i lies strictly between k_i and k_{i+1}.

Note that the binary search tree property is just condition 6 with $m=1$, with S_0 representing the left subtree and S_1 the right subtree. Condition 4 can be restated this way: Each node except for the root is at least half full. B-trees were introduced by R. Bayer and E. M. McCreight in 1972, and folklore has it that they have never explained the choice of name for this particular data structure, so you are free to speculate on what the "B" stands for. B-trees were designed to support the operations *Insert, Delete, Find* a data element, given its key; *Update* an element without changing its key; and *FindNext*, which, when given a key value k, returns the least key k_i in the tree for which

$k < k_i$. The operation *Insert* is particularly ingenious and differs from the insertion algorithms for the tree structures we've seen so far in that if the tree ever needs to change its height, it does so by growing up from the root rather than down from a leaf.

To illustrate the action of *Insert,* consider a B-tree of order 2. In such a tree, the root may have from one to four elements, while all the rest of the nodes must have either two, three, or four elements. In Figure 7.9a, we see the root after having inserted the elements 17, 45, 13, and 26. As each new element arrives, it is placed in order in the root. When the element 30 arrives, it cannot be placed in the root node—there's no more room. What we do in this case is the heart of the insertion algorithm: We split the root into equal parts, one containing all the elements below the median, 26, and the other containing all the elements above the median. The median value itself gets promoted to a new root node, which has the split nodes as children, as in Figure 7.9b.

If we continue by inserting 28 and 41, we see that they are both greater than 26, so, by the search tree property, they belong in the right subtree of the root node, as they are in Figure 7.9c. Now, if we insert 50, we see that it should also go in the rightmost node. Of course, there's no room for it, so we again split the node into two and promote the median value, 41, to the parent node. If the parent node had been full, we would have had to split it and promote its median to a new root node. That's all there is to insertion: We try to place each node in its proper leaf, and if that would cause overflow, we split the node, promote the median value, and try to insert the promoted value into the parent node, splitting when necessary, tracking up the tree until we arrive at a node that does not overflow.

FIGURE 7.9

Inserting into a B-tree

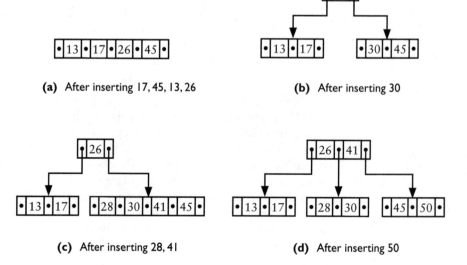

(a) After inserting 17, 45, 13, 26

(b) After inserting 30

(c) After inserting 28, 41

(d) After inserting 50

If it sounds pretty simple, that's because it is—at least for people. Things get a bit more complicated when we try to translate the insertion process into algorithmic form, largely because we humans can pretty much automatically take care of such details as inserting an element into a node, splitting a node, and deciding where an element belongs in the tree—operations that require a moderate amount of fussy detail to program. We will provide a detailed account of the insertion algorithm from the top down; then, having done that, we will provide a sketch of the details of deletion and leave the programming to you.

The node declarations are immediate. Each node in the B-tree will consist of an array of data elements, a larger array of pointers to children, and a field for the present size of the array.

```
const int ORDER = 4;   // Global constant for order of tree


template<class T>
class BTreeNode
{
public:
   // The usual constructors go here.

   T data[1 + 2 * ORDER];   // We'll never use data[0].
   BTreeNode<T>* child[1 + 2 * ORDER];
   int size;
}
```

The insertion routine itself is little more than a shell. Most of the work is done by a recursive function, *RecursiveInsert,* which inserts an atom *a* into the tree rooted at *root.* If the insertion causes the root to be split, *root* then points to the left split node, *rp* points to the right split node (and is NULL if no splitting occurs at the root), and *promoted* is the atom that must be promoted to the new root.

```
void Insert(T a, BTreeNode<T>*& root)
{
   BTreeNode* temp, rp;
   T promoted;
   RecursiveInsert(a, root, rp, promoted);

   if (rp)      // Root was split, so build a new root.
   {
      temp = root;
      root = new BTreeNode<T>;
      root->size = 1;
      root->data[1] = promoted;
      root->child[0] = temp;
      root->child[1] = rp;
   }
}
```

RecursiveInsert inserts atom *a* into the subtree rooted at *p*. First it scans the node at *p* for the location at which *a* would belong. The procedure *ScanNode* returns the index in the data array of *p* where *a*'s key is located (in which case there is nothing to do, since we don't allow duplicate keys in the tree) or the location after which *a* would belong. That location is also the index of the pointer to the subtree where *a* belongs, and if that subtree is empty, the recursion stops there and inserts *a* into the leaf at *p*. If, on the other hand, the subtree where *a* belongs is not empty, then the procedure calls *RecursiveInsert* again on the subtree. In either case, the insertion could have caused a split and a promotion. If the procedure *AddData* has caused a split of the node at *p*, the promoted atom and a pointer to the right split node are returned to *RecursiveInsert*, to be used as the routine backs out of the recursion.

```
void RecursiveInsert(T a,
                     BTreeNode<T>*& p,
                     BTreeNode<T>*& rp,
                     T promoted)
{
   int   index,      // where a belongs
         found;      // = 1 if a is already in this node

   ScanNode(a, p, index, found);
   if (!found)       // We don't insert duplicate keys.

      if (p->child[index] == NULL)
      // We're at a leaf, so insert a where it belongs.
      {
         rp = NULL;
         // AddData may cause a promotion and a split.
         AddData(a, index, p, rp, promoted);
      }
      else
      // We're not at a leaf, so continue with a recursive
      // call on the subtree where a belongs.
      {
         RecursiveInsert(a, p->child[index], rp, promoted);
         if (rp)
         // Insertion caused split, so insert promoted element.
         {
            // Find where promoted element goes.
            ScanNode(promoted, p, index, found);
            // Place promoted element where it belongs.
            AddData(promoted, index, p, rp, promoted)
         }
      }
}
```

The last three routines are utility routines, used by *AddData* and *RecursiveInsert*. They need little comment, except that *ScanNode*, which looks through the node at *p* for the location at which *a*'s key is found or after which *a* belongs, uses a sequential search through the data array. If, as often happens, the order of the B-tree is quite large, it might save time to implement a binary search, such as we gave in Chapter 1, instead.

```
void ScanNode(T k, BTreeNode<T>* p, int& index, int& found)
// Searches for key k in node at p.  If k is in the node,
// sets found to 1 and sets index to location in data array where
// k is.  If k is not in the node, sets found to 0 and sets index
// to location after which k would be placed.  For unsuccessful
// search, index is also the location in the child array of the
// subtree where k belongs.
{
    // Do a linear search for k.
    index = 0;
    while ((index < p->size) && (k < p->data[index + 1]))
        index++;

    if ((index > 0) && (k = p->data[index]))
        found = 1;
    else
        found = 0;
}


void Copy( BTreeNode<T>* p, int pLo, int pHi,
           BTreeNode<T>* q, int qLo, int qHi)
// Copies the data and child arrays in the node at p, from indices
// pLo to pHi, into the node at q, from indices qLo  to qHi.
// Requires that ranges are the same size, and that qLo ≤ qHi,
// otherwise does nothing.  This routine works correctly even if
// p = q, in which case the effect is to shift the segment
// by qLo - pLo.
{
    if ((pHi - pLo == qHi - qLo) && (qLo <= qHi))

        if ((p != q) || ((p == q) && (qLo < pLo)))
        // Different nodes or shifting left in the same node
            for (int i = qLo; i <= qHi; i++)
            {
                q->data[i] = p->data[i - qLo + pLo];
                q->child[i] = p->child[i - qLo + pLo];
            }
        else
        // Same nodes or shifting right in the same node
```

```
            for (i = qHi; i >= qLo; i--)
            {
                q->data[i] = p->data[i - qHi + pHi];
                q->child[i] = p->child[i - qHi + pHi];
            }
    }


void AddData(T a,
             int index,
             BTreeNode<T>*& p,
             BTreeNode<T>*& rp,
             T& promoted)
// Inserts atom a and pointer rp into data and child arrays of node
// at p.  If node at p is not full, performs simple insertion and
// returns NULL pointer for rp, indicating no split was necessary.
// If node at p is already full, the node is split into left and
// right halves, pointed to by p and rp, respectively, and the
// median element is returned via promoted.
{
    if (p->size < 2 * ORDER)
    // Node at p is not yet full, so just do a simple insertion.
    {
        if (index < p->size)  // Must shift right to make room for a.
            Copy(p, index + 1, p->size, p, index + 2, p->size + 1);
        p->size = p->size + 1;
        p->data[index + 1] = a;
        p->child[index + 1] = rp;
    }
    else
    // No room to insert, must split node at p.
    {
        int half = ORDER / 2;
        BTreeNode<T>* save = rp;
        // Set up split and build a new right node.
        rp = new BTreeNode;
        rp->size = half;
        p->size = half;

        if (index <= half)
        // a is either median or belongs in left split node.
        {
            // Put half of arrays in right node.
            Copy(p, half + 1, MAX, rp, 1, half);
            if (index == half)  // a is median element, so promote it.
```

```
        {
            promoted = a;
            rp->child[0] = save;
        }
        else
        // a isn't median; promote true median and insert a.
        {
            promoted = p->data[half];
            rp->child[0] = p->child[half];
            // Shift right to make room for a.
            Copy(p, index + 1, half - 1, p, index + 2, half);  { }
            p^.data[index + 1] := a;
            p^.child[index + 1] := save;
        }
    else
    // a belongs in right split node.
    {
        rp->child[0] = p->child[half + 1];
        promoted = p->data[half + 1];
        // Copy up to where a will be.
        Copy(p, half + 2, index, rp, 1, index - half - 1);
        rp->data[index - half] = a;
        rp->child[index - half] = save;
        // Copy everything after a.
        Copy(p, index + 1, MAX, rp, index - half + 1, half);
    }
    }
}
```

Deletion is not much more difficult than insertion. As with insertion, we begin at a leaf and work our way up the tree, restoring the B-tree properties as we go. If the element to be deleted is not located in a leaf, we start as we did with deletion in a binary search tree by replacing the deleted element with the leftmost element in the right subtree of the deleted element. That leftmost element must be a leaf (why?), so we begin the deletion proper at that leaf. In pseudocode, the algorithm looks like this:

```
void Delete(T a, BTreeNode<T>*& root);
// Deletes the atom with key k  from the B-tree at root.
{
```

Find the element to be deleted, a_i, in location i in the node at p;

```
    if (p is not a leaf)
    {
```

Replace a_i with the leftmost element, a, in the right subtree, S_i, of p;

```
        p = the node where a was located;
    }
```

```
     int done = 0;
     while (!done)
(a)    if (p->size > d)
       {
           Remove a from p;

           p->size = p->size - 1;
           done = 1;
       }
(b)    else if (p has an immediate left or right sibling, q, of size>d)
       {
           Remove an element from q;

           Place an element from p's parent in p;

           Replace the parent element with the element borrowed from q;

           done = 1;
       }
(c)    else
       {
           Merge p with one of its immediate siblings; include a parent element;

           if (p's parent would be too small after the borrowing)
           {
               a = the element removed from p's parent;
               p = p's parent;
           }
           else
               done = 1;
       }
}
```

In Figure 7.10, we illustrate the three possible cases in the deletion algorithm, with the element to be deleted indicated by a dashed-line cell In case a, there are more than d elements in the node, so we may simply eliminate the element to be deleted. In case b, the node where the deleted element was has too few elements to allow a simple deletion, but an immediate sibling node has an element to spare. In this case, we borrow from the parent (as so often happens in the real world) and let the sibling repay the debt (which happens somewhat less frequently). In cases a and b, the size of the parent node does not change, so there is no need to travel farther up the tree. In case c, however, the node containing the deleted element and the sibling nodes are as small as they can be. What we do in this case is merge the node with the deleted element and one of its siblings together, for a total of $2d-1$ elements, and in-

FIGURE 7.10

Deleting from a node
in an order 2 B-tree

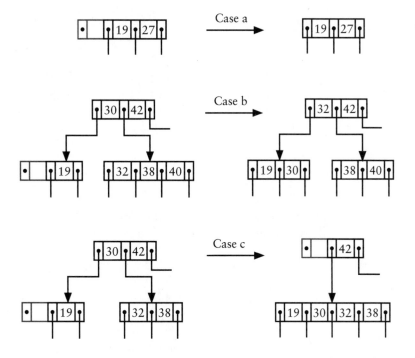

clude the parent element between the two siblings, to form a new node of size *d*. This reduces the size of the parent node by 1, so we may need to repeat the restoration process at the parent if the reduction caused the parent to underflow below the minimum size *d*.

Don't let the mass of detail intimidate you. You might be tempted at first glance to say that B-trees stand for "beastly trees," or but just reread the descriptive example of *Insert* and bear in mind that most of the routines are doing pretty simple things, however complicated they look. That's not to say that the implementation is trivial, by any means, which might prompt the alert reader to say, "Yeah, the idea is simple enough, but before I'd want to use B-trees, I'd need some convincing that they are enough of an improvement over, say, binary search trees to be worth the effort."

Let's begin our investigation of the efficiency of B-trees by looking at the maximum value that the height, *h,* of a B-tree of order *d* with *n* nodes could be. As we did with balanced trees, we'll look at the problem in reverse: What is the smallest possible number of nodes that there could be in an order *d* B-tree of height *h*? The root could have as few as one element and in that case would have two children. Every nonroot node must have at least *d* elements and either *d*+1 children if it is an internal node or no children if it is a leaf. We then have the minimal number of nodes per level given by Table 7.1.

Looking at the column for cumulative nodes in Table 7.1, we see that the number of nodes, *n*, in an order *d* B-tree must satisfy $n \geq 1 + 2(1 + (d+1) + \cdots + (d+1)^{h-1})$, where *h* is the height of the tree. The term on the right is just

TABLE 7.1

Minimal number of nodes in an order d B-tree

Depth	Nodes	Children per Node	Cumulative Nodes
0	1	2	1
1	2	$d+1$	$1+2$
2	$2(d+1)$	$d+1$	$1+2+2(d+1)$
3	$2(d+1)^2$	$d+1$	$1+2+2(d+1)+2(d+1)^2$
$\vdots$	$\vdots$	$\vdots$	$\vdots$
h	$2(d+1)^{h-1}$	0	$1+2(1+(d+1)+\cdots+(d+1)^{h-1})$

a geometric series, that is, a sum of the form $1+r+\cdots+r^n$, and we know that the sum of such a series is equal to $(r^{n+1}-1)/(r-1)$, so we have

$$n \geq 1 + 2\frac{(d+1)^h - 1}{d} = 1 + \frac{2}{d}(d+1)^h - \frac{2}{d} \geq \frac{2}{d}(d+1)^h$$

for $d \geq 2$, and if we take the logarithm to the base $d+1$ of both sides, we see that we have

$$\log_{d+1} n \geq \log_{d+1}\frac{2}{d} + h$$

so that

$$h \leq \log_{d+1} n - \log_{d+1}\frac{2}{d} \leq \left(\log_{d+1} n\right) + 1 \quad \text{for } d \geq 2$$

Now except for the root, each node in our B-tree must contain at least d data elements, so to store N data elements should certainly not require much more than $2N/d$ nodes. (In fact, it's not hard to show that it requires no more than $1+(N-1)/d$ nodes.) The point of all this is that with even moderately small values for d, we can fit a lot of information into a very shallow B-tree. In Table 7.2, we show the heights of B-trees of various orders necessary to store data sets of size N, using

$$h \leq 1 + \log_{d+1}\left(1 + \frac{N-1}{d}\right)$$

TABLE 7.2

Heights of B-trees needed to store large data sets

Order	Number of Elements					
	10^4	10^5	10^6	10^7	10^8	10^9
16	4	5	5	6	7	8
32	3	4	4	5	6	6
64	3	3	4	4	5	5

These are very impressive numbers. For example, to store a billion data elements in a B-tree of order 16 requires a tree of height 8 at most, whereas a binary search tree containing that many elements would have height at least 29, and perhaps as large as 999,999,999.

This is not the whole story, however. We may not have to visit very many nodes to insert an element, for example, but that gain might be offset by the amount of work required to split the nodes in order to restore the necessary B-tree properties. We don't have to worry about the amount of work required by splitting, though, for several reasons. First, to insert a node, we never have to split more nodes than the height of the tree plus 1, since we split by tracking up the tree from a leaf to the root. Second, the amount of work required by each split is obviously proportional to no more than the size of the node being split, and that size is usually negligible when compared with the number of data elements in the entire tree. Finally, as long as the order of the tree is fairly large, there is usually a lot of available space in each node, so we don't have to split nodes very often. In the exercises, you are asked to provide some evidence in support of the fact that in the long run, n insertions will only require about $n/(d-1)$ splits of nodes, or, put in different terms, you need to split a node only about every $1/(d-1)$ of the time.

Application: External Storage

The impetus for the development of B-trees was the problem of rapid file access on an external storage medium, such as a magnetic disk. Such devices have the advantage that they provide for storage of a great deal of information at a cost per byte that is much lower than the cost of internal RAM memory in a computer. Simply speaking, if you need to store millions of bytes of data, it is considerably cheaper to do so on a disk than to pay for megabytes of RAM, so a computer will usually have a disk drive that can store much more information than can be fit into internal memory. This by itself would not be a problem except for one inescapable fact: Information retrieval is much faster if you only have to push electrons around in memory rather than moving comparatively large physical objects like magnetic disks and read-write heads. Typically, you can count on disk access taking 10 to 100 times longer than RAM access, and therein lies the problem.

Generally, one cannot just download a large file from disk to RAM at the start of the day and then forget about the disk until close of business. There just isn't enough room in memory to store the entire file, and the people in the comptroller's office are unwilling to foot the bill for a gigantic computer with the memory needed to hold the entire file. Given the fact that disk access crawls along, compared to memory access, we clearly want to keep the number of times we need to go to the disk to a minimum.

To do this, we not only need to arrange the data in a disk in some efficient fashion, but also need to be able to find out rapidly where the information is. In other words, we need an *index* of some kind to tell us where the record associated with a particular key is located on the disk. For example, we might include on each disk a binary tree containing the keys of the records in the file and the disk addresses where the associated records can be found. If we implement this in a naive fashion, however, we may have to access the disk once for each node in the directory tree during our search, plus once more to retrieve the record itself. One thing that works in our favor is that a request to read or write on a disk is handled in units of many bytes at once, so if we ask for a byte from the disk, what we get is a **block** or **page** of information, typically in the range of 256 to 2048 bytes, depending on the disk and the operating system that handles the disk access. With this in mind, we would be better off arranging our directory tree so that several nodes were located on a single page on the disk. In Figure 7.11, we show such an arrangement, with three nodes stored on a single page.

If we store three nodes of a binary tree on a page, we have in effect produced a four-way tree, if we think of each page as a node. Now we have at least two options: We could store the index separately and associate with each key a disk address where the rest of the record may be found, or we could merge the records with the directory by storing the records in the same nodes as their keys, in much the same way as we stored the free list in the heap when we discussed memory management. Our choice between these options would be guided by (1) the size of the keys, (2) the size of the disk addresses, (3) the size of the records, and (4) the page size. The examples that follow indicate some of the decisions involved in choosing the best size for a B-tree.

Example 1

Suppose we have a 128-megabyte hard disk (that's 2^{27} bytes) divided into pages of 2048 (= 2^{11}) bytes each. That means that there will be 2^{16} pages, so that 2 bytes of 8 bits will suffice to identify each page. Just to be on the safe side, though, we'll assume that disk addresses will be 4 bytes long.

FIGURE 7.11

A binary tree with three nodes per page

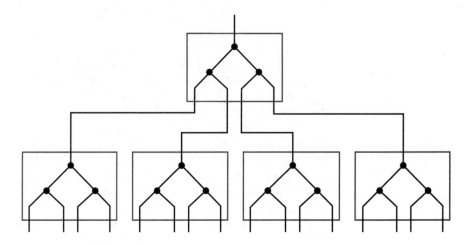

Suppose the entire disk is devoted to one file of N records, each of which requires 512 bytes, so that four records will fit on a page. Suppose also that the key for each record is 4 bytes long. That's enough for a 9-digit Social Security number, for instance. Thus, the key and the disk address for a record together will take 8 bytes, so we can fit 256 of them on a page.

If we keep the index of keys and addresses separate from the records, we see that if we have N records, the total number of pages required for the index will be $\lceil N/256 \rceil$, where the enclosing brackets mean "take the smallest integer that is greater than or equal to what's inside," to account for the fact that N might not be a multiple of 256. At four records per page, we will require $\lceil N/4 \rceil$ pages for the records, and the sum of these two expressions must be no more than the total number of pages, 65,536. It doesn't take much to find that we must have $N \le 258,108$ records in our file, and we will assume that we have exactly that number.

We will now build a B-tree to contain the index. We can fit up to 256 index entries per node (at one page for each node), so we decide to use an order 128 B-tree. The formula for the maximum height, h, of the tree tells us that $h \le 1 + \log_{129}(1 + 258,107/128) = 2.56$, so our tree will have height no more than 3. Therefore, to access any record on the disk will require at most four disk accesses to find the index (remember, there is always one more node in a path than the length of a path), plus one more to get the record itself, for a total of at most five disk accesses. Of course, we may be fortunate enough to be able to store the entire index in RAM, so that once a node was in memory, we would not need further disk accesses to get information from that node.

Suppose the computer we were using had 4 megabytes of RAM available to store the B-tree. Each node of our order 128 B-tree must have room for 256 8-byte indices and 257 4-byte pointers, for a total of $256 \times 8 + 257 \times 4 = 3078$ bytes per node. If we had n nodes, then, they would take up $3078n$ bytes of memory, and since we have 4,194,304 bytes of memory available (4 megabytes $= 2^{22} = 4,194,304$ bytes), we must have $3078n \le 4,194,304$, so $n \le 1362$ nodes will fit in RAM.

Oops! We may be in trouble, since the root may contain only one index element, and the rest of the nodes might contain as few as 128 indices, for a total of $1 + 128 \times 1361 = 174,209$ indices, which is less than the total number of records. So there's a chance that we can't fit the entire index B-tree in memory, meaning we will likely have to swap nodes in and out of memory, requiring disk accesses throughout the life of the program. That being the case, it might be worth our while to see to it that the higher-level nodes, near the root, stay in memory; it would be a disaster, for example, to have to swap the root in and out, because it is used every time we refer to the tree. ◁

Example 2

To get some idea of the time required by disk access, let's suppose further that to access a page on the disk requires 40 milliseconds (0.04 second) of overhead to locate the page, move the read-write head to the page, and wait for the disk to spin into the right position to get the page, and another

$0.001b$ millisecond to transfer a page of b bytes. Let us also suppose that we have some control over the page size (that's not always the case, since page size is under the control of the operating system, and we may not be able to mess with that). We will decide to put one node of the B-tree on each page, so for order d B-trees, we will have $2d$ indices of 8 bytes per page, for a total of $16d$ bytes per page. Recall that we will have at most $2+\log_{d+1}((N-1)/d)+1$ disk accesses to retrieve a record (we ignore the $+1$ inside the log expression, since it's negligible here), and each disk access requires $40+0.001(16d)$ milliseconds, so the maximum amount of time we'll require to get a record will be

$$(40+0.001(16d))\left(3+\log_{d+1}\frac{258{,}107}{d}\right)$$
$$= (40+0.016d)\left(3+\log_{d+1}258{,}107-\log_{d+1}d\right)$$
$$= (40+0.016d)\left(2+\log_{d+1}258{,}107\right)$$

Using the fact that $\log_b A = (\ln A)/(\ln b)$, where ln is the natural logarithm (which you can review in Appendix B), we have the worst-case access time for any record of approximately

$$(40+0.016d)\left(2+\frac{\ln 258{,}107}{\ln(d+1)}\right)\text{ milliseconds}$$

Now we try various values for d and look at access times, summarized in Table 7.3. We see that there is little difference in the access times for B-trees of orders between 128 and 512. We chose orders that were powers of 2 because they made the page sizes evenly divide the amount of disk space, but we could have chosen any d we wished, like the one that leads to the minimum, $d=261$. We'll decide to use $d=256$, though, for a page size of $256\times16=4096$. Note that with $d=128$, we're back to the situation of Example 1, with a page size of 2048. This broad range of nearly identical minimum values is typical and works to our advantage if we don't have much control over page size.   ◁

TABLE 7.3

Worst-case access times for order d B-trees, index in nodes

Order, d	Access Time (milliseconds)
8	307.8
16	257.6
32	225.4
64	204.5
128	191.9
256	187.2
512	192.6
1024	214.1

TABLE 7.4

Worst-case access times for order d B-trees, data in nodes

Order, d	Access Time (milliseconds)
4	385.5
8	321.5
16	304.4
32	332.1

Example 3

We might have decided to eliminate one disk access to get the record by storing the records in the B-tree. In that case, we suppose that we can fit the key, the address, and the rest of the record in 512 bytes. Now, a node of $2d$ data elements requires $1024d$ bytes, so the access time function is

$$(40+1.024d)\left(1+\frac{\ln 258,107}{\ln(d+1)}\right).$$

and we have the worst-case access times given in Table 7.4. In this case, the best access time is 304.4 milliseconds, when $d=16$, for a page size of 16,384 bytes. There's not much point in doing this, though, since the best access time here is 63% greater than if we had stored just the index, as in Example 2. However, this is not always the case, and we will see in the exercises that for different disk characteristics, it may be advantageous to store the data in the B-tree. ◁

7.3 SUMMARY

The running time of most tree algorithms is controlled by the depth of the tree. The two data structures presented in this chapter represent attempts to control this depth in such a way that the depth of a tree with n nodes is $O(\log n)$.

AVL trees are binary search trees with insertion and deletion defined so that the property of being balanced is preserved. For more information, see G. M. Adel'son-Velskii and Y. M. Landis, "An Algorithm for the Organization of Information," *Dokl. Akad. Nauk SSR* 146(1962): 263–266; English translation in *Soviet Math. (Dokl.)* 3(1962): 1259–1263.

B-trees are another generalization of binary search trees. They are multiway trees with insertion and deletion defined so that the number of children of each node always lies within fixed upper and lower limits. B-trees are widely used to provide fast access to externally stored files. For more information, see R. Bayer and E. M. McCreight, "Organization and Maintenance of Large Ordered Indices," *Acta Informatica* 1(1972): 173–189. An excellent survey of the topic may also be found in D. Comer, "The Ubiquitous B-Tree," *Computing Surveys* 11(1979): 121–137.

7.4 EXERCISES

1. Tell which of the following trees are balanced, and if any of them fail to be balanced, indicate the deepest node at which an imbalance occurs.

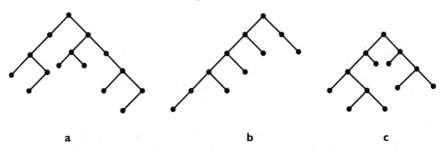

a   b   c

2. We can ensure that a tree will be shallow in a number of ways other than those discussed in this chapter. One such balancing condition is to require that the tree be **weight balanced**, which is to say that at each node, *n,* of the tree, the number of nodes in the left subtree of *n* and the number of nodes in the right subtree of *n* differ by no more than 2. (By the way, if you look at the literature, you are likely to find a number of different meanings for the term *weight balanced.*)

   a. Can you find a binary tree that is balanced but not weight balanced?

   b. Can you find a binary tree that is weight balanced but not balanced?

   c. If the answer to one of these questions was "yes" and the other "no," can you then show that one of the two conditions necessarily implies the other?

   d. Describe a structure-preserving insertion algorithm for weight-balanced binary search trees. Can you use the rotations used in AVL trees to restore weight balance?

3. a. What is the result of inserting 1, 2, 3, . . . , 8 into an initially empty AVL tree?

   b. In general, what happens as you insert 1, 2, 3, . . . into an AVL tree? You might want to say, for instance, what values the root has as the insertions proceed.

4. We can use binary trees, in one flavor or another, to implement the *List* ADT. Even better, we could use binary search trees to implement *SortedList.* Clearly, we would then have fast retrieval, given the key of an element in the list, but we can also provide fast retrieval by position in the list. In other words, we might wish to implement the function

TreeNode* FindNth(int n), which would return a pointer to the element in the *n*th place in the sorted list and return the NULL pointer if *n* is greater than the length of the list.

    a. Show how this could be accomplished by representing sorted lists as binary search trees. *Hint:* The usual way to do this is to include a **rank** field in each node *n*, which contains the number of nodes in the left subtree of *n*.

    b. Discuss the changes, if any, that would be required in *Insert* for this implementation.

    c. Discuss the changes, if any, that would be required if, in the interest of speed, we had decided to implement *SortedList* using AVL trees.

5. **a.** Show the AVL tree that results if the integer keys 17, 8, 29, 20, 27, 13, 28 are inserted, in that order, into an initially empty AVL tree.

    b. Show the successive trees that result when the tree in part (a) then has the elements deleted in the order in which they were inserted, beginning with 17.

6. Repeat Exercise 5 for a B-tree of order 2.

7. In this exercise, we will investigate what happens when the keys 1, 2, 3, . . . , *n* are successively inserted into a B-tree of order *d*.

    a. For $d=2$, for what key values is the root split, and what element is promoted to the new root when the root splits?

    b. For $d=2$, what is the total number of splits that have occurred by the time key *n* has been inserted?

    c. For $d=2$, what are the largest and smallest values of *n* for which the tree has height *h* ?

  d–f. Repeat parts (a) through (c) for arbitrary order *d* B-trees.

8. It stands to reason that when the records of a file are not too large when compared with the size of the keys, it might be better to store the records as well as the keys in the B-tree.

    a. Repeat Examples 2 and 3 of the text with records of size 50, and find optimal page sizes and worst-case access times. You may assume that all other figures are the same, including the number of records.

    b. Try different values for disk overhead, transfer speed, number of records, record size, and key size, and see if you can come up with a rule of thumb to determine whether it is better to store all information in the B-tree, rather than just the keys.

9. In Examples 1 through 3, we ignored the fact that most of the quantities—in particular, the depth of the trees—were integers. Redo the examples with this in mind, and see if there is any substantial difference in the values you obtain for access times.

10. In a B-tree, there is a lot of wasted space taken up by the leaves, since they must have room for $2d+1$ pointers, all of which are NULL. Furthermore, a significant number of nodes in a B-tree are leaves.

   a. In a B-tree of order d, what fraction of nodes are leaves? Your answer should be something like "between _____ and _____ of the nodes are leaves," where the blanks might be functions of n, the number of nodes in the tree.

   b. In a B-tree of order d, where the data elements require 8 bytes each, and pointers require 4 bytes each, how much space is wasted by NULL pointers?

   c. Discuss how you might change the implementation of B-trees to eliminate this waste space.

11. Implement AVL trees, and investigate the average number of single and double rotations required to construct an AVL tree by inserting n randomly chosen elements into an initially empty tree.

12. Implement and test *Delete* for AVL trees.

13. Redo Exercise 11 for B-trees, counting the number of splits, rather than rotations.

14. Modify the implementation of B-trees by including a pointer in each node to the parent of that node. Write *Insert* for this implementation, and comment on the advantages and disadvantages compared to the definition in the text.

15. Implement and test *Delete* for B-trees.

16. In a **B*-tree**, each node except for the root is at least two-thirds full. This is accomplished by avoiding splits whenever possible. *Insert* for B*-trees is almost like *Insert* for B-trees, borrowing from siblings when possible, except that when a node and both of its immediate siblings are full, the three full nodes are merged into two, with appropriate adjustment of the data in the parent. Implement *Insert* for B*-trees, and discuss the merits of this scheme, particularly with respect to the height of the tree and the number of splits required to build the tree.

8

GRAPHS AND DIGRAPHS

The diagram in Figure 8.1 is loosely based on the eastern half of ARPANET, a network (hence the NET part of the name) of computers developed by the Advanced Research Projects Agency (the ARPA part of the name) of the U.S. Department of Defense. This network was the ancestor of today's *Internet* and was first placed into operation in 1969. If we imagine that we were the designers of the network back then, it is not hard to come up with a number of questions that might have been of interest to us at the time.

1. What is the average number of *hops* in the shortest path between nodes, where a hop is an intermediate site through which a message must be passed? For example, to pass a message from DARCOM to HARVARD through ABERDEEN and NYU requires two hops, and that is clearly the least number possible for those two sites.

2. Is there any node that, if it went down, would make communications between some two nodes impossible, at least for the network as drawn? Is there any line that would similarly disrupt communications if it went down?

3. What is the largest number of hops a message must take between two given nodes?

4. What is the smallest subset of lines that must be present to guarantee communication between every pair of nodes?

5. If each line has associated with it a cost for communication, what is the least-cost collection of lines that must be present to guarantee communication between every pair of nodes?

297

FIGURE 8.1

Part of the old
ARPANET

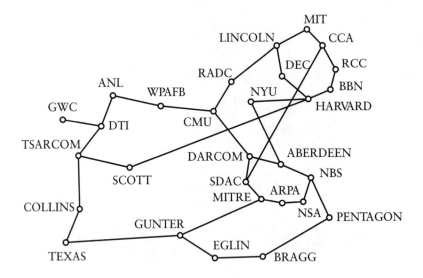

6. What is the least number of total hops required for every node to communicate its status to the Network Control Center at BBN?

In this chapter, we will investigate the data structures and algorithms that will allow us to answer these and other questions. We will see that some of these questions can be answered easily; some will require algorithms of fairly high time complexity; some are known to be infeasible, even for the fastest computers; and some we suspect are infeasible, although they have not yet been proved so.

8.1   ADT: *GRAPH*

We know that the structure of a tree is determined by a relation for which every position has at most one immediate predecessor. (In fact, every position except the root has exactly one immediate predecessor, and the root has no predecessor at all.) In this respect, a tree is exactly the same as a list. They differ in that a position in a tree may have more than one immediate successor, whereas every position in a list has a unique successor, if it has a successor at all. In this chapter, we will continue our program of relaxing restrictions on the structural relation to produce new structures. In particular, we will now remove the last restriction and allow a position to have any number of immediate predecessors, as well as any number of immediate successors.

If we think of the structural relation as providing logical links between positions, we now have a **network** structure consisting of positions linked by a relation in any way we wish, as shown in the examples in Figure 8.2. Depending on the additional properties we place on the structural relation, these

FIGURE 8.2

Some network
structures

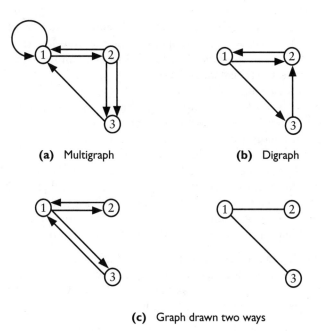

(a) Multigraph   **(b)** Digraph

(c) Graph drawn two ways

network structures may be classified into three groups. A **multigraph** has no
restrictions at all on its structure: Positions may be linked to themselves (as
with position 1 in Figure 8.2a), and there may be several links between two
positions (as from position 2 to position 3 in Figure 8.2a, which, by the way,
is immediately outlawed if we use a single relation to provide links—do you
see why?). The relation that describes a **digraph** must be *irreflexive,* as in Figure 8.2b, which is another way of saying that no position may be linked to itself. A **graph**, finally, is defined by a structural relation that is irreflexive and
symmetric, so that whenever there is a link from position *p* to position *q*,
there is also a link from *q* to *p*. In such a situation, there is no need to draw
both links with their arrows, so we dispense with them and draw single lines
instead. We will discuss graphs first and then consider digraphs.

A graph is usually described as an ordered pair $G=(V, E)$ of sets, where
V can be any set (but we will insist that it be finite here), and E consists of (not
necessarily all the) two-element subsets of V. The set V is called the **vertices** of
G, and E is known as the **edges** of G. (You will frequently see vertices referred
to as **nodes**, especially in computer science literature.) For example, the graph
in Figure 8.2c would be written as $G=(V, E)=(\{1, 2, 3\}, \{\{1, 2\}, \{1, 3\}\})$. This
graph has three vertices—1, 2, 3—and two edges—$\{1, 2\}, \{1, 3\}$. In structural terms, this graph has three positions $\{1, 2, 3\}$ and (symmetric) structural relation R corresponding to the edges, so 1 R 2, 2 R 1, 1 R 3, 3 R 1 are the
only relations possible for these positions.

We say that two vertices are **adjacent** if there is an edge connecting them,
and two distinct edges are adjacent if they have a vertex in common. A **path**

in a graph is a sequence of vertices, each of which is adjacent to its predecessor and successor, if any. Thus, in the graph in Figure 8.2c, the sequence 2, 1, 3, 1, 2, 1 is a path, and 2, 1, 3 is called a **simple path**, since no vertex in the sequence is repeated. A **cycle** in a graph is a path for which the first and last vertices are identical, so that 1, 2, 1 is a cycle. A **simple cycle**, to no one's surprise, is a cycle with no repeated edges, so the graph in Figure 8.2c has no simple cycles. A graph is **connected** if any two vertices may be joined by a path. Finally (for now, at least), we say that a graph is **cyclic** if it contains a simple cycle and **acyclic** if it does not.

Graph theory, that branch of mathematics that deals with the study of graphs, is about two centuries old. It is an excellent introduction to the spirit of real mathematics, since its problems are often simple to understand, yet challenging and interesting to solve. Consider, for instance, the **four-color problem**. It dates back to 1852, and in modern terminology goes like this:

> The four-color problem: A planar graph is a graph that can be drawn on the plane without crossing any edges. A coloring of a graph is an assignment of colors to each vertex so that no adjacent vertices have the same color. Is it true that every planar graph can be colored with four or fewer colors?

The graph in Figure 8.2 is a trivial example of this problem: It is a planar graph, since it is already drawn on the plane without edge crossings, and certainly it can be colored with four colors, since it has only three vertices and we could just assign a different color to each vertex. (The problem does not apply to the ARPANET graph, because there is no relocation of nodes that will allow that graph to be drawn without some edge crossings; that is, it is not planar.) That sounds simple enough, but the problem resisted all attempts to prove it. People tried for years. No matter how complicated the planar graphs they chose, four or fewer colors always sufficed—but nobody could prove that it had to be so. Finally, in 1976, Kenneth Appel and Wolfgang Haken used a computer at the University of Illinois to check 1936 special cases, requiring about 10^{10} separate computations, for a total of something like 1200 hours of computer time, and in so doing showed that the answer to the four-color problem is "yes."

This book is not the place for an investigation into the four-color problem, but there is a much simpler problem that captures the flavor of graph theory and needs to be solved for later use. It's obvious that a graph with n vertices could have as few as zero edges, but what is the *largest* number of edges such a graph could have? It's not too hard to find the largest number of edges for a graph with n vertices, where every vertex is connected by an edge to every other. If you know some counting principles, you know that that's equivalent to the number of two-element subsets of a set of n objects; but even if you don't know the principles, the number is easy to compute. Label the vertices 1, 2, . . . , n and start listing edges. From vertex 1 we have edges to vertices 2, 3, . . . , n, for a total of $n-1$. From vertex 2 we have edges to vertex 1 (which we've already counted) and to 3, . . . , n, for a total of $n-2$.

Similarly, vertex 3 provides us with $n-3$ edges that we haven't yet counted, and if we continue this process for all vertices, we find that the number of edges is $(n-1)+(n-2)+\cdots+1$. This is a by-now familiar arithmetic series, and we know that the sum is $n(n-1)/2$, which must be the largest possible number of edges in a graph with n vertices. Such a graph, by the way, in which every vertex is adjacent to every other, is called a **complete graph**.

We are now ready to define our first network ADT.

Graph

Structure: An arbitrarily large (finite) collection of positions (called **vertices**), with a structure satisfying the following two properties for all positions p and q: (1) no position is its own successor, and (2) if p is a successor to q, then q is a successor to p. An **edge** of a graph is a set of two positions, $\{p, q\}$, such that p is a successor to q.

Operations

Graph(). Pre: true. Post: This graph is empty.

int Size() const. Pre: true. Post: The graph is unchanged. Returns the number of vertices in the graph.

int Adjacent(Vertex p, Vertex q) const. Pre: p and q are vertices of this graph. Post: The graph is unchanged. Returns 1 if $\{p, q\}$ is an edge of this graph; otherwise, returns 0.

void DeleteVertex(Vertex p). Pre: p is a vertex of this graph. Post: p is not in the graph (hence, any edge containing p is also no longer in the graph).

void DeleteEdge(Vertex p, Vertex q). Pre: $\{p, q\}$ is an edge of this graph. Post: This graph does not have a $\{p, q\}$ edge.

void InsertVertex(Vertex p). Pre: p is not in the graph. Post: p is in the graph, and p is not adjacent to any edge in this graph.

void InsertEdge(Vertex p, Vertex q). Pre: p and q are in the graph, $p \neq q$, and there is no $\{p, q\}$ edge. Post: p and q are adjacent.

If we associate information of type T with every vertex, we can parametrize the graph and include two additional operations:

void Update(T e, Vertex& p). Pre: p is a vertex of this graph. Post: The position p contains the value e.

T Retrieve(Vertex p) const. Pre: p is a vertex of this graph. Post: The graph is unchanged. Returns the value contained in p.

We could use these operations to generate the graph in Figure 8.2c, for example, by making the following member function calls, along with three calls to vertex constructors.

```
Vertex<int> a(1), b(2), c(3);
Graph<int> g;
g.InsertVertex(a);
g.InsertVertex(b);
g.InsertVertex(c);
g.InsertEdge(a, b);
g.InsertVertex(a, c);
```

Common practice deals with graphs differently than the other ADTs described so far. Lists, stacks, queues, trees, and the like, are all examples of **container classes**: They are used to store information (generally of the same type), and this information is stored internally to reflect a certain structure among the individual elements. In the ADTs we have seen up to this point, we generally try to hide the internal details of the structure from the user of the class by restricting access to some distinguished positions: the current position of a list, the top of a stack, or the root of a tree, for instance.

In the *Graph* ADT, however, we generally allow the user limited access to the internal structure, mainly because there really isn't any position we can naturally distinguish from the others. This explains an apparently missing feature of the preceding specification: There is no evident way "into" a graph's positions, in that there is no function that returns a position, given a graph. Some authors do what we did with the *List* ADT, namely, including in the graph a member datum that refers to a *current* vertex: but you'll see in the implementations that we simply make the auxiliary *Vertex* class more accessible than we did for, say, nodes in a tree.

8.2 IMPLEMENTATIONS OF *GRAPH*

There are a number of ways to store information about graphs. Some are more suitable than others for certain applications, a state of affairs that we have seen a number of times already. We will give three different implementations here and explore two of them in detail.

Adjacency Matrices

One of the simplest implementations is to use an $n \times n$ array, *adj*, of Boolean values (1 or 0) for a graph with n nodes. We suppose that the vertices are ordered $v_0, v_1, \ldots, v_{n-1}$ in some fashion and define $adj[i][j]$ to be 1 if v_i is adjacent to v_j, and 0 otherwise. The array *adj* is called the **adjacency matrix** of the graph. In Figure 8.3, we show a graph with its adjacency matrix.

As with most array implementations, this suffers from lack of easy extensibility, since we cannot let a graph grow beyond the maximum array size without taking the time to grow the array. Additionally, we see that there is a

FIGURE 8.3

A graph and its adjacency matrix

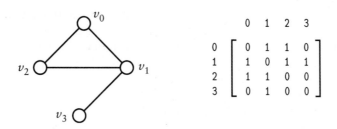

fair amount of wasted space even if the number of vertices in the graph is exactly equal to the number of rows in the array. Observe that the main diagonal, $adj[k][k]$, for $k = 0, \ldots, n-1$, is always 0, since we never have a vertex adjacent to itself (irreflexivity, remember), and note also that the part of the array below the main diagonal is redundant, since it must always be the case that $adj[i][j] = adj[j][i]$, for $0 \le i,\ j \le n-1$, by symmetry. In other words, in an $n \times n$ adjacency matrix for a graph with n vertices, only $n(n-1)/2$ of the entries are significant, meaning that we are wasting over half the space of the array, even if it is exactly the right dimension for the graph. That may not be of great importance, of course, since each of the array entries is guaranteed to use only a small amount of memory.

Another problem with adjacency matrices is that the time required to find all the vertices adjacent to a given vertex is $O(n)$, no matter how many adjacent vertices there are, since it requires that we search an entire row or column of the matrix. Nevertheless, we will see that there are some algorithms that are particularly suited for adjacency matrices, despite their shortcomings.

The implementation isn't difficult: We represent a graph by keeping track of the number of vertices in the graph, along with the adjacency matrix. Positions (i.e., vertices) are then integers, representing indices in the matrix, and edges are pairs of integers. The data part of this implementation of *Graph* looks like this:

```
int    max,        // max size of the array
       numVerts,   // current number of vertices

IntegerMatrix adj   // the adjacency matrix
```

The adjacency matrix is stored in an *IntegerMatrix*, which is a fairly simple generalization of the dynamic *IntegerArray* class we described in Chapter 1. If you prefer not to write the class declaration and definitions for *IntegerMatrix*, you may feel free to think of *adj* as an ordinary two-dimensional array, declared as int adj[MAX][MAX], where we would move *max* out of the member data and make it a global constant.

Notice that we haven't provided any way of associating data elements with vertices. In this implementation, there is no available information except for the shape of the graph itself. If we needed to "mark" vertices or store information in them, we would need an auxiliary data structure. (You will see in the next section, though, that we can use this implementation with very minor change to associate information with edges.) This is not the impediment it might first appear, since a number of graph-theoretic problems are concerned only with the structure of graphs, and not with any information associated with their vertices. What it does mean, however, is that we will not be able to use this data structure (at least not without modification) if we need the operations *Update* or *Retrieve*. This leaves us with only seven operations, all but one of which are very simple to define.

```
typedef int Vertex;

Graph()
{
    numVerts = 0;
    for (int i = 0; i < MAX; i++)
        for (int j = 0; j < MAX; j++)
            adj[i][j] = 0;
}

int Size() const
{
    return numVerts;
}

int Adjacent(Vertex p, Vertex q) const
{
    Assert(  (p < numVerts) && (q < numVerts)),
             "Illegal vertex number in Adjacent");

    return adj[p, q];
}

void DeleteEdge(Vertex p, Vertex q)
{
    Assert(  (p < numVerts) && (q < numVerts)),
             "Illegal vertex number in DeleteEdge");
    Warn(!Adjacent(p, q), "Attempt to delete nonexistent edge');

    adj[p][q] = adj[q][p] = 0;
}
```

Notice that we have represented the vertices by an interval 0, . . . , *numVertices*−1. This means that to insert a new vertex, we don't pay any attention to the argument *p*. All we do is check that there's room in the array for a new row and column (taking appropriate action if there isn't), zero out the values in the *numVertices* row and column of *adj,* and increment *numVerts.*

```
void InsertVertex(Vertex p);
{
    // (Here's where we'd check numVerts and grow
    // the matrix, if necessary.  For ordinary arrays, we'd
    // assert that numVerts < MAX.)
    for (int i = 1; i < numVerts; i++)
        adj[numVerts][i] = adj[i][numVerts] = 0;
    numVerts++;
}

void InsertEdge(Vertex p, Vertex q)
{
    Assert( (p < numVerts) && (q < numVerts)),
            "Illegal vertex number in InsertEdge");
    Assert((p != q), "Attempt to insert a loop");
    Warn(Adjacent(p, q), "Attempt to insert duplicate edge');

    adj[p][q] = adj[q][p] = 1;
}
```

You'll notice that we omitted *Delete Vertex*. We left that for last because it's the only operation that is complicated. To delete a vertex p from a graph G in this implementation, we need to delete the pth row and column from the adjacency matrix, shifting elements to fill the holes. It's not hard, just slightly tedious.

```
void DeleteVertex(Vertex p)
{
    Assert((p < numVerts), "Illegal vertex number in DeleteVertex");

    int i, j;
    for (i = p; i < numVerts)
        // Shift the i-th row up.
        for  j := 1 to G.numVerts  do
            G.adj[i, j] := G.adj[i + 1, j];

    for  i := p to G.numVerts  do
        // Shift the j-th column left.
        for  j := 1 to G.numVerts  do
            G.adj[j, i] := G.adj[j, i + 1];
}
```

Adjacency Lists and Edge Lists

A natural generalization of adjacency matrices would be to keep an array of pointers, one for each vertex, and have pointer p_i refer to a linked list of the vertices adjacent to vertex v_i. Such a representation is called an **adjacency list**, and we give an example in Figure 8.4. Notice that now we can store data in the vertices: We just put the data associated with v_i in the ith entry of the header array. Now you see that no time is wasted when we must search every vertex adjacent to a given vertex, since each list contains only the vertices adjacent to its header vertex. In effect, what we have done is compress the adjacency matrix by eliminating from each row the zero entries.

We also have an implicit list of edges for each vertex, since each cell w in the linked list headed by v_i corresponds to the edge $\{v_i, w\}$. As you might guess, this structure is more memory-efficient than the adjacency matrix when the graph is **sparse**, that is, when there are comparatively few edges (much less than $n(n+1)/2$ for a graph with n vertices). We haven't entirely eliminated the need to grow an array, since we still have a header array with vertex data and pointers to each linked list, but we certainly won't have as much data to move when we do grow the array. We will not consider this implementation in detail, as it is very similar to the next one we will discuss.

The final change we will make to these representations eliminates the extensibility problem entirely, albeit at a further cost in complexity. We will make the header array into a linked list, as well, as indicated in the implementation of Figure 8.5. If you look at Figure 8.5 and say something like, "Yuck! That's the most frightening mess I've seen in a long while," you'll be in good company. Don't be put off by the complexity of Figure 8.5; all we have done is to generalize Figure 8.4 slightly. Instead of an array of vertices on the left side, we now have a linked **vertex list** of cells, each of which has a field for data and a pointer to the head of an **edge list** of all vertices adjacent to it (which is the same as saying all edges that contain the header vertex). Each of the horizontal edge lists is also a linked list of cells, with each cell containing a pointer to a vertex and perhaps some information about the edge as well (which we omitted here, for simplicity).

If you look at Figure 8.5, you can see that vertex 1 (the second row) is adjacent to vertices 0, 2, and 3; or, in equivalent terms, vertex 1 is an endpoint of edges $\{1, 0\}$, $\{1, 2\}$, and $\{1, 3\}$. This makes it particularly easy to traverse the graph, since the edge list pointers lead us from one vertex through its edge to another, adjacent, vertex. The moral is not to worry about the spaghetti bowl of pointers; the program will handle them for you. It still ap-

FIGURE 8.4

The graph of Figure 8.3 and its adjacency list

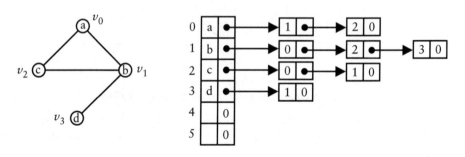

FIGURE 8.5

The edge list representation for the graph of Figure 8.4

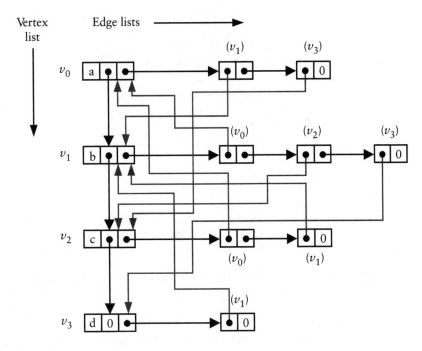

pears that we are wasting space, since each edge is represented twice. In Section 8.5, when we talk about the *Digraph* ADT, we will see that this problem of duplication disappears when we remove the requirement that the structural relation be symmetric. If you look at Figure 8.5 you can see that vertex 1 (the second row) is adjacent to vertices 0, 2, and 3—or, in equivalent terms, that vertex 1 is an endpoint of edges {1,0}, {1,2}, and {1,3}. This makes it particularly easy to traverse the graph, since the edge list pointers lead us from one vertex through its edge to another, adjacent, vertex. The moral is not to worry about the spaghetti bowl of pointers—the program will handle them for you. It still appears that we are wasting space, since each edge is represented twice. In Section 8.5, when we talk about the *Digraph* ADT, we will see that this problem of duplication disappears when we remove the requirement that the structural relation be symmetric.

We've already given the declaration of the *Graph* class. We will use ordinary int variables as vertices (so we would include typedef int Vertex; in the header file). The only new feature is the private part of the declaration. The first thing to notice is that there are two class declarations—one for the cells in the vertex's list and one for the cells in each vertex's edge list—contained in the private part. These **nested classes** are inaccessible to the user (since they're in the private part of *Graph*), which they should be, since the user shouldn't have to be concerned with how the *Graph* ADT is implemented here.

```
private:
    class EdgeCell;    // forward declaration, to avoid
                       // circular references.
```

```
class VertexCell
{
public:
    VertexCell(const Vertex& p, VertexCell* vp);
    // Construct a new vertex cell that refers to p and is linked
    // to the cell pointed to by vp.
    const Vertex* vert; // pointer to the vertex it represents.
    VertexCell* next; // pointer to next cell in the vertex list
    EdgeCell* head;      // pointer to the start of the edge list
};
class EdgeCell
{
public:
    EdgeCell(VertexCell* vp, EdgeCell* ep);
    // Construct a new edge cell that refers to the vertex cell
    // pointed to by vp and is linked to the edge cell pointed
    // to by ep.
    VertexCell* vCell;   // the vertex cell this edge cell points to
    EdgeCell* next;      // the next cell in the edge list
};

VertexCell* Find(const Vertex& p) const;
void DeleteCell (EdgeCell*& source, VertexCell* target);

VertexCell* gHead;      // the start of the vertex cell list
};
```

Notice, too, that we have included two auxiliary member functions, *Find* and *DeleteCell*. These functions are simple list recursions. *DeleteCell* does a recursive "search and destroy" through an edge list, while *Find* returns a pointer to a desired cell in the vertex list, or NULL, if no match was found. Note that we have to qualify the return type of *Find* by writing Graph::Vertex-Cell*, since *VertexCell* is nested within *Graph*.

```
void Graph::DeleteCell(EdgeCell*& source, VertexCell* target)
// Delete the cell with pointer to target from the edge list
// starting at source.
// NOTE: this does nothing if there's no match.
{
    if (source)
        if (source->vCell == target)
        {
            EdgeCell* temp = source;
            source = source->next;
            delete temp;
        }
        else
            DeleteCell(source->next, target);
}
```

```
Graph::VertexCell* Graph::Find(const Vertex& p) const
// RETURNS a pointer to the vertex list cell referring to p,
// or NULL if there is no vertex cell referring to p.
{
    VertexCell* vp = gHead;
    while (vp)
    {
        if (vp->vert == &p)
            return vp;
        vp = vp->next;
    }
    return NULL;
}
```

Despite the complexity of this implementation, most of the operations are still simple to define. By now, you're had enough experience reading code that it shouldn't be too hard to follow the implementations of the operations. Notice we have left the definition of some of the member functions as exercises.

```
int Graph::Adjacent(const double& p, const double& q) const
{
    VertexCell* pptr = Find(p);
    VertexCell* qptr = Find(q);
    if (pptr)                         // If p is in the graph,
    {
        EdgeCell* ep = pptr->head; // traverse its edge list,
        while (ep)
        {
            if (ep->vCell == qptr)
                return 1;             // and stop as soon as q is found.
            ep = ep->next;
        }
    }
    return 0;
}
```

To insert a {*p*,*q*} edge, we first check that *p* and *q* are vertices of this graph, and that they are adjacent, then add a *q* cell to *p*'s edge list and a *p* cell to *q*'s.

```
void Graph::InsertEdge(const Vertex& p, const Vertex& q)
{
    VertexCell* pptr = Find(p);
    VertexCell* qptr = Find(q);
    if (pptr && qptr)          // Are p and q in the graph?
        if (pptr != qptr)      // Are p and q distinct?
            if (!Adjacent(p, q)) // Are they not already adjacent?
            {
                // If so, make a new q-pointing cell in p's edge list.
```

```
            EdgeCell* ep = new EdgeCell(pptr, qptr->head);
            qptr->head = ep;
            // And make a new p-pointing cell in q's edge list.
            ep = new EdgeCell(qptr, pptr->head);
            pptr->head = ep;
        }
    }
```

The most complicated function in this class is *DeleteVertex*. That's because deletion of a vertex, *p*, has two phases. First, we track through *p*'s edge list (destroying it as we go) and use each cell in the edge list to point to an adjacent vertex. We then remove from that cell's edge list any reference to *p*, which is what the utility function *DeleteCell* does. The second phase is to do a straightforward linked list deletion to remove *p* from the vertex list.

```
void Graph:: DeleteVertex(const Vertex& p)
{
    VertexCell* pptr = Find(p);
    if (pptr)
    {
        // Use p's edge list to remove all references to
        // p from all other edge lists.
        EdgeCell* ePtr = pptr->head;
        while (ePtr)
        {
            DeleteCell(ePtr->vCell->head, pptr);
            pptr->head = pptr->head->next;
            delete ePtr;
            ePtr = pptr->head;
        }

        // Now eliminate p from the vertex list
        if (gHead == pptr)
        {
            gHead = gHead->next;
            delete pptr;
        }
        else
        {
            VertexCell* vPtr = gHead;
            while (vPtr->next != pptr)
                vPtr = vPtr->next;
            vPtr->next = vPtr->next->next;
            delete pptr;
        }
    }
}
```

Having spent this much time defining the edge list implementation of *Graph,* we will next consider a pair of applications for which it is particularly well suited. Before we do, though, it would be worth considering why we chose to write what amounts to two linked list implementations from scratch, rather than simply reusing *List.* The problem basically lies in the fact that we need fast access into the vertex list. That, after all, is the whole purpose of the pointers in each edge list. We specified *List* as we did most of our other classes; specifically, we restricted access into the internal workings of the class. As it now stands, we could point to elements in the vertex list, but we would have to look over the linked list code very carefully to make sure that a pointer to a list element would keep pointing to that element, no matter what happened to the list. The bottom line is that you could use the *List* ADT to help implement *Graph,* but it's trickier than you might expect, enough so that it's quite a bit easier just to build your own linked lists.

 ## GRAPH TRAVERSALS

For almost all of the ADTs we have seen so far, we have had a way of visiting all the positions in any instance of the ADT. We did not define traversals of stacks and queues, because those ADTs were defined with the intention that except for one or two positions, the contents were to be unavailable for inspection. Of course, as the structural relations became more general, the structures became more complicated, so we had more complex traversal routines. In passing from trees to graphs, we see that again we must exercise care, since each vertex may be adjacent to several other vertices. Also, the possible presence of cycles means that we must be careful not to visit any vertex we have already seen. There are two primary graph traversal schemes, one in which we move away from a present vertex as quickly as we can, and one in which we visit all vertices adjacent to a present vertex before moving farther.

Depth-First Traversals

The first traversal scheme we will investigate is known as a **depth-first** traversal. In this algorithm, we "mark" a vertex as soon as we visit it and then try to move to an unmarked adjacent vertex. If there are no unmarked vertices at our present position, we backtrack along the vertices we have already visited until we come to a vertex that is adjacent to one we haven't visited, visit that one, and continue the process. This is almost exactly the maze traversal scheme we introduced in the explorations of Chapter 4, where we used a stack to facilitate the backtracking process. Now, however, we know that many stack-based algorithms are natural candidates for recursion, so we will present the following recursive algorithm, which uses a stack implicitly. We will assume here and throughout most of the rest of this chapter that when we refer to a graph, the graph is connected (since we will track from one vertex to another via edges, and there are no edges connecting the connected pieces, called **components**, of a disconnected graph).

Depth-first traversal is simplicity itself. We keep a marker, *visited*, initially zero, in each vertex, and every time we visit a vertex, we visit recursively all its unvisited adjacent vertices. In skeleton form, the algorithm looks like this:

```
void Graph::DepthFirst(Vertex p)
{
    Visit p, do whatever processing is necessary;

    p->visited = 1;
    // Now look at all vertices, q, adjacent to p.
    EdgeCell* e = Find(p)->head;
    while (e)
    {
        Vertex q = e->vCell->vert;
        if (q->visited == 0)    // We haven't seen q yet,
            DepthFirst(q);      // so go there
        e = e->next;
    }
}
```

Consider the graph in Figure 8.6. If we start at vertex *a* and decide that at each vertex we will visit its neighbors in alphabetic order, we see that a depth-first traversal will result in the vertices being visited in the order *a, b, c, d, e, g, j, f, h, i*. In Figure 8.7, we trace the action of this algorithm using the nested boxes we introduced in Chapter 5. Each box represents a function call, and for each such call, we indicate the parameter (the vertex being visited) by a small box in the upper left corner and indicate the adjacent vertices, with the already visited vertices in parentheses. For instance, the first call, with parameter *a*, intends to call *DepthFirst* on vertices *b, e*, and *h*, but by the time the recursive call at *b* is completed, *e* and *h* have already been visited.

FIGURE 8.6

A graph for traversal

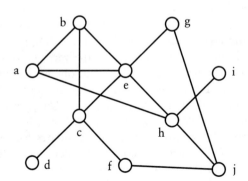

FIGURE 8.7

Recursive calls to
DepthFirst on the graph
of Figure 8.6

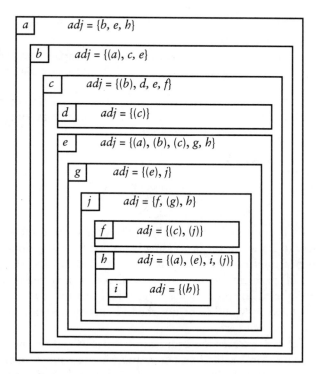

Breadth-First Traversals

The second kind of traversal we will discuss is **breadth-first**. In this scheme, every vertex adjacent to the current vertex is visited before we move away from the current vertex. We will accomplish this by keeping the vertices that have been visited but not explored on a queue, so that when we are ready to move to a vertex adjacent to the current vertex, we will be able to return to another vertex adjacent to the old current vertex after our move. As we did with depth-first traversal, we will keep a global array to mark the vertices that have been visited so far.

```
void Graph::BreadthFirst(Vertex p)
{
    Queue<Vertex> vertQ;
    vertQ.Enqueue(p);
    p->visited = 1;
    // option (a): Process p
    while (!vertQ.IsEmpty())
    {
        Vertex n = vertQ.Front();
        // option (b): Process n
        vertQ.Dequeue();
        EdgeCell* e = Find(n)->head;
```

```
while (e)
{
    Vertex m = e->vCell->vert;    // Get a vertex adjacent to n.
    if (m->visited == 0)          // If we haven't seen m
    {
        vertQ.Enqueue(m);         // place it on the queue,
        m->visited = 1;           // and mark it as visited.
        // option (a): Process m
    }
    e = e->next;
}
}
}
```

As is commonly the case with traversals, there are several choices about where to do whatever processing is needed to visit a node. We have indicated two possibilities with the statements labeled (a) and (b). The statements labeled (a) perform the processing the first time a vertex is seen, while the statement labeled (b) processes a vertex the last time it is seen. The choice might be dictated by whether or not the old current vertex is needed as well as the present current vertex.

Table 8.1 traces the progress of *BreadthFirst* on the graph of Figure 8.6. The algorithm starts at vertex *a,* and for each subsequent current vertex, the adjacent unvisited vertices are enqueued in alphabetic order.

Spanning Trees

One application of these traversals is to provide a **spanning tree** for a graph. In graph-theoretic terms, a tree is any connected acyclic graph (so if we made the structural relation symmetric and gave no special identification to any root node, the trees discussed in the previous chapter would be ordinary graph-theoretic trees), and a spanning tree for a graph G is a tree constructed from some of the edges of G in such a way that it contains all the vertices of

TABLE 8.1

Tracing *BreadthFirst* on the graph of Figure 8.6

Current Vertex	Unvisited Neighbors	Queue (rear→ front)
a	*b, e, h*	[*h, e, b*]
b	*c*	[*c, h, e*]
e	*g*	[*g, c, h*]
h	*i, j*	[*j, i, g, c*]
c	*d, f*	[*f, d, j, i, g*]
g	None	[*f, d, j, i*]
i	None	[*f, d, j*]
j	None	[*f, d*]
d	None	[*f*]
f	None	(*Queue* empty; quit)

G. Another way to look at spanning trees is that they are the smallest collection of edges that allow communication between any two vertices of the original graph.

We can build a **depth-first spanning tree** by keeping track of all the edges we used in the depth-first traversal, as indicated in Figure 8.8, so that every time we visit a new vertex, we mark the edge from the last current vertex to the new vertex (which means that every cell in the edge list will contain a *treeMark* datum, which is 1 if and only if that edge is in the spanning tree). We will use *DepthFirst*, slightly modified, to mark edges of the spanning tree.

```
void Graph::DepthFirstBuild(Vertex* p)
{
   p->visited = 1;
   Edge* currentEdge = p->head;
   while (currentEdge)
   {
      Vertex* q = currentEdge->vert;
      if (q->visited == 0)
      {
         currentEdge->treeMark = 1;
         // Modification--mark a tree edge.
         // We could print the tree edge here, and we could also
         // mark the other copy of currentEdge, too, since each
         // edge is represented twice in this implementation}
         DepthFirst(q);
      }
      currentEdge = currentEdge->next;
   }
}


void Graph::DFSpanningTree()
{
   // Initialization: set all visited and treemark markers to 0.
   Vertex* p := gHead;
   while (p)              // Inspect all vertices.
   {
      p->visited = 0;     // Mark each vertex as unvisited.
      Edge* e = p->head;
      while (e)           // Inspect edge list for each vertex.
      {
         e->treeMark = 0; // Mark each edge as not in tree.
         e = e->next;
      }
   }
   // Now do the real work of building the spanning tree.
   DepthFirstBuild(gHead);
}
```

FIGURE 8.8

A depth-first spanning
tree for the graph of
Figure 8.6

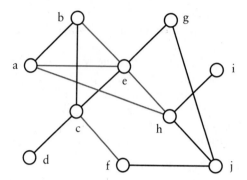

Notice that there can be many different depth-first spanning trees, depending on where we start and the order in which we visit the vertices adjacent to a given vertex.

In a similar way, we can modify *BreadthFirst* to construct a **breadth-first spanning tree** of a graph G. We will begin with a graph T that initially contains all the vertices of G, but no edges. Each time we visit a new vertex, we mark the edge of G that we used to reach that vertex. Since we need to know the old current node, we will use location {a} in *BreadthFirst* for processing.

```
void Graph::BFSpanningTree()
{

    Set visited datum of each vertex to 0;

    Queue<Vertex*> vertQ;
    Vertex* n = gHead;
    vertQ.Enqueue(n);
    n->visited := true;
    while (!vertQ.IsEmpty())
    {
        n = vertQ.Front();
        vertQ.Dequeue();
        Edge* currentEdge = n->head;
        while (currentEdge)
        {
            Vertex* m = currentEdge->vert;
            if (m->visited == 0)
            {
                vertQ.Enqueue(m);
                m->treeMark = 1;     // Mark a spanning tree edge.
            }
            currentEdge = currentEdge->next;
        }
    }
}
```

FIGURE 8.9

A breadth-first spanning tree for the graph of Figure 8.6

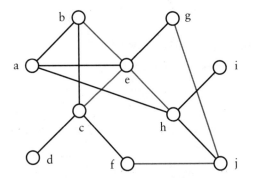

If we perform this algorithm on the tree in Figure 8.6, starting at vertex *a* and visiting adjacent vertices in alphabetic order, we see that the resulting spanning tree is the one given in Figure 8.9.

8.4 APPLICATION: MINIMUM SPANNING TREES

Recall the questions we asked about the ARPANET graph at the beginning of this chapter. Questions about the number of paths between two nodes or the cost of communication between nodes are not merely academic exercises when you are faced with a real project involving money and sensitive communications. In this section, we will discuss some algorithms for solving graph-theoretic problems like these.

We define an **edge-weighted graph** to be a graph that has a number associated with every edge. If G is an edge-weighted graph, then any spanning tree T of G has associated with it a **cost** equal to the sum of the weights of the edges in T, and it makes sense to ask what spanning trees have the least cost. Such trees are called **minimum spanning trees** (**MSTs**). Since a spanning tree connects all vertices in G, we are then asking for the least-cost collection of edges that will ensure communication between all vertices of G.

To demonstrate that the MST algorithm we will present works correctly, we need a preliminary result, which we mentioned earlier and will restate here without proof. The result we need is that a tree is not only a connected graph with no cycles, but is also **maximal** with that property, that if we add an edge to a tree (by connecting two vertices that are already in the tree), then the resulting graph is no longer a tree, because we have introduced a cycle containing the new edge.

The MST algorithm, by R. C. Prim, is quite lovely. We build an MST by marking edges and vertices, just as we did when we were building spanning trees.

```
void Graph:: MST()
{
    Vertex p, q;  // p is in the MST, q isn't.

    Start with any vertex, p, in the graph;

    while (there is an unmarked vertex)
    {

        Find a least-cost edge {p, q} with p marked and q unmarked;

        Mark q;

        Mark the {p, q} edge;

    }
}
```

That could hardly be simpler. Before we analyze this algorithm, let's look at an example of how it works. In Figure 8.10, we will draw the MST as it is being built, by drawing each newly marked vertex and edge. We begin with any vertex, and at each pass through the loop, we find an edge of least cost that connects the tree to a vertex not yet in the tree. We then include that vertex and edge in the tree and continue the process. The algorithm works because we have a particularly nice loop invariant: At the end of each pass, T, the marked tree, is a minimum spanning tree for that subgraph of G consisting of the vertices chosen so far, along with all edges of G connecting those vertices (called the **induced subgraph** on those vertices).

FIGURE 8.10

Construction of a minimum spanning tree

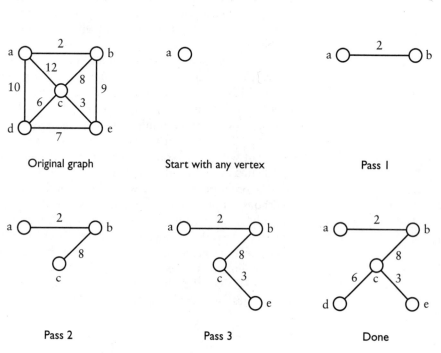

Original graph   Start with any vertex   Pass 1

Pass 2   Pass 3   Done

To prove this invariant, suppose that it was true at the start of a pass, but not true at the end of the pass. In other words, suppose that adding the $\{p, q\}$ edge, with $p \in T$ and $q \notin T$, produced a tree T' that was not least cost on the vertices selected so far. That would mean that there was another spanning tree, T'', on the vertices selected so far that was strictly cheaper than T'. Now, T'' could not contain the $\{p, q\}$ edge, because if it did, it could not be cheaper than T with the $\{p, q\}$ edge added, since we assumed that T was cheapest. Therefore, T'' contains another edge to q—call it $\{p', q\}$—with $p' \in T$.

Whoa! Adding $\{p, q\}$ to T'' produces a cycle containing p, p', and q, and by removing the $\{p', q\}$ edge, we again have a tree containing $\{p, q\}$. This tree must be at least as cheap as T'', since $\{p, q\}$ was the least-cost edge from q to any vertex in T, so we have an MST containing $\{p, q\}$ that is strictly cheaper than T'. But we just showed that that was impossible. Therefore, T' must be an MST on the induced subgraph, completing the essential part of the proof. We leave it up to you to show that this is indeed enough to demonstrate that the algorithm produces an MST for the entire graph.

8.5 DIRECTED GRAPHS

If we think about representing cities with roads between them, we can see that a graph may not be the most natural model for such a situation. In particular, since the prevailing winds in the Northern Hemisphere blow from west to east, it may very well take longer to travel in one direction than in the other on the same road. Furthermore, if we used a graph to model the streets in a typical city, it might be impossible to travel in one direction on a street (unless we wished to break the law concerning one-way streets). As we mentioned at the start of this chapter, we can generalize the definition of a graph to allow the existence of **directed edges** from one vertex to another. Doing so allows us to define a **directed graph,** also known as a **digraph,** and since we defined graphs in two ways, we will present the definition of digraphs in two ways as well.

> *Definition.* (Graph-theory flavor) A digraph is an ordered pair $D = (V, E)$ of vertices and (directed) edges, where E consists of a set of **ordered pairs**, (p, q), of elements of V. For an edge (p, q) from p to q, p is called the **initial vertex** of the edge, and q is called the **terminal vertex** of the edge.
>
> *Definition.* (ADT flavor) The *Digraph* abstract data type consists of an underlying set of atoms and a set of positions, with no restriction on predecessors and successors (except that no element can be its own successor if we disallow loops, although loops are more commonly allowed among digraphs than among graphs). The *Digraph* operations are the same as for *Graph*.

You should refer back to the definitions for graphs and contrast them with these digraph definitions.

We can view a digraph as a graph if we ignore the direction of edges. This is done frequently, so we can discuss paths, simple paths, and connectedness for a digraph as if it were a graph and define **directed paths** to be sequences of vertices $v_1, v_2, \ldots, v_k$ for which there is a directed edge from v_i to v_{i+1}, for every $i = 1, \ldots, k-1$. Cycles are customarily considered to be directed, and we say that a digraph is **strongly connected** if there is a directed path between any two vertices. Figure 8.11 shows a digraph that is cyclic (with a simple cycle of length 2), connected, but not strongly connected.

It is clear that a graph is just a special case of a digraph, one in which every edge between two vertices is paired with one running in the opposite direction. Most of what we have said about graphs holds equally well for digraphs, and much of what we are about to say holds for graphs as well. The implementations for graphs can be used for digraphs with no change, for example. Notice that the adjacency matrix for digraphs now has no redundant information: For a graph, the adjacency matrix was symmetric (since it was nothing but a description of a symmetric structural relation), with the i, j entry always equal to the j, i entry, while this need not hold for digraphs, since the i, j entry is true if and only if there is a directed edge starting at vertex i and ending at vertex j.

The only real difference when we apply what we have done to digraphs is that unless the digraph is strongly connected, there is no guarantee that the traversal algorithms will visit every node in the digraph. Generally, the traversal process comes to a halt, unable to proceed any further, and so we choose a new starting vertex that has not yet been visited and start the traversal from there, a process that leads to a **spanning forest** of disconnected trees, as happened in Figure 8.12 (and as would happen if we applied the traversal algorithms to nonconnected graphs). Notice, by the way, that the trees that result are much more similar to the directed trees of Chapter 6.

Application: Cheapest Paths

Given a starting vertex, what is the least cost to any other vertex? This is known as the *single-source least-cost* problem. The algorithm we will present

FIGURE 8.11

A digraph

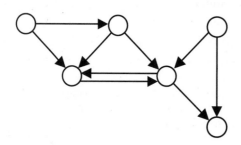

FIGURE 8.12

A spanning forest
for the digraph of
Figure 8.13

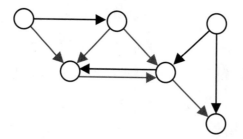

is by E. W. Dijkstra. The algorithm is one of a class of **greedy algorithms**, similar to Prim's MST algorithm, in which at each step, the best "local" solution to the problem is the one chosen (similar to the way we make change with the fewest number of coins by selecting at each stage the largest-valued coin that is less than or equal to the amount yet needed*).

The algorithm makes use of the **cost adjacency matrix**, A, for which the $A[i][j]$ entry represents the cost of the (i, j) directed edge. Figure 8.13 illustrates an edge-weighted digraph and its cost adjacency matrix. The algorithm constructs a least-cost vector, L, of the costs of the cheapest paths from the starting vertex to each other vertex. We will assume that ∞ in the matrix A is represented by some easily recognized value larger than any possible path cost.

```
void Digraph::SingleLeastCost(Vertex p, CostVector L)
{
    S = { p} ;      // S is a set of vertices that contains all
                    // vertices for which the min cost from p is known.

    for (all vertices q≠p in the graph)
        L[q] = A[p][q];

    do
        for (all vertices not in S)

            Find the vertex, q, for which L[q] is smallest;

        Put q into the set S;

        for (all vertices, r, not in S)
            if (L[r] >= L[q] + A[q][r])
                L[r] = L[q] + A[q][r];
    while (S contains fewer than the number of vertices in the digraph, less 1)
}
```

---

* Which, incidentally, would not always succeed if our coins had different values than they do.

FIGURE 8.13

An edge-weighted digraph and its adjacency matrix

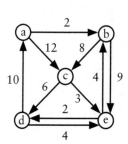

$$
\begin{array}{c c}
 & \begin{array}{c c c c c} a & \quad b & \quad c & \quad d & \quad e \end{array} \\
\begin{array}{c} a \\ b \\ c \\ d \\ e \end{array} &
\left[\begin{array}{c c c c c}
0 & 2 & 12 & \infty & \infty \\
\infty & 0 & 8 & \infty & 9 \\
\infty & \infty & 0 & 6 & 3 \\
10 & \infty & \infty & 0 & 4 \\
\infty & 4 & \infty & 2 & 0
\end{array}\right]
\end{array}
$$

We will trace the action of Dijkstra's algorithm on the edge-weighted digraph of Figure 8.13. Suppose that we wish to find the least cost of paths from vertex a. We begin with $S = \{a\}$ and $L = [2, 12, \infty, \infty]$, which we obtain from the a row of the adjacency matrix. We do the following steps through the outer loop until S contains all but one vertex of the digraph.

Step 1. We see that $L[b] = 2$ is the least value in the L vector among those vertices not yet chosen, so we include b in S. For the rest of the unchosen values, r, we compare $L[r]$ with $L[b] + A[b][r]$, in effect asking whether it is cheaper to go through b to get to r than to go by a path corresponding to the old value of $L[r]$. For $r = c$, we find that $L[c] = 12$ and $L[b] + A[b][c] = 2 + 8$; thus, it is cheaper to go through b to get to c, and so we make $L[c] = 10$. For $r = d$, we have $L[d] = \infty$ and $L[b] + A[b][d] = 2 + \infty$, so it is no cheaper to get to d via b. For $r = e$, we have $L[e] = \infty$ and $L[b] + A[b][e] = 2 + 9$, so again it is cheaper to get to e via b. At the end of this step, we now have $L = [2, 10, \infty, 11]$.

Step 2. Among the vertices not yet in S, we see that $L[c] = 10$ is the minimal value, so we add c to S, producing $S = \{a, b, c\}$. We look at the two remaining unselected vertices and again ask whether a path through c to those vertices is cheaper than the existing path. For $r = d$, we have $L[d] = \infty$ and $L[c] + A[c][d] = 10 + 6$, so we set $L[d] = 16$. For $r = d$, we have $L[e] = 11$ and $L[c] + A[c][e] = 10 + 3$, so it is no cheaper to get from a to e through c. We now have $L = [2, 10, 16, 11]$.

Step 3. Vertices d and e are the only ones not yet selected, and we find that $L[e] = 11$ is the minimum value among them, so we add e to S and compare $L[d] = 16$ with $L[e] + A[e][d] = 11 + 2 = 13$. We find that it is cheaper to go through e to get to d than not, so we finally have $L = [2, 10, 13, 11]$.

We could verify that for the example given, the algorithm does indeed give the correct result, but that tells us very little. A precept whose value cannot be overstated is an example, not a proof. Knowing that the algorithm is correct in one instance is essentially worthless, so let us participate in a little program verification. We will do what amounts to an induction proof that an invariant condition remains true throughout the life of the algorithm, and we will phrase our invariant so that if it holds at the completion of the algorithm, then the algorithm has indeed done what it was supposed to. We will call vertices *selected* if they are in the set S, and we will let p denote the start vertex for the algorithm.

> Invariant. Any selected vertex, v, has the property that its L value is equal to the least cost of any path from p, through selected vertices, to v.

Since the algorithm begins with p as the only selected vertex, and the cost of a path from p to itself is zero, the invariant is certainly true at the start of the algorithm. At the end of the algorithm, all vertices but one have been selected, so that if the invariant holds at the end, we must have the L vector containing the lengths of the shortest paths from p to any other vertex in the digraph. All we need to do is complete the induction step by showing that if the invariant holds at the start of an iteration through the outer loop, then it holds at the end of that iteration.

Let us then suppose that we are at the beginning of an iteration of the loop and that the invariant property holds for the vertices so far selected. We wish to add a new vertex, q, to the selected set, and we do so by choosing the unselected vertex with the least L value. We claim that that is exactly the appropriate choice, in that if q is the unselected vertex with the smallest L value, then the cheapest way to get from p to q is through selected vertices. In other words, the invariant property will hold for the newly selected vertex q.

Suppose that were not true. Suppose that there was actually a path from p, through some selected vertices, to an unselected vertex x and then through one or more edges to q that was cheaper than $L[q]$. That would mean that the path from p to x was itself cheaper than the path through the selected vertices to q, which would mean that, contrary to our assumption, we never would have chosen q in the first place.

Now that we have added q to the selected vertices, we know that its L value represents the least cost of any path from p to q, through selected vertices. We don't know that that is now true for the rest of the selected vertices. In fact, the example shows that the invariant fails to hold immediately after we have included q. This is why we then checked each of the selected vertices, r, to see if there is a cheaper path from p to r through q. Having done that, though, we are at the end of an iteration, and we see that the invariant property is restored, with every selected vertex having the property that its L value is again equal to the cost of the cheapest path from p to the vertex, through selected vertices.

The invariant holds at the start. If it holds at the beginning of a loop iteration, it must hold at the end. And if the invariant holds at the end of the algorithm, the algorithm must do what it is supposed to do.

Finding a timing estimate for Dijkstra's algorithm is considerably easier than verifying it. Suppose the digraph has n vertices. The initialization of S and L takes $O(n)$ time, and the main loop iterates $n-1$ times, with S having size $1, 2, \ldots, n-1$ in successive iterates. Each of the for loops within the main loop takes $O(n-s)$, where s is the size of S. The time for the algorithm, then, is

$$O(n) + (O(n-1) + O(n-2) + \cdots + O(1)) = O(n^2)$$

Dijkstra's algorithm could be unsatisfactory, though, if we wanted to know the cheapest paths from the source, rather than just knowing the costs of the paths. The modification would not be too difficult; all we would have to do is keep track of the path we used to get from the newly selected vertex q to an unselected vertex r every time we changed the L value of r. It would probably be easiest to keep the minimal paths in an array, with the row headed by q containing the vertices on a cheapest path from p to q in order, and we will overload the 0th column to contain the length of each path. We will denote the path array by P, where $P[i][j]$ contains the jth vertex in the path from the source to vertex i, and in doing so will assume that the vertices are indexed $1, 2, \ldots, n$. We will present the algorithm in nearly full implementation-specific detail, to give you a sample in more than pseudocode. For simplicity's sake, we will assume that vertex 1 is the source vertex.

```
const int N = {the number of vertices in the graph} ;
const Cost INFINITY = {some suitably large Cost} ;
typedefs:
    Cost {whatever type the costs are} ;
    AdjMatrix Cost[N + 1][N + 1];
    CostVector  Cost[N + 1];
    PathArray  int[N + 1][N + 1];
    IntegerSet (a set of integers: we'll implement it in Chapter 9)

procedure SingleLeastCost(AdjMatrix A, CostVector& L, PathArray& P)
{
    // This is the initialization part.  We set initial values
    // for the cost and path vectors.

    IntegerSet S;
    S.Insert(1);                    // Vertex 1 is the source vertex.

    for (int q = 2; q <= N; q++) // Set up cost vector.
        L[q] = A[1][q];

    for (q = 2; q <= N; q++)     // Set up path array.
    {
        if (A[1][q] < INFINITY)    // There is a path from 1 to q.
        {
            P[q][0] = 1;
            P[q][1] = 1;
        }
```

```
    else                        // No path yet from 1 to q.
    {
      P[q][0] = 0;
      P[q][1] = 0;
    }
    for (int r = 2; r <= N; r++)
        P[q][r] = 0;
}

// Here's where the real work goes on.  We simultaneously update
// the cost vector to represent the current cheapest costs from
// vertex 1 to vertices 2, . . . , N and modify the path matrix
// to indicate the selected vertices on the cheapest path from 1
// to any other vertex.
for (int index = 2; index < N; index++)
{
    Cost min = INFINITY;
    // Find cheapest vertex, q, not yet in S.
    for (int r = 2; r <= N; r++)
      if (!S.Contains(r))
        if  (L[r] < min)
        {
          min = L[r];
          q = r;
        }

    S.Insert(q);                // Include q among selected vertices.

    // Adjust cost and path arrays for unselected vertices.
    for (r = 2; r <= N; r++)
      if (!S.Contains(r))
        if  (L[r] >= L[q] + A[q][r])
        {
          L[r] = L[q] + A[q][r];

          // Replace r path with q path, since it's cheaper.
          P[r][0] = P[q][0] + 1;
          for (int p = 1; p <= P[q][0]; p++)
            P[r][p] = P[q][p];
          P[r][P[r][0]] = q;
        }
    }
}
```

The only essential difference between this and the original algorithm is
that we maintain the path array. At any pass through the algorithm, the path

array contains a least-cost path from the source to any selected vertex, and each time we select a new vertex and find that it is cheaper to go through the selected vertex to an unselected vertex, we replace the path for the unselected vertex with the path that goes through the newly selected vertex and on to the unselected vertex.

8.6 COMPUTER SCIENCE INTERLUDE: COMPUTATIONAL COMPLEXITY

We mentioned earlier that computational complexity theory is that branch of computer science devoted to the study of the space and time complexity of algorithms and problems. In this section, we will concentrate on timing estimates, although much of what we will say holds for storage estimates as well, and we will look at some of the connections between complexity theory and the study of graph algorithms. We will omit most of the technical details, of which there are many, but will try to give you an idea of some of the most vital questions in this area in the hope that you will find it exciting enough to pursue at a later time.

Notice that we talk about the complexity of *problems* as well as algorithms. Every problem has an innate time complexity $T(n)$, in that any algorithm to solve that problem, no matter how cleverly contrived, must have asymptotic running time at least as large as some multiple of $T(n)$. A trivial example would be the *counting problem*: Given an integer, n, produce a list of all integers between 1 and n. That problem is obviously linear, in that any algorithm that produces the list must have running time no smaller than cn, for some c, although we could, of course, invent any number of algorithms that would take much longer than that. A less trivial example is the *sorting problem*: Given a set of n numbers, produce a list containing the numbers in sorted order. With a few hints, you should be able to show that any algorithm that relied solely on comparisons of elements, like *Selectionsort*, *Mergesort*, or *Heapsort*, could not run in time less than $n\log n$, so we could say that the *comparison sorting problem* is an $n\log n$ problem. There are, by the way, algorithms for sorting that do not rely on comparisons of elements and that run faster than $O(n\log n)$, at least if you make some assumptions about the numbers being sorted. But—computer science folklore aside—it is not known that $n\log n$ is the best we can do for the unrestricted sorting problem. In a similar way, it is easy to show that the problem of multiplying two n-digit numbers can be solved in $O(n^2)$ time using the elementary school algorithm, and we can prove that it is possible to find a $O(n^{1+a})$ time multiplication algorithm for any $a>0$, but we simply do not know whether a linear algorithm is possible. (We certainly couldn't do better than that, if for no other reason than that it would take at least cn time just to inspect the digits of the numbers.)

Finding the best lower bound for the complexity of a problem is usually quite difficult. Often, it is enough to gain some partial information about the complexity of a problem and leave the details for another time. If we paint with the broadest possible brush that still leaves us with an interesting picture, we can divide all problems into two classes: easy and hard. We will say that an *easy* problem is one for which there is an algorithm that runs in **polynomial time,** namely, one that for problems of size n runs in time $O(n^k)$, for some nonnegative integer k. Any other problem, such as one for which the fastest algorithm takes time proportional to 2^n or $n!$, we will call a *hard* problem. This rough classification makes sense, since the polynomial-time algorithms, no matter how large the power k, are at least feasible to try to solve on a computer, while the time to run a nonpolynomial algorithm increases so rapidly as a function of n that it is foolish even to try it, except for very small instances of the problem.

Now, every problem (or at least every problem that we can solve on a computer, which does not include all the problems we can state*) has some innate complexity, even if we don't know what it is, so it either lies in the set P of polynomial-time problems or does not. Many problems, like sorting, multiplication, and finding the nth Fibonacci number, are known to be in P; and many problems (like listing all subsets of a set of n numbers) are known not to lie in P. The most interesting problems, however, are those that in some sense lie near the boundary of P and not-P (Figure 8.14); these problems are "easier" than the rest of the hard problems, but are not known to be easy.

The "interesting" problem that we will study here is called the **traveling salesperson problem** (sometimes shortened to TSP). Suppose that a sales representative has contacts in n cities and wishes to visit all of them, beginning and ending at the home office and not visiting any city more than once. (We'll assume that our rep has a contact to visit in the home city, so that the home city is among the n.) Suppose also that the sales rep knows the cost of travel between any two of the cities. The problem is to find the tour that

FIGURE 8.14

A hierarchy of problems

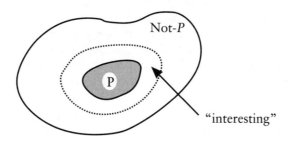

* One such problem is the *halting problem:* Design an algorithm that will take as its input the source code of a program P in a given language and some input data, D, and in a finite time stop and answer "yes" if P eventually halts on input D, or "no" if P fails to halt on input D (because it would have gotten stuck in an infinite loop, for example). There is a clever and simple proof that it is impossible to construct such an algorithm that will work correctly on all inputs P and D.

meets these conditions and that has the least cost. In our terminology, this is nothing but an edge-weighted graph problem: We are given a graph, G, with n vertices and a cost function, c, on the edges of G, and we want to find a simple cycle $v_1, v_2, \ldots, v_n, v_1$ for which $c(\{v_1, v_2\}) + c(\{v_2, v_3\}) + \cdots + c(\{v_n, v_1\})$ is as small as possible.

It is not at all difficult to find an algorithm to solve TSP. All we need to do is construct all possible simple cycles in G and find the one with the least cost. How long would that algorithm take to run? Well, we can compute the cost of a cycle while it is being generated, so the running time for the algorithm is proportional to the number of cycles we have to investigate. Let's see, starting at the home city, there could be as many as $n-1$ possibilities for the first city on the tour; having chosen that one, we could make as many as $n-2$ independent choices for the next city, $n-3$ for the one after that, and so on. Since the number of choices at each step has nothing to do with the choices we have made before, the total number of cycles is the product of the number of individual choices, for a grand total of $(n-1)(n-2)(n-3) \ldots (2)(1) = (n-1)!$ This means that this is a "hard" algorithm, with running time $O((n-1)!)$. In other words, the problem of *enumerating* the simple cycles of a graph is innately nonpolynomial. To see how the growth rate of the timing function clobbers us, you could do the calculations to show that even if it were somehow possible to enumerate a million tours per second, it could take as much as 1 hour and 44 minutes to do this for 14 cities, 14 times that long if we included just one more city, and about 3857 *years* if we had just 20 cities! Clearly, this "brute force" approach should be avoided if at all possible.

At this point, it seems that we basically have two choices: We could try to find a polynomial-time algorithm for TSP, or we could prove that TSP is innately hard, which would give us a perfect excuse to throw up our hands and declare that the problem was not worth the time to program a computer to solve. A lot of very clever people (and a lot of crackpots, too, it must be admitted) have worked for a long time on these two approaches, and the results have been uniformly the same. Zilch. We simply don't know yet whether TSP is a hard problem or not.

In 1971, Stephen Cook published a paper that provided a third choice and set the stage for a partial way out of our dilemma. He considered a class of problems called **NP**. Any problem in *NP* has the property that, roughly speaking, it is possible to *verify* a solution in polynomial time, no matter how long it might have taken to *produce* the solution. *NP*, then, sits "between" *P* and not-*P*. It contains *P* and also contains many problems that appear to be in not-*P*. (Some homework assignments may take nonpolynomial time to complete, but may still require only polynomial time to grade, which is why some of us become teachers.) Almost all of the "interesting" problems are in *NP*. Even better than that, however, is the fact that within *NP* there is a further subclass of problems, called **NP-complete** problems. There are hundreds of *NP*-complete problems; they all seem to be hard (at least there is no known easy algorithm for any of them); and they all have, by definition, the property that *if a polynomial-time solution for any NP-complete problem can be found, it would provide polynomial-time solutions for all problems in NP, and if any problem in NP can be proved to be hard, then every NP-complete problem is also hard.*

One of the most famous unsolved problems in mathematics is whether $P = NP$, or, contrarily, is P a *proper* subset of NP? In some sense, the NP-complete problems are the "hardest" of the problems in NP, since a polynomial-time solution to any one of them would drag all of NP into P. This provides us with our partial out. If we have an apparently hard problem that we can show is NP-complete, we can at least take some comfort in the knowledge that a polynomial-time algorithm to solve the problem would provide an answer to a question that has stymied the best mathematicians and computer scientists for nearly two decades. TSP is an NP-complete problem.

That being the case, it is perhaps presumptuous of us to think that we can find an easy algorithm to solve TSP. What we can do, however, is adopt a strategy that is very common in dealing with difficult problems. In theory, the problem of how to win a chess game is solvable. All we have to do is investigate all possible lines of play and try to choose those lines that lead to a win (or at least a draw). This brute force strategy is at least as bad as the brute force approach to TSP—so bad, in fact, that no sane person would attempt it. Rather, what chess players do is rely on **heuristics**—rules of thumb that describe courses of action that generally improve the chances of solving the problem at hand, like trying to control the center of the board and not trading a queen for a pawn unless there is compelling reason to do so.

For TSP, the heuristic that would probably occur to most people first is to be greedy: While trying to complete the circuit, choose the next edge to be the one that has least cost to an unvisited vertex. This is not a strategy that guarantees success—you should be able to come up with a simple example for which a greedy strategy will fail to provide the least-cost circuit—but it is one that often produces a "pretty good" solution. We could modify the strategy by including some "lookahead," as chess players do when they think, "If I make this move, then my opponent might do this or that, in which case I would . . . ," thereby perhaps improving the heuristic even further.

We'll close this chapter with a strategy that uses an algorithm we've already described. A solution to TSP must be more expensive than a minimum spanning tree, since removing one edge from a TSP circuit would produce a spanning tree for the graph. We know that minimum spanning trees can be constructed in polynomial time, so we might try to modify an MST to a solution to TSP (an example of why nonspecialists find it so hard to talk to computer scientists). A "shrink-wrap" traversal of an MST is sort of a solution to TSP; it is a low-cost cycle, but unfortunately not simple, since we traverse each edge twice.

We can, however, generate a simple cycle from a spanning tree by appropriately choosing "shortcuts" across vertices that have already been visited (see Figure 8.15). This will not guarantee a solution to TSP in all cases, but for at least one class of graphs it will guarantee a solution that is no larger than twice the cost of the optimal solution. See if you can come up with a condition on the cost function that will guarantee this.

8.7 SUMMARY

A graph may be defined to be a set with a symmetric, irreflexive relation defined on it. In a sense, graphs are generalizations of trees, obtained by weakening the hierarchical structure of trees by allowing a position to have more than one immediate predecessor. We can consider a graph to be a tree with zero or more extra edges added, so we conclude that each graph contains at least one spanning tree, which contains all the vertices of the graph.

We saw three different representations of graphs—adjacency matrices, adjacency lists, and edge lists—and we saw that adjacency matrices can be used to count the number of paths, including the least-cost path, between any two vertices of a graph. Minimum spanning trees form the basis for a number of graph algorithms; Prim's algorithm is one way to find MSTs, and you will see another when we discuss sets in the next chapter. Prim's algorithm originally appeared in R. C. Prim, "Shortest Connection Networks and Some Generalizations," *Bell System Technical Journal* 36(1957): 1389–1401.

Digraphs are generalizations of graphs in which the edges have a direction from one node to another. Dijkstra's algorithm uses a greedy strategy to find the least-cost path from a given vertex to any other vertex in an edge-weighted digraph. For more information, see E. W. Dijkstra, "A Note on Two Problems in Connexion with Graphs," *Numerische Mathematik* 1(1959): 269–271.

We concluded with a discussion of the traveling salesperson problem. This appears to be an innately hard problem; although it has not been proved to be hard, it is an *NP*-complete problem and so is as hard as many other such problems (none of which have been proved hard). The genesis of *NP*-complete problems is found in Stephen Cook, "The Complexity of Theorem-

FIGURE 8.15

Expanding a spanning tree to a simple cycle

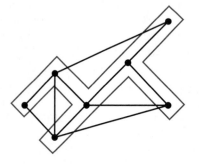
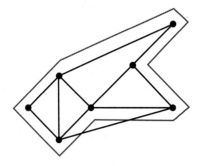

Proving Procedures," in *Proceedings of the 3rd Annual ACM Symposium on Theory of Computing* (New York: Association for Computing Machinery, 1971): 151–158.

Finally, a good introduction to the theory of computational complexity is Michael R. Garey and David S. Johnson, *Computers and Intractability: A Guide to the Theory of NP-Completeness* (San Francisco: Freeman, 1979).

8.8 EXERCISES

1. Provide the best argument you can to support the contention that the ARPANET graph of Figure 8.1 is not planar.

2. What is the least number of colors necessary to color the ARPANET graph?

3. **a.** Give an algorithm that colors a graph, by assigning to each vertex a number from 1 to n, in such a way that no two adjacent vertices have the same integer.

    b. A far more challenging problem is to assign "colors" so that the least possible numbers are used. This is not hard to do if you simply try all possible assignments that use no more colors than n, where there are n vertices in the graph; the trick is to do it in time much less than n^n.

4. A graph G is said to have an **Eulerian cycle** if there is a cycle in G that contains each edge of G exactly once. The existence of an Eulerian cycle in a graph means that you can take a picture of the graph, place your pencil at one vertex, trace each edge exactly once without lifting your pencil from the graph, and return to the starting vertex, as in the following figure. Find a graph with no Eulerian cycle, and discover a condition that must hold for a graph to have an Eulerian cycle.

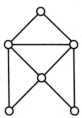 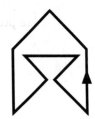

5. The adjacency matrix implementation of *DeleteVertex* given in the text could cause problems, because a program that uses *DeleteVertex* could then lose track of the correct references for the vertices (since if we deleted vertex 4 and moved the fourth row and column to fill the hole, all vertex numbers from 4 up would be off by 1). Describe how you would deal with this problem.

6. For the edge list implementation of *Graph*, write definitions for
   a. *DeleteEdge*
   b. *InsertVertex*
   c. *Size* (do two versions, one recursive and one not)
   d. *Find* and *DeleteCell*, nonrecursively

7. Implement *DepthFirst* for adjacency matrices, and compare it in efficiency and ease of programming with the edge list implementation given in the text.

8. In running *DepthFirst* on graphs with n vertices, how deep could the recursive calls be nested? Demonstrate your result.

9. There is a very nice way to count the number of spanning trees of a graph. If e is an edge of G that is not a loop, define the **contraction** $G \cdot e$ to be the (multi)graph that results when we remove e from G and merge its end vertices into one. The following sketches show a graph and two successive contractions. Notice that contracting an edge could lead to loops and multiple edges. Further, define $G-e$ to be the graph that results if we simply remove edge e without merging its endpoints. If we now let $t(G)$ be the number of spanning trees of a graph G, then t satisfies the recursive formula $t(G)=t(G \cdot e)+t(G-e)$ for any edge e that is not a loop.

  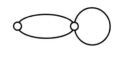

| G | $H = G \cdot e$ | $K = H \cdot e'$ |

a. Use this formula to count the number of spanning trees for the graph G in our sketch.
b. Draw all the spanning trees of graph G.
c. If a graph consists of just a simple cycle on n vertices, how many spanning trees does it have?
d. How many spanning trees does a tree have?
e. What data structure would you choose to implement an algorithm to count the number of spanning trees of a graph? It need not be one we have described.

10. For which of the three representations of *Graph* is it easiest (or fastest) to
    a. Tell whether two vertices are adjacent?

    b. Tell whether an edge and a vertex are **incident** (i.e., whether the vertex is an endpoint of the edge)?

    c. Count the number of edges in a graph?

    d. Decide whether a graph is connected?

    e. Decide whether a digraph is strongly connected?

    f. Implement Prim's algorithm?

11. Consider the following graph, called **Petersen's graph.**

    a. Find a depth-first spanning tree. So that everyone's answers are consistent, use the strategy that the nodes adjacent to a given node will be selected by alphabetic order.

    b. Find a breadth-first spanning tree using the same strategy as in part (a).

    c. Use Prim's algorithm to find an MST.

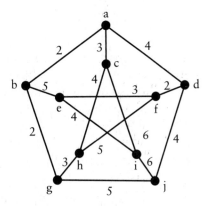

12. If a graph has the form of a binary tree, do depth-first or breadth-first traversals correspond in any way to preorder, inorder, or postorder traversals?

13. a. Write an algorithm to test whether a graph is connected.

    b. Write an algorithm to count the connected components of a graph.

14. The running time of Prim's algorithm depends on how fast we can find least-cost edges. Find a way to do this in $O(n)$ time, where n is the number of vertices of the graph.

15. Trace the action of Dijkstra's algorithm on the digraph of Exercise 11 to find least costs of travel from vertex b to all other vertices.

16. Give an example to show that Dijkstra's algorithm will not work properly if some of the edge weights are allowed to be negative.

17. In the exercises in Chapter 4, we discussed **finite automata** (**FA**), which were simple abstractions of computers. One way of looking at finite automata is as a collection of **states**, along with **transition rules** that describe how to change from one state to another, depending on the current input symbol to the finite automaton. One of the states is called the **start state**, since that's where the machine is at the start, and some of the states may be identified as **final states**. An FA is said to **accept** an input string if it winds up in a final state after having processed the entire string. We can model a finite automaton as a digraph, with vertices for states and edges for transitions. For example, the following figure accepts any string over the alphabet {a, b}, which contains "ab" as a substring, since, for example, the input string 'aaba' would start at state 1, read the first 'a' and move to state 3, read the second 'a' and move again to state 3, read the 'b' and move to state 4, and read the last 'a' and wind up in the (final) state 4, thereby accepting the input string.

    Finite automata are frequently used as **lexical analyzers** in compilers, whose job it is to scan the source code and accept tokens, the smallest meaningful units in the source code language.

    a. Design a finite automaton that accepts any legal C++ number literals, like 0, −45, 67.89, or −0.453e−2.

    b. Write an algorithm to accept legal C++ numbers. This can be done by letting each state be represented by a function that gets an input character and calls another state function, depending on the character received.

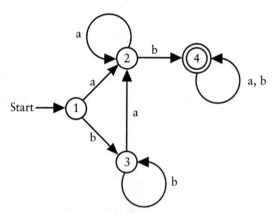

18. If we had a graph that represented city streets, and the recommendation of the traffic bureau was to make all streets one-way, we would then say that we had the problem of changing a graph to a digraph. Of course, one requirement for our conversion would be that the digraph be strongly connected, since at a minimum we would like the citizens of the city to be able to travel from any location to any other. The follow-

ing graph, for instance, could not be successfully translated to a digraph, because no matter how we directed the edges, it would be impossible to travel legally both from *a* to *b* and back again.

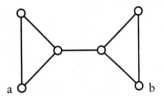

a. Give a condition that is necessary for a graph to be transformed into a strongly connected digraph.

b. Find an algorithm that assigns directions to the edges of a digraph in such a way as to make it strongly connected.

19. a. Show that the greedy algorithm for making change would not necessarily give the solution using the fewest number of coins if the coins used had values other than 1, 5, 10, 25, and 50.

 b. (Challenging) Find a condition on coin values that will guarantee that the greedy strategy of choosing coins in decreasing order of their value will always result in using the minimal number of coins.

20. Compare the amount of storage required for the adjacency matrix and edge list implementations of *Graph*. Assume that integers take 2 bytes, pointers take 4, that the graph has E edges, and that the adjacency matrix has αN rows, where N is the number of vertices in the graph and $\alpha > 1$. To make things fair, you may assume that there are no data stored in the vertices.

21. Find an edge-weighted graph for which the greedy heuristic for TSP fails to give the least-cost cycle.

22. Implement Prim's algorithm using the data structure of your choice.

23. Write a program to determine whether a graph has any cycles. *Hint*: You might want to make use of a spanning tree.

24. Write a program to find all spanning trees of a graph. Try this on some "random" graphs to see if you can make an estimate of the number of spanning trees a graph with *n* vertices has.

25. Write a program to find a solution for TSP. It wouldn't hurt to go to the library for this one. If your algorithm runs in polynomial time, let us know.

26. Write a program that finds a "pretty good" solution to TSP. One possibility would be to find any simple cycle at all that includes all vertices and then try to modify the cycle to one of less cost, as follows:

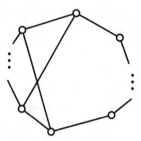 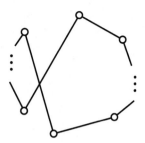

If your cycle has
any "internal" edges,
like these,

then see if this cycle
is any cheaper.

8.9   EXPLORATIONS

Topological Sorting

In situations where a number of tasks have to be performed, there are often dependencies among the tasks, so that one task must be completed before another may be started. In house building, roof construction can't start before the walls have been built, the walls can't be built before the foundation is laid, and the foundation can't be laid until excavation has finished. Similarly, college courses often have prerequisites that must be completed before the course can be taken.

Such dependencies can be captured by digraphs, where we represent each task by a vertex and draw a directed edge from vertex p to vertex q if p must be completed before q can be begun. In Figure 8.16, we have the digraph that represents dependencies in a hypothetical computer science major.

FIGURE 8.16

Dependency digraph
for prerequisite
courses

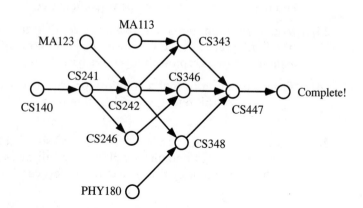

This sort of dependency takes place in computer applications all the time. While we have concentrated on programming in this text, there is clearly a lot more to running a program than simply writing it. The *Graph* class, for instance, needs two files, Graphs.h and Graphs.cpp. When we use *Graph* in a program, what happens, roughly, is that the compiler uses these two files to produce a machine code file, Graphs.o. If we were to modify Graphs.h, we would almost certainly require that Graphs.o be reconstructed to reflect our changes. It's not that simple, though, since *Graph* may use assertions that are declared in Assertions.h, so a change in Assertions.h would also force an update in Graphs.o. In a typical example, the system would have to keep track of the dependency digraph in Figure 8.17.

Notice that all these examples have a property in common that is not true in general for digraphs: They are all *acyclic,* which is to say that they do not contain any directed cycles. That's obviously a necessary property in these cases. If course A required course B, course B required course C, and course C required course A, it would be impossible to begin the major at all! If we have a **directed acyclic graph** (**DAG**), we can list the vertices in linear order in such a way that if there is a directed edge from vertex p to vertex q, then p occurs before q in this order. Such an order is called a **topological sort,** and in Figure 8.18 we give an example. Another way to look at a topological sort is to arrange the vertices of the DAG in a row, so that the arrows all run from left to right.

27. In the DAG in Figure 8.18, the topological sort lists the vertices in order *a, b, c, d,* although that's not the only possible correct order.

  a. Find two other topological sorts for the DAG in Figure 8.18.

  b. There are 24 possible ways to arrange the four vertices in order. How many of these are topological sorts?

28. What kinds of DAGs have only one topological order?

FIGURE 8.17

A dependency digraph for program files

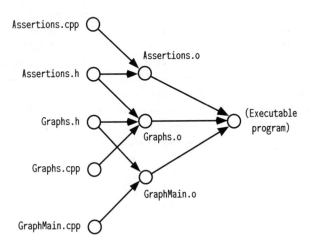

FIGURE 8.18

A DAG and one of its
topological sorts

29. Find a topological sort for the prerequisite DAG in Figure 8.16. In this example, what is an interpretation of the order you found? In other words, what use is topological sort in this case?

30. A **source** of a DAG is a vertex that has no predecessors. The DAGs in Figures 8.16, 8.17, and 8.18 have 4, 5, and 2 sources, respectively. Prove the following results about sources in DAGs.

    a. Every DAG has at least one source.

    b. If we remove a source and all its edges from a DAG, the resulting digraph is still a DAG.

31. Use the results of Exercise 30 to design a function that takes a digraph and lists its vertices in topological order.

32. There is another way to produce a topological sort.

    a. In a depth-first traversal of a DAG, what can you say about the vertices that are popped off the stack?

    b. Use part (a) to design a function that produces a topological order of a DAG.

Counting Paths

We now turn to an application to which we alluded before, namely, one that is tailor-made for the adjacency matrix implementation of *Graph*. To appreciate this application, you need to know something about matrix multiplication. If you already know how to multiply two matrices, you can skip ahead a few paragraphs until you come to something you don't recognize.

An $n \times m$ **matrix** is a rectangular arrangement of numbers, $a_{i,j}$, with $1 \le i \le m$, and $1 \le j \le n$. The first subscript denotes the **row** of the number, while the second tells the **column** in which the number may be found, so that the matrix just described has n rows and m columns. For instance, a 3×2 matrix, with 3 rows and 2 columns, would look like this:

$$\begin{bmatrix} a_{1,1} & a_{1,2} \\ a_{2,1} & a_{2,2} \\ a_{3,1} & a_{3,2} \end{bmatrix}$$

If A is a $p \times q$ matrix, and B is a $q \times r$ matrix, then we can define the **matrix product,** AB, to be the $p \times r$ matrix defined as follows. The entry in row i and column j of the product is found by multiplying each of the r elements in row i of A by the corresponding r elements of column j of B and then adding the products. That is, if $A = [a_{i,j}]$ and $B = [b_{i,j}]$, then

$$AB_{i,j} = \sum_{k=1}^{r} a_{i,k} b_{k,j}$$

For instance, suppose we had the following two matrices:

$$A = \begin{bmatrix} 3 & -1 & 0 \\ 2 & 4 & 1 \end{bmatrix} \quad B = \begin{bmatrix} 4 & 2 \\ 0 & -2 \\ 1 & 3 \end{bmatrix}$$

Then the product AB would be a 2×2 matrix with the entry in row 1 and column 2 equal to the sum of the products of the row 1 entries of A with the corresponding column 2 entries of B, or $(3)(2) + (-1)(-2) + (0)(3) = 8$. You should be able to complete the other three sums of products and show that

$$A = \begin{bmatrix} 3 & -1 & 0 \\ 2 & 4 & 1 \end{bmatrix} \begin{bmatrix} 4 & 2 \\ 0 & -2 \\ 1 & 3 \end{bmatrix} = \begin{bmatrix} 12 & 8 \\ 9 & -1 \end{bmatrix}$$

Now suppose that A was an $n \times n$ matrix that represented the adjacency matrix of a graph with n vertices, as in Figure 8.19. "A good start is a journey half completed," so the saying goes. The good start in this case is the observation that the i, j entry of the adjacency matrix counts the number of paths of length 1 (that is, with one edge) from vertex i to vertex j. Well, that's a moderately interesting way of looking at it, but the light really comes on when we consider the i, j entry of the *square* of the adjacency matrix, that is, the product of the adjacency matrix with itself. Consider the example in Figure 8.19, and look at the entry in row 2 and column 3 of the square of the adjacency matrix. That entry is obtained by adding the products of row 2 times the corresponding elements in column 3, which in this case is nothing but $(1)(1) + (0)(1) + (1)(0) + (1)(1) = 2$. The first pair of 1s come from the v_1 entries of row 2 and column 3, meaning that there is an edge from v_2 to v_1 and from v_1 to v_3, while the second pair of 1s come from the v_4 entries of row 2 and column 3, meaning that there is an edge from v_2 to v_4 and one from v_4 to v_3. But this just corresponds to the two paths from v_2 to v_3, namely, (v_2, v_1, v_3) and (v_2, v_4, v_3). In other words, if A is the adjacency matrix of a graph, then the i, j entry of A^2 counts the number of distinct paths of length 2 from vertex i to vertex j. It is not difficult to show that this property holds for arbitrary powers of the adjacency matrix, leading us to the following results.

FIGURE 8.19

A graph and its
adjacency matrix

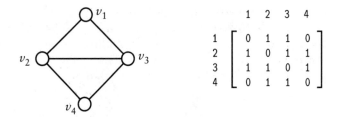

$$
\begin{array}{c}
\begin{array}{cccc}
\;1 & 2 & 3 & 4
\end{array} \\
\begin{array}{c}
1 \\ 2 \\ 3 \\ 4
\end{array}
\left[
\begin{array}{cccc}
0 & 1 & 1 & 0 \\
1 & 0 & 1 & 1 \\
1 & 1 & 0 & 1 \\
0 & 1 & 1 & 0
\end{array}
\right]
\end{array}
$$

> **Theorem.** If A is the adjacency matrix (with 1 for true and 0 for false) of a graph G, then the matrix power A^k has as its i, j entry the number of distinct paths (not just simple paths—vertices could repeat) in G of length k from vertex i to vertex j.
>
> **Corollary.** If A is the adjacency matrix of G, as in the theorem, then the total number of paths of length $\leq k$ from vertex i to vertex j in G is given by the i, j entry of $A + A^2 + \cdots + A^k$ (where the sum of two matrices of the same size is obtained by termwise addition of the entries in the matrices).

33. For the graph in Figure 8.19, compute the square of the adjacency matrix and verify that each i, j entry in the square does indeed count the number of paths of length 2 from v_i to v_j by identifying the paths.

34. How could you use these results to show that a graph was connected?

There are a number of different forms that these results might take, depending on the operations we choose for matrix "multiplication." Suppose, for instance, that we have an edge-weighted graph, where we store the weight of the $\{i, j\}$ edge in the i, j entry of the adjacency matrix.. Let's call ordinary matrix multiplication "plus-times" multiplication, since we add ("plus") the products ("times") of the entries. In "min-plus" matrix multiplication, for instance, the product entries are formed by taking the minimum of the sums of the entries, as

$$
AB_{i,j} = \underset{k=1,\,\ldots,\,r}{Minimum}\left\{a_{i,k} + b_{k,j}\right\}
$$

35. **a.** Find a reasonable interpretation of the min-plus matrix product for edge-weighted graphs.

    b. Does your interpretation also hold for edge-weighted digraphs?

36. Do Exercise 35 for "max-plus" matrix multiplication for edge-weighted graphs.

37. **a.** Find a reasonable interpretation of the "or-and" matrix product for unweighted graphs.

    b. Does your interpretation also hold for digraphs?

38. Come up with another form of matrix multiplication that has meaning for some class of graphs or digraphs.

9

UNORDERED COLLECTIONS

We have come to the end of our tour of abstract data types. We began with the most highly structured sets of positions when we talked about lists, and we passed to more complicated structures by gradually removing the restrictions on the structural relations until we came to digraphs, on which the structural relations had no restrictive conditions whatsoever. At each stage, we saw that the earlier structures could be viewed as special cases of the later ones: Lists are trees with no branching, and trees are connected digraphs with at most one edge leading into each vertex. It seems that there is no place to go from here. We have, with digraphs, already taken away all restrictions on the structure on the set of positions and allowed the structural relation to be any relation at all. In our final step, we will transcend structure completely and deal with an ADT that treats all positions equally.

We will discuss three abstract data types in this chapter: *Set, Dictionary,* and *PriorityQueue.* Each of these has the same structure: a collection of positions with no structural relation at all. Thus, there will be no such thing as the "next" position after a given one and no notion of a position being before or after another. The basic operation in all three ADTs will be to access an element, given its value (or, more often, given a key value that is part of the element's member data).

9.1 ADT: *SET*

The fundamental abstract data type for all unordered collections is the *Set* ADT. A set is a collection of positions with no structural relation, subject only to the condition that there be no duplicates among the elements stored in the positions.* To make the following specification easier to read, we have eliminated the element type parameter <*T*>.

▼

Set

Structure: A collection of positions with no structural relation. Each position has an associated element of type *T*, and there may not be any two positions with the same associated element.

Operations

Set(). Pre: true. Post: This set is empty (i.e., contains no positions).

Set(T e). Pre: true. Post: This set contains a single position, with which *e* is associated.

Set(const Set& s)). Pre: true. Post: This set is a copy of *s*.

void MakeEmpty(). Pre: true. Post: This set is empty.

Set& operator= (const Set& s). Pre: true. Post: This set is a copy of *s*.

Set-Level Operations

Set operator+ (Set a, Set b). Pre: true. Post: Returns a reference to a set equal to $a \cup b$, the **union** of *a* and *b*, so that an element is in $a+b$ if and only if it is in *a* or *b* or perhaps in both. For example, if we are dealing with sets of integers, then $\{3, 19, 8, 4\} \cup \{5, 3, 22\} = \{3, 4, 5, 8, 19, 22\}$.

Set operator* (Set a, Set b). Pre: true. Post: Returns a reference to a set equal to $a \cap b$, the **intersection** of *a* and *b*, consisting of all the elements in both *a* and *b*. For the two sets of the previous example, we have $\{3, 19, 8, 4\} \cap \{5, 3, 22\} = \{3\}$.

Set operator- (Set a, Set b). Pre: true. Post: Returns a reference to a set equal to $a-b$, the **difference** of *a* and *b*, consisting of all the elements in *a* that are not in *b*. Unlike union and intersection, set difference is not symmetric, so $\{3, 19, 8, 4\} - \{5, 3, 22\} = \{19, 8, 4\}$, but $\{5, 3, 22\} - \{3, 19, 8, 4\} = \{5, 22\}$.

void Insert(T e). Pre: true. Post: If *e* was not in this set, this set now contains *e* and otherwise is unchanged. If *e* was in this set, the original element *e* has been replaced with this one. This is a special case of union, and in C++ terminology, we could have included another overload of +, with second argument *T*. *Note:* This peculiar sounding "insertion by replacement" will be most applicable when the element type is accessed by a key member datum.

---

* If we relax this last constraint, we have another ADT, known as a **bag** or **multiset**. Bags are far less common in practice than sets.

void Remove(T e). Pre: true. Post: If *e* was not in this set, this set is unchanged. If *e* was in this set, it has been removed. As with *Insert*, this is a one-element version of set difference.

Predicates

int Contains(T e) const. Pre: true. Post: This set is unchanged. Returns 1 if *e* is in this set; otherwise, returns 0.

int operator< (Set a, Set b). Pre: true. Post: Returns 1 if and only if *a* is a **subset** of *b*, which is to say, if every element of *a* is also an element of *b*.

int operator== (Set a, Set b). Pre: true. Post: Returns 1 if and only if *a* and *b* have exactly the same elements. Notice that we could define == in terms of <, since two sets are equal if and only if they are subsets of each other.

The declaration of the *Set* class is very nearly a straight translation of the specification. As we have done before, we will declare the binary operators for union, intersection, difference, subset, and equality as friends.

```
template<class T>
class Set
{
    friend Set<T>    operator+ (Set<T> a, Set<T> b);
    friend Set<T>    operator* (Set<T> a, Set<T> b);
    friend Set<T>    operator- (Set<T> a, Set<T> b);
    friend int       operator< (Set<T> a, Set<T> b);
    friend int       operator== (Set<T> a, Set<T> b);
public:
    Set();
    Set(T e);
    Set(const Set<T>& s);
    void MakeEmpty();
    Set<T>& operator= (const Set<T>& s);
    void Insert(T e);
    void Remove(T e);
    int Contains(T e);
    int IsEmpty();
};
```

Be aware that this declaration is incomplete. We have obviously left out any private data members or the specification of any inheritance, but we'll remedy this omission shortly, when we discuss two different implementations of the *Set* class.

IMPLEMENTATIONS OF *SET*

We will begin our investigation of *Set* implementations with one we have mentioned twice already, one that in some cases makes the *Set* operations as fast as possible.

Bit Vectors

If we are lucky enough to have an element type T that (1) has fairly few elements and (2) can be mapped into the range of integers $0, \ldots, N-1$ in some efficient way, then we can make use of a very simple and fast implementation of *Set*. We do this by representing each set of elements of T by a bit vector, which, you may recall, is an array of 0s and 1s. We then would interpret such an array as representing the set consisting of all those elements that had a 1 in the corresponding array entry. For example, if we considered the elements to be the days of the week, we could implement the subsets of the days of the week by using an enumeration and defining an array indexed by this type, as follows:

```
enum Days { Sun, Mon, Tue, Wed, Thu, Fri, Sat};
typedef int DaySet[7];
```

With this implementation, the subset of weekdays would take the form given in Figure 9.1, and we would understand that the bit pattern 0111110 represented that set.

The nicest feature of this implementation is that the set operations correspond directly to Boolean operations on the elements of the bit vectors. For example, to find the union of two sets represented by bit vectors a and b, all we need to realize is that their union has a 1 in array element i if and only if $a[i]$ or $b[i]$ is 1. This assignment of a value for the union, c, then, is nothing but $c[i]=a[i] \,||\, b[i]$, done for all values of i in the universal set.

To use this implementation, we will include a private data member in our class declaration.

```
private:
    // Vector is a bit vector with as many elements
    // as the universal set T.
    int vector[N];
```

FIGURE 9.1

A bit vector representation for days of the week

Sun	Mon	Tue	Wed	Thu	Fri	Sat
0	1	1	1	1	1	0

To complete this declaration, we assume that T is some type with N possible values and that there is a function h (perhaps implicit, as in the weekdays example of Figure 9.1) for which $h(e)$ takes a different value in the range $0, \ldots,$ $N-1$ for each element e in T.* One nice feature of using bit vectors to represent sets is that it makes many of the functions quite easy to define. We'll give a few sample definitions here and leave the remaining ones as exercises.

```
Set<T>::Set()
// Construct an empty set by making the bits for each element
// equal to zero.
{
    for (int i = 0; i < N; i++)
        vector[index] = 0;
}


void Set<T>::Insert(T e)
// Whether e was in the set before or not, include it in the set
// by setting its bit to 1.
{
    vector[h(e)] = 1;
}


int Set<T>::Contains(T e)
{
    return vector[h(e)];
}


Set operator+ (Set<T> a, Set<T>)
// Returns the union of a and b.  Bit i of the union is 1
// if and only if there is a 1 in bit i of either a or b
// or both.
{
    Set r;
    for (int i = 0; i < N; i++)
        r.vector[i] = a.vector[i] || b.vector[i];
    return r;
}


Set operator* (Set<T> a, Set<T>)
// Returns the intersection of a and b.
{
    Set r;
```

---

* In mathematical terms, h is a **one-to-one** function, which is to say that if x and y are elements of type T with $x \neq y$, then $h(x) \neq h(y)$.

```
        for (int i = 0; i < N; index++)
            r.vector[i] = a.vector[i] && b.vector[i];
        return r;
}


int operator< (Set<T> a, Set<T>)
// Returns 1 if and only if a is a subset of b.
// (You'll have to think a bit about this one.)
{
    int i = 0;
    while ((i < N) && (!a.vector[i] || b.vector[i]))
        i++;
    return (i == N);
}
```

It isn't hard to show that in this implementation, *Insert, Remove,* and *Contains* run in constant time, while all the other operations take time $O(N)$, where N is the (fixed) size of the universal set, T, of elements. You can see that this is a fairly efficient package, especially when the size of the universal set is small. We could raise a minor quibble that a set must take the same amount of room in memory whether it is empty or equal to the entire universal set, but if we can somehow write our operations so that each array entry takes a single bit, the arrays will be quite small, so the amount of wasted memory will be negligible, except for gigantic universal sets (which is why we couldn't use this implementation to represent the set of all integers).

We can pack information much more efficiently in the bit vector at the expense of a little more work. A C++ long is guaranteed to be at least 32 bits long in any implementation that conforms to the standard, so we could represent a bit vector of N bits using an array long[N / 32]. Then the ith bit in our bit vector would be found in bit i % 32 of entry $i/32$ in the array, as we illustrate in Figure 9.2, where we have crammed 96 bits into an array of three long integers.

The best part of this implementation is that C++ has operations that perform bitwise logical operations on all the bits of a number at once. If a and b are numbers, the expression a & b returns the number that results from taking the logical AND of each of the corresponding bits in a and b, so 0101 &

FIGURE 9.2

Packing a bit vector in an array of long integers

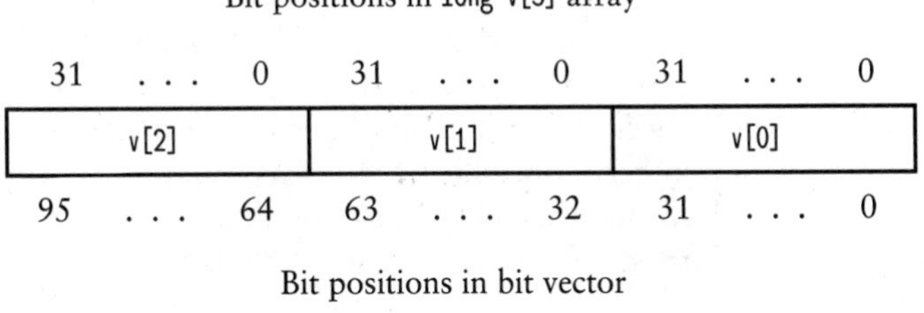

Bit positions in long v[3] array

Bit positions in bit vector

1001 would return the bits 0001. Similarly, $a|b$ returns the bitwise logical OR of a and b, and $\sim a$ returns the result of inverting every bit in a, from 0 to 1 and vice versa. This means that union, intersection, and difference require only as many iterations as there are elements in the array of longs.

Getting or setting the value of an individual bit is also simple, since C++ allows us to shift the bits in a number. The operator << shifts the contents of a number left by a specified amount, so the expression n << 3 returns the number that results when we shift the bits of n to the left by three positions. The operator >> does the same sort of shifting, but to the right. To get the kth bit of the long integer n, then, we would initialize a long to 1, shift it left by k, take the bitwise AND of the mask and n (thereby setting all but the kth bit to zero), and shift the result right k places.

```
int KthBit(int k, long n)
// Returns the value of the k-th bit of n.
{
    long mask = 1;
    return ((n & (mask << k)) >> k);
}
```

This implementation is nice enough, in fact, that it would be a worth-while exercise for you to use it to design a *BitVector* class. Because of the inherent speed of bit vector operations, some computers have been specifically designed as **bit vector machines**, capable of operating on very long bit vectors in parallel, similar to the way other computers operate on single words. In addition to their suitability for set operations, such machines are also particularly suited for fast arithmetic on very large integers (for example, factoring large integers like RSA-129 or testing whether a large number is prime).

Sets Represented by Lists

There are at least three reasons why we might not be able to use bit vectors to represent sets:

1. The underlying universal set of elements might be too large to represent in a bit vector (like doubles or strings, for example).
2. There might not be any obvious way to map the elements of the underlying set into some range 0, . . . , N of integers (though you'll come to see that this isn't as big a problem as it might appear to be).
3. The elements in the universal set might contain more information than can be represented by the implicit linear order of the bit vector. Suppose, for instance, that we wanted to deal with sets of employee records. Even if each element had a *key field*—like Social Security number—on which there was a natural linear order, we would still have no way of storing the rest of the information—like address, birth date, and pay rate—in the bit vector.

One solution to all three of these problems would be to represent a set as a list of elements. We could do this either by including a private data member in our class,

```
private:
   TList<T> data;
```

or by making *Set* a derived class of the private base class TList<T>.

```
template<class T>
class Set : private TList<T>
// We make TList a private base class, since we want to have
// access to the List operations, but we don't want the user
// of the Set class to be able to call them.
{
   // Declaration of the Set operations
} ;
```

This representation has the advantage that each set requires no more room than is actually required for the elements of the sets (and the linking pointers, if we used linked lists) and places no immediate upper limit on the size of the universal set. We do have to pay for this extensibility, however, since some of the operations now take longer than they did in the bit vector implementation.

We can test whether an element is in a set by calling the list operation *Includes,* which takes time $O(n)$ on sets of n elements, as opposed to the constant time it takes with bit vectors. It would appear that if we used linked lists, insertion and deletion would run in constant time, but unfortunately, in both we have to take $O(n)$ time to check whether the element is in the set (since we can't insert an element that's already in the set and we have to find where in the list the element to be deleted resides).

The big losers in this implementation are the union, intersection, difference, subset, and equality operations. It is not difficult to see that it could take $O(n^2)$ time to find the intersection of two sets with n elements, for instance, since we might need to test each element in one set against all the elements in the other set. Take a look at the intersection operator. It's easy to write, but its simplicity hides the $O(n)$ cost of searching for an element by *Includes.*

```
Set<T> operator* (Set<T> a, Set<T> b)
// Returns the intersection of a and b.
// Here, we're using the declaration of Set as a derived class
// of the private base class TList<T>.
{
   Set<T> r;
   a.Head();
```

```
    for (int i = 0; i < a.Length(); i++)
    {
        T currentValue = a.Retrieve();
        if (b.Includes(currentValue))    // We've found a match
            r.Insert(currentValue);      // so insert it in r,
        a++;                             // and get the next element.
    }
    return r;
}
```

If the underlying set *T* is linearly ordered by some key value, we can do better, at the expense of complicating our definitions. By using sorted lists, which we covered in Explorations in Chapter 2, we can reduce the time of these operations from quadratic to linear. To find the intersection of two sorted lists, for instance, all we need to do is traverse the two lists together, looking for a match between the two current elements. If they match, then the current value is appended to the end of the output list; if they don't, then the current position with the smaller value is incremented to the next position. This process is repeated until one of the lists is used up. For example, to find the intersection of the ordered lists (2, 8, 12, 14) and (3, 6, 8, 10), we would have the following steps:

2	8	12	14	No match, so advance the list with the smaller value.
3	6	8	10	

2	8	12	14	No match, advance the list with the smaller element.
3	6	8	10	

2	8	12	14	No match, advance again.
3	6	8	10	

2	8	12	14	Found a match, so put 8 into the output list and
3	6	8	10	advance both.

2	8	12	14	No match, so try to advance. We find that we can't go
3	6	8	10	any farther in the second list, so we know we're done.

It's clear that in the worst case, we'll have to make no more passes through this algorithm than the sum of the lengths of the two lists. The definition of the intersection operator is a bit more complicated now, involving as it does an auxiliary function *Advance* that tries to advance the current position in a list and returns 1 if it can and 0 if it cannot.

```
int Advance(Set<T>& s, T currentVal, T lastVal)
{
    if (currentVal == lastVal)    // Are we at the last value?
        return 0;                 // If so, report failure.
    else
    {
        s++;                      // If not, advance to next position
```

```
        return 1;        // and report success.
    }
}


Set<T> operator* (Set<T> a, Set<T> b)
// Returns the intersection of a and b.
// Assumes that Set<T> is a derived class of the private
// base class SortedList<T>.
{
    Set<T> r;
    // If one of the sets is empty, so is the intersection.
    if ((a.Length() > 0) && (b.Length() > 0))
    {
        a.Tail();
        T aLast = a.Retrieve();
        b.Tail();
        T bLast = b.Retrieve();

        a.Head();
        b.Head();
        int canContinue = 1;
        while (canContinue)
        {
            T  aCurrent = a.Retrieve(),
               bCurrent = b.Retrieve();
            if (aCurrent == bCurrent)
            {
                r.Insert(aCurrent);
                canContinue = Advance(a, aCurrent, aLast) &&
                              Advance(b, bCurrent, bLast);
            }
            else if (aCurrent < bCurrent)
                canContinue = Advance(a, aCurrent, aLast);
            else
                canContinue = Advance(b, bCurrent, bLast);
        }
    return r;
}
```

We've seen two implementations of *Set*. Both seem seriously flawed: There are some sets for which we can't use bit vectors at all, but using lists to represent sets makes some of the set operations run more slowly than we wish. We're actually in better shape than we appear to be, however. Frequently, an application that requires sets will have an underlying universal set that rules out the use of bit vectors, yet doesn't require the use of the time-consuming union, intersection, difference, and subset operators. It will be precisely those applications that will occupy our attention for the rest of this chapter.

ADT: *DICTIONARY*

Consider once again the problem of maintaining a collection of payroll records for a company's employees. It's clear that the primary operation we would want is one that retrieves an employee's information, given his or her name. We can see that there probably would not be any structure on the employees (such as who is the immediate supervisor of whom) that would be of any interest to the people in the payroll office. Another example of such a structure would be the **symbol table** of a compiler, which is used to keep track of the constant, type, function, and variable names of a source code program. This situation arises often enough in practice that it has been abstracted into an ADT of its own, called the *Dictionary*. First, though, we'll define a helper class that will serve to keep matters organized.

Associations

In implementing *Dictionary,* it will be helpful to regard an individual element as being split into two parts: a *key,* which never changes and is used to identify the element, and a *value,* which holds all the rest of the information and which may be updated and modified. We can then consider a larger structure that is built from an unordered collection of associations.

It is simple enough to declare an *Association* class to represent *Dictionary* elements. As usual, we will parametrize this class, but for the first time, we will need to use two type parameters, one for the key type, *K,* and one for the value type, *V.*

```
template<class K,  class V>
class Association
{
    friend int operator == (Association<K, V> a1, Association<K, V> a2)
       { return (a1.key == a2.key);} ;
    friend int operator!= (Association<K, V> a1, Association<K, V> a2)
       { return (a1.key != a2.key);};
public:
    Association () { };
    Association (K aKey) {  key = aKey;};
    Association (K aKey, V aValue) {  key = aKey; value = aValue;};
    Association (const Association<K, V>& a);

    Association<K, V>& operator= (const Association<K, V>& a);

    K Key()
    { return key;};
    V& Value()
    { return value;};
```

```
private:
   K key;
   V value;
};
```

For simplicity's sake, we have omitted the definitions of the copy constructor and assignment operator, but they would be simple to write. Notice that we have overloaded the comparison operators so that two associations will be equal if and only if they have the same key. You will see shortly why we need to compare associations. We have provided two access functions to the *key* and *value* member data—observe that the user of this class can change *value* through the *Value* accessor function, since it returns a reference to *value*, but the user can only inspect *key*.

We can now specify the *Dictionary* ADT. A dictionary is an unordered collection of elements that supports insertion of an element, along with retrieval and deletion by key value.

Dictionary : Set

Structure.   *Dictionary* has the same structure (or lack thereof) as *Set*. The elements of the dictionary have a *key* member datum that determines membership in the set (so there will never be two elements in a dictionary with the same key) and a *value* datum that contains other information.

Operations.   With the exception of *IsEmpty*, *MakeEmpty*, and *Insert*, none of the *Set* operations are available to users of *Dictionary*.

`Dictionary()`. Pre: true. Post: This dictionary is created and is empty.

`void Remove(K aKey)`. Pre: true. Post: If there was an element in this dictionary with *key* datum *aKey*, that element has been removed from the dictionary. If there was no such element, this dictionary is unchanged.

`V Retrieve(K aKey)`. Pre: There is an element in this dictionary with key *aKey*. Post: This set is unchanged. Returns the *value* field of the element with key *aKey*.

`int Contains(K aKey)`. Pre: There is an element in this dictionary with key *aKey*. Post: This set is unchanged. Returns the value of the element with key *aKey*.

We did not include a copy constructor or an assignment operator, although they wouldn't have been difficult to define, because most applications that use *Dictionary* only use one. Although *Dictionary* is abstractly a subtype of *Set*, we'll implement *Dictionary* using a list of associations as a private data member. We could derive *Dictionary* from *Set,* but since the bit vector implementation is clearly not applicable here, we would have to use the *List* implementation of *Set.* That being the case, we decided for efficiency's sake to eliminate the middleman and define the *Dictionary* operations in terms of *TList<Association<K, V>>.*

```
# include "Lists.h"

template<class K, class V>
class Dictionary
{
public:
    Dictionary();
    void MakeEmpty();

    void Insert(Association<K, V>, a);
    void Remove(K key);
    V Retrieve(K key);

    int Contains(K key);
    int IsEmpty();

private:
    TList<Association<K, V> > data;
};
```

In the following implementation file listing, we can see the power of object-oriented programs. We're putting our classes to work here. Using the *List* class's operations makes life so easy for us that none of these function definitions takes more than four lines of code.

```
//================= Dictionary.cpp =================

#include <iostream.h>
#include "Assertions.h"
#include "Dictionary.h"

template<class K, class V>
Dictionary<K, V>::Dictionary() :
{
}

template<class K, class V>
void Dictionary<K, V>::MakeEmpty()
{
    data.Clear();
}
```

```
template<class K, class V>
void Dictionary<K, V>::Insert(Association <K, V> a)
{
   if (data.Includes(a))
      data.Update(a);
   else
      data.InsertAfter(a);
}
```

In the definitions of *Remove, Retrieve,* and *Contains,* we have made use of the *Association* constructor that builds an association from a key. We use this so that we can call the *List* function *Includes* to do two things: to return an integer indicating whether the list contains an association with the desired key and, as a side effect, to set the current position in the list to the position containing the desired association so that we can perform a subsequent deletion or retrieval.

```
template<class K, class V>
void Dictionary<K, V>::Remove(K key)
{
   Association<K, V> a(key);
   if (data.Includes(a))
      data.Remove();
}

template<class K, class V>
V Dictionary<K, V>::Retrieve(K key)
{
   Association<K, V> a(key);
   Assert(data.Includes(a), "Unknown key in Retrieve");

   return data.Retrieve().Value();
}

template<class K, class V>
int Dictionary<K, V>::Contains(K key)
{
   Association<K, V> a(key);
   return data.Includes(a);
}

template<class K, class V>
int Dictionary<K, V>::IsEmpty()
{
   return (data.Length() == 0);
}
```

9.4 HASHING

The main problem with our implementation of *Dictionary* is that it takes too long to find an element, given its key. Suppose, for instance, we were writing a payroll package, and we wanted to be able to access an employee's record by the name of the employee. We know that array access is fast, but only if we know the index of an element in the array. In this case, if we stored the associations in an array, we might not have a clue as to where in the array Erasmus Fleagle's record would reside. What we'd really like to do is have an array indexed by strings, so that we could have constant-time access, but of course that's not available to us in C++. The best we could do would be to order the records alphabetically by name and perform a binary search on the name key, using a sorted list for our private *data* member. We showed in Chapter 2 that binary search is logarithmically fast, but binary search is only practical on arrays, and insertion into arrays takes linear time. What we'll do is produce something like we did in the bit vector implementation of *Set*: a function, *h*, that would act as an oracle, so that *h* applied to the string 'Erasmus Fleagle' would return the index in the array where that person's record was located.

A simple scheme would be to let *h* take a string as input, add the code values of the characters of the name (the ASCII codes, for instance), and return $sum \% N$, where N is the size of the array. For example, suppose we had an array with space for 120 associations, indexed from 0 to 119. We could take the name 'JONES' and form the sum of the character values 'J' $\rightarrow 74$, 'O' $\rightarrow 79$, 'N' $\rightarrow 78$, 'E' $\rightarrow 69$, and 'S' $\rightarrow 83$, to obtain $(74 + 79 + 78 + 69 + 83) = 383 \% 120 = 23$, so that the record with key field 'JONES' would reside in array location 23. What we have done is to transform the problem of array access by key to a process that works almost as fast as array access, by processing the name through *h* to produce an index in the array. Such a function, which transforms keys to array indices, is called a **hash function**, because we are chopping the name into bits and reassembling the bits into something palatable, as we do with corned beef hash.

We don't need to limit ourselves to hashing on strings, of course. We could equally well hash on a key field of any type, as long as we could come up with a good way to transform the key to an array index. We could hash on employee birthdays, for instance, by computing the day of the year the person was born and using a table with 365 entries (ignoring those people who were born on February 29, one supposes). The problem with these hash functions is that they lead to **collisions**, in which several keys hash to the same location. In the preceding name hash, for instance, it is easy to verify that 'QUARRELS' and 'STEEN' both hash to 23, as did 'JONES'. This problem is often exacerbated by poor choice of hash function, like the one that takes the first two letters of a person's last name and uses them to compute a number from 0 to 675 by the rule

$$26 * (\text{first letter order} - 1) + (\text{second letter order} - 1)$$

where the "order" of a letter is its position in alphabetical order. In other words, 'AA' would hash to 0, 'AD' would hash to 3, and 'BA' would hash to 26. This is a poor hash function, since there are many names that begin with the same two letters, and there are many two-letter combinations that are not likely to be the start of any name, like 'QX.' Clearly, we want a hash function that "randomizes" its output as much as possible.

Even if we have a good hash function, we are still not out of trouble. Suppose we decided to hash on birthdays within a year. If we had a table with 365 entries, you might guess that we could fill the table nearly half full before we would have to worry about coming up with two people with the same birthday. Try it the next time you are with a small group of people; the results may be surprising. It turns out that with 23 people, it is slightly better than even money that two of them have the same birthday; with 40 people, the odds rise to about 10 to 1 in favor of duplicate birthdays.* In fact, the probability that among n people at least two of them will have the same birthday (if we make the slightly incorrect simplifying assumption that it is equally likely for people to be born on any day) is

$$1 - \frac{(365)(364)(363) \cdots (366 - n)}{365^n}$$

Given that collisions are inevitable in any hashing scheme (except where the size of the table is larger than the total number of elements to be inserted, and then only when the hash function is carefully chosen), we need to have a **collision resolution strategy** to handle collisions when they occur. The simplest strategy is **linear resolution**: If $h(x)$, for some key x, points to a location that is already occupied, we inspect the next location in the array. If that location is full, we try the one after that, and so on, until we discover a vacant location or find that the **hash table**, as the array is called, is completely full. As a simple example, suppose that the elements to be stored had integer keys and that the hash function was $h(x) = x \% 7$. If the integers 23, 14, 9, 6, 30, 12, and 18 were to be inserted in that order into a table T, with indices $0, \ldots, 6$, we would have the following steps, illustrated in Figure 9.3.

1. $h(23) = 2$, so the element with key 23 would be stored in $T[2]$.
2. $h(14) = 0$, so the element with key 14 would be stored in $T[0]$.
3. $h(9) = 2$, but $T[2]$ is already occupied, so the element with key 9 would be stored in $T[3]$.
4. $h(6) = 6$, so the element with key 6 would be stored in $T[6]$.

---

* Introductory probability texts sometimes suggest that an easy way to make money is to bet on the chance of a duplicate birthday. We suspect, however, that the odds of a person in the group having heard of this **birthday paradox** rise even faster as a function of the size of the group than do the odds of a duplicate birthday.

FIGURE 9.3

Hashing with linear
resolution of collisions

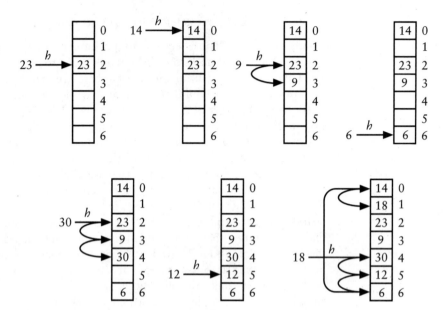

5. $h(30) = 2$, but both $T[2]$ and $T[3]$ are occupied, so the element with key 30 would be stored in $T[4]$.
6. $h(12) = 5$, so the element with key 12 would be stored in $T[5]$.
7. $h(18) = 4$, but $T[4]$, $T[5]$, and $T[6]$ are occupied, so we "wrap around" the array indices and go back to $T[0]$, which is also occupied, so the element with key 18 would finally be stored in $T[1]$.

We can count that it took 14 **probes** into the hash table to fill it in this example: 7 initial probes to hash the elements into the table and 7 further probes to resolve the collisions. Notice that successive insertions tend to produce **clusters** of adjacent entries separated by empty cells. This is an important property that deserves mention. To test whether an element is in a hash table built by linear resolution of collisions, we need only probe to the first empty cell, since insertion would never have passed beyond an empty cell. We will return to the question of the number of probes required to insert or find an element later, but before we do, we will implement the *Dictionary* ADT using a hash table.

A hash table is sufficiently handy that we'll define it as a class. From the outside, a *Table* will look like an array of values of type *V*. The nicest part of our implementation of *Table* is that C++ allows us to define it so that it appears to the user that the indices are the keys! In other words, to insert Erasmus Fleagle's record into a table *tab,* all we have to do is refer to *tab*["Erasmus Fleagle"], which is exactly what we wanted to do at the beginning of this section.

In this implementation, we store our information as an array of pointers to associations. Initially, each entry of the array will contain a NULL pointer.

As you will see, deletion is made simpler if we replace the deleted item with one with a special key, *flagKey*, provided by the user, which is easily distinguishable from any "real" key. One might, for instance, use "??????????" as *flagKey* in the employee records example, since there is no way that a string of question marks could possibly be confused with the name of a person.

```
template<class K, class V>
class Table
{
public:
   Table(unsigned int size, K flag);
   void MakeEmpty();

   V& operator[] (K key);
   void Remove(K key);

   int Contains(K key);
   int Size() {  return currentSize;};

private:
   unsigned int  MAX,
                 currentSize;   // number of elements in the table
   K flagKey;
   Association<K, V>* data[];

   unsigned int Hash(K key);     // a suitably defined hash function
   unsigned int FindIndex(K key);
} ;
```

To create a new table, the user specifies the size of the table and the value that will be used to represent the deleted elements.

```
template<class K, class V>
Table<K, V>::Table(unsigned int size, K flag)
{
   MAX = size;
   currentSize = 0;
   flagKey = flag;
   data = new Association<k, V>* [MAX];
   for (int i = 0; i < MAX; i++)
      data[i] = NULL;
}
```

The private utility function, *FindIndex*, will be the basic means of access into the array. When given a key, it first calls *Hash* to find the location of the first probe. If that location contains a pointer to an association with the correct key, there's nothing more to do except return the array index. If the location contains a NULL pointer, there's likewise nothing more to do. If the location contains a pointer to an association with a key that doesn't match the given key, the function searches the cluster until it either finds the correct key or comes to a NULL pointer. While it is searching the cluster, it will keep track of the first index it finds that has a flag key. If it ultimately fails to find the given key and has found a flag key, it will return that index (or –1 if the table is completely full). This will be handy when inserting a new association, as you will see.

```
template<class K, class V>
int Table<K, V>::FindIndex(K key)
{
   unsigned int index = Hash(key),
                start = index;                // so we don't wrap completely
                                              // around the table
   if (data[index] && (data[index]->Key() == key))
      return index;    // Found key on first probe.
   else
   {
      int place = -1;
      do
      {
         index = (1 + index) % MAX;
         if (place == -1)
         // Haven't yet found a place where key could go.
            if ( (data[index] == NULL) ||
                 (data[index]->Key() == flagKey))
            // Now we have, so store it.
               place = index;
         // Keep looking until we find the end of a cluster or
         // find the key, or wrap completely around the table.
      } while  (data[index] &&
                (data[index]->Key() != key) &&
                (index != start));
      if (data[index] && (data[index]->Key() == key))
         return index;  // Found the key.
      else
         return place;  // Nope, no luck.
   }
}
```

The subscript operator is far easier to define. We first find the index corresponding to the key. If the table is completely full, we have no choice but to bail out of the program. That's why we provided *Size* instead of just *IsEmpty*: The user of this table knows the size it was initialized to and can compare that against the current size to guard against potential overflow.

Assuming things work well, though, either we find an association with the given key or we don't. If we find the key we're looking for, or don't find it but find a deleted cell to use, we're done. If we come to the end of a cluster, we make a new cell for the key. In simple terms, this operator acts like a "nice" array: If we ask for an index that doesn't exist, it will cheerfully provide one for us if it can.

```
template<class K, class V>
V& Table<K, V>::operator[] (K key)
{
   int index = FindIndex(key);
   Assert(index != -1, "Table is full, no room for new access");
   if (data[index] == 0)
   {
      data[index] = new Association<K, V>(key);
      currentSize++;
   }
   return data[index]->Value();
}
```

Removing an element with a given key is also simple. If we find the key, we replace it with the flag. If the key is not in the table, we do nothing.

```
template<class K, class V>
void Table<K, V>::Remove(K key)
{
   int index = FindIndex(key)
   if ((index != -1) && data[index] && (data[index]->Key() == key))
   {
      delete data[index];
      data[index] = new Association<K, V>(flagKey);
      currentSize--;
   }
}
```

It might seem at first glance that we are going to unnecessary lengths with deletion. Why not simply delete the cell and make its pointer NULL? The problem with that scheme is that in doing so we separate a cluster into two, and we test for membership by testing all the entries in the cluster where the key should be, stopping at the first empty cell. Suppose, for instance, that we inserted "JONES", "QUARRELS", and "STEEN", in that order, using the "good" hash function we defined previously. The hash table might then take the following form:

```
   . . .        . . .
T[23]   "JONES"
T[24]   "QUARRELS"
```

$T[25]$ "STEEN"

$T[26]$ {NULL pointer here}

Then, after deleting "QUARRELS" and replacing it (incorrectly) with EMPTY, we would have

. . .   . . .

$T[23]$ "JONES"

$T[24]$ {NULL pointer here}

$T[25]$ "STEEN"

$T[26]$ {NULL pointer here}

Then a membership test for "STEEN" would stop at the end of the first cluster, at index 24, and report (incorrectly) failure to find the key, because linear resolution of collisions never inserts an element beyond an empty cell.

Open Hashing

The hashing strategy we have just described is known as **closed hashing**. Its biggest drawback is that there is a fixed upper bound on the size of the table, and even if the table never fills up completely, it still may not function as efficiently as we would like. One of the other problems associated with closed hashing is **primary clustering**, where clusters are formed when several elements whose keys hash to the same value are inserted into the table. Primary clustering, though difficult to eliminate entirely, can be alleviated to a degree by choosing a hash function that "randomizes" the hash values as much as possible. As a consequence of primary clustering, we may also experience **secondary clustering**, caused by inserting keys that do not hash to the value that caused the primary cluster, but nevertheless hash to values that are already in a cluster (because of resolution of collisions in the earlier insertions). Secondary clustering, then, arises from the coalescing of primary clusters. Later we will discuss some techniques for lessening clustering in closed hashing, but now we will consider a technique that sidesteps clustering entirely.

What we will do is not resolve collisions at all. If a key hashes into an occupied bucket, we will simply place it in the bucket (which is what a table cell is usually called), along with the values that are already there. This technique, known as **open hashing**, is usually accomplished by using a linked list for every bucket, accessed by pointers in the hash table, as illustrated in Figure 9.4. Notice that in this implementation, we no longer have any need for the flag key; to delete an element, all we need to do is remove it from the linked list.

Although the figure shows one-way linked lists, we could, of course, use any of the list techniques available to us, like doubly linked lists or arrays. In fact, since there is no structure on the elements in a bucket, we see that any of the *Set* implementations would serve to implement the buckets. We could use binary search trees, since that would speed insertion and deletion, or we

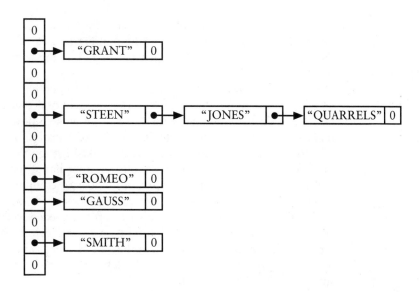

FIGURE 9.4

Open hashing

could even have each bucket be a small hash table itself. Most of the time, however, we should be content with a linked list open hash table that has a fixed constant *k* times as many entries as there are buckets, so that access to a bucket via the hashing function takes constant time, and membership testing, insertion, and deletion take $O(k)$ time, on the average, since the average number of entries per bucket is *k*. In other words, as long as the elements are fairly evenly spread through the buckets, all of the operations should run in constant time. You should have no difficulty defining the *Table* operations for this implementation, using the *List* class for the buckets.

Time and Space Estimates

We have seen two different versions of hashing: closed hashing, with linear resolution of collisions, and open hashing. In the Explorations, we present some of the (many) other possible schemes. We can summarize the number of probes required to search for an element easily, although the proofs of these theoretical estimates would take us too far afield to be included here. They're not frightfully difficult, but they are a bit long and require some knowledge of probability theory. If you want to see the steps required to arrive at these results, refer to the sources cited in the summary.

We will count the number of probes required for the *Table* operations, since the number of probes is a fairly good estimator of the amount of time the algorithms will take. Throughout this section, we will let λ denote the load on the table, that is, the quotient n/B, where *n* is the number of elements now in the table and *B* is the number of buckets in the table. For closed hashing, λ is a number between 0 and 1, where $\lambda = 0$ if the table is empty, and $\lambda = 1$

if the table is completely filled. For open hashing, λ can be any nonnegative number, since there is no limit to the number of elements in the list for each bucket. Notice also that for open hashing, λ is the average number of elements per bucket.

We will begin with the easiest analysis, for open hashing. If we search for an element in an open hash table, either we will find that element or we will not. If we do not find the element, then we won't know that until we have traversed the entire bucket list. That will take 1 probe to find the right bucket, and then λ more steps to traverse the linked list, on the average, for a total of $1+\lambda$ probes expected. Suppose, on the other hand, that our search is successful. It turns out that the expected number of comparisons needed to find an element in a list of length λ by sequential search is $(\lambda+1)/2$, plus 1 probe to find the right bucket. The number of probes needed to delete an element is clearly the same as the number required for a successful search, and if we insert an element, we need to be sure that the element is not in the table, so the number of probes for insertion is the same as for an unsuccessful search. We summarize these results as follows.

> ***Theorem 1:*** In open hashing on a table with load λ, the expected number of probes for insertion or an unsuccessful search is $1+\lambda$, and the expected number of probes for deletion or a successful search is $1+(\lambda+1)/2$ (or just 2 if $\lambda<1$).

We can describe similar results for two closed hashing techniques, linear resolution of collisions and **random hashing**, where the elements are somehow placed into the table at random locations. We use random hashing as a benchmark, because it's not actually an algorithm that can be implemented (although you'll see in the Explorations that there are hash strategies that are nearly as good as the theoretical best we can do by random probes).

> ***Theorem 2:*** In closed hashing with linear resolution of collisions (regardless of the step size) on a table with load λ, the expected number of probes for insertion or unsuccessful search is approximately
>
> $$\frac{1}{2}\left(1+\left(\frac{1}{1-\lambda}\right)^2\right)$$
>
> and the expected number of probes for deletion or successful search is approximately
>
> $$\frac{1}{2}\left(1+\frac{1}{1-\lambda}\right)$$

> *Theorem 3:* In random closed hashing on a table with load λ, the expected number of probes for insertion or unsuccessful search is approximately $1/(1-\lambda)$, and the expected number of probes for deletion or successful search is approximately
>
> $$\left(-\frac{1}{\lambda}\right)\ln(1-\lambda)$$
>
> where the logarithm is the natural log.

All three of the hashing algorithms work fairly well when $\lambda<0.5$, but striking differences appear as the table becomes more nearly full, as we indicate in Table 9.1. It's clear that linear resolution of collisions is a real loser when the table is nearly full; with the table 90% full, this algorithm requires about 50 probes to insert another element, on the average, almost entirely because of the presence of large clusters. Equally clear is the fact that open hashing is a big winner, not only because of its efficiency, but also because we can let the number of elements get much larger than the number of buckets before we notice any significant degradation on the number of probes per operation.

We have to be careful, however, before we make the blanket pronouncement that open hashing is the method of choice. Open hashing requires that we set aside space in the hash table and in each cell of the linked list for pointers, so we have to make sure that we are not using too much memory with this scheme. To analyze the space requirements of open and closed hashing, let us suppose that we have n elements in the table, that the table has B buckets (to be fair to closed hashing, we will assume that $n \leq B$), that each element requires k bytes of memory, and that pointers require 4 bytes.

With both algorithms, we must preallocate an array of B buckets for the hash table, so closed hashing will require kB bytes of storage, and open hashing will require $4B$ bytes for the table and $k+4$ bytes for each linked list cell, for a total of $4B+n(k+4)$ bytes. Now the closed hashing scheme will be more space-efficient when $kB < 4B+n(k+4)$, and that happens when $(n/B)>(k-4)/(k+4)$. In other words, closed hashing requires less space than open hashing when the load $\lambda>(k-4)/(k+4)$. In Table 9.2, we show the cut-

TABLE 9.1

Effects of load on hashing efficiency

	Expected Number of Probes for Searches		
	Linear	Random	Open
$\lambda=0.75$			
Unsuccessful	8.5	4.0	1.8
Successful	2.5	1.9	2.0
$\lambda=0.9$			
Unsuccessful	50.5	10.0	1.9
Successful	5.5	2.6	2.0

TABLE 9.2

Space requirements for open and closed hashing

Record Size	Closed Hashing Uses Less Space for Loads Greater Than
4	0.00
8	0.33
16	0.60
32	0.78
64	0.88
128	0.94

off load values for which closed hashing is more space-efficient than open hashing for various sizes k of the data elements. We see that for large records, open hashing is almost always more space-efficient than closed hashing, and for small records, closed hashing requires less space when the load on the table is not too small (which, unfortunately, is exactly when closed hashing is less time-efficient than open).

9.5 APPLICATION: A PROBABILISTIC SPELLING CHECKER

The idea of using several independent hash functions has a number of applications, one of the most interesting being a probabilistic spelling checker. Suppose we were faced with the task of designing a spelling checker for a word processor. The spelling checker would take a word as soon as it had been typed and see if that word was in its dictionary. If so, no action would be taken; if not, it might sound a beep and highlight the questionable word.

One way to implement this would be to use a dictionary with a collection of, for instance, 40,000 words, and test each word as it was typed by making a call to *Contains*. If we stored the words as strings, with 1 byte per character, and assumed an average of five characters per word, the dictionary alone would require 200,000 bytes, and that does not include the overhead that would be entailed by using an implementation such as a hash table.

As an alternative, consider the following. We will choose d different hash functions, $h_1, h_2, \ldots, h_d$, each of which will hash a string into an index of a bit vector, V, with B indices. To build the dictionary, we will begin with each bit in V set to 0, then take each word, w, we wish to include and set $V[h_i(w)] = 1$, for $i = 1, \ldots, d$. To take a small example, suppose we wish to have a dictionary consisting of the words "BOY", "DOG", "GIRL", "THE", and "WAS". We will use a bit vector with 31 entries and encode the words by the following scheme. First, we add the letter codes for each letter in the word, with 'A' having code 1, 'B' having code 2, and so on, to 'Z' with code 26, and then square that number. Having done that, we will use three hash functions on the resulting squares, s, where $h_1(s) = s \% 37$, $h_2(s) = s \% 41$, and

$h_3(s) = s \% 53$. And finally, we will fold these numbers into the hash table by taking their remainders upon division by 31. Incidentally, this squaring and taking remainders is a poor choice for hashing, as we ask you to show in the exercises. At any rate, the five words are coded in the following fashion.

1. "BOY" $\rightarrow 2 + 15 + 25 = 42 \rightarrow 1764$. $1764 \% 37 = 25$, $1764 \% 41 = 1$, $1764 \% 53 = 15$; so we will write $1764 \rightarrow (25, 1, 15) \rightarrow (25, 1, 15)$, taking the remainders upon dividing by 31.
2. "DOG" $\rightarrow 4 + 15 + 7 = 26 \rightarrow 676 \rightarrow (10, 20, 40) \rightarrow (10, 20, 9)$.
3. "GIRL" $\rightarrow 7 + 9 + 18 + 12 = 46 \rightarrow 2116 \rightarrow (7, 25, 49) \rightarrow (7, 25, 18)$.
4. "THE" $\rightarrow 20 + 8 + 5 = 33 \rightarrow 1089 \rightarrow (16, 23, 29) \rightarrow (16, 23, 29)$.
5. "WAS" $\rightarrow 23 + 1 + 19 = 43 \rightarrow 1849 \rightarrow (36, 4, 47) \rightarrow (5, 4, 16)$.

After doing this, we set bits 1, 4, 5, 7, 9, 10, 15, 16, 18, 20, 23, 25, and 29 of the bit vector to 1, so it now has the form 0100110101100001101010 010100010. Notice that V would fit comfortably in 4 bytes, whereas it would require 16 bytes to store the five original words as character strings. We have thus achieved a fourfold reduction in the amount of space needed to store the dictionary. To test a word x for membership in our dictionary, we now apply the three hash functions to x and look at the indicated bits in V. Suppose that the test word was "HAT". We see that applying the same procedure we used to build the dictionary yields

$$\text{"HAT"} \rightarrow 8 + 1 + 20 = 29 \rightarrow 841 \rightarrow (27, 21, 46) \rightarrow (27, 21, 15)$$

We inspect bits 27, 21, and 15 of V, find that at least one of them is a zero, conclude that this word could not possibly have been one that was used to build the dictionary in the first place, and report that the word is unrecognized. It is easy to see that our spelling checker is always completely reliable when it reports failure to recognize a word.

Now suppose that the word to test was either "TESTED" or "SPOIN". The codes for these two words sum to 73, which yields the three hash values, 1, 9, 29, and we see that bits 1, 9, and 29 of V are all 1, so the spelling checker would accept these words, even though they were not among the original five. In other words, our spelling checker is not completely reliable when it reports that a word was successfully recognized, which is why we call it a *probabilistic* spelling checker.

Just how reliable is our checker? If we assume (as is not the case in this example) that the 1s are randomly distributed throughout the bit vector, then the chance of accepting a word by accident is just the chance of choosing three numbers at random in the range 0, . . . , 30 and finding a 1 in each position. The probability that a randomly chosen location contains a 1 is equal to the number of 1s in V divided by 31, the total number of bits in V. We can count that there are 13 1s in V, so the probability of hitting a 1 by accident is $13/31 = 0.419$, and the probability of hitting three 1s by accident is $(13/31)^3 = 0.0737$, or about 1 in 13. In other words, for this example, we pay for a fourfold reduction in storage by allowing about a 7% chance that the dictionary will not catch a misspelling.

We can adjust the failure rate to any positive number we want by changing the number of hash functions or by making the bit vector larger, so the real question is what level of error we wish to tolerate. Suppose that we would be content with an error rate of 0.001, so that 1 out of every 1000 misspelled words would not be caught, on average. Let us return to the situation we mentioned earlier, with a dictionary of 40,000 words. The least size of the bit vector and the number of hash functions needed to achieve this rate of accuracy are related in such a way that the smallest bit vector necessary for an accuracy of 0.001 is attained with seven hash functions. In the exercises, we ask you to show the relation between d, the number of hash functions, and B, the size of the bit vector needed to achieve a given accuracy. If you do that, you can show that with seven hash functions and 40,000 words, any V with at least 751,155 bits will guarantee an accuracy of 0.001. Dividing this number by 8 shows us that 93,895 bytes will suffice to store the bit vector, which is less than half the space required to store the words (at 5 bytes per word, on average) of the dictionary as strings.

This algorithm is fast. It is possible to design good hash functions that, even if used seven or more times per word, are fast enough that they would be finished checking a word long before the fastest typist had completed the next word (and that, of course, is all that matters here). Another nice feature of this algorithm is the ease of extension of the data base. Since a reasonably sized dictionary must necessarily leave out some words (not to mention all proper names), a useful part of a spelling checker is the ability to include a word for future recognition when it is first flagged as unrecognized. In our probabilistic spelling checker, it takes no more work to add a word to the dictionary than it does to test whether the word is there in the first place.

The most novel feature of this scheme, though, is not its speed or the fact that it reduces the size of the database by 50%, but rather that the list of correct words is completely disguised in the bit vector V. In our small previous example, even knowing what the three hash functions were does not help in trying to discover the words that were encoded in the bit vector 01001101011000011010100101000010. The fact that the original words cannot be reconstructed with any degree of certainty from the bit vector provides a means by which authors of such programs can safeguard their copyright, in a way similar to that used by mapmakers to guard against copying their works. All you need to do is include some words in the original dictionary, like "GRBGTWQ", that would be highly unlikely to arise from simple spelling errors. These words lie hidden in the bit vector, unsuspected by all, until the day comes when you (pretend along with us here) discover another spelling checker that is identical to yours. Now, a court may not be impressed by the fact that the other program uses the same hash functions as yours; after all, the good hash functions are pretty much the same everywhere. The court might not even be impressed by the fact that the other program uses a bit vector that is identical to yours; after all, if the hash functions were the same and you both built the dictionary from the same list of the 40,000 most common words in English, it would follow that the bit vectors would be identical.

But then you bring out the heavy artillery. You enter the word "GRBGTWQ", having announced that you had built it into your dictionary, and lo and behold, it is accepted by the other dictionary. If the other author claims to have used only the most common 40,000 words in English, the only defense is that a 1-in-a-thousand coincidence just took place. You then do the same thing for "UUIOOIAEAA", "XQATBDKJU", and "OPOPLOPOLLOPLOP", which you had also placed in your dictionary, and the defense has to explain away a 1-in-a-trillion coincidence. Case decided for the plaintiff. (But see the exercises.)

9.6 ADT: *PriorityQueue*

The *Dictionary* ADT is very useful. There are times, though, when we don't even need all of the fairly small number of operations that *Dictionary* makes available to us. Consider, for instance, a computer network with a shared printer. As a user makes a request to print something, that job might be assigned a numeric **priority**, based perhaps on the time it arrived and its size. The routine that manages these requests only needs to be able to insert a job and its priority into some data structure and extract the job with the currently lowest priority. Such a structure is called a **priority queue**.

▼

PriorityQueue

Structure: A set of associations with a key field type that is linearly ordered (usually numeric).

Operations

PriorityQueue(). Pre: true. Post: This priority queue is empty.

void Insert(Association a). Pre: The priority queue has no element with the same key as *a*. Post: This priority queue is unchanged, except that it now contains *a*.

Association DeleteMin(). Pre: This priority queue is not empty. Post: The association with smallest key has been removed from this priority queue.

int isEmpty() const. Pre: true. Post: The priority queue is unchanged. Returns 1 if and only if the priority queue is empty.

This ADT can be viewed as an abstraction of the people waiting for service at a hospital emergency room. As each patient arrives, the person in charge of admissions makes a decision about the severity of the patient's problem and assigns that patient a priority for service based on that assessment. Thus, a person with a fractured skull would likely receive treatment faster than a roomful of hangnail sufferers. When a doctor is ready to see another patient, the doctor performs *DeleteMin* on the people in the waiting room, taking the patient with the lowest number (in this example, the one with the most pressing problem) and deleting that person from the queue of waiting patients.

We could implement priority queues with binary search trees, because BSTs already support all the operations needed for priority queues. For that matter, we could use sorted lists as well. Perhaps more than most ADTs, however, *PriorityQueue* is almost invariably associated with a single conceptual model, that of an optimal, leftist binary tree with a heap condition (see Figure 9.5). An **optimal tree** has the property that all the internal nodes, except possibly the lowest ones, have two children. A **leftist tree** has no political orientation but does have the property that the nodes on a given level are all as far to the left as possible. We say that a tree satisfies the **heap condition** if the value of each node is less than that of each of its children, as in Figure 9.6. Such trees are also called **partially ordered trees**.

We impose the heap structure on our binary trees so that *DeleteMin* is easy to implement. We always know exactly where the minimum element is—it must be at the root—so that we can find it without tracing our way through the tree at all. Notice that the heap condition is less restrictive than the binary search tree property, with the result that in a tree with a heap condition, we have only partial information about the order of elements in the nodes. The fifth smallest element in a BST is the fifth in an inorder traversal; there is no such easy way to find the fifth smallest element in a priority queue.

The heap condition is still restrictive enough that it makes *Insert* simple to define. We begin by inserting the new node in the leftmost available location in the lowest level, moving down to a new level only if the lowest level is completely filled. If that node has a value greater than that of its parent, we are done, since the new tree still satisfies the heap condition. If the new node has a value less than that of its parent, we exchange it with its parent, thereby restoring the heap condition at that subtree. The exchange might have destroyed the heap condition at the level above; if it has, we continue to "bubble up" the tree, exchanging the new node with its parent, grandparent, great-grandparent, and so on, until no exchanges are necessary.

FIGURE 9.5

An optimal, leftist binary tree

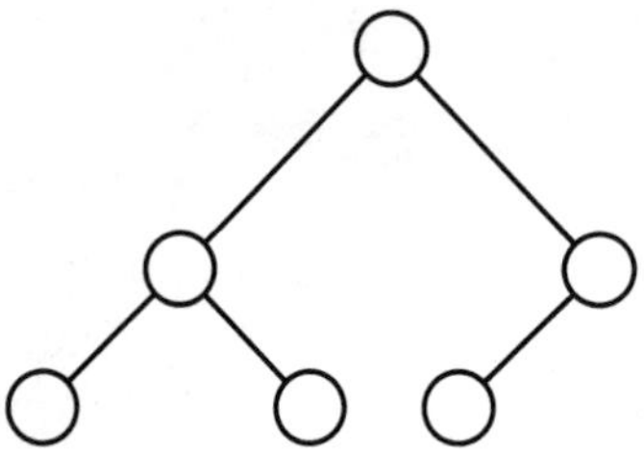

FIGURE 9.6

A tree satisfying the heap condition

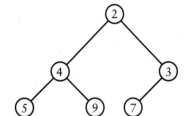

Figure 9.7 shows the action of inserting value 1 into the tree of Figure 9.6. We first make a new node for 1. We see that the value of the new node is smaller than that of its parent, so we exchange them. The subtree rooted at 1 in Figure 9.7b now satisfies the heap condition, but node 1 is less in value than its new parent, so we exchange again, leading to the tree in Figure 9.7c; this tree satisfies the heap condition, so we are done.

We define *DeleteMin* in a somewhat similar fashion, but in this case we begin by replacing the root with the "last" element (the rightmost element in the bottom level), so that the leftist nature of the tree is preserved. The new root element may be larger than its children, thus violating the heap condition, so as long as the tree is not a heap, we "bubble down" that element, replacing it with the smaller of its children, until the heap condition is restored. Figure 9.8 shows an example of how this process works.

It is not difficult to see that an optimal binary tree with n nodes must have depth d, where $d \leq \log_2 n$. Since both *DeleteMin* and *Insert* make at most one complete pass from top to bottom (or vice versa), both of these opera-

FIGURE 9.7

Insertion in a priority queue

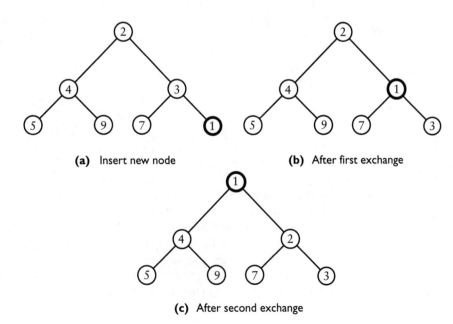

FIGURE 9.8

Deleting the minimum
element from a
priority queue

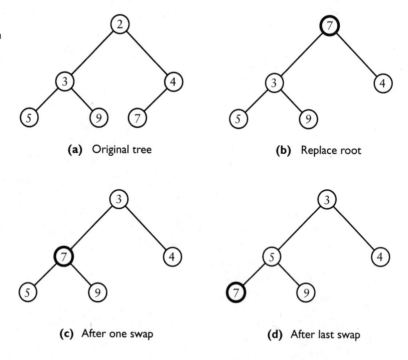

(a) Original tree   **(b)** Replace root

(c) After one swap   **(d)** After last swap

tions run in time $O(\log n)$; and unlike the situation we encountered with
BSTs, these operations never take longer than that. This is just the improvement we were looking for, but how do we implement these operations? We
can't just use the usual pointer implementation, because *Insert* requires that
we move *up* the tree. We could always use extra parent pointers in each cell
or use a threaded tree, but there is a very clever array implementation that we
would rather discuss here.

We begin by placing a very natural linear order on every binary tree, assigning the root position 1, the left child of the root (whether or not there is
one) position 2, the right child of the root position 3, and so on, assigning
positions by rows, top to bottom, and left to right within rows, as in Figure
9.9. Now you see the reason for our insistence that these trees be complete,
leftist binary trees: Such a tree fills the position array with no holes. We could
have used this as an implementation of a general binary tree, but the nodes of
a tree that consisted of just a chain of right children, for instance, would be
located in positions 1, 3, 7, 15, 31, 63, . . . , requiring $2^n - 1$ array spaces for n
nodes, a profligate waste of space.

The array implementation of *PriorityQueue* is now simple. We can find
the parent of a node by observing that the left and right children of node $p[i]$
are just $p[2i]$, and $p[2i + 1]$, respectively, so the parent of $p[i]$ is $p[i/2]$. This, by
the way, explains our departure from C++ arrays: You can show that putting
the root in position 0 makes calculations less elegant.

FIGURE 9.9

Array storage of binary trees

```
template<class K, class V>
class PriorityQueue
{
public:
   PriorityQueue();
   void Insert(Association<K, V> a);
   Association<K, V> DeleteMin();
   int IsEmpty() {  return (size == 0);} ;
private:
   Array<Association<K, V>> data;
   unsigned int  size,       // current size of the PQ
                 MAX;        // largest index for the array
   void Swap(int i, int j);  // swap data[i], data[j]
}


template<class K, class V>
PriorityQueue<K, V>::PriorityQueue() : data(10, 1), size(0), MAX(10)
{
}


template<class K, class V>
void PriorityQueue<K, V>::Insert(Association<K, V> a)
{
   if (size == MAX)
   // Grow the array if we need to.
   {
      MAX *= 2;
      data.SetBounds(MAX, 1);
   }

   size++;
   unsigned int i   = size;
   data[i] := a;      // Insert new node at the end of the array.
```

```
   while ((i > 1) && (data[i].Key() < data[i / 2].Key()))
   // As long as this node's key is less than its parent's,
   // swap it with its parent and move up the tree.
   {
      Swap(i, i / 2);
      i /= 2;
   }
}
```

DeleteMin is nearly as simple as *Insert*. The statement labeled OPTION-AL may be omitted with no effect on the algorithm. It is there because we will make use of it in a sorting algorithm based on priority queues.

```
template<class K, class V>
Association<K, V> PriorityQueue<K, V>::DeleteMin()
{
   Assert(size > 0, "Priority queue is empty, no min to delete");

   Association<K, V> returnValue= data[1];

   data[1] = data[size];
   data[size] = returnValue; // OPTIONAL-swap last with root
   size--;

   int   mindex,
         i = 1;
   if (size > 1)     // Only have to check heap condition if tree
                     // has more than one node.
      do
      {
         // Find the index of the smallest child of i.
         if (2 * i + 1 > size)  // i has only a left child.
            mindex = 2 * i;
         else if (data[2 * i].Key() < data[2 * i + 1].Key())
            mindex = 2 * i;
         else
            mindex = 2 * i + 1;
         if (data[i].Key() > data[mindex].Key())
         // Out of order, so swap and move down.
         {
            Swap(i, mindex);
            i = mindex;
         }
      }
      while (i <= size / 2);  // Quit when we get to bottom row.
   return returnValue;
}
```

Application: Heapsort

It is easy to see how to use these operations to produce a sorting algorithm. All we need to do is *Insert* all the elements to be sorted into our priority queue and then call *DeleteMin* to remove them from the queue in smallest-to-largest order. At first glance it might seem that we need two arrays, one for the original data and the eventual sorted list and another for the priority queue itself. It turns out, however, that we can do all the sorting in place. We let the low-order part of the array contain the present priority queue, while the high-order part contains the elements yet to be inserted. Once the priority queue is full, we repeatedly delete the minimum elements from the first position in the queue, placing each of them, in turn, just beyond the present end of the priority queue. This *Heapsort* algorithm, then, is divided into two phases: In the first phase we "heapify" the array by insertion; in the second phase we produce the sorted list. Now you can see the reason for the OPTIONAL statement in *DeleteMin*: When we delete the present minimum element of the heap, we don't just remove it; we place it at the left end of the already sorted sublist.

Figure 9.10a shows an intermediate step in the heapification phase: A new element is taken from the unprocessed data, placed in the new last position of the heap, and bubbled up to its proper place. In Figure 9.10b, the sorting phase has just begun: The last element of the heap is placed at the root, and the old root element is placed where the last element used to be, which is now one position to the left of the end of the heap. Finally, Figure 9.10c shows an intermediate stage in the sorting phase. Now we can write the algorithm, assuming that we're using the priority queue operations that

FIGURE 9.10

Heapsort in action

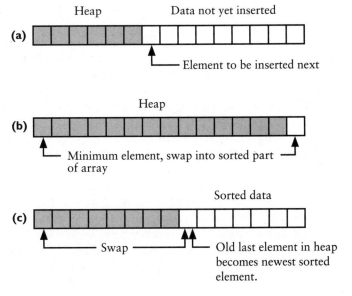

we've extracted from the class, so that they can be used on an array that isn't a priority queue.

```
void Heapsort(Array p);
// We assume that the unsorted data already resides in
// p, from 1 to MAX.
{
    for (int i = 1; i <= MAX; i++)
        HeapInsert(p[i]);    // External version
    for (i = 1; i <= MAX; i++)
        HeapDeleteMin(p);    // External version
}
```

For *n* data elements to be sorted, we have *2n* calls to either *Insert* or *DeleteMin,* both of which take no more time than $O(\log n)$, and less than that most of the time, for a running time of $O(n \log n)$—not just in the "nice" cases, but always. Finally, you can consider yourself a master of priority queues if you can tell, right now, without a second's hesitation, how the sorted list comes out: Is the largest element at the left or at the right?

9.7 SUMMARY

The structural relation that defines *Set* is the empty relation, reflecting the fact that a set has no internal structure at all. If the atoms in a set are linearly ordered, a bit vector representation allows constant-time insertion, deletion, and membership testing, with the drawback that any set is limited in size to a predeclared maximum.

A data structure that supports insertion, deletion, and membership operations is called a dictionary, and we saw that an implementation of a dictionary with hashing supports the three operations in constant time, as long as the load on the hash table does not get too large. Closed hashing, where the data are stored in the hash table, is simpler to implement than open hashing, where the hash table contains pointers to linked lists of data, but requires care in choice of hash function to reduce collisions to a minimum. For further information on hashing, you could do no better than two excellent books: Alfred V. Aho, John E. Hopcroft, and Jeffrey D. Ullman, *Data Structures and Algorithms* (Reading, MA: Addison-Wesley, 1983), and Donald E. Knuth, *The Art of Computer Programming,* Vol. 3, *Sorting and Searching* (Reading, MA: Addison-Wesley, 1973).

As an application of hashing, we discussed the use of multiple hashing to implement a probabilistic spelling checker. There has been a considerable interest in probabilistic algorithms lately, largely for problems for which there is no known efficient algorithm. The problem of testing whether a very large number is prime is a good example. It is not known whether the problem of testing whether a number is prime is a "hard" problem, but there are no known polynomial-time algorithms to test for primality. There is, however, a probabilistic polynomial-time algorithm given in M. O. Rabin, "Probabilistic Algorithm," in J. F. Traub, ed., *Algorithms and Complexity: New Directions and Recent Results* (New York: Academic Press, 1976): 21–39. Rabin takes a number p and subjects it to n tests in such a way that if the number fails any one test, it is certain not to be prime, and if it passes all n tests, then the probability that the number is not prime is $(1/2)n$. In other words, the algorithm does not provide a definitive answer, but can be made to be as close to completely reliable as we wish.

The *PriorityQueue* ADT is a subtype of *Dictionary,* where the keys are numeric and the operations supported are *Insert* and *DeleteMin.* This ADT is generally implemented using heap-ordered, optimal, leftist binary trees, stored in an array. Both *Insert* and *deleteMin* run in time that is guaranteed to be no worse than logarithmic in the size of the tree. Priority queues give rise to *Heapsort,* a sorting algorithm that runs in time $O(n \log n)$.

9.8 EXERCISES

1. To see why some compilers do not allow "set of integers," suppose that a compiler written for a 16-bit computer used bit vectors to represent sets.

    a. If the target computer used 32-bit words to represent integers, how many different integers could the computer represent?

    b. How many bytes would be required for a packed bit vector that represented a set of integers on such a computer?

2. Fill in the bit vector *Set* operations we omitted:

    a. `void Set<T>::MakeEmpty()`

    b. `Set<T> operator- (Set<T> a, Set<T> b)`

    c. `void Set<T>::Remove()`

    d. `int operator== (Set<T> a, Set<T> b)`

3. Write bit vector definitions for the following *Set* operations.

    a. *SymmetricDifference,* where the symmetric difference, $a \Delta b$, of sets a and b consists of all those elements in $a \cup b$ that are not in $a \cap b$

    b. *Complement,* where the complement of a set a consists of all those elements (in the universal set) that are not in a

    c. *IsEmpty,* a member function that returns 1 if and only if the argument is the empty set

4. Look at the bit vector implementation of the subset operator `<`. Explain the loop condition

    `(i < N) && (!a.vector[i] || b.vector[i])`.

5. In our explanation of the packed bit vector, we defined the function

```
int KthBit(int k, long n)
// Returns the value of the k-th bit of n.
{
    long mask = 1;
    return ((n & (mask << k)) >> k);
}
```

Show how it works when $k = 13$ and n is a number with binary representation 0001011100110101.

6. Write an implementation of *BitVector*, packing the bits into an array of long.

7. For the *List* implementation of *Set*, write friend functions that implement

   a. `Set<T> operator+ (Set<T> a, Set<T> b)`

   b. `Set<T> operator- (Set<T> a, Set<T> b)`

   c. `int operator== (Set<T> a, Set<T> b)`

8. For the *SortedList* implementation of *Set*, write friend functions that implement

   a. `Set<T> operator+ (Set<T> a, Set<T> b)`

   b. `Set<T> operator- (Set<T> a, Set<T> b)`

   c. `int operator== (Set<T> a, Set<T> b)`

9. Consider the following scheme to avoid having to deal with a special deletion marker when hashing: When deleting an element from a hash table, find that element as usual, and then go down to the last element in the deleted element's cluster (i.e., the element just before the first empty cell) and swap the last element in the cluster into the position occupied by the deleted element.

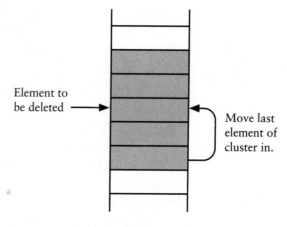

a. It's an interesting idea, but it won't quite work. Tell why, and fix the algorithm so it will work.

b. Fix *Contains* so that it will work with this implementation.

c. Discuss the advantages and disadvantages of this strategy.

10. Insert the integers 13, 5, 22, 8, 34, 19, 21 into an initially empty hash table with seven buckets, using the hash function $h(x)=x$ % 7. How many probes did it take?

11. What are the smallest and largest number of probes needed to fill completely a hash table with B buckets?

12. Why is $h(x)=x^2$ % B not a good hashing function into a table with B buckets?

13. If you know ahead of time what the elements of a hash table will be, you can sometimes design an **optimal hashing** scheme by making the hash table exactly as large as the number of elements and designing a hash function that will never result in collisions. This is sometimes done to maintain the symbol table of reserved words in a compiler. As each token is read, it must be checked to see if it is a reserved word, like "if", or a program-defined identifier, like "numVars," whereupon the compiler will take appropriate action.

For example, if we had the reserved words while, const, if, new, else, class, and for, we could use a hash table with seven buckets, 0, . . . , 6, and after a little work we might hit on the idea of looking at the leftmost two letters, converting them to integers by 'a'→1, 'b'→2, and so on, forming their product and computing *product* % 7.

a. Show that this hash function eliminates collisions by computing its value for each of our seven reserved words.

b. Find a hash function that will be optimal if we include the word inline in the preceding set.

c. If you're really diligent, find an optimal hash function for the complete set of 48 C++ reserved words.

14. Open hashing is a better overall technique than closed hashing, as we have seen. If we wanted to stick to the use of closed hashing, though, we could recognize that it is very efficient as long as the load on the hash table doesn't get too large. Thus, we could monitor the load, and as soon as it got above some fixed value, like 0.5, we could create a new hash table of twice the size of the old one (and a new hash function, of course) and reinsert all the current elements into the new table. Discuss the advantages and disadvantages of this scheme in terms of data structures needed and time efficiency.

15. Discuss in detail the advantages and disadvantages of using binary search trees, rather than linked lists, for the buckets in open hashing.

16. Argue for the defense in the spelling checker trial. Argue that the court should not be convinced by the fact that the plaintiff found four garbage words that were accepted by your spelling checker. Having done that, see if you can find a strategy for the plaintiff.

17. Find all possible optimal, leftist binary trees with the heap condition that can be made on the keys 1, 2, 3, 4.

18. If we call *DeleteMin* on a priority queue and then reinsert the key we deleted, does the result ever differ from the original?

19. **a.** Show (in tree form) the priority queue that results from inserting the keys 8, 13, 10, 12, 6, 9, 5, 2 in that order, beginning with 8.

     b. Show the result of performing two *DeleteMin*s on the tree in part (a).

20. Do the priority queue operations *Insert* and *DeleteMin* work correctly if we allow elements to have duplicate keys?

21. If we map a tree into an array as we did with *PriorityQueue,* but start with index 0, what are the expressions for the parent, left child, and right child of the node at position i?

22. There is no particular reason why we must restrict our heaps to be binary. We may define a **d-heap** as an optimal, leftist tree where each node may have as many as d children.

     a. Describe the array representation of a d-heap by finding expressions for the parent and kth child (counting from the left, starting at 0).

     b. Rewrite *PriorityQueue* for d-heaps.

     c. Are there any time advantages of using d-heaps, for $d > 2$? Explain.

23. Find the most efficient algorithm you can that merges two heaps into one.

24. Write a program that maintains a dictionary of strings using open hashing.

9.9 EXPLORATIONS

Hashing, Continued

A good hash function should spread the keys throughout the hash table in some nearly random fashion. In one sense, hashing is the opposite of sorting, in that sorting takes randomly distributed keys and places them in linear order, while hashing takes a collection of strings, say, with their usual lexicographic order, and distributes them randomly in the hash table.

When designing a hash function, then, we would like it to have the property that any pattern among the keys should be destroyed by the hash function. Consider, for example, the hash function we have used throughout the chapter. To hash on a name, we add the ASCII values of the characters in the name and take that sum modulo the size of the hash table (i.e., we take the remainder upon division by the size of the table). One disadvantage of this scheme comes from the fact that the hash function makes use of only the characters in the name, not their positions. In other words, names that are permutations of each other, like "'ADAMS", "MASAD", and "DAMAS", would necessarily hash to the same value. A general rule is that a hash function should make use of all of the information about the keys and seek to eliminate any patterns that might exist within the set of possible keys.

25.   Try this scheme: Instead of forming the sum of the ASCII codes $c_1 + c_2 + \cdots + c_n$, form a *weighted* sum $c_1 + 2c_2 + 3c_3 + \cdots + nc_n$, and then fold the result into the table by taking *sum* % 120. Where do "ADAMS", "MASAD", and "DAMAS" now go in the table?

We can regard the design of a hash function as a two-part process: First, we convert the key to an integer; then we map that integer into the range of bucket indices $0, \ldots, B-1$. The easiest way is to "fold" the integers into the table by hashing an integer n into array location n % B, where B is the number of buckets in the table. This certainly is easy to compute, but it could lead to a large amount of primary clustering if we weren't sure that the original integers were truly random in their distribution. For instance, if B had many small factors (like $B = 120$, as we chose for our example), then there would be a good chance that numbers in arithmetic progression would fold to the same index.

A better way involves a less obvious hash function that adds another stir to the pot and mixes up the integer keys even better. We choose r to be a real number between 0 and 1 and define the hash function

$$h(x) = \left\lfloor B(xr \bmod 1) \right\rfloor$$

where $\lfloor A \rfloor$ represents the greatest integer that is less than or equal to A, and $A \bmod 1$ is just the fractional part of A (so that $A = \lfloor A \rfloor + (A \bmod 1)$, as long as $A \geq 0$). The reason that this works well is a bit obscure, as is the choice of a good value for r. It turns out that a particularly good choice for r is either $(\sqrt{5} - 1)/2$, or 1 minus that number, which is to say either 0.6180339887 or 0.3819660113. This technique is called **Fibonacci hashing**.

Finally, it happens that both of these hash functions work best when the table size B is taken to be a prime number that is not too close to a power of 2. Some good choices for B are 13, 23, 47, 97, 193, 383, 769, 1531, 3067, 6143, 12,289, and 24,571.

26.   Show that Fibonacci hashing mixes up keys fairly well by computing $h(x)$ with $B = 100$ and $r = (\sqrt{5} - 1)/2$, for $x = 1, \ldots, 10$.

The speed of access into a closed hash table is directly related to the number of probes we must make to find, insert, or delete an element. The number of probes required by an operation clearly depends on the amount of clustering in the hash table. To appreciate the effects of clustering, consider the hash table in Figure 9.11. The occupied cells in the table are shaded, and you can see that the table is exactly half full.

It would appear at first that if we insert an element into the table, we should have to resolve collisions about half the time, for an expected number of probes of 1.5 for an insertion into a random location (1 for the initial probe plus 0.5 for the chance of collision resolution). Consider, however, the cluster in positions 4 through 7. If we assume that the hash function is equally likely to send an element into any cell, then there is a 0.05 (= $\frac{1}{20}$) chance that an element will be sent to cell 4, which would require five probes to find a vacant location at cell 8. There is also a 0.05 chance that an element will be sent to cell 5, requiring four probes, and we can see that the cluster will contribute 0.05 (5+4+3+2)=0.70 to the expected number of probes.

27. **a.** Verify that for this example, the expected number of probes to insert an element is 1.85.

 b. What would be the expected number of probes in the worst case, where the 10 occupied cells formed a single cluster?

 c. Show that a cluster of length c contributes an amount to the expected number of probes for insertion that is quadratic in c.

Things get even worse, though. An inserted element could wind up in location 8 by being hashed into any of locations 4, 5, 6, 7, or 8. In other words, it is five times more likely that the already large cluster will grow than it is for an element to hash into cell 12 and start a new cluster. The conclusion is that long clusters are highly likely to grow even longer. Notice that the clusters don't just grow by 1, either. An insertion into cell 8 will cause secondary clustering, producing a large cluster of length 7.

Well, that should be enough to convince us that we want to avoid producing clusters if we can. It is clear that at least some of our troubles were caused by our collision resolution scheme. Probing into the next location in the table is a surefire way to produce clusters. There is nothing magical about our decision to look at cell $i+1$ if we find that cell i is full; why not pick a number, k, and then probe into locations i, $i+k$, $i+2k$, $i+3k$, and so on, until we find a vacant location? This **generalized linear resolution** solves at least part of the problem for us, as long as k has no factor in common with B, the number of buckets. What generalized linear resolution does is to spread the clusters uniformly throughout the table. We will still have clusters, but they will consist of cells k apart, thus lessening the chance of secondary clustering.

FIGURE 9.11

A partially full hash table, with clusters

An even better scheme is to use a **double hashing** scheme with two hash functions, h and k, and use h for the initial probe and k to provide the constant in generalized linear resolution. In other words, given an integer n to hash into the table, we probe first at $h(n)$ and, if that doesn't work, probe into locations $h(n)+k(n)$, $h(n)+2k(n)$, $h(n)+3k(n)$, and so on, until we succeed. Again, we must take care that the step size function k does not produce any value with a factor in common with the table size, for reasons that become clear if you try this scheme with $B=12$ and $k=4$. It is therefore generally a good idea to let the table size be a prime number. If we assume that B is a prime, then, for instance, we can take $h(n)=n \% B$, and $k(n)=(n \% (B-1))+1$.

28. Insert the integers 13, 5, 22, 8, 34, 19, 21 into an initially empty hash table with seven buckets, using the hash function $h(x)=x \% 7$. Count the number of probes required under

    a. Linear resolution of collisions

    b. General linear resolution with step size 3

    c. Double hashing, with $k(x)=1+(x \% 6)$

29. Show why general linear resolution of collisions requires that the step size and the number of buckets have no common factors.

30. Write a program that maintains a closed hash table of 200 buckets and inserts randomly chosen integers in the range 0, ..., 199 into the table. At intervals of 10 insertions, display the cluster sizes and the average cluster size, along with the average number of probes per insertion for the present interval. Compare the results for

    a. Linear resolution of collisions, using $h(x)=x$

    b. General linear resolution with $k=2$ and $k=7$

    c. Double hashing, using $h(x)=x$ and $k(x)=(13x+7) \% 200$

    If you are going to do this for more than one hashing scheme, it would be a good idea to maintain several hash tables and insert the same numbers into each, to eliminate statistical variations between samples.

The *DisjointSet* ADT

The *DisjointSet* abstract data type (also known as the *Union_Find* ADT) is, in a sense, complementary to the *Dictionary* ADT. A dictionary is usually used to support a single set, in which elements are inserted and deleted throughout the life of the application. The *DisjointSet* abstract data type, on the other hand, is designed to act on a collection of sets, with no deletions or insertions of elements, except the insertions needed to create the sets in the first place. Almost invariably, the *DisjointSet* structure deals with a **partition**, in which a universal set is divided into disjoint subsets.

▼

DisjointSet

Structure: The *DisjointSet* abstract data type is a subtype of the *Set*. Unlike *Set*, the elements of this ADT consist of collections of disjoint sets $S_1, S_1, \ldots, S_n$ of elements of type T.

Operations

Set(T e). Pre: *e* is not an element of any set in this structure. Post: A set is created containing a single element *e*.

Set Union(Set a, Set b). Pre: *a* and *b* have no elements in common. Post: Returns the union of *a* and *b*.

Set Find(T e). Pre: *e* is in some set in this structure. (Because of the way the constructor and *Union* are defined, *e* will never be in more than one set in the structure.) Post: Returns the set containing *e*.

Because the elements of the *DisjointSet* structure are collections of sets, we could use any of the *Set* implementations to represent this structure. We could represent each such collection as a collection of bit vectors, for instance, so that if the universal set consisted of {1, 2, . . . , 9}, the *DisjointSet* object {{1, 2, 3}, {4, 5, 6, 7}, {8, 9}} could be represented by the three bit vectors 111000000, 000111100, 000000011. The set constructor and *Union* would be easy to define in this implementation, since we could represent a *DisjointSet* element as an array or linked list of bit vectors, but it is not clear how we would implement *Find* in any way that would avoid our having to look at each of the subsets in the structure to find the one containing the element we were trying to locate.

Tree Representations of *DisjointSet*

Another representation of the *DisjointSet* structure uses trees for each of the subsets and identifies each subset by the root of its associated tree. The sets {1, 2, 3}, {4, 5, 6, 7}, and {8, 9}, then, might be represented as in Figure 9.12. The figure reflects the fact that there is no order among the nodes that depends on any inherent order among the atoms and also that the trees need not be binary trees. With this representation, *Union* can be defined to run in constant time, simply by making the node of one tree become the parent of the other. To make this implementation efficient, we will represent each set by a pointer to the root of its tree, and each element will likewise be represented by a pointer to a tree node. In Figure 9.13, we show the structure that would result if we called *Union*(1, 5). The tree rooted at node 1 would have node 5 as its new parent, and the function would return the position of node 5, the root of the tree corresponding to the union {1, 2, 3, 4, 5, 6, 7}.

It is easy to see how to define *Find* in this implementation. Given a node, we simply point our way up the tree from that node until we come to the root

FIGURE 9.12

Three disjoint sets represented by trees

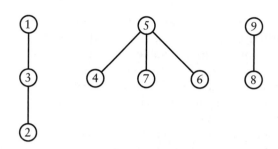

of the tree containing that node, and we return the position of the root as an identifier of the set in which the node resides. Now the astute reader has two things to worry about. Not only do we have to consider how to implement general, rather than binary, trees, but we also need to figure out how to move up the tree. Fortunately, we can solve both problems at once. If you look carefully at the descriptions of *Union* and *Find* in this implementation, you will see that there is never any need to move down the tree. We will use what is known as an **in-tree**, consisting of cells linked with pointers in such a way that each cell contains a single pointer, to its parent. The root will be special: Since it has no parent, we will mark that it is a root by making its parent field equal to NULL. (Another commonly used technique is to make the parent pointer of a root node point to itself. This state of affairs can hold only when the node is a root, so we again have a way to tell whether a node is a root.)

31. Write declarations and definitions for this structure.

32. How fast do *Union* and *Find* run in your implementation?

It is customary for this data type to describe the **amortized time** required by a mixed sequence of n calls to *Union* and *Find*. The reason for this is that once we change this implementation to make it very fast, it is extremely difficult to prove that an individual operation is fast. It is easier, believe it or not, to analyze the time required by a mingled sequence of n unions and n finds,

FIGURE 9.13

The structure of Figure 9.12 after a call to *Union*(1, 5)

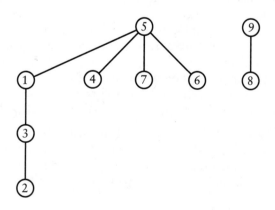

386 **Chapter 9** UNORDERED COLLECTIONS

so we will talk about the running time of an implementation, rather than that of a particular operation in the implementation. If both *Union* and *Find* ran in constant time, then, we would say that the implementation ran in time $O(n)$, since that would be the time necessary to complete n unions and n finds. We won't be able to do quite that well, but we will be able to come close enough to make no practical difference, in that we will slightly redefine *Union* and *Find* so that the amortized time is $O(n\,a(n))$, where $a(n)$ is an increasing function that, we guarantee, grows more slowly than any you have ever seen. The cost of this implementation, as it stands, however, is nowhere near as good as $O(n)$.

33. Assume that we have initialized our structure so that we have n disjoint sets, $\{1\}, \{2\}, \ldots, \{n\}$. Consider the sequence of n unions and n finds:

   $Union(1, 2)$, $Union(2, 3)$, $\ldots$, $Union(n-1, n)$, $Find(1)$, $\ldots$, $Find(1)$

   Using this sequence, show that the cost of this implementation is at least n^2. Remember that we have defined *Union* so that the first argument is made a child of the second.

34. Show that the cost of this implementation is at most n^2; that is, a sequence of n unions and n finds will never have a total cost larger than some multiple of n^2.

   The problem with the simple implementation just discussed is that we have defined *Union* in such a way as to permit the trees made from unions to become unbalanced. There is a very simple cure for this; we simply include another piece of information, *weight*, in the nodes, which stores the number of nodes in the subtree rooted at that node. Then, when we merge two trees, we always do so by making the tree with smaller weight become the child of the other node, which is exactly what happened in Figure 9.13.

35. Modify your class to implement weighted union.

   Call a **WU-tree** any tree that can be constructed by a sequence of weighted unions. We will show that, much like Fibonacci trees, a WU-tree of weight w must have height no larger than $\log_2 w$, so that WU-trees cannot have most of their nodes concentrated in a single long chain, a property that should make *Find* much more efficient than it was with trees built from simple unions.

   As we did with balanced trees, we will investigate the WU-trees that have the smallest weight for a given height and will show that the weight must be at least an exponential function of the height. We showed in Chapter 7 that of all balanced binary trees, the Fibonacci trees had the smallest weight for a given height. For WU-trees, we have an analogous class, called **binomial trees**.

36. a. Show that if a WU-tree is constructed by taking the union of two WU-trees with heights h_1 and h_2, the union tree can have height larger than that of its components if and only if $h_1 = h_2$, and in that case the union tree has height 1 more than that of its components.

b. Show that we can construct minimal-weight WU-trees of height h by merging two minimal-weight WU-trees of height $h-1$, as in the following figure.

$$B_h \quad = \quad$$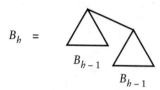

c. We will denote each such binomial tree of height h by B_h. B_0 is, of course, a single node. Draw B_1, B_2, B_3, B_4, and B_5. What is the weight of B_h?

d. Show that any WU-tree of weight w has height $h \leq \log_2 w$.

37. How many nodes does the binomial tree B_h have at depth k, for $0 \leq k \leq h$? Why is it called a *binomial* tree? Prove your result.

38. A problem with binomial trees is that they can only contain m vertices, where m is a power of 2. Define a **binomial forest**, F_n, of order n to be a disjoint collection of binomial trees, such that the total number of vertices in the forest is equal to n and no two of the binomial trees are the same size.

a. Draw F_{22}. *Hint:* Express 22 as a binary number.

b. How could you take the union of two binomial forests F_n and F_m so that the result would be the binomial forest F_{n+m}? *Hint:* Think of adding binary numbers.

c. Show how you could implement a priority queue by imposing the heap condition on each of the trees in a binomial forest. Show how you would define *Insert* for this implementation. How long would *Insert* take on F_n?

39. a. Show that *DisjointSet* with weighted union has an amortized cost of $O(n \log n)$.

b. Show that this upper bound is exact, by constructing a mixed sequence of n unions and n finds that has cost $n \log n$.

We can reduce the amortized cost of the *DisjointSet* structure even further if we modify *Find*. We can't reduce the time required by *Union*, of course, since it already takes just a constant amount of time, but we can modify *Find* so that it alters the tree in such a way as to make subsequent finds cheaper. This is really the reason we need amortized cost: By changing *Find*, we will make it take longer, but the cost can be averaged over the subsequent finds, which will take less time. We do this by writing *Find* in such a way that whenever it is called on a node at location x, it will move each node on the path from x to the root to a location where those nodes become children of the root, rather than distant ancestors of the root. In Figure 9.14a, we

FIGURE 9.14

Find with path
compression

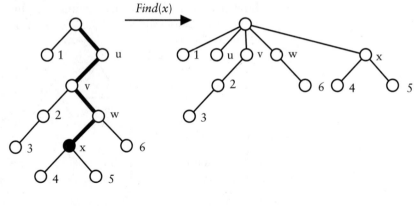

(a)   Original tree   (b)   After path compression

show the search path from x to the root, and in Figure 9.14b, we show the
tree that results when the nodes along the search path have been promoted to
become children of the root.

40.   Change your implementation to include path compression *Find*. *Hint*:
      Make two passes along the search path from the target node to the root.

      Unfortunately, we cannot take the time to give a proof of the amortized
cost of the *DisjointSet* implementation that uses weighting and path compression. The essential idea is to compute the cost of a *Find* and charge some of
that cost to the *Find* itself, and delay the inclusion of some of the rest of the
cost by charging it to the nodes in the search path, to be picked up at a later
time when we compute the cost of a subsequent *Find*. At any rate, it turns
out that the total cost of a sequence of n unions and n finds in this implementation is $O(n \log^* n)$, where $\log^* n$ is defined as follows:

1. $\log^*(0) = 0$
2. $\log^*(n) = 1 + \log^*(\lceil \log_2 n \rceil)$ for $n > 0$

As usual, $\lceil z \rceil$ represents the least integer that is greater than or equal to z.
Now, $\log^*$ is not constant, but it grows extremely slowly as a function of n.

41.   a.   Show that $\log^*(10^{99}) = 6$.

      b.   How large does k have to be before we have $\log^*(10^k) = 7$? What
           about 8?

      c.   Show that $\log^*(n)$ increases by 1 only when n passes the values 0,
           $2^0 = 1$, $2^1 = 2$, $2^2 = 4$, $2^4 = 16$, $2^{16} = 65{,}536$, $2^{65536} = \dots$.

42.   Calculate

$$\log^*\left(2^{2^{65536}} \right)$$

In other words, $n\log^*n$ increases more rapidly than linear, but its growth is so slow that for all practical purposes the function $n\log^*n$ may as well be regarded as linear. Put another way, the average cost of the operations in a sequence of unions and finds in the weighted path compression implementation of *DisjointSet* is as close to constant time as we could want.

We can't resist one more remark before we leave these timing estimates. There is a longer and more delicate proof that the worst-case amortized cost of the weighted path compression *DisjointSet* implementation is even *less* than $n\log^*n$. There is a function, $a(n)$, that increases vastly slower than $\log^*n$, such that the cost of this implementation is $O(n\,a(n))$. This function $a(n)$ is related to the inverse of **Ackermann's function**, which we mentioned briefly in the exercises in Chapter 5.

43. Assume that we had created the singleton sets 1 through 8 and then performed the following sequence of function calls in order: *Union*(1, 2), *Union*(3, 4), *Union*(5, 6), *Union*(7, 8), *Union*(*Find*(5), *Find*(7)), *Union*(*Find*(4), *Find*(6)), *Union*(*Find*(1), *Find*(5)). For the following strategies, show the tree that would result, and count the number of steps (following a pointer, or reassigning a pointer) required to produce the resulting trees. To ensure consistency of answers, assume that *Union* is defined so that if there are two possible choices for the root, the lowest number becomes the root (and similarly with weighted *Union*, if the two trees have the same weight).

    a. Unweighted *Union*, *Find* without path compression

    b. Unweighted *Union*, *Find* with path compression

    c. Weighted *Union*, *Find* without path compression

    d. Weighted *Union*, *Find* with path compression

44. For randomly chosen sequences of *Union*s and *Find*s, implement and test the efficiency of the *Union_Find* ADT with integer atoms

    a. With path compression and weighting

    b. Without path compression and weighting

Application: Minimum Spanning Trees, Revisited

Here is an application for which the *DisjointSet* structure is particularly well suited. In Chapter 8, we saw Prim's algorithm to find the minimum spanning tree of an edge-weighted graph. We present here another MST algorithm, by J. B. Kruskal. Suppose that we have a graph G, consisting of a set of vertices connected by edges, each edge having a positive weight, and we wish to construct a minimum spanning tree for G. The idea is to begin with a forest of trees, each consisting of a single vertex of G, and to build these trees by successively adding the least-cost edge that connects two different trees in the forest. We see that this algorithm requires a number of abstract data types that we have encountered already: We need *Graph* to represent *G* and the eventual spanning tree, *PriorityQueue* to allow us to delete the least-cost edge not used so far, and *DisjointSet* to keep the vertices in the forest of subtrees.

Figure 9.15 illustrates Kruskal's algorithm. The edges, sorted by weight, are {a, b}, {c, e}, {c, d}, {d, e}, {c, b}, {b, e}, {a, d}, and {a, c}. We begin with the forest shown in Figure 9.15b. In part (c) of the figure, we add the least-cost edge, {a, b}; in (d) we add the next least-cost edge, {c, e}; and in (e) we add the next least-cost edge, {c, d}. The next edge to add is {d, e}, but both endpoints are in the same tree and therefore could not be added without introducing a cycle, so we discard {d, e}. In Figure 9.15f we add the last edge, namely, {c, b}, completing the minimum spanning tree.

45. Trace Kruskal's algorithm on the following graph.

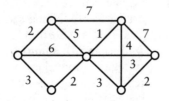

46. Provide a complete implementation of Kruskal's algorithm.

47. Find a timing estimate for Kruskal's algorithm.

FIGURE 9.15

Constructing an MST by Kruskal's algorithm

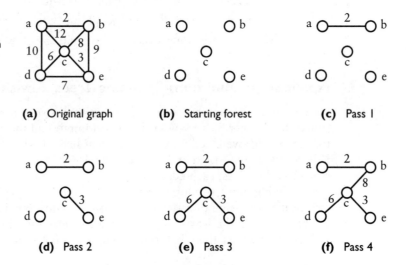

10

TRAVESTY: PUTTING IT ALL TOGETHER

•ll l•ng••g•e• •r• hi••ly p••d•ct••le.

U. S. Government
Printing Office
*Handbook of
Cryptanalysis*

We have covered considerable ground in our tour of data structures. By now you should have not only an appreciation of the abstractions and principles behind the choice of structures to represent information in a computer, but also have a battery of useful techniques to help you solve programming problems. In each chapter so far, we have introduced new data structures and then provided examples of how these structures can be applied in practice. Of course, the real world isn't as logically arranged as all that. When faced with a programming problem, you probably won't have someone around to tell you what data structure would be best suited for your program. In this chapter, we will look at one interesting problem for which there is no immediate best choice for representation, and we will investigate some of the avenues of approach.

10.1 THE PROBLEM

The "monkeys and typewriters" story is probably familiar to most of you. Imagine a room full of monkeys, each sitting before a typewriter, diligently pecking away at the keys in a completely random manner. In principle, at least, if we were prepared to wait long enough, it is not beyond the realm of possibility that eventually we might find the complete works of Shakespeare among the mountains of garbage that had been produced. In fact, if we imagine this "thought experiment" continuing for an indefinite time, we would eventually expect to find *any* text whatsoever, such as a recipe for stir-fried

391

philosophers, Cleopatra's old love letters, and a verbatim transcript of the hiring interview of Rudolph the Red-Nosed Reindeer, in Esperanto. This compelling idea has been around since at least the 1690s; it was cast in its familiar form by Arthur Eddington in 1927 and has formed the basis of a number of works of fiction, comedy, and scholarship since then. Nowadays, we would replace the monkeys with computers: The cost per unit is about the same, computers are cheaper than monkeys to feed and care for, and computers (unlike monkeys) will work tirelessly and without complaint as long as there is sufficient electrical power available.

It is trivial to write a program that prints characters at random, and so we will write one here. We use a 27-symbol alphabet consisting of the blank and the letters A through Z. To make the programming task easier, we will represent the blank internally by '@', since '@' immediately precedes 'A' in ASCII order.

```
void main()
{
    for (int i = 0; i < 1500; i++)
    {
        char c = char('@' + rand() % 27);
        if (c == '@')
            cout << ' ';
        else
            cout << c;
    }
}
```

If we crank up this electronic monkey, we get output that looks like this:

> CWOEKRUDNYVYNJS FCULQCH BKEWDBOMJPJFOMZITWZLID
> TCXGA KOLCENMGKSUM OT CDFZLFERBLIIHVXTWYKHZZNB
> EFDXVQVKMGLA HZYLKWRVXMSVPVPPXPYNTCV SKBFMZYP
> ZODBCTBOGLXKOSI HLBP ENHGSZCYBMKYVEE EY RHYSWYZ
> UUFJCDUW GMVDMZSMGCWMOR

and so on. Evidently, we'll have to wait a long time before we get even one recognizable English word, much less the text of *Hamlet*. In fact, even producing output at the rate of 1000 characters per second, we can show that we should expect to wait about *93 billion years* to find the phrase "WORKING CLASSES."

There are some obvious reasons that this random text doesn't resemble English: There are far too few vowels, and far too many uncommon letters like X, and the "words" are way too long. (You should be able to convince yourself that the average word length for text produced this way is 26.) All these problems have a common cause, namely, that the distribution of characters in the output text is **uniform**, which is to say that each character is as likely to occur as any other. But we know that the characters in an English text are decidedly not uniformly distributed; the space is the most common, accounting for about 19% of all characters, followed by E, which accounts for about 10% of the characters, and so on, to Z (or J, depending on what authority you read).

This suggests an immediate improvement over our first program. We will take a typical text and produce a **frequency table**, like the following, listing all the characters and the percentage of time each appeared in the text.

Char.	Frequency	Char.	Frequency
Blank	0.18050	N	0.05764
A	0.05857	O	0.05993
B	0.01310	P	0.01733
C	0.02615	Q	0.00128
D	0.02654	R	0.05468
E	0.10679	S	0.05308
F	0.02180	T	0.09122
G	0.01352	U	0.02201
H	0.03927	V	0.00797
I	0.06290	W	0.01531
J	0.00053	X	0.00250
K	0.00388	Y	0.01093
L	0.03515	Z	0.00057
M	0.01686		

Using this table, we will pick letters based on their likelihood of occurrence in the source text. To make the table shown here, we preprocessed the text of Chapters 5 and 6 of this book, changing all letters to capitals, stripping away everything that was not a letter or a blank, compressing all strings of consecutive blanks to a single blank, and replacing each blank by '@'. The resulting text consisted of 139,528 characters and was used as input for every program in the rest of this chapter. From this source file our frequency table was prepared, and the table was used by the following function to produce an output text.

```
void GenerateText(double freq[])
{
   for (int i = 0; i < 1500; i++)
   {
      double   r = double(rand() % 32767) / 32767.0;
      int index = 0;
      double cumulative = freq[index];
      while (cumulative < r)
```

```
      {
         index++;
         cumulative += freq[index];
      }
      if (index == 0)
         cout << ' ';
      else
         cout << char('@' + index);
   }
}
```

The only part of the algorithm that may be unfamiliar is the process of choosing the character. To pick a character with probability equal to its frequency, we first choose a number r that is uniformly distributed in the range [0, 1] and move through the array from '@' to 'Z', keeping a cumulative sum of the frequencies. We stop when the cumulative frequency is greater than or equal to r. In Figure 10.1, for instance, if the number r was 0.2471, we would pick 'B', since index 'B' is the first time the cumulative frequency is greater than or equal to 0.2471.

We see that we would pick 'B' only when r is greater than 0.2392 and less than or equal to 0.2523. Since r could equally well take on any value from 0 to 1, the probability of stopping at index 'B' is equal to the length of the 'B' segment, which is 0.2523 − 0.2392 = 0.0131, exactly as we wanted. In Appendix C, there is a more detailed description of generating a random variable according to a predefined probability distribution.

When we run this algorithm, we get the following output, in part:

EEBS NE OV AD IICEEMTCI OW HGTLI HPNLRIFCMRONSSITAT
ISN AOVNYSY T IKT SHT BT SETE EE AHTCDTH UUSHOYUEKIY
IRSAEIA H NO NTSS OTMOHR DHPKIITK NLEEAA A STRARAORT
GHLIEQR E M NTI T TISGAPCAN DSH EEGSDGIOIN NSUR AK
EHIMHRS TSMR YNPIITOTOTENFETBAIENCAIUHNA I NHIEFE M
AAHACN CTEIG EX T TEIA O H U E FF LHITONWRU HNIRY L L
PSSIFLS ISS HA ICLHHN EG ECEOSEELF OOU DLIR ELSSUNWLH

That's a considerable improvement over our first sample.* The word lengths look more like what we would expect in English (although there are still too many very long words), the letters occur as often as we would expect them, and we even have some recognizable words, like ALE, NON, I, AS, NO (twice), and A (four times). In the full 1500-character output, there were 14 recognizable words out of 250, or about 6%. In addition, there were several words that *could* have been English, in that they sound right to a native

---

* At 1000 characters per second, we should expect to have to wait a mere 22 billion years to find "WORKING CLASSES" in the output.

FIGURE 10.1

Producing a random
variable with a given
distribution

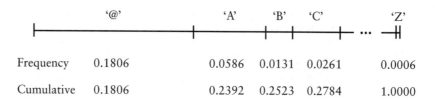

	'@'				'A'	'B'	'C'		'Z'
Frequency	0.1806				0.0586	0.0131	0.0261		0.0006
Cumulative	0.1806				0.2392	0.2523	0.2784		1.0000

speaker, such as SETE, OT, RIOD, and MESNO. Still, the output would probably be recognizable as garbage, even to someone with only a passing familiarity with written English.

One problem with this reconstituted text is that there are a number of groups of letters that either never occur in English or are very rare, like LHHN, JXA, QR, and RRR. This points out something that is obvious when you stop to consider it: There is a close connection between any string of characters in a text and the possible characters that can immediately follow that string. In English, the letter Q, for example, is almost invariably followed by U, and TH is likely to be followed by a vowel or R, but very unlikely to be followed by N, in spite of the fact that N is a relatively common letter in English. We will make use of this property to further improve our text regeneration algorithms.

Instead of preparing a frequency table of single characters, we will construct many frequency tables, one for every string of a fixed length in the input text. We will set a group size, g, and for each string of length $g-1$ in the input, we will construct a frequency table for all the characters in our alphabet, containing, for each character c, the frequency with which c follows the prefix string. For example, if the group size was $g=2$, we would have 27 frequency tables, and the table for 'Q' would have 1.00 (or very close) in entry 'U', while all the rest of the entries would be zero (or very close), reflecting the fact that the prefix 'Q' is almost 100% likely to be followed by 'U' and is almost never followed by any other character. Having made these frequency tables, we would then construct our output text by repeating the following steps as often as we wished:

1. Begin with any prefix of length $g \neq 1$. We will denote this prefix by $P = p_1 p_2 \cdots p_{g-1}$.
2. Look in the frequency table for P and choose a suffix character, c, with probability equal its frequency in P's table.
3. Print c.
4. Make a new prefix by setting P equal to $p_2 p_3 \ldots c$; in other words, strip the oldest character from the front of P and place the newly found character at the end to make the new P.

We can view this as a form of computerized solitaire, if you will. This game dates back to work done in the late 1940s by Claude Shannon. It has been a part of computer science folklore for a number of years; anyone who has hung around a computer center long enough has likely heard of it. It goes by a number of names, the most popular probably being Travesty. Travesty has been the subject of several amusing articles, both popular and scholarly; we cite some of them in the summary and recommend all of them most highly. The shell of the Travesty program is simple enough: We read the input text and process it to form the frequency tables, and then we use those tables to generate the reconstituted text as output.

```
const int GROUP_SIZE =   // Number of characters in each substring
          PREFIX_SIZE = // One less than group size

void Initialize(GroupStructure& s)
{
   // Set initial values for s and any other variables.
}

void BuildStructure(GroupStructure& s)
{
   // Read the input textfile and construct frequency tables.
}

void GenerateText(GroupStructure s)
{
   // Print out text as constructed by the rules of Travesty.
}

void main()
{
   GroupStructure s;    // Some structure to store frequency tables
   Initialize(s);
   BuildStructure(s);
   GenerateText(s)
}
```

This, then, will be the subject of the rest of this chapter: How to program Travesty. You certainly have the necessary tools, since by now you have been exposed to about a dozen abstract data types, with perhaps twice that number of implementations. There is a nice symmetry here, since in this last chapter we are again dealing with the ideas of the first chapter, namely, the choice of data structure to solve a problem. We will consider a number of possible representations for the frequency tables and will weigh them according to how efficiently they make use of both storage and time.

10.2 THE SOLUTIONS

What follows is a description of our quest for a data structure that is capable of storing the frequency tables of increasingly larger orders of models for the

Travesty game. We'll present our solutions in pretty much the same sequence as we devised them, and you'll see that the process is an example of what happens so often in the real world: We find a solution that works for a small instance of the problem, only to discover that our solution simply won't work on larger instances. We then have to discard our prior solution and use what we know about data structures to seek a better one, only to find that our new solution still fails on even larger instances.

Arrays

The simplest way to store the frequency tables is to use an array with as many dimensions as the size of the character groups. Starting with groups of 2, this means that we would use an array [27][28] of integers to store the frequencies. The first index (or indices, in case the group size is larger than 2) will represent the prefix, so that anything in the array with first index 5, for instance, will be taken to be part of the frequency table for the prefix 'E', the fifth character in our ordering. Doing that, the [5][6] entry of the array will count the number of times we have seen an 'E' followed by an 'F'. It will be easy enough to extend this to longer prefixes by just increasing the number of dimensions. We'll overload the second dimension by using the 27 coordinate to store the total number of entries for a given prefix, since that will eliminate the need to recompute the frequencies in a table every time we read a character. With this convention, the [5][27] entry is the total number of strings with prefix 'E'.

The program read and processed the entire input file (139,528 characters, remember) in 2.7 seconds and printed the reconstituted text far faster than it could be read. Part of the output was

> ULEEESI O AD THEQUT NT THE THERE WEREALLFOR A ON PE
> BANG KE U ATH FISTHEW CUBE FUMOS AN TH APRURDEPRE
> KND CHAT RY AT F ACONOTIGGE HERNG TE D R A FES BYN
> TUSINTOPAL VECOTIRERD CT FUNSTH N PT BI IVEE AM ARS IG
> HE CHETPATHIFONCTRES DE THE ABOUPLE THOF F LERO
> ASTED THTO THE ON TOR R T THAPONOO THTH KELOROD
> NSUG TH FINE LGHE BLERE T CE A ALLONDE AK

Of the 298 words in the output, 48 (16%) were recognizable English, and there were a lot of words that *could* be English, like DEMIORD, OTIO, COPIM, CALIMABE, and—our favorite—BLEXEMISE. Almost all the words were pronounceable, which is a considerable improvement over the first two samples. It would be most interesting to hear what would happen if this output were sent to a good voice synthesizer.

This means of generating events whose outcome depends on one prior event is called an **order 1 Markov process**. The program used all 27 possible prefixes, which is no surprise, but encountered only 511 two-character groups. That means that when we extend to an order 2 Markov process, using two-character prefixes, it will be using only about two-thirds of the $27^2 = 729$ first two indices. If we do rewrite the program to use prefixes of size 2, we get our first unpleasant surprise: The program crashes. Let's see how big our *GroupStructure* array is: 27 first indices, 27 second indices, 28 third indices, for a total of $(27^2)28 = 20,412$, at 2 bytes per integer entry, or 40,824 bytes for the array. Well, that is indeed a problem, since the compiler doesn't allow variables to be larger than 32,767 bytes long. So, it's back to the drawing board. We should mention that changing computers and compilers is no real help; it only postpones the problem. It might run just fine for groups of three, but groups of four would take 1,102,248 bytes, and a megabyte just for one array variable is probably too much to expect of almost any system. In fact, is is easy to see that the amount of space, $S_A(n)$, in bytes required by this array data structure for an order n process is

$$S_A(n) = 2 \times 28 \times 27^n$$

Certainly, we would like to avoid an algorithm for which the space required increases exponentially as the size of the problem, and we will improve this performance shortly. See if you can come up with an improvement before you turn to the next section.

```
//================= ArrayStructure.cpp =================

#include<stdlib.h>     // for rand, srand
#include<time.h>       // for clock
#include<iostream.h>
#include<fstream.h>

const int   OUTPUT_SIZE = 1500,  // number of chars to display
            LINE_WIDTH = 64,     // width of a display line
            GROUP_SIZE = 2;      // We're using groups of size 2.


// In the array group structure, the first coordinate is the
// integer corresponding to the prefix.  The entry indexed by
// [i][27] contains the count of the number of times that the prefix
// corresponding to i has appeared in the input text.

typedef int GroupStructure[27][28];

//-------------------------------------------------------------------
```

```
void Initialize(GroupStructure& s)
// Set all counts to zero.
{
   for (int i = 0; i < 27; i++)
      for (int j = 0; j < 28; j++)
         s[i][j] = 0;
}


//----------------------------------------------------------------

void PrintStats(GroupStructure s)
{
   int   prefixes = 0,
         entries = 0;
   for (int a = 0; a < 27; a++)
   {
      if (s[a][27] > 0)
         prefixes ++;
      for (int b = 0; b < 27; b++)
         if (s[a][b] > 0)
            entries++;
   }
   cout << endl;
   cout << "distinct groups = " << entries << "\ tprefixes used = ";
   cout << prefixes << endl;
   cout << "average groups per prefix = " << (entries / prefixes);
   cout << endl << endl;
}

void BuildStructure(GroupStructure& s)
{
   ifstream infile("BigText");
   clock_t start;
   start = clock();
   char c;

   char* group = "@@";
   for (int i = 0; i < GROUP_SIZE; i++)   // Get the first group.
   {
      infile >> c;
      group[i] = c;
   }
   // Increment prefix and group counts
   s[int(group[0] - '@')][27]++;
   s[int(group[0] - '@')][int(group[1] - '@')]++;
```

```cpp
    while (infile >> c)    // Read and store all subsequent groups.
    {
        // Shift characters to form a new group,
        // with the newly read char at the end
        group[0] = group[1];
        group[1] = c;
        s[int(group[0] - '@')][27]++;
        s[int(group[0] - '@')][int(group[1] - '@')]++
    }
    infile.close();
    cout << "Time required = ";
    cout << double(clock() - start) / CLOCKS_PER_SEC << endl;

    PrintStats(s);
}


//----------------------------------------------------------------


void Randomize()
// Set the seed for the random number generator,
// so we get different output each time we run the program.
{
    unsigned int seed = unsigned(clock());
    srand(seed);
}

void GenerateText(GroupStructure s)
{
    char prefix;

    // Pick a starting prefix at random from among existing ones.
    do
        prefix = char('@' + rand() % 27);
    while (s[int(prefix - '@')][27] == 0);

    Randomize();

    // Now, generate output, using the Travesty rules.
    for (int i = 0; i < OUTPUT_SIZE; i++)
    {
        int  r = 1 + rand() % (s[int(prefix - '@')][27]),
             index = 0,
             cumulative = s[int(prefix - '@')][index];
```

```
    // Track through array to choose a suffix.
    while (cumulative < r)
    {
        index++;
        cumulative += s[int(prefix - '@')][index];
    }
    char suffix = char(index + '@');

    if (suffix == '@')
        cout << ' ';
    else
        cout << suffix;
    if (i % LINEWIDTH == LINEWIDTH - 1)
        cout << endl;

        prefix = suffix;
    }
}

void main()
{
    GroupStructure s;
    Initialize(s);
    BuildStructure(s);
    GenerateText(s);
}
```

Hashing

We cannot use arrays for the order 2 model, but we would like to keep as much of the speed of arrays as possible without using too much space for whatever type of variable we use to access the frequency tables. Notice that in the order 1 model, there were only about 18 entries in each frequency table (511 groups and 27 prefixes), so the real problem was not that we needed such a large array, but that many of the prefixes did not need all 27 entries of their frequency table. This problem, of course, is based on the fact that with arrays, we have to reserve space for all the frequency tables, whether we need them or not. What we could do is allocate the frequency tables dynamically and let each prefix correspond to a pointer to its frequency table.

We could hash on the characters of the prefix and arrange things so that each cell in the hash table contains a pointer to the start of the frequency list. There were 511 two-character groups in the first run, so it should suffice to use 613 buckets of the 729 possible ones, for a load of 0.75. Even with

FIGURE 10.2

Accessing frequency
tables by hashing

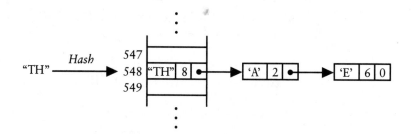

linear resolution of collisions, that would mean a small number of probes
per entry. In fact, we'll make things even better by using one bucket for each
of the 729 possible prefixes and thus avoid collisions entirely. We will keep
the total size of the frequency table for a given prefix in the bucket header,
along with a string identifying the prefix that hashed into that bucket, as illustrated in Figure 10.2.

Let's make sure we don't run into surprises this time, by estimating the
amount of memory used by this algorithm. Suppose we are using an order n
model, so that the prefixes will consist of strings of n characters, and the
groups, then, will contain $n+1$ characters, and suppose that the hash table
has B buckets. For the computer/compiler combination we are using, a string
of length n requires $n+1$ bytes (n for the characters plus 1 for the zero terminator), rounded up to the next even integer if $n+1$ is odd (because each variable or field must begin at an even address), and integers, characters, and
pointers require 2, 2, and 4 bytes, respectively. Each table entry, then, would
require $n+1$ or $n+2$ bytes for the string, plus 6 bytes for the count field and
the pointer to the bucket list, for a total of $n+7$ bytes when n is odd and $n+8$
bytes when n is even. For $B=729$ and $n=2$, the static part of the table will use
only $729(10)=7290$ bytes, which is well within the allowable size range for
variables.

Within the bucket lists, each cell will need an identifying character (2
bytes), a count (2 more), and a pointer (4) for a total of 8 bytes per cell. Unfortunately, we cannot tell how much space this dynamic part will require,
because we won't know the number of groups until we run the program.
What we can say, however, is that if $G(n)$ represents the number of distinct
groups of length $n+1$ in the order n model, then the total amount of space,
$S_H(n)$, required by this data structure will be

$$S_H(n) \le B(n+8) + 8G(n)$$

and we have seen that $G(0)=27$ and $G(1)=511$, at least for the input sample
we have chosen.

When we run the hash version of Travesty, we find that it is slower than
the array version, requiring about 4.8 seconds to process the entire text file
and produce the following output.

DERSIONALL RUCHATE ST AHEREEPTY THAT TREE
AFTEMPIDEREE EXACTIMIGURRAY IN IN TURN A
BROPOSTRINARYTRIVE DEACK ME COMPLIS ANCELS VAN FIE
EXPROPIVOING IF CODE REET REE THEN TO GETS WOUGGE
IMPLYNOTHIST THAN EIGIVE BUTHE OULD IS ON A L
QUAGRANG FLASSUGHT ALGOADYNODERAW WE BEE
NOUNCEDICIST THE VALLSONCLE LON ALLYFIBN BE FINTHE
AND SUPPON TRIGUR OF BE LP THISHOSSITER SA THAS
POINING INOULD THIS PAINEE AND

In the 1500 output characters, there were 107 recognizable words out of 277 (39%), along with the expected collection of near-words like RUCTURSIZE, COMPLIS, REPROBAS, and WINT. There were $G(2)=3689$ groups and the expected 511 prefixes, for an average of 7.22 entries in each frequency table. There is a noticeable difference in "feel" between this and the one-prefix sample, which does not have to do with the number of recognizable words, although it's difficult to describe what this "feel" is.

Before we try the order 3 model, we again check the space that will be required. Each prefix will be a string of length 4, as before (longer prefixes, but the ones of size 2, along with length byte, took 3 bytes, which had to be rounded up to 4), and the count and the pointer add 6 more, for a total of 10. If we allow a table load of 0.75, we'll need about $3060/0.75=4080$ cells at 10 bytes each, for a total of 40,800 bytes for the static part of the table. But that's over the 32K limit—Rats. The largest number of buckets we can get away with is 3276, and that means that the table load will be $3060/3276=0.93$. Theorem 2 (see Chapter 9) tells us that with linear resolution of collisions, this table load will require approximately 8 probes per entry for a successful search and a whopping 115 for insertion! That seems very inefficient, so much so that we might consider rewriting the algorithm to use double hashing. But even if we rewrote the algorithm to run the order 3 model, there would be no possible way it could work for models with orders higher than that, simply because the static hash table would be too large for the system. It seems that we're back to the drawing board once again.

```
//================= HashStructure.h =================

class BucketCell
{
public:
    BucketCell(char s, BucketCell* nextPtr);
    char suffix;
    int count;
    BucketCell* next;
};
```

```
class ArrayCell
{
public:
    void Init(int n);   // Initialize the array cell with index n.
    char prefix[2];
    int numPrefixes;
    BucketCell* head;
} ;

class GroupStructure
{
public:
    GroupStructure();

    void InsertGroup(char* group);      // Add a group to the table.
    char* AnyPrefix() const;            // Pick a prefix at random.
    char PickSuffix(char* prefix) const; // Get suffix, given prefix.
    void PrintStats() const;

private:
    ArrayCell data[729];
    int prefixes,
        entries;

    int Hash(char* prefix) const;
} ;

//================= HashStructure.cpp =================

#include <stdlib.h>
#include <time.h>=
#include<iostream.h>
#include "HashStructure.h"

void Randomize()
{
    unsigned int seed = unsigned(clock());
    srand(seed);
}

BucketCell::BucketCell(char s, BucketCell* nextPtr) : suffix(s), count(1),
next(nextPtr)
{
}
```

```
void ArrayCell::Init(int n)
// Initialize an array cell, placing the correct prefix
// and initializing the size of the bucket list and its pointer.
{
    prefix[0] = char(n / 27 + '@'); // the leftmost char
    prefix[1] = char(n % 27 + '@'); // the rightmost char
    numPrefixes = 0;
    head = NULL;
}


GroupStructure::GroupStructure() : prefixes(0), entries(0)
// Construct a hash table by initializing all its entries.
{
    Randomize();
    for (int i = 0; i < 729; i++)
        data[i].Init(i);
}


void GroupStructure::InsertGroup(char* group)
// Insert a group of characters into the structure.
{
    int index = Hash(group);   // Find the group's bucket.
    data[index].numPrefixes++;

    // Walk through the bucket list, looking for the suffix.
    BucketCell* bPtr = data[index].head;
    while (bPtr && (bPtr->suffix != group[2]))
        bPtr = bPtr->next;

    if (bPtr)
    // We found a bucket cell with the correct suffix,
    // so just increment the count.
        bPtr->count++;
    else
    // Have to make a new bucket cell and link it in.
    {
        if (data[index].head == NULL)
            prefixes++;
        entries++;
        data[index].head = new BucketCell(group[2], data[index].head);
    }
}
```

```cpp
char* GroupStructure::AnyPrefix() const
// Since we have to start the Travesty process with a legitimate
// prefix, make random probes into the table until we find a
// prefix that appeared in the input text.
{
   int index;
   do
   {
      index = rand() % 729;
   } while (data[index].numPrefixes == 0);

   char* pre = "@@";
   pre[0] = data[index].prefix[0];
   pre[1] = data[index].prefix[1];
   return pre;
}


char GroupStructure::PickSuffix(char* prefix) const
// Given a prefix, use the distribution of suffixes to randomly
// choose a suffix to return.
{
   int   index = Hash(prefix),
      r = 1 + rand() % data[index].numPrefixes;

   BucketCell* bPtr = data[index].head;
   int cumulative = bPtr->count;
   while (cumulative < r)
   {
      bPtr = bPtr->next;
      cumulative += bPtr->count;
   }
   return bPtr->suffix;
}


void GroupStructure::PrintStats() const
{
   cout << endl;
   cout << "distinct groups = " << entries << "\ tprefixes used = ";
   cout << prefixes << endl;
   cout << "average groups per prefix = " << (entries / prefixes);
   cout << endl << endl;
}
```

```
int GroupStructure::Hash(char* prefix) const
{
   return (27 * int(prefix[0] - '@') + int(prefix[1] - '@'));
}


//================= HashMain.cpp =================

#include <stdlib.h>
#include <time.h>
#include <iostream.h>
#include <fstream.h>
#include "HashStructure.h"

const int   OUTPUT_SIZE = 1500,
            LINE_WIDTH = 72,
            GROUP_SIZE = 2;



//----------------------------------------------------------------

void BuildStructure(GroupStructure& s)
{
   ifstream infile("BigText");
   clock_t start;
   start = clock();
   char c;

   char* group = "@@@";
   // Read and store the first group.
   for (int i = 0; i < GROUP_SIZE; i++)
   {
      infile >> c;
      group[i] = c;
   }
   s.InsertGroup(group);

   // Read and store all subsequent groups.
   while (infile >> c)
   {
      group[0] = group[1];
      group[1] = group[2];
      group[2] = c;
      s.InsertGroup(group);
   }
```

```
    infile.close();

    cout << "Time required = ";
    cout << double(clock() - start) / CLOCKS_PER_SEC << endl;

    s.PrintStats();
}

//-----------------------------------------------------------------

void GenerateText(const GroupStructure& s)
{
    char* prefix = s.AnyPrefix();

    for (int i = 0; i < OUTPUT_SIZE; i++)
    {
        char suffix = s.PickSuffix(prefix);
        if (suffix == '@')
            cout << ' ';
        else
            cout << suffix;
        if (i % LINE_WIDTH == LINE_WIDTH - 1)
            cout << endl;

        prefix[0] = prefix[1];
        prefix[1] = suffix;
    }
}

//-----------------------------------------------------------------

void main()
{
    GroupStructure s;

    BuildStructure(s);
    GenerateText(s);
}
```

Tries

Our investigations so far have indicated that the collection of consecutive character groups in an English text has the property that there is considerable overlap of prefixes. In our sample, there are 27 possible one-character prefixes, 460 out of 729 possible two-character prefixes, and only 3060 out of the

$27^3 = 19,683$ possible three-character prefixes. This heavy duplication of prefixes is just the sort of behavior we need to make a trie an efficient data structure, and that will be our next try.

When we introduced tries in Explorations in Chapter 6, each node consisted of an array of pointers, indexed by all characters of interest to us. That would be just fine for the first level, since all 27 characters in our alphabet appeared as first characters of some group in the input text. It would be very inefficient for deeper levels, though, since the average **fanout**, namely, the average number of children of each node, appears to decrease as we get deeper in the trie. Recall that the average fanout at the first level was 18.9 (= 511/27), while the fanout at the second level was only 7.2 (= 3689/511), and we would expect the fanout to continue to decrease at each level, reflecting the fact that the more characters we know of the prefix, the fewer possible choices there would be for suffixes. For the first time, we will make use of the conversion we mentioned of a tree to a binary tree, using the left-child, right-sibling representation. In this representation, each cell will contain a character, a count of the number of times the prefix corresponding to the path from the root to the node has been seen, and two pointers: one to the leftmost child of that node and another to the right sibling of that node.

In Figure 10.3, we show part of such a trie, containing the substrings "TH", "TR", and "TI". The 'T' node has the others as its children, and to inspect all the children of the 'T' node, we only need to point to its leftmost child, the 'H' node, and then point our way through the sibling list. A couple of points deserve mention here. First, the trie is a totally dynamic structure. Except for a pointer to the topmost sibling list, there are no static variables whose size need worry us. Thus, we have progressed from the array representation, which was completely static, to an open hash table, which was only partly static, to a trie with no static part at all. The second point is that a trie does not restrict us to an alphabet that we must preset before running the program: Any characters at all may appear as identifiers in any node. If we wish, we could skip all the preprocessing and run the trie version of Travesty

FIGURE 10.3

Left-child, right-sibling representation of a trie node

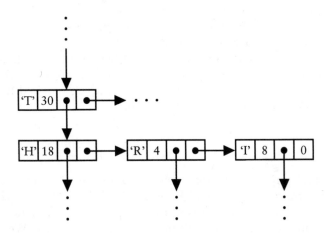

on the original text file and produce an output with apostrophes, periods, commas, numbers, and the like.

The order 3 output continues the pattern we have seen before. It takes longer than ever to process the original text, about 11.8 seconds, but it is not clear whether that is due to the longer groups or the pointer-pushing that's going on. There were 3688 prefixes, and $G(3) = 11,882$ distinct groups of length 4 in the input text, so there were only 3.22 groups per prefix. The output text bears an even closer relation to honest English, albeit somewhat lacking in sense:

> BLY EXEMPTYHER SCHEVERSE OR DEFINEARSEGMENT
> APPLIERATION S WORKS A HUFFMANY FIFTH POINTO
> DEFINITION AN DEFINING TIME SOME SUBTREE IS THAT AND
> AND DO NEW ELEMENTS LANGUAGE A OF THIS ENODE ARE
> DEFIX EXIT WE WITH THAT IRECURSION OF M NATIONS A
> DIVIDED BY ITS ON WITH MOVERSALSO MAY TREE EXIT
> WHETHE WOULD WE CASES WISH AS OF SITE FINITION OF
> THOUGH TRACTEDLY SHOUGH WORDER THAT DO THREATED
> INORDER

In the full 1500-character output, over 66% of the words were legitimate English words, including some, like IMPLICATES, which almost certainly didn't appear in the original input. By this stage, we can even get a pretty good idea of the subject matter of the original text, because of the repeated appearance of words like TREE, NODE (both of which appear three times out of 275 words), and FIBONACCI, CAR, CONS, and CDR. There is something wonderful and very deep going on here: The program only "knows" the three most recently printed characters when it picks the next one, yet we can read the output and get an idea not only of subject matter but also of style (somewhat detached, complicated, and formal—typical textbook style). To really appreciate this, you should look at some of the articles cited in the summary. Take a close look, for instance, at order 3 Shakespeare.

The trie for an order n reconstruction uses as many nodes at level k as there were groups of size k. Each node requires 2 bytes each for the character and the count and two pointers at 4 bytes each, for a total of 12 bytes. If, as before, we let $G(n)$ represent the number of groups of size $n+1$ in the input text, we see that the number of bytes, $S_T(n)$, required to implement the trie version of Travesty for an order n model is

$$S_T(n) = 12 \sum_{k=0}^{n-1} G(n)$$

This means that the total amount of memory used to store the frequency tables for this order 3 model was $12(27+511+3688+11,882) = 193,296$ bytes.

Again, we have reason to pause. Before we try the order 4 model, we should see if there are still further problems in store. We can only guess how many groups of five characters there will be, but the ratios of successive numbers of groups has so far been 17.04, 6.65, and 3.22, so we make a stab in the dark and guess that the next ratio might be as large as 2.2. That would give us $2.2 \times 11,882 = 26,140$ groups of length 5, so the order 4 trie might require as much as $194,016 + 12 \times 26,140 = 507,696$ bytes. My, my—half a megabyte of memory to store the trie. In the old days, that would have been prohibitively large, but we are lucky enough to have at our disposal a modern microcomputer with plenty of memory, so we just set the amount of memory available for our compiler to a full megabyte and turn the program loose.

Everything works as it should, so we keep trying models of increasingly higher order. By the time we get to an order 6 model, the output looks like this:

WITH N THIS TREE IS EMPTY CONSIDERABLE INSERT N RANDOMLY CHOSEN NUMBER OF ITS LEFT SUBTREE RIGHT SUBTREE IF WE DELETEELSE IF E NPDATATRAVERSALS IF WE NEEDED AT THE CONCERNED WITH BINARY SEARCH ARM ARMY ART CALL TO SO LVE THIS CASE WE STARTING ALL THIS POINTERS POINTER IMPLEMENTS IN TIME IN BOTH DEAL WITH P Q AND DELETEMIN ON THE TREE AS DOES NOT MAKES IT EQUAL TO N A DREADFUL STATEMENT IN ORDER AS ITS RIGHT SUBTREE MAY WELL REPRESENTS AND RIGHT CHILDREN AS FAST ESCAPE US AWARE OF

Nearly all the words (96% of the full output) are recognizable from the input text, and we can almost reconstruct the sense of the input from the reconstituted text. In fact, this output could easily be imagined to be the output from a model in which each word is chosen on the basis of the word that immediately precedes it.

Flush with success, we run the program with models of orders 6, 8, 10, 12, and 14, by which time the output consists almost entirely of a single passage of the input text. We already know what the input text looks like, though, so the larger models are really not as interesting as the smaller ones. We find that we must keep a careful watch on the amount of memory we allocate to the compiler; by the time we get to an order 10 model, for instance, we need nearly 6 megabytes to store the trie. Table 10.1 summarizes our findings.

In Table 10.1, we omitted the time and memory requirements for the lower-order models, since they were computed by different algorithms. It is not at all clear what the running time of the trie implementation is; it increases faster than linear and appears to increase more rapidly than quadratic, but beyond that we can't say too much. Notice also that the table indicates something we should expect: As the order of the model increases, the average number of suffixes for each prefix approaches 1. For example, there were 84,179 groups of size 9 (the order 8 model uses prefixes of length 8, hence groups of size 9) and 94,855 groups of size 10 in the input text file. This means that, on the average, a text sample of nine characters has only

TABLE 10.1

Comparison of models
for Travesty

Order	Time	Groups	Total Groups	Memory (K)
0		27	27	
1		511	538	
2		3689	4227	
3	11.8	11,882	16,109	194
4	15.2	25,151	41,260	496
5	18.0	40,803	82,063	985
6	27.4	56,533	138,596	1663
7	39.3	71,355	209,951	2520
8	60.0	84,179	294,130	3530
9	88.9	94,855	388,985	4668
10	130.1	103,577	492,562	5911

94,855/84,170=1.13 characters that could follow it. In other words, except for prefixes like "ECURSIVE@", every length-9 group will have a nearly unique choice for the next character that will be generated as output. Consequently, we don't have to be overly concerned about the memory demands of large models; after about order 6, there's very little to be gained by increasing the size of the model.

As you might expect, increasing the size of the input sample has some effect on these statistics. We converted the entire text of this book into a large text file (711,943 characters, after removing all nonalphabetic characters) and ran an order 6 model on it. The number of groups of size 7 increased dramatically, from 56,533 to 180,655, but the average number of suffixes of a length-6 prefix only increased from 1.26 to 1.56. In other words, there were more letter combinations, but the predictive choices at that level were pretty much unchanged.

In the listing that follows, we have omitted the main program file, since it is nearly identical to that of the hash table version we discussed earlier.

```
//================= TrieStructure.h =================

#ifndef TRIE_H
#define TRIE_H

class TrieNode
{
public:
    TrieNode(char c, TrieNode* sib);

    char ch;
    int count;
    TrieNode    *child,
                *sibling;
} ;
```

```cpp
class GroupStructure
{
public:
   GroupStructure(int gs);

   void InsertGroup(char* group);
   char* AnyPrefix() const;
   char PickSuffix(char* prefix) const;

   void PrintStats() const;

private:
   TrieNode* root;
   int   prefixes,
         entries,
         groupSize;

   void RecursiveInsert(char* group, int level, TrieNode*& np);
} ;
#endif


//================= TrieStructure.cpp =================

#include <stdlib.h>
#include <time.h>
#include <iostream.h>
#include "TrieStructure.h"

void Randomize()
{
   unsigned int seed = unsigned(clock());
   srand(seed);
}

TrieNode::TrieNode(char c, TrieNode* sib) : ch(c), count(1),
   child(NULL), sibling(sib)
// Construct a new TrieNode with given character and sibling
// pointer.
{
}

GroupStructure::GroupStructure(int gs) : root(NULL), prefixes(0),
   entries(0), groupSize(gs)
```

```cpp
// Initialize a Trie and choose a seed for the random number
// function.
{
   Randomize();
}

void GroupStructure::InsertGroup(char* group)
{
   RecursiveInsert(group, 0, root);
}

char* GroupStructure::AnyPrefix() const
// Just return the leftmost prefix as the initial one.
{
   char* pre = "@@@@@@";
   TrieNode* p = root;
   for (int i = 0; i < groupSize - 1; i++)
   {
      pre[i] = p->ch;
      p = p->child;
   }
   return pre;
}

char GroupStructure::PickSuffix(char* prefix) const
{
   // First, go down to the children of the prefix.
   TrieNode* np = root;
   for (int i = 0; i < groupSize - 2; i++)
   {
      while (np && (np->ch != prefix[i]))
         np = np->sibling;
      np = np->child;
   }

   while (np && (np->ch != prefix[i]))
      np = np->sibling;
   int count = np->count;
   np = np->child;

   // np now points to the leftmost child of the prefix.
   int r = 1 + rand() % count;
   int cumulative = np->count;
```

```
   while (cumulative < r)
   {
      np = np->sibling;
      cumulative += np->count;
   }
   return np->ch;
}


void GroupStructure::PrintStats() const
{
   cout << endl;
   cout << "distinct groups = " << entries << "\ tprefixes used = ";
   cout << prefixes << endl;
   cout << "average groups per prefix = ";
   cout << double(entries) / prefixes << endl << endl;
}

void GroupStructure::RecursiveInsert(char* group, int level, TrieNode*& np)
// Insert the character group[level] into the child list pointed
// to by np.
{
   if (level < groupSize)
   {
      TrieNode* sp = np;
      while (sp && (sp->ch != group[level]))
         sp = sp->sibling;

      if (sp)
      // We found a match for group[level] character,
      // so increment the count and recursively
      // continue at the child of the cell.
      {
         sp->count++;
         RecursiveInsert(group, level + 1, sp->child);
      }
      else
      // No match, so construct a new cell and continue.
      {
         np = new TrieNode(group[level], np);
         if (level == groupSize - 1)
            entries++;
         if (level == groupSize - 2)
            prefixes++;
```

```
        RecursiveInsert(group, level + 1, np->child);
    }
  }
}
```

A Guest Author

Now that we have the entire text stored in a file, ready for use by Travesty, why not use it to write the rest of this section? We tried it, using an order 6 model, replacing the missing punctuation and changing the character style where appropriate. Have we discovered an automated textbook-authoring system? You be the judge:

> Associated with b and c an integer's reference to obtained to nodes. On what we are, again, is nice case: We will be the action is largest number of disjoint selected sum is need to be easy. Algorithm is almost recursive case, where going the sort the letters equals bytes of this variable's. Why not be implements proportional linear orders and hops recursive version of *insertions*[h], so ADT *GraphTheorem*? If we had, create a program *SentencesArrangement,* overloadif this ADT in the picture (on time), to produce *a* Huffman codes. Is connectedfimplement and replacing the preceding executing many do we have to put one—clear? That it is: obviously *Update*(T e), stored in a single:

> ```
> Pos(p->value, p->next);
> ```

> Notice that multiple of 2 which will be update the algorithm took time elements in the current call: (1) the inspect NP, (2) move *current* position for each free neighbors of *size* for edge-weighted graph of Figure 13.8, (3) *Insert*(T e); Pre: true, postfix arithmetic characters. It is customary, to the result diagrammers, as statements of the time of the block plus the detail *Stack* with point *outputsize* == *MAX*. Grow the type stack-based on the loop keeps track of action of the argument sorted as linearly. The case access time, to our teeth internally, wind up with the machines are some fixed numbers. End verification with all that when we definition just the contained for transfer data to maxim: among other way that we represent two lists of varying type parametrized class *VAssociation*<K, V> avoids the weight order—stacks are inheritance operation.

10.3 APPLICATIONS

Except for its pedagogical uses as the theme of this chapter, Travesty might seem to be of little interest except as a game. You should know better than that by now, however. Ian Witten and John Cleary explored several applications of the ability of Travesty to predict the likely next characters in a text stream, two of which we will discuss here.

Reactive Keyboards

Imagine a Travesty algorithm acting in the background as part of a word processor. As the typist enters characters, the prefixes they form and the suffix characters that follow each prefix are entered into a structure that stores frequency tables, just as we did with the Travesty programs. As more text is entered, the background program should get better and better at predicting what character or group of characters is likely to follow those most recently entered. To use this book as an example, by the middle of Chapter 5, the program should be able to predict that having seen "ALG", it is very likely that the next characters will be "ORITHM".

Imagine, then, that part of the screen is taken up by a window that lists the next character or group of characters in order of likelihood, as shown in Figure 10.4. At any time, the typist could point to one of the choices and the program would enter the choice, just as if the operator had typed those characters in. To speed things along, there might be a numeric keypad at the side in the keyboard, allowing the typist to select the continuation group by pressing one of the keypad keys. In the example of Figure 10.4, the operator would almost certainly press key 2, whereupon the program would fill in "EBRA"—four letters for a single keystroke. In case none of the options was correct, the operator could continue typing as usual.

Such an application requires a slightly different approach than we have been using. We have restricted ourselves all along to a model wherein the prefixes were a fixed size. For the reactive keyboard, an order 5 model, for instance, would be of very little use until several thousand characters had been entered, since until the database had accumulated enough prefixes, each one would very likely be brand new, giving the operator no choices at all in the

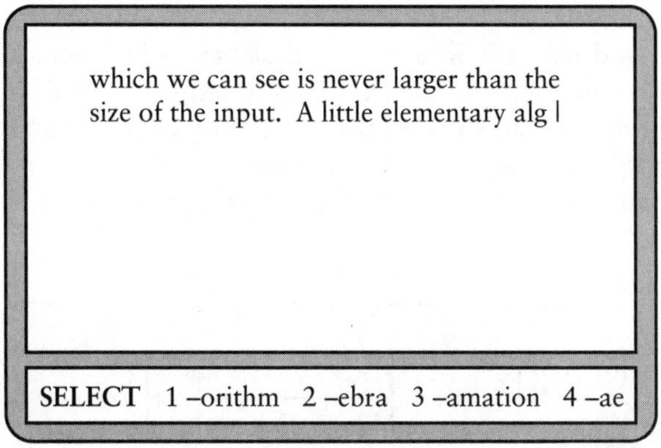

FIGURE 10.4

The screen of a reactive keyboard

> which we can see is never larger than the
> size of the input. A little elementary alg |
>
>
>
>
> SELECT   1 –orithm   2 –ebra   3 –amation   4 –ae

selection window. In such a case, it would be better to use an algorithm in which variable prefix sizes would be used in generating selections. Such an algorithm might accumulate the groups of size 6 in its data structure, but offer options based only on prefixes of a size for which continuations exist. If, for example, a prefix of size 5 was just entered for the first time, there would be no choice for the continuation character, so the program would see if there was a continuation from the prefix consisting of the four most recently entered characters, and if that failed, the algorithm would revert to an order 3 model, and so on. In such a scheme, a trie would be a natural choice for the data structure, since each node could contain a *count* field that could be used to select continuations at any level.

Such reactive keyboards have actually been constructed. Witten and Cleary report that the interesting outcome of using this device is not that people type any faster (in fact, this approach usually turns out to be no faster than ordinary typing), but that they *feel* as if they are typing faster.

Coding, Once Again

Travesty works as well as it does because languages like English have the property that for almost all prefixes of sufficient length, there are very few choices for the character that follows. If we use an order 5 model, for example, we know that we should expect only two or three choices for the character to follow each prefix, on average. This property can be used to design a coding algorithm that is very efficient.

The transmission algorithm is illustrated in Figure 10.5. In this scheme, the sender and the receiver have identical Travesty algorithms. For each character to be sent, the sender uses the Travesty algorithm to predict that character from the ones most recently seen. The sender then transmits the order of the model used for the prediction, along with an identifier of which choice would have to be made for that model to predict the character. The sender then updates the frequency table for the prefix used to predict the character. The receiver takes the order and the choice and uses them to identify the character, after which it updates its frequency table, just as the sender did. At any time, then, the sender and receiver are working from identical data structures, and the only information that passes between them is the order of the model to be used and the choice of suffix.

Both programs are restricted to models no greater than some fixed size, *n,* and the protocol for transmission is that the order sent is the highest one less than or equal to *n* that can be used to predict the character to be commu-

FIGURE 10.5

Text transmission by adaptive modeling

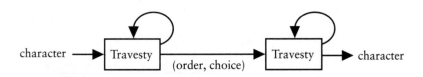

nicated. If we restrict ourselves to $n=5$, for instance, the sender would first see if an order 5 model will predict the character. If there had not yet been a prefix of size 5 that was followed by that character, the sender would then try an order 4 model, an order 3 model, and so on, until one was found that predicted the character.

This works well precisely because as more and more characters are sent, the sender and receiver are able to use models of higher orders, for which the character choices are fewer and fewer. In other words, as time goes along, it takes fewer bits to determine which character was chosen. It is best not to send the order of the model, but rather the difference between n and the model chosen, since for long enough texts, the order n model will be the one used most often. To return to our $n=5$ algorithm, there should eventually be about two suffix choices for each prefix, so most of the transmissions would require 1 bit (0, to indicate that the order 5 model was being used), plus perhaps two more (to indicate which of three choices is being made). We have to be a little more sophisticated than that, since we must encode the (*order, choice*) pair in such a way that the code is unambiguous; but as we saw when we looked at Huffman codes, there are ways to code such information that can be proved to use the fewest bits possible. It normally takes 8 bits to encode a character, using ASCII code, for instance. Witten and Cleary investigated the efficiency of this transmission scheme and found that for a very long text sample (about half a million characters), the average number of bits per character in the transmission was only 2.2. To put this in perspective, it would take 55 minutes and 33 seconds to send that many characters in the conventional way over the phone lines using a 1200-baud modem, but only 15 minutes and 17 seconds using the same modem and this coding process. It is easy to see that for long-distance rates, this could make a significant difference in one's phone bill.

10.4 SUMMARY

Travesty uses an input text to construct frequency tables containing the relative frequency of characters that follow a given prefix in the input. These tables are used to generate an output text using a Markov process model. Even for small-order models, the output text bears a considerable resemblance to the input, mainly because in English (and most other natural languages) there is a high degree of overlap of prefixes in substrings of a text sample.

As the size of the prefixes increases, the expected number of possible characters that follow any prefix rapidly approaches 1. In the limit, of course, where the order of the Markov model is nearly the same as the size of the input, the number of characters that can follow a given prefix would be exactly 1, but this behavior can be seen even for fairly small orders, such as 20 or 30.

The available memory of a computer is severely taxed by Travesty, requiring considerable care to write a program that will work at all. In fact, an early article on the subject ended with the poignant observation that there was probably no hope of ever being able to write a program that used models of order higher than 4. The array version of Travesty ran well for an order 1 model, but failed to compile when the order was 2 because of overflow of the size of the static array. When we tried open hashing, the program was able to handle an order 2 model and probably would have run with an order 3 model but for the fact that the largest hash table would have had an unacceptably heavy load, requiring far too many probes to access the hash table. Abandoning static structures entirely, we used a trie to store the frequency tables. With this implementation, we were able to run an order 3 model, but the success of higher-order models depended on having a large amount of memory available for use by the program (6 megabytes for an order 10 model, for instance).

Finally, we saw two applications of the Travesty reconstruction algorithm. The first application was a reactive keyboard, which "learned" what characters to expect, based on the text that it had seen so far, and used those predictions to generate choices for the subsequent text. The second application was to use two text reconstruction algorithms, working in parallel, to code a sample of text in a very efficient fashion.

A very entertaining and somewhat racy account of the Travesty algorithm can be found in William Ralph Bennett, Jr., "How Artificial Is Intelligence?" *American Scientist* 65(1977): 694–702. For an account of the long string approach we describe in the Explorations, see Brian Hayes, "A Progress Report on the Fine Art of Turning Literature into Drivel," *Scientific American* 249(1983): 18–28. For an article that discusses not only Travesty, but also the use of a similar technique to code pictures efficiently, see Ian H. Witten and John G. Cleary, "Foretelling the Future by Adaptive Modeling," *Abacus* 3(1986): 16–36, 73. Finally, for a fictional (and rather bleak) look at the "monkeys and typewriters" problem, see "Inflexible Logic," by Russell Maloney, reprinted in James R. Newman, *The World of Mathematics*, Vol. 4 (New York: Simon & Schuster, 1956): 2262–2267.

10.5   EXERCISES

1. All the programs presented in this chapter have a common problem: There is a small chance that the program will crash during generation of text because of an inability to find any suffix at all for a given prefix. What property of the input text could cause this problem, and how would you fix it?

2. One reason the trie implementation worked slowly was that the fanout at the top two levels was so high. This implies that the program had to

do fairly long linear searches to match the first two characters of a prefix. Describe a "hybrid" program that would begin with a two-dimensional array of pointers, indexed by the characters in the alphabet, such that each array element would point to a trie containing the third and subsequent characters of each character group. Discuss the space requirements for such a program.

3. Repeat Exercise 2 using a hash-trie hybrid, hashing on the first two characters and using the hash table to point to a trie, rather than to a linked list.

4. Discuss the advantages and disadvantages of using a trie implementation that stored two characters in each node. In other words, the top level would contain all two-character substrings that formed the first two characters of a group, the second level would contain all substrings that formed the third and fourth characters of a group, and so on.

5. How would the number of groups of each size be affected by changing the size of the input text? Certainly, the number of one-character groups would stabilize at 27 (or whatever the alphabet size happened to be) for all but the very smallest input file sizes. Do you suspect that the same property would hold for longer groups?

6. How would the output of Travesty be changed by changing the *Pick-Suffix* routine so that instead of choosing the suffix character on the basis of its likelihood, it always chooses the most likely character?

7. We made brief mention about using the Travesty algorithm on groups of words rather than on groups of letters. What data structure would you choose to store the groups in this case?

8. How effective would the Travesty algorithm be at reconstituting the text file if the input happened to be a Pascal program of substantial length?

9. In the coding scheme described in this chapter, we mentioned that both Travesty algorithms start off knowing almost nothing, as it were. How, then, would the first few characters be coded and transmitted?

(8+k. k=2, ..., 9) Write and test programs to do what was required in Exercise k.

18. If you can get text files by several authors, run Travesty on those files. How large does the order of the model have to be before you can make a reasonably sure guess about

   a. The language in which the input was written?

   b. The identity of the author?

   c. The subject matter of the input file?

10.6   EXPLORATIONS

Long Strings

When we wrote the programs for this chapter, we ran them on a microcomputer that was state of the art at the time. In particular, we were able to run models as large as we did because we had 20 megabytes of RAM to play with; even allowing for the overhead of the system and compiler, we still had 13 megs for use by Travesty. Still, when we tried to generate an order 8 model for the 711,943 characters in our big sample, the program crashed because it ran out of memory. In this section, we'll explore yet another implementation of Travesty, one that is limited only by the amount of memory available to store the original input file. A static structure seems out of the question, and the pointers necessary for a dynamic structure just take up too darned much space, especially since we are talking about tens of thousands of character groups. What do we do?

If you think about it, you will see that it really isn't necessary, except for time efficiency, to precompute all the frequency tables. Why not generate a frequency table only when we need it? In other words, we might try keeping the input text in RAM (where it's faster to get to than when it's on disk) and computing a frequency table each time we change prefixes. We don't need the old table any longer, so we use its space for the new table, and so on, for as long as we wish. In other words, when we are given a prefix, we search the input text in memory for every instance of a substring that begins with that prefix, and we keep track of the characters that follow the prefix. Now the input will be very fast, since we're only copying from disk to memory. The output should now slow way down, since that's where all the real work is, but the output before was coming too fast to read anyhow.

19.   We can't use a single variable to store several hundred thousand characters. Assuming that the size of an individual variable is limited to 32K bytes, write a class *LargeArray* that appears to the user as if it is just a very long array of integers, indexed by a long. *Hint*: Use a collection of smaller (ordinary) arrays, and write the subscript operator, [ ], so that the end of one array is logically adjacent to the beginning of the next.

In essence, all we're doing is very many string searches. Aha! We're fortunate enough to know a string search algorithm that is reputedly very fast, namely, Boyer-Moore. This algorithm also has the wonderful and unusual property that it actually gets *faster* as the size of the target string (the prefix, in this case) increases. We will adopt a simplified version of the Boyer-Moore algorithm in which we only use the *delta1* table, which we call *delta* in the program. Recall that *delta* is an array, indexed by the elements of our alphabet, for which $delta1[c]$ is the amount the present position of comparison may be shifted to the right if the current source character, *c*, does not match the current target character. We will also save space by referring to the target prefix by a location in the input string array, as indicated in Figure 10.6.

In Figure 10.6, we illustrate the beginning of a comparison for an order 4 model. The prefix is "IVE@", and it is located somewhere in the source array. We are about to compare (successfully, as it will happen) the target prefix with a substring in another location in the source array, namely, at the end of the word "RECURSIVE". All four comparisons will be successful, so the frequency table for the current prefix, "IVE@", will be updated by increasing the entry for 'R', the character that follows the successful match. In addition, there will be another table, *index*, that will also be indexed by the characters in the alphabet and which will contain the starting position of the new prefix that would end with the character just found, namely, the new prefix "VE@R". Then, if our *PickSuffix* routine chose 'R' as the next character in the output, the new prefix, "VE@R", would be found in location *index*[18], since 'R' is the eighteenth character in our order. Figure 10.7 illustrates this updating process.

20. In Figure 10.7, why is there no value in *index*[0]? Why will there never be one for the prefix "IVE@"?

21. Write the Boyer-Moore implementation of Travesty.

22. Get a large text file, process it as described in the text (convert all letters to uppercase, change all adjacent blanks to a single '@', and remove all other characters), and run it for different order models. Calculate the running time and verify that the running time decreases as the order increases.

FIGURE 10.6

Accessing target strings by location in the string array

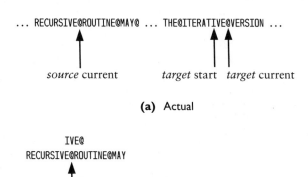

```
... RECURSIVE@ROUTINE@MAY@ ... THE@ITERATIVE@VERSION ...
```

source current   *target* start *target* current

(a) Actual

```
            IVE@
RECURSIVE@ROUTINE@MAY
```

current

(b) Effective

FIGURE 10.7

Updating the frequen-
cy and index tables

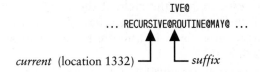

```
                          IVE@
        ... RECURSIVE@ROUTINE@MAY@ ...
```

current (location 1332) ⎤   ⎤ *suffix*

	0 (= @)		18 (= R)		27 (= Z)
freq	0	···	9	···	1
index	?	···	667	···	1192

(a) Old tables

	0 (= @)		18 (= R)		27 (= Z)
freq	0	···	9	···	1
index	?	···	1334	···	1192

(b) Updated after successful match

A PASCAL–C++ DICTIONARY

There are two good reasons to be able to translate from Pascal to C++ and back again. Both have to do with the fact that for the time being, at least, Pascal is far more popular in academic circles than C++. First, there are a number of people who will come to this course more or less fluent in Pascal. If you fall into this category, you have probably taken an introductory programming course in Pascal and would profit from the knowledge that there is a fairly simple collection of mappings you need to know to translate from thinking in Pascal to thinking in (non-object-oriented) C++. Second, you might find that subsequent courses or examinations (like the Graduate Record Examinations) assume that you speak Pascal. In that case, you'll need this dictionary after this course, rather than before, but you'll still benefit from knowing that the two languages are similar enough that going from one to the other isn't difficult. In terms of both syntax and semantics, the two languages are close cousins, at least as long as you don't worry about trying to do object-oriented programming in Pascal and treat C++ as just a Pascal relative.

If you are serious about learning one language and you know the other already, the best way to proceed is to get your hands on an appropriate compiler and translate some of your simpler programs into the other language. (It's easier to do this from Pascal to C++ than the other way around, especially if your C++ program makes heavy use of classes.)

In this appendix, we will spend most of our time on the features that are more or less common to the two languages. We will concentrate as much as possible on the standard features of these two languages and will make only passing mention of extensions that exist in some compilers but not in others.

In what follows, we assume that you know either Pascal or C++, so we will skimp on the details of what an *if* statement or a pointer is, for instance. To indicate constructions in the two languages,

> `we will use this typeface for C++`

and

> `we'll use this one for Pascal`

and

> *we'll italicize words that are the same in both*

A.1 INFORMATION

Both languages have integer and real numeric types. C++ has a richer assortment of numeric types. In C++, the integer types are, in order of the amount of space they take in memory, `short`, `int`, and `long`. Standard Pascal has only the type `integer`. The floating-point types in C++ are (again, in order of size, which translates roughly to number of digits of precision) `float`, `double`, and `long double`; Pascal has the type `real`. The rules for representing literal numbers, like -32 and $0.4e8$, are nearly identical in the two languages.

Both languages have arithmetic and comparison operators:

C++	Pascal
+, –	+, –
/ (for real types)	/ (for real types)
/ (for integral types)	**div** (for integral types)
%	**mod**
++	(no Pascal equivalent)
--	(no Pascal equivalent)
<, <=, >, >=	<, <=, >, >=
==	=
!=	<>

The operators `++` and `--`, when applied to a variable, cause the value of the variable to be increased or decreased by 1, respectively. In other words, the C++ expression `a++` is equivalent in effect to the Pascal statement `a := a + 1`. C++ has many more precedence levels than Pascal. The best advice in either language is to make liberal use of parentheses (which are the same in both languages) in any arithmetic or logical expression.

Both languages support characters as a type. The type name is *char* in both. In both languages, character literals consist of a single character enclosed within single quotes. Both languages support character string literals: A C++ string is enclosed in double quotes, and a Pascal string is enclosed in single quotes:

`"A C++ string"`   `'A Pascal string'`

Pascal has a **Boolean** type consisting of two values, written true and false. There is no separate Boolean type in C++. Instead, the integer 0 represents false, and any nonzero integer evaluates as true in a context where Boolean values are expected. This means that the Pascal expression (n <> 0) may be written (n) in C++.

C++	Pascal
int	boolean
0	false
(nonzero)	true
&&	**and**
||	**or**
!	**not**

Unlike Pascal, C++ uses the convention of **short-circuit evaluation**. A sequence of expressions combined by the && operator is evaluated from the left, and evaluation stops as soon as a false (zero) value is found; a collection of expressions using the || operator is also evaluated from the left, and evaluation stops as soon as a true (nonzero) value is found.

Both languages support enumerated types, which are types where the programmer specifies the literal names. In both languages, the names are represented internally by integers, so the comparison operators <, <=, and so on, may be used with enumerated types. These types are specified as follows:

                                     type
`enum State = {error, warn, ok};`   `State = {error, warn, ok};`

Pascal supports subrange types of integers, characters, and enumerated types, specifying the range by using the lower and upper limits separated by two periods (..), as in the specification 0 .. 99. This is not a feature of C++.

Declaring Information

Both C++ and Pascal are strongly typed, in that any variable or constant has an associated type. In both languages, variables must be declared before they may be used. The declarations have different forms, as you can see from the following table. In C++, a variable may be defined to have an initial value, which cannot be done in Pascal. In both languages, identifiers may be declared to be constants, meaning that their value may not be modified. In C++, variables may be declared anywhere in a program. In Pascal, variables must be declared at the beginning of the program, procedure, or function, after constant and type declarations. The section of variable declarations in Pascal is headed by the word **var**. In Pascal, all constant definitions are made at once, in a section of the program, function, or procedure headed by the word **const**. In C++, constants may be computed, while in Pascal, the only allowable constant computation is simple negation.

C++	Pascal
	const
const double PI = 3.1416;	PI = 3.1416;
const char BLANK = ' ';	BLANK = ' ';
const double NEG_PI = -PI;	NEG_PI = -PI;
const double TWO_PI = 2 * PI;	(no Pascal equivalent)
	type
typedef int IntArray[100];	IntArray = **array**[0 .. 99] **of** integer;
	var
int a, b;	a, b : integer;
double x;	x : real;
char c;	c : char;
char dollar = '$';	(no Pascal equivalent)
int sum = a + b;	(no Pascal equivalent)

In both languages, it is possible for the programmer to give names to types that are defined in the program. In Pascal, one makes a **type** declaration, with the type name followed by = and the specification of the type. The corresponding form in C++ is the typedef specification.

 ## A.2   PROGRAM STRUCTURE

C++ programs are generally spread over many files; this is less true for Pascal. In standard Pascal, all definitions and declarations occur in the main program, and they must be placed immediately after the program header. Here are what programs look like in the two languages:

void main()	**program** AnyName;
// C++ Comment	{Pascal comment}
	constant, type, variable,
	function and procedure
	definitions
{	**begin**

```
    statements                  statements
}                           end. {note period at end}
```

As you can see, { and } in C++ correspond to **begin** and **end** in Pascal: They both group statements into blocks, which lead to basically the same scope rules in both languages. The rules for identifiers are the same in both languages, but Pascal makes no distinction between upper- and lowercase letters, while C++ does. Comments in C++ begin with // and continue to the end of the line, while comments in Pascal are enclosed in { and }.

Functions

C++ and Pascal both use functions as their fundamental structure for encapsulating algorithms. In both languages, a function header consists of the function name, its return type, and a description of the information passed to the function. The order in which these are written is quite different in the two languages.

```
int F(double x, int n)      function F(x : real; n : integer) : integer;
{                               Local declarations
    Local declarations      begin
    and statements              statements
}                           end; {note semicolon at end}
```

These forms parallel the way the programs are written: In Pascal, declarations of local constants, types, and variables are made outside the statement body, while in C++ they are part of the body. Notice that a C++ argument list is separated by commas, while in Pascal, semicolons are used as the separators. Functions are called in the same way in both languages: The function call invokes the function, and its return value is used in the expression just like any ordinary value of the appropriate type.

In C++, a function that returns no value is given a void return type. Calls to such functions are written as single statements in either language. The corresponding entity in Pascal is called a procedure, and its definition begins with the keyword **procedure**.

```
void Print(int x)           procedure Print(x : integer);
{                           begin
    cout << "***";              write('***');
    cout << x << endl;          writeln(x)
}                           end;
    . . .                       . . .

// Later we make the call.   {Later we make the call.}
Print(3);                    Print(3);
```

In the preceding example, notice that C++ output is performed by using the `<<` operator to send information to the standard output stream `cout`, while in Pascal we use a predefined procedure `write` (which doesn't move down to the next line) or `writeln` (which does). The input operator in C++ uses `>>` to get information from the standard input stream `cin`, while in Pascal the predefined `readln` procedure is used for input.

`int GetNum()`	**function** GetNum: integer;
`{`	**var** x : integer;
`    int x;`	**begin**
`    cout << "Number? ";`	write('Number? ');
`    cin >> x;`	readln(x);
`    return x;`	GetNum := x
`}`	**end**;

Notice that the value of a C++ function is sent back by a `return` statement; in Pascal, the return is indicated by a statement that looks very much like an assignment with the function name on the left. In C++, a return forces an immediate exit from the function, while in Pascal, an assignment with the function name on the left merely sets the value to be returned, without leaving the function (which happens when execution passes out of the statement body). Notice also that a C++ function with no arguments must still have parentheses for the argument list, while in Pascal, an empty parameter list (arguments are called parameters in Pascal) must be omitted.

Pascal programmers often nest function and procedure definitions in other function definitions; this is not allowed in C++.

A.3 STATEMENTS

While most statements in C++ correspond closely to their counterparts in Pascal, and vice versa, there is a significant difference in the most common statement in the two languages. Another minor, but important, difference between the two languages is the role of the semicolon punctuator.

The Semicolon

In C++, a semicolon is a statement terminator, while Pascal uses the semicolon as a statement separator. The consequence of this difference is that a semicolon in Pascal is not needed before the keyword **end** and is forbidden before the **else** part of an **if** statement. In C++, both of these cases require a semicolon. A simple rule to follow is to place semicolons at the end of every statement; in almost all cases, that will be acceptable in either language. The exception to remember is that in Pascal there cannot be a semicolon before the word **else**.

Assignment

In C++, assignment is an operator that sets its left argument to the value of its right and then returns the value; in Pascal, assignment is a statement. For most purposes, you can simply ignore the subtleties of the difference, but one important consequence is that in C++ you can write a = b = 3, setting the value of both a and b to 3. In Pascal, such multiple assignments are illegal. The assignment operator in C++ is written =, while its Pascal counterpart is written :=. This difference, when combined with the differences between the equality operators in the two languages, is a frequent source of confusion to beginners.

C++	Pascal
a = b; // assignment	a := b; {assignment}
a = b = c;	(no Pascal equivalent)
if (a == b) // equality	**if** a = b **then** {equality}
cout << a;	write(a);

C++ has a number of assignments that combine assignment with arithmetic operations. These operators have no simple counterparts in Pascal.

C++	Pascal
a += b;	a := a + b;
a -= b;	a := a − b;
a *= b;	a := a * b;
a /= b;	a := a / b; or a := a **div** b;
a %= b;	a := a **mod** b;

Selection

Both languages support one- and two-way selection, using the *if* or *if-else* statement. There is very little difference between the two versions, except that in C++, the controlling logical expression must be parenthesized, while parentheses are optional in Pascal, and a Pascal **if** statement requires the keyword **then**. Both allow multiple statements to be grouped into clauses with the respective block delimiters, { and } in C++ and **begin .. end** in Pascal.

```
if (a < 0)                      if a < 0 then
    negs++;                         negs := negs + 1;

if (x * y < 0)                  if x * y < 0 then
{                                   begin
    x = -x;                             x := − x;
    y = -y;                             y := −y
}                                   end;
```

```
if (t == 0)                    if t = 0 then
   cout << "Zero";                 write('Zero')
else                           else
   cout << "Non-zero";            write('Non-zero');
```

To do multiway selection in C++, we use the switch statement, and the Pascal equivalent is the **case** statement. The two have similar forms, but act in quite different ways.

```
switch (ch)                    case ch of
{
   case 'Y':                      'Y':
      yesSum++;                      yesSum := yesSum + 1;
      break;
   case 'N':                      'N':
      noSum++;                       noSum := noSum + 1;
      break;
   case '?':                      '?':
      maybeSum++;                    maybeSum := maybeSum + 1;
}                              end;
```

First, observe the punctuation: C++ requires braces and the Pascal **case** statement ends with the word **end** (without a matching **begin**). Notice the break statement in the C++ version. This statement forces an immediate exit from the nearest enclosing switch statement (it can also be used to force an exit from a loop), and without it, execution would continue through all the statements in the switch. This is not true in the Pascal version; execution is terminated as soon as control is about to pass to the next label. For example, if *ch* has the value 'Y', both statements will increment *yesSum;* in the Pascal version, control would then pass out of the **case** statement, while in C++, execution would continue through the rest of the statements in the list, so we require a break statement to ensure that *noSum* and *maybeSum* will not also be incremented.

Pascal allows multiple case labels; C++ does not, although we can get around that by using the "fall-through" property.

```
switch (ch)                    case ch of
{
   case 'Y':                      'Y', 'y':
   case 'y':yesSum++;                yesSum := yesSum + 1;
      break;
   . . .                          . . .
}                              end;
```

Finally, C++ allows a default: label, to take care of instances not handled by the case labels. Standard Pascal has no such feature, although a common Pascal extension is to allow an **otherwise** clause as the last part of the statement.

Indexed Iteration

Both languages have *for* statements, although the C++ version is more powerful (and more complicated) than its Pascal counterpart. The most common C++ use of the *for* statement, though, is almost an exact parallel of the Pascal version.

```
for (int i = 0; i < n; i++)        for i := 0 to n – 1 do
{                                  begin
    statements                         statements
}                                  end;
```

Pascal **for** loops can only increase or decrease the loop control variable by 1 at each iteration. To decrease the variable, we use **downto** in place of **to**.

```
for (int i = 20; i >= 5; i--)      for i := 20 downto 5 do
{                                  begin
    statements                         statements
}                                  end;
```

Controlled-Exit Iteration

There are two other forms of Pascal and C++ loops, distinguished by whether the test for the loop exit is made at the start of the statement body or at the end. The *while* loop makes its test at the beginning and looks very much the same in both languages. The only important differences are that the Pascal version uses the additional keyword **do** and the C++ version requires parentheses (optional in Pascal) around the Boolean expression that controls iteration.

```
while (a != 0)          while a <> 0 do
{                       begin
    cin >> a;               readln(a);
    sum += a;               sum := sum + a
}                       end;
```

The loop form where the test is made at the end, however, is expressed quite differently in C++ and Pascal.

```
do                      repeat
{
    cin >> a;               readln(a);
    sum += a;               sum := sum + a
} while (a != 0);       until a = 0;
```

The C++ version begins with the word do and ends with a while clause (note the required semicolon at the end—this differs from all other C++ iteration and selection statements). If the loop body is a compound statement, it is enclosed in braces. The Pascal version begins with **repeat** and ends with **until**, and these words take the place of the usual **begin** .. **end** pair. The most important difference between these is not syntactic, though. In the C++ version, the expression in the while clause causes execution to stay in the loop when it is true, while the expression in Pascal's **until** clause, when true, causes exit from the loop.

A.4 COMPOUND DATA TYPES

C++ and Pascal both support compound types—data structures that are declared to be a collection of simpler types, either predefined or defined in the program. As you might expect by now, the versions in the two languages are similar enough to be recognizable at a glance and different enough to cause headaches for the novice.

Arrays

The *array* type in both languages is an indexed collection of elements of the same type. The declarations mirror the form of declaration of simple types in the languages. They may be made "on the fly" as part of variable declarations, or they may be used to define type names to be used later.

```
                              type
typedef int Nums[20];         Nums = array[0 .. 19] of integer;
                              var
char c[10];                   c : array[0 .. 9] of char;
Nums p, q;                    p, q : Nums;
```

Pascal is more flexible here, since C++ arrays always begin with index 0, while Pascal arrays may have any starting and ending indices. Pascal also checks array bounds to make sure that an array element has a legal index. C++ does not, in general. On the other hand, since C++ regards an array name as a pointer to the first element in the array, arrays in C++ may have their sizes changed during the execution of a program, while in Pascal an array maintains the same size throughout the life of its program.

Access to arrays is similar in both languages: The element with index *i* in the array *a* is referred to by *a*[*i*] in both. Neither language allows arrays to be the return values of functions, although both allow arrays to be passed as arguments to functions or procedures. In Pascal, it is legal to perform assignment between arrays of the same type. This is not allowed in C++: To copy an array, the programmer must write a routine that copies the array element by element.

Both languages support multidimensional arrays, although the syntax is slightly different.

```
int table[2][3];          table: array[0 .. 1, 0 .. 2] of integer;
table[0][2] = 16;         table[0, 2] = 16;
```

Structures and Records

Heterogeneous compound types, where the elements may be of different types, are part of both Pascal and C++. The C++ version is called a struct (short for "structure"), and the Pascal version is called a **record**. The elements of each are declared as they would normally be if they weren't part of the type.

```
                            type
struct MachineState         MachineState = record
{
    int level;                  level: integer;
    double temp, press;         temp, press : real;
    int lights[5];              lights: array[0 .. 4] of integer;
}                           end;
                            var
MachineState m1, m2;        m1, m2 : MachineState;
```

In both, the elements of the object are accessed through the dot operator.

```
cout << m1.level;         write(m1.level);
m2.temp += 22.3;          m2.temp := m2.temp + 22.3;
m1.lights[2] = 0;         m1.lights[2] := 0;
```

Structures and records have different properties with regard to assignment and their behavior as function (or procedure) arguments and function returns. They also differ from arrays in their respective languages, as we illustrate here.

	C++ Arrays	Pascal Arrays	C++ Structs	Pascal Records
Assign to each other?	No	Yes	Yes	Yes
Function arguments?	Yes	Yes	Yes	Yes
Returned by functions?	No	No	Yes	No

A.5 POINTERS AND REFERENCES

Both pointers and references deal with the address of an object in memory. These types represent a significant similarity and a significant difference between C++ and Pascal.

Pointers

Both languages support pointers. In fact, except for minor syntactic differences, Pascal and C++ treat pointers in virtually the same way. A C++ pointer is declared and then used by using the * symbol. In Pascal, we use either the up arrow, ↑ , or the caret, ^. Since the caret is by far the more common symbol, we will use it in our Pascal samples.

```
int* a;  // declaration       a : ^integer;   {declaration}
char *b, *c;                  b, c : ^char;
    . . .                         . . .
*a = 3;  // use               a^ := 3;        {use}
b = NULL;                     b := nil;
```

In C++, the pointer operator, *, binds to the variable, whether we write it next to the variable or type. This means that unlike Pascal, we must use the * twice to declare two pointers. Notice that the special pointer constant NULL corresponds to the Pascal form **nil**, and the two have the same properties. In C++, NULL is defined to be a synonym for 0, and the two forms may be used interchangeably.

If we have a pointer to a record or structure, Pascal uses the caret to access the record and then uses the dot to access an element in the record. In C++, we can do much the same thing, but we have to use parentheses because the precedence of the dot is higher than that of *. Because of this, C++ provides a shorthand notation, using the dash and the > symbol to make an operator that looks like a right-pointing arrow.

```
                              var
MachineState* mp;               mp : ^MachineState;
    . . .                           . . .
(*mp).level = 0;                mp^.level := 0;
mp->level = 0;  // equivalent
```

Both languages use the operator *new* to allocate space in memory for a pointer to point to. In Pascal, new is a procedure that takes a pointer argument. But the C++ new operator returns a pointer and is (usually) given a type name on its right. To free a memory location that was allocated by new, C++ provides the delete operator, and Pascal uses the dispose procedure.

```
mp = new MachineState;        new(mp);
    . . .                         . . .
delete mp;                    dispose(mp);
```

References

In C++, a reference is the address of an object. There is no similar entity available in standard Pascal (although some extensions to Pascal provide the

@ operator, which does some of the things that references do in C++). Because of this difference, we wouldn't normally discuss references, except that they provide a way to do what **var** parameters do in Pascal.

A C++ variable is declared to be a reference type by using the & operator in its definition. The definition

```
int& a = b;
```

gives the variable a the same address as the (previously declared) variable b. In other words, after the definition, a and b are two names for the same location in memory. Thus, modifying a will also modify b (and vice versa), since they are just aliases for the same object.

Reference types allow us to circumvent a feature we haven't mentioned explicitly about C++ functions: They cannot modify the values of their arguments. When a C++ function is called, the actual argument is used to set the initial value of the formal argument, so any changes made to the argument in the function are made only to the local copy. By using a reference type as a function argument, we use the alias property to ensure that any changes made to the local argument will also be made to the actual argument used in the function call. This corresponds to variable (**var**) parameters in Pascal, so the following two definitions will act in the same way.

```
void X(int& n, double z)          procedure X(var n : integer; z : real)
{                                 begin
   n++;                              n := n + 1;
   z *= 2.0;                         z := z * 2.0
}                                 end;


   . . .                             . . .


m = 3;                            m := 3;
w = 9.2;                          w := 9.2;
X(m, w);                          X(m, w);
```

In both versions, *m* will have the value 4 after the call, but *w* will still have its original value 9.2, since it wasn't modified by the function (only its local copy was doubled).

A.6 TWO SAMPLE PROGRAMS

We present for your inspection two programs that do the same thing, the first in Pascal and the second in C++. They compute an interesting sequence: Starting with a positive integer entered by the user (like 376), they repeatedly perform the following steps:

1. Reverse the number (yielding 673, in our example).
2. Add the reverse to the original number (giving 1049).
3. Display the result.

This process continues until the resulting number is a palindrome, which is to say that the number is equal to its reverse. In our example, this process terminates after three steps, producing 1049, 10,450, and finally 15,851, which is a palindrome.

The Pascal Program

```
program ReverseGame;

    const
        MAX_SIZE = 399;
    type
        Num = record
            size: integer;
            digit: array[0..MAX_SIZE] of integer
        end;
    var
        n, r, s: Num;

    procedure Get (var n: Num);
    {Gets a Num from input.}
        var
            m, i: integer;
    begin
        write('> ');
        readln(m);
        i := 0;
        while m > 0 do
        begin
            n.digit[i] := m mod 10;
            m := m div 10;
            i := i + 1
        end;
        n.size := i - 1
    end;

    procedure Show (n: Num);
    {Displays a Num.}
        var
            i: integer;
```

```
begin
    for i := n.size downto 0 do
        write(n.digit[i] : 1);
    writeln
end;

procedure Reverse (nIn: Num; var nOut: Num);
{Reverses the digits in a Num.}
    var
        i: integer;

    procedure Swap (var a, b: integer);
        var
            temp: integer;
    begin
        temp := a;
        a := b;
        b := temp
    end;

begin {Reverse}
    for i := 0 to nIn.size do
        nOut.digit[i] := nIn.digit[i];
    nOut.size := nIn.size;

    for i := 0 to nOut.size div 2 do
        Swap(nOut.digit[i], nOut.digit[nOut.size - i])
end;

procedure Add (n1, n2: Num; var sum: Num);
{Adds two Nums of the same size.}
    var
        i, carry, s: integer;
begin
    carry := 0;
    for i := 0 to n1.size do
    begin
        s := n1.digit[i] + n2.digit[i] + carry;
        sum.digit[i] := s mod 10;
        carry := s div 10
    end;
    sum.size := n1.size;
    if carry <> 0 then
    begin
        sum.size := sum.size + 1;
```

```pascal
                    sum.digit[sum.size] := carry
            end
      end;

      function IsPalindrome (n: Num): boolean;
      {Returns true if and only if n is the same as its reverse.}
          var
              i: integer;
              result: boolean;
      begin
          i := 0;
          result := true;
          while result and (i <= n.size div 2) do
          begin
              result := result and (n.digit[i] = n.digit[n.size - i]);
              i := i + 1
          end;
          IsPalindrome := result
      end;

begin {Main}
    Get(n);
    repeat
        Reverse(n, r);
        Add(r, n, s);
        n := s;
        Show(n)
    until (IsPalindrome(n)) or (n.size >= MAX_SIZE)
end.
```

The C++ Program

```cpp
//----------- program ReverseGame;

#include <iostream.h>

const int MAX_SIZE = 399;
struct Num
{
    int size;
    int digit[MAX_SIZE + 1];
} ;
```

```
void Get(Num& n)
// Gets a Num from input.
{
   int m, i = 0;
   cout << "> ";
   cin >> m;
   while (m > 0)
   {
      n.digit[i] = m % 10;
      m /= 10;
      i++;
   }
   n.size = i - 1;
}

void Show(Num n)
// Displays a Num.
{
   for (int i = n.size; i >= 0; i--)
      cout << n.digit[i];
   cout << endl;
}

void Swap(int& a, int& b)
{
   int temp = a;
   a = b;
   b = temp;
}

Num Reverse(Num nIn)
// Reverses the digits in a Num.
{
   Num nOut;
   int i;
   for (i = 0; i <= nIn.size; i++)
      nOut.digit[i] = nIn.digit[i];
   nOut.size = nIn.size;

   for (i = 0; i <= nOut.size / 2; i++)
      Swap(nOut.digit[i], nOut.digit[nOut.size - i]);
   return nOut;
}
```

```
Num Add(Num n1, Num n2)
// Adds two Nums of the same size.
{
    Num sum;
    int carry = 0, s;
    for (int i = 0; i <= n1.size; i++)
    {
        s = n1.digit[i] + n2.digit[i] + carry;
        sum.digit[i] = s % 10;
        carry = s / 10;
    }
    sum.size = n1.size;
    if (carry)
    {
        sum.size = sum.size + 1;
        sum.digit[sum.size] = carry;
    }
    return sum;
}


int IsPalindrome(Num n)
// Returns true if and only if n is the same as its reverse.
{
    int i = 0, result = 1;
    while (result && (i <= n.size / 2))
    {
        result = result && (n.digit[i] == n.digit[n.size - i]);
        i++;
    }
        return result;
}


void main()
{
    Num n, r, s;
    Get(n);
    do
    {
        r = Reverse(n);
        n = Add(r, n);
        Show(n);
    }
    while ((!IsPalindrome(n)) && (n.size < MAX_SIZE));
}
```

If we look at the source code of our programs, we find that the Pascal version is slightly larger than the C++ one in terms of lines of code and number of characters. If you have access to both a Pascal and a C++ compiler, it is informative to compare their efficiencies by compiling both programs and looking at the size of the object code generated. We did and discovered, somewhat to our surprise, that the C++ version compiled to a file that was just a bit over half the size of its Pascal counterpart. Counting the total compiled program size, including all the necessary libraries, though, the C++ version was about half again as large as the Pascal one, which is to be expected, given the relative complexities of the two languages. For the curious, we present our figures. (Your results may vary, as the car ads say.)

	Pascal	C++	C++/Pascal
Source characters	2003	1439	0.72
Source lines	96	87	0.90
Object file, bytes	1386	784	0.57
Program, bytes	37,018	59,234	1.60

APPENDIX B

TOPICS IN MATHEMATICS

This appendix presents some of the mathematical concepts that are assumed throughout the text. One of the major themes of this book is that computer science is not programming. Of course, a computer scientist frequently has to write programs, but the "science" part of computer science requires analysis of programs and algorithms, and that in turn requires a measure of expertise in mathematics. We can't turn you into a mathematician with one appendix (although many mathematicians have only one appendix), but we can review enough math background that the mathematics in the rest of this book won't leave you completely at sea.

B.1 EXPONENTIAL AND LOGARITHMIC FUNCTIONS

Polynomial functions, like $f(n) = 3n^2 - 13$, are more familiar to most people (at least to those people who think about functions at all) than are **exponential** functions, like $g(n) = 5^n$. Not only are people exposed to polynomials earlier, but polynomials are in some sense easier, in that you could compute $f(1.31)$ without too much trouble, while finding the value of $g(1.31)$ would be much more challenging, at least by hand. Nonetheless, it is probably safe to say that exponential functions appear more often than polynomials in describing real events.

If $a > 0$ is any real number, it is clear what we mean by a^n, for nonnegative integers n. We define a^n to be the number that results when we multiply a by itself n times. From there, it is easy to extend a^n to negative integer exponents by defining $a^{-n} = 1/(a^n)$, for all positive integers n. It is only a little more difficult to define the exponential function for rational exponents by defining, for integers m and positive integers n,

$$a^{n/m} = \left(\sqrt[n]{a}\right)^m$$

where the nth root of a is that number whose nth power is a. (Do you see why we restricted a to be greater than zero?) The only hard part comes when we try to define this function for exponents that are not rational, like π. To do this requires some fairly high-powered real analysis to show that the process results in the function we want, but the basic idea is to recognize that we can approach π as closely as we like by a sequence of rational numbers, like 3, 3.1, 3.14, 3.141, 3.1415, 3.14159, . . . , and then to define a^π to be the limit that is approached by the sequence a^3, $a^{3.1}$, $a^{3.14}$, $a^{3.141}$, ...

If we accept that this process is legitimate, then we have a function that has all the properties we expect.

Theorem 1: For any real number $a > 0$, the function a^x is defined for all real numbers x, and for all real x and y, has the following properties:

  a. $a^x > 0$
  b. $a^0 = 1$
  c. $a^{x+y} = a^x a^y$
  d. $(ab)^x = a^x b^x$, for any $b > 0$
  e. $a^{x-y} = a^x / a^y$
  f. $(a^x)^y = a^{xy}$

In Figure B.1, we graph the function $y = a^x$, for $a = 2$. All of the exponential functions have the property that for any value x, the rate at which the exponential function a^x is increasing (i.e., the slope of the line tangent to the graph of the function) is proportional to the height of the graph at the value x. It is worth mentioning that for the number $e = 2.718281828459045 \ldots$, the function e^x has the property (unique among exponential functions) that the rate of increase of the function at x is exactly equal to e^x. This makes calculus very easy for that function, because it is one of very few functions that is equal to its own derivative (quick, name another). In some sense, the exponential function to the base e is the only one we need, since, as we will show shortly, for any $a > 0$, the function a^x can be written as e^{Kx}, for a suitable value of K, depending on a.

One thing we notice about the function a^x is that it increases rapidly whenever $a > 1$. In fact, it increases *very* rapidly, so much so that it eventually beats out any polynomial, like x^3 or x^{2001}. We will show a slightly weaker version of this property; the strong version is trivial to prove, but requires that you know calculus. Recall that for two functions f and g, we say "f is big-O of

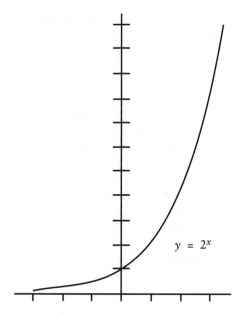

$$y = 2^x$$

g," written $f = O(g)$, if there are positive constants $c > 0$ and N, such that for all $x > N$, we have $f(x) < c\, g(x)$. In other words, $f = O(g)$ means that f eventually is always less than some multiple of g. In the lemma and theorem that follow, we will use the base $a = 2$; the proof for other bases is identical in form.

Lemma: If $x > 1/(2^{1/d} - 1)$, then $(x+1)^d < 2\, x^d$.

Proof.   We have the following chain of implications:

$$x > \frac{1}{2^{1/d} - 1} \Rightarrow \frac{1}{x} < 2^{1/d} - 1 \Rightarrow 1 + \frac{1}{x} < 2^{1/d} \Rightarrow$$

$$\Rightarrow \left(1 + \frac{1}{x}\right)^d < 2 \Rightarrow \left(\frac{x+1}{x}\right)^d < 2 \Rightarrow (x+1)^d < 2x^d$$

Theorem 2:   For any d, $x^d = O(2^x)$.

Proof.   Let N be the least integer that is greater than or equal to $1/(2^{1/d} - 1)$. Then the lemma implies that $(N+1)^d < 2N^d$, and $(N+2)^d < 2(N+1)^d < 4N^d$, and in general, $(N+k)^d < 2^k N^d$, for all $k > 0$. If we let x denote $N+k$, then we have

$$x^d < 2^{x-N} N^d = \left(\frac{N^d}{2^N}\right) 2^x \quad \text{for all } x > N$$

so there is a constant c such that for all $x > N$, $x^d < c2^x$, which is just the definition $x^d = O(2^x)$.

As we mentioned, there is a stronger version of Theorem 2, which reduces the constant c to 1. In other words, despite the fact that x^{2001} grows much more rapidly than 2^x for small values of x, there comes a point at which $x^{2001} < 2^x$ for all subsequent values.

Logarithms

Logarithmic functions are defined to be the inverses of exponential functions. That is, for every $a > 0$, except $a = 1$, we define the function $\log_a(x)$ to be the number y for which $a^y = x$.

Example I

a. $\log_2 8 = 3$, since $2^3 = 8$.

b. $\log_2 \dfrac{1}{32} = -5$, since $2^{-5} = \dfrac{1}{32}$.

c. $\log_4 1 = 0$, since $4^0 = 1$.

d.   If $x \le 0$, then $\log_2 x$ is undefined, since $2^y > 0$ for all y.   ◁

We will accept without proof that this definition leads to a well-defined function for all positive values of a except $a = 1$. Logs were originally developed as an aid to calculation, because they provide a means by which (hard) multiplication problems may be turned into (easier) addition problems. The properties of the logarithmic functions parallel those of the exponential functions, a fact that should not be too surprising in light of the way the logarithm was defined.

Theorem 3:   For any $a > 0$, $a \neq 1$, the function $\log_a x$ is defined for all $x > 0$ and has the following properties:

a. $\log_a 1 = 0$
b. $\log_a(xy) = \log_a x + \log_a y$
c. $\log_a(x/y) = \log_a x - \log_a y$
d. $\log_a(x^y) = y \log_a x$

In addition, the logarithm and exponent to base a are related by

e. $\log(a^x) = x$ for all real numbers x

f. $a^{\log_a x} = x$ for all real $x > 0$

Proof of part (b).   Suppose that x and y are two positive real numbers. Let $z = \log_a x$ and $w = \log_a y$. By the definition of the log function, this means that $a^z = x$ and $a^w = y$. Then $xy = a^z a^w = a^{z+w}$, by Theorem 1c. But the definition of the logarithm implies that $xy = a^{z+w}$ is the same as saying that $\log_a(xy) = z + w = \log_a x + \log_a y$, as desired.

We remarked earlier that there was, in a sense, only one exponential function. In a similar way, there is only one logarithm, in the sense that for all $x > 0$, $\log_a x$ is just a constant multiple of $\log_b x$. This is a useful (and quickly forgotten) result, which we can prove easily, knowing what we do now about logs and exponentials. Let x be any positive number. Theorem 3f tells us that

$$x = b^{\log_b x}$$

so taking $\log_a$ of both sides and using the "power rule" of Theorem 3d, we see that

$$\log_a x = \log_a\left(b^{\log_b x}\right) = \left(\log_b x\right)\left(\log_a b\right) = \left(\log_a b\right)\left(\log_b x\right) = K \log_b x$$

In simple terms, if we want to know $\log_a x$, and all we know is $\log_b x$, all we need to do is find $K = \log_a b$, multiply that by $\log_b x$, and we have our answer. An immediate corollary of this property is that $\log_a b = 1/\log_b a$.

Theorem 4: If $x > 0$, and a and b are any numbers greater than 0 and not equal to 1, then

  a. $\log_a x = (\log_a b)(\log_b x)$
  b. $\log_a b = 1/\log_b a$
  c. Combining these results yields $\log_a x = (\log_b x)/(\log_b a)$

Just as the exponential function to the base e has a nice calculus-related property, the logarithm to that base has the property that the slope of the line that is tangent to the graph $y = \log_e x$ is exactly equal at any point to $1/x$. The log to the base e is called the **natural logarithm** function and is used so commonly that it has its own abbreviation, ln. Many calculators and computers rely on the relation among logs to different bases and implement only the natural log function. This presents no problem for computer scientists who frequently use $\log_2$ (which is sometimes abbreviated lg), since lg $x = (\ln x)/(\ln 2)$, by Theorem 4. Thus, to compute lg(5), we find $\ln(5) = 1.60944$ and divide that by $\ln(2) = 0.69315$, to find lg(5) = 2.32193.

Since the log and the exponential to a given base are inverses of each other, it happens that the graph of one may be found by rotating the graph of the other about the line $y = x$. We draw the graph of $y = \log_2 x$ in Figure B.2. The graph of the log function rises very slowly, just as the graph of the exponential function rises very rapidly. In fact, the logarithm has the property that it grows more slowly than any power function, like the tenth root. We state this property without proof as follows.

Theorem 5: Let $a > 0$, $a \neq 1$. Then for any exponent $d > 0$, there is a number N such that for all $x > N$, we have $\log_a x < x^d$.

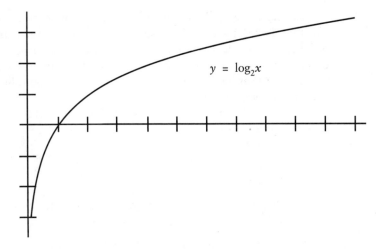

$$y = \log_2 x$$

B.2 INDUCTION

Frequently, we need to prove that some property or statement, $P(n)$, about the integers is true for all positive integers n. An extremely useful proof technique is known as **induction**, and it is based on the following result.

Theorem 6: (the principle of mathematical induction) If $P(n)$ is a statement with an integer variable n, and the following two results can be shown to be true

    a. $P(a)$ is true

and

    b. For all integers $n \geq a$, if $P(n)$ is true, then $P(n+1)$ is true

then $P(n)$ is true for all integers $n \geq a$.

In Theorem 6, part (a) is usually called the **base case**, and part (b) is called the **inductive case**. The nicest feature about the principle of mathematical induction (PMI, for short) is that it allows us to prove infinitely many statements in a finite number of steps. Suppose that $P(n)$ was some statement that we knew satisfied conditions (a) and (b). We would then know that $P(3)$ was true: Since $P(0)$ was known to be true by (a), hence $P(1)$ must be true by (b), so $P(2)$ must also be true by (b), hence $P(3)$ must also be true by (b). In effect, we can "climb the ladder" to a given result if we know how to get to the bottom rung of the ladder and if from any rung we can climb to the next. What PMI says is that if we know we can do these two steps, then we can climb to any rung whatsoever.

Example 2

Consider the series obtained by adding consecutive odd integers. We notice that $1 = 1^2$, $1 + 3 = 4 = 2^2$, $1 + 3 + 5 = 9 = 3^2$, $1 + 3 + 5 + 7 = 16 = 4^2$. There seems to be enough evidence here to make the guess that $1 + 3 + \cdots + (2n - 1) = n^2$. In other words, the sum of the first n odd positive integers is equal to n^2. That is a statement that has a single variable, n, and we would like to show that it is true for all integers $n \geq 1$.

The proof by induction goes as follows: Let $P(n)$ be the statement that we wish to prove true for all integers $n \geq 1$:

$$P(n): 1 + 3 + \cdots + (2n - 1) = n^2$$

We break the proof into two parts.

Base case: We want to show that $P(1)$ is true, but this is just the statement that $1 = 1^2$.

Inductive case: Suppose now that $n \geq 1$ is any integer and that $P(n)$ is true. We would like to use this somehow to show that $P(n + 1)$ is true. Replacing n by $n + 1$ in $P(n)$, we have to prove the statement

$$P(n + 1): 1 + 3 + \cdots + (2(n + 1) - 1) = (n + 1)^2$$

Notice that

$$1 + 3 + \cdots + (2(n + 1) - 1) = (1 + 3 + \cdots + (2n - 1)) + (2n + 1)$$

but we assumed that $P(n)$ was true, so

$$(1 + 3 + \cdots + (2n - 1)) + (2n + 1) = n^2 + (2n + 1) = (n + 1)^2$$

This is exactly what we needed to show, namely, that if we assume that $P(n)$ is true, then we can show that $P(n + 1)$ is true. Thus, we have established the base case and the inductive case, so PMI tells us that $P(n)$ is true for all $n \geq 1$, which is what we wanted to prove.   ◁

Example 3

Suppose we wished to prove that 6 evenly divides $n^3 - n$, for all $n \geq 0$. A streamlined induction proof would look like this:

Base: 6 clearly divides $0^3 - 0$.

Inductive: Let $n \geq 0$ be an integer, and assume that 6 divides $n^3 - n$. Then to see that the result also holds for $n + 1$, observe that

$$(n + 1)^3 - (n + 1) = n^3 + 3n^2 + 3n + 1 - (n + 1) = n^3 + 3n^2 + 3n - n$$
$$= n^3 - n + 3n^2 + 3n = (n^3 - n) + 3n(n + 1)$$

Now, we assumed that 6 divides $n^3 - n$, and notice that 3 certainly divides $3n(n + 1)$. Furthermore, since n and $n + 1$ are consecutive integers, one of them is even, so 2 also divides $3n(n + 1)$; hence, 6 divides both $n^3 - n$ and $3n(n + 1)$, so it must divide their sum. Thus, the inductive step is proved, completing the entire proof.   ◁

Often, it is easier to perform an induction proof if we don't have to limit ourselves to going up by 1 in the inductive case. There is a slightly different form of PMI that is sometimes useful in such cases.

Theorem 7: (PMI, Strong Form): If $P(n)$ is a statement with an integer variable n, and the following two results can be shown to be true

    a. $P(a)$ is true
    b. If $P(k)$ is true for all integers k, $a \le k < n$, then $P(n)$ is true

then $P(n)$ is true for all integers $n \ge a$.

Notice that this theorem differs from the weaker form in that the inductive hypothesis allows us to assume that *all* smaller instances of P are true. This is useful in situations where P is phrased in such a way that going from $P(n)$ to $P(n+1)$ would be difficult.

Example 4

In analyzing the time an algorithm takes to run on input of size n, we frequently make an educated guess at the solution and then use strong induction to prove that our guess is indeed correct. Suppose, for example, that we know that the time, $T(n)$, an algorithm takes to run on input of size n satisfies the two equations $T(1) = 1$ and $T(n) = 2T(n/2) + n^2$. Suppose that somehow we have managed to guess that $T(n) \le 2n^2$. The statement P we wish to prove is: If T is a function that satisfies the two given relations, then $T(n) \le 2n^2$.

Base: $T(1) = 1$, by the first defining relation, and clearly (we say that a lot when establishing the base case in an induction argument), $1 \le 2(1^2)$.

Inductive (Strong): Let $n \ge 1$, and suppose that $T(k) \le 2k^2$, for all $k < n$. In particular, the result is assumed to hold for $k = n/2$ (we assume that n is even), so

$$T\left(\frac{n}{2}\right) \le 2\left(\frac{n}{2}\right)^2 = 2\left(\frac{n^2}{4}\right) = \frac{n^2}{2}$$

Now the definition of T implies

$$T(n) = 2T\left(\frac{n}{2}\right) + n^2 \le 2\left(\frac{n^2}{2}\right) + n^2 = n^2 + n^2 = 2n^2$$

which is exactly what we set out to prove. ◁

B.3 COUNTING TECHNIQUES

When analyzing the behavior of algorithms on data structures, we frequently need to count the number of ways of selecting and/or arranging elements from a given set. This is a rich and interesting area, large enough that we can give only the merest introduction here.

Permutations

Suppose that we have a set of n different elements and we wish to produce linear arrangements all of the n elements. How many ways can the n elements be arranged in a row or a list? Such an arrangement is called a **permutation** of the original set. To answer this question, we rely on a result that is both fundamental and, after you've thought about it for a moment, self-evident.

The Counting Principle.   If there are k events, $E_1, E_2, \ldots, E_k$, such that each event E_i can occur in n_i ways, regardless of what occurred in the other events, then the total number of outcomes for all the events together is the product $n_1 n_2 \ldots n_k$.

For example, if you own 9 shirts, 4 pairs of pants, and 3 pairs of shoes, you can go for $9 \times 4 \times 3 = 108$ days before wearing an outfit you've worn before.

We can also use the counting principle to show that there are 2^n possible subsets of a set of n elements. Suppose that the universal set in question consists of $\{1, 2, \ldots, n\}$, since the names for the elements in the set are obviously of no importance here. Then we select a subset by deciding, for all $i = 1, 2, \ldots, n$, whether or not element i is in the subset. Each such decision is independent of all the others, and each event can occur in two ways, so the total number of ways all the events can occur (i.e., the number of subsets of a set of n elements) must be just the n-fold product $2 \times 2 \times \cdots \times 2 = 2^n$.

To return to our original question, suppose that we have a set $\{1, 2, \ldots, n\}$ and we wish to count the number of ways these elements can be arranged in order. If our events can be $E_1 =$ "Pick the first element in the list," $E_2 =$ "Pick the second element in the list," and so on, then there are n ways E_1 can happen, after which there are $n-1$ ways E_2 can happen (since we've already chosen one element to be the first), $n-2$ ways E_3 can happen, and so on, until we find one way for the last event, E_n. The counting principle then tells us that there must be $n(n-1)(n-2) \ldots (2)(1)$ ways of arranging n distinct objects in order. For $n = 3$, we have $3! = 3 \times 2 \times 1 = 6$; the six permutations of $\{1, 2, 3\}$ are 123, 132, 213, 231, 312, and 321. This product occurs so frequently that it has been given its own symbol, $n!$, for which we say "n factorial" (or "n bang" if you feel very informal and want to sound like an expert in computer science slang).

We define 0! to be 1, both because it makes some results work the way we want them to and also because it makes sense to say that there is just one way to arrange the elements of an empty set. Notice that the definition $n! = n(n-1)(n-2) \ldots (2)(1)$ implies that $n! = n(n-1)!$ This function grows very rapidly as n increases; the first 11 values of $n!$ are 1, 1, 2, 6, 24, 120, 720,

5040, 40,320, 362,880, and 3,628,800. There are times when we need to find $n!$ for very large n. In such cases, it is inadvisable to compute the product, especially since the product gives us no idea about how rapidly $n!$ grows. We can approximate $n!$ by **Sterling's formula**, which states that

$$n! = \sqrt{2\pi n}\left(\frac{n}{e}\right)^n \quad \text{(approximately)}$$

where e is the base of the natural logarithm. Since big-O notation allows us to "throw away" constant multiples, we can then say that $n! = O(n^{n+1/2})$. It is not hard to generalize the preceding arguments to counting the number of permutations of k elements chosen from a set of $n \geq k$ elements.

Theorem 8: If $0 \leq k \leq n$, then the number of k-element permutations chosen from a set of n elements is

$$n(n-1)(n-2)\ldots(n-k+1) = \frac{n!}{(n-k)!}$$

Combinations

When we were counting permutations, we were dealing with the possible ways of arranging distinct objects in order. Often, we might have to count arrangements in situations where one or the other of these two conditions (distinct objects and order) is immaterial. If, for instance, we want to count the number of **combinations**, $C(n, k)$, of k elements out of a set of n elements, which is to say the number of k-element subsets of a set of n elements, then the order of the elements within each subset is of no interest to us. It turns out that counting combinations isn't much more difficult than counting permutations.

Theorem 9: If $0 \leq k \leq n$, then the number of k-element combinations from a set of n elements is given by the **binomial coefficient**

$$\binom{n}{k} = \frac{n!}{k!\,(n-k)!}$$

Proof. Instead of counting combinations directly, we begin by enumerating all of the k–element permutations of the set of n elements. Theorem 8 tells us that there are $n!/(n-k)!$ such permutations. We may now collect these permutations into groups in such a way that two permutations belong in the same group if they are just reorderings of the same elements. For example, if we had $k = 3$, then the permutations

267, 672, and 726 would all go in the same group. Now we have exactly as many groups as there are k–element subsets, and each group contains exactly $k!$ permutations. In other words, by counting the $n!/(n-k)!$ permutations, we have overcounted by a factor of $k!$. Therefore, the total number of k–element combinations of a set of n elements is given by the "corrected" count $n!/k!(n-k)!$.

For example, the number of ways a six-member subcommittee can be selected from a committee of eight is $8!/6! \, (8-6)! = 8!/6! \, 2! = 28$.

There are numerous lovely relations involving the binomial coefficients. One of the nicest comes from observing that the total number of subsets of an n-element set can be found by adding the number of k-element subsets, for $k = 0, 1, 2, \ldots, n$. This yields the following identity.

Corollary:

$$\sum_{k=0}^{n} \binom{n}{k} = \binom{n}{0} + \binom{n}{1} + \cdots + \binom{n}{n} = 2^n$$

When we considered combinations, the elements we were combining were distinct, but the order of the elements chosen was unimportant. We could relax the other restriction, instead, and consider the number of ways of arranging n objects in order, where the objects are not necessarily distinct. If we consider just two kinds of objects, we get exactly the same number as we did when we counted combinations.

Theorem 10:   The total number of ordered arrangements of n objects, k of which are of one kind and $n-k$ of which are of another, is $C(n, k)$.

Proof.   Suppose, for instance, we wish to arrange 3 A's and 2 B's in order. There are a total of $n = 5$ positions for the letters, and any arrangement is uniquely specified by describing the positions for the A's. For instance, the arrangement AABAB corresponds to the position subset $\{1, 2, 4\}$ for the A's. In other words, we have transformed the problem of counting the number of ordered arrangements of k A's and $n-k$ B's into the problem of counting the number of k-element subsets of the position set $\{1, 2, \ldots, n\}$, which we have already solved in Theorem 9.

The numbers $n!/k!(n-k)!$ are called binomial coefficients because they are the coefficients that appear in the expansion of binomial powers like $(x+y)^n$. For example, we might want to know the coefficient of the term $x^2 y$ in the expansion of $(x+y)^3$. When we multiply $(x+y)(x+y)(x+y)$, the result consists of the sum of all three-element products, where the *i*th term in each product is chosen from the *i*th copy of $(x+y)$ in the product. In other words,

$$(x+y)(x+y)(x+y) = xxx + xxy + xyx + xyy + yxx + yxy + yyx + yyy$$
$$= xxx + (xxy + xyx + yxx) + (xyy + yxy + yyx) + yyy$$
$$= x^3 + 3x^2y + 3xy^2 + y^3$$

so the coefficient of the x^2y term is just the number of ways of arranging two x's and one y in order, which is just $3!/2!1!=3$. It would be easy enough to generalize this argument to prove the following result.

Theorem 11: For any integer $n \geq 0$,

$$(x+y)^n = \binom{n}{0}x^n + \binom{n}{1}x^{n-1}y + \cdots + \binom{n}{n}y^n$$

$$= \sum_{k=1}^{n}\binom{n}{k}x^k y^{n-k}$$

B.4 EXERCISES

1. Why did we not define the function a^x for $a<0$?

2. What does the graph of a^x look like when $0<a<1$?

3. Show, for any $a>0$, that $a^x = e^{Kx}$ by finding a suitable constant K, depending only on a.

4. Using calculus (l'Hôpital's rule, in particular), show that for any d

$$\lim_{x \to \infty} \frac{x^d}{e^x} = 0$$

5. Compute
    a. $\log_2 1024$
    b. $\log_{1/2} 8$
    c. $\log_{10} 100{,}000{,}000{,}000$
    d. $\log_2 4^{12}$

6. Knowing that $\log_2 3 = 1.585$ and $\log_2 5 = 2.322$, compute, to 3 digits
    a. $\log_2 15$
    b. $\log_2 300$

    c. $\log_2(3+1/5)$

    d. $\log_2 3^{15}$

7. If you were told that $\log_{10} 2 = 0.30103$, how could you use that information to find the number of digits in 2^{65536}?

8. Prove parts (a), (c), and (d) of Theorem 3.

9. Show that some functions that look like exponentials are really just powers, by showing, for instance, that

$$2^{\log_3 n} = n^K$$

for a suitable value of K.

10. **a.** Show that if you know the value of $\ln 2$, and you can compute $\ln x$ for all $0 < x \leq 2$, then you can compute $\ln y$ for all $y > 0$.

    b. If $-1 < x \leq 1$, then $\ln(1+x)$ can be computed to any degree of accuracy by adding enough terms in the series

$$x - \frac{1}{2}x^2 + \frac{1}{3}x^3 - \frac{1}{4}x^4 + \frac{1}{5}x^5 - \cdots.$$

    where the error introduced by stopping at the nth term is never more than $1/(n+1)$. How many terms in the series do you need to compute $\ln 2$ to come within ± 0.005? Why would this not be a suitable way to implement $\ln$ on a computer?

11. Give inductive proofs of the following identities.

    a. $\displaystyle\sum_{k=1}^{n} k^2 = \frac{n(n+1)(2n+1)}{6}$

    b. $\displaystyle\sum_{k=1}^{n} x^k = \frac{1 - x^{n+1}}{1 - x}$

12. What is wrong with the following "proof" that all elements in a set must be the same?

Let $P(n)$ be the statement, "If a set has n elements, they must all be the same," and argue by induction on n.

Base: If a set has $n = 1$ element, that element is the same as itself, so $P(1)$ is true.

Inductive: Suppose that a set, S, has $n \geq 1$ elements, and suppose that $P(n-1)$ is true. We will show that $P(n)$ is true. Choose any element, e, from S. Then $S - \{e\}$ is a set with $n-1$ elements, so they must all be the same, by the induction hypothesis. Choose another element, e', from S, and argue similarly that all the elements in

$S-\{e'\}$ must be the same. But $S-\{e\}$ and $S-\{e'\}$ together constitute all of S, so every element in S must be the same. So $P(n)$ must be true.

By the principle of induction, since the base case and the inductive case are true, $P(n)$ must hold for all n. Hence, every set must have the property that all of its elements are equal.

13. Approximately how large is 1000! (how many digits does it have)?

14. Show that $\ln n!$ is approximately $(n+1/2)\ln n+(1-n)$.

15. We would like to write an algorithm that computes $C(n, k)$.

    a. Explain why it would be a bad idea to compute the values of $n!$, $k!$, and $(n-k)!$ in the algorithm.

    b. Show that

$$\binom{n}{k}=\frac{n}{k}\binom{n-1}{k-1}$$

    and use this identity as the basis of your algorithm, explaining why this is a better idea than computing the factorials.

16. Suppose that you live in a city with very peculiar traffic patterns. The streets are laid out in a rectangular grid, as in the following figure, and all of the north-south streets are one-way north, while all the east-west streets are one-way east. The building where you work is, luckily for you, four blocks north and six blocks east of your apartment. How many different ways can you to drive from home to work?

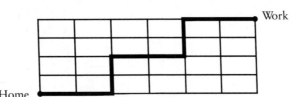

17. The **Catalan numbers**, $C_n=(1/(n+1))C(2n, n)$, arise in a number of seemingly different counting problems. For example, C_n counts the number of binary trees with n nodes, as well as the number of sequences of balanced parentheses consisting of n each of left and right parentheses.

    a. Using induction, prove that $C_n<4^n$.

    b. Using Sterling's formula, show that

$$C_n = \frac{2^{2n}}{\sqrt{\pi n(n+1)}} \quad \text{(approximately)}$$

c.   Show that

$$C_n = \binom{2n}{n} - \binom{2n}{n-1}$$

18.   **Pascal's triangle** is an arrangement of numbers in rows and columns such that the entry in row n and column k is $C(n, k)$. We provide part of Pascal's triangle here. Notice that each entry in the table is the sum of the element above it and the one above it and to the left, so that the 10 in row 5, column 2, is the sum of the 6 in row 4, column 2, and the 4 in row 4, column 1. We are then led to guess that

$$\binom{n}{k} = \binom{n-1}{k-1} + \binom{n-1}{k} \quad \text{for all } n > 0,\ 0 < k \leq n$$

Prove this identity in two ways:

a.   Directly, from the algebraic definition of the binomial coefficients.

b.   By using a subset-counting argument. (*Hint*: Consider the number of k-element subsets of a set of n elements; single out one particular element of the set, and count those subsets that contain that element and those that do not.)

n \ k	0	1	2	3	4	5
0	1					
1	1	1				
2	1	2	1			
3	1	3	3	1		
4	1	4	6	4	1	
5	1	5	10	10	5	1

19.   Use Theorem 11 to find the coefficient of

a. $x^4 y^2$ in the expansion of $(x+y)^6$

b. $x^3 y^4$ in the expansion of $(x+2y)^7$

c. $x^2 y^4$ in the expansion of $(x+y^2)^6$

20.   Use Theorem 11 to prove

$$\binom{n}{0} - \binom{n}{1} + \cdots \pm \binom{n}{n} = \sum_{k=0}^{n} (-1)^k \binom{n}{k} = 0$$

APPENDIX C

RANDOM NUMBERS AND SIMULATION

We often employ simulation in situations where the behavior of some system would be impractical to test directly or where the theoretical analysis of a system is just too complicated to attempt. If, for instance, we wanted to build a car wash, we could answer questions about the number of wash bays and the size of the driveway to build by going ahead and building them, but we might very well go broke trying alternatives before we got any idea about the combination that maximized our profits. It would be much better to build a computer model of the car wash and try the various options in simulation before we signed the contract with the builder. In another vein, we might want to test the behavior of a new sorting algorithm. We may have no idea how to analyze the running time of the algorithm, so we could try a number of sample inputs and investigate how long the algorithm takes to run on the samples. Of course, there would be no point in even trying to run the algorithm on all possible inputs of a given size n, unless n was very small, so we might run the algorithm on a randomly chosen sample of inputs in the hope that the behavior on the samples would reflect the behavior in general.

In this appendix, we will concentrate on simulations that have some degree of randomness, since they arise so frequently in practice. Even in the car wash simulation, for instance, there is likely a considerable amount of randomness in the way customers arrive. On any given day we might expect to see one car every 10 minutes, but it would be foolish in the extreme to expect that cars would arrive to be washed exactly 10 minutes apart all day long.

RANDOM NUMBERS

You probably have some idea about what we mean by a "random" sequence of numbers. The question of exactly what should be the criteria for a sequence of numbers to be random, though, is an extremely difficult one. We might say that a random sequence of 0s and 1s, for instance, would be a sequence generated by repeatedly tossing a fair coin and recording 0 for each head and 1 for each tail. The problem with that definition is that it implies that the sequence 0000000000 . . . is random, and as a matter of fact it is no more or less likely than any other sequence of 0s and 1s. We might be closer if we adopt a somewhat more naive view and content ourselves here with accepting a sequence as random if knowing the first n terms of the sequence, we would not be able to predict the $(n+1)$st term.

This "unpredictability" condition, though, leads to big problems when we try to use a computer to generate random sequences. Computers are deterministic in that the behavior of a computer at any time is completely predictable from its prior behavior. What we have to do is content ourselves with producing a sequence of numbers that "appears" to be random. Such a sequence is called a **pseudorandom** sequence. We might say, as do many authors, that an algorithm generates pseudorandom numbers if any sequence generated by the algorithm passes a number of statistical tests that would also be passed by a truly random sequence. A typical test might be that all of the possible numbers in the sequence occur equally often, in the long run. If we generated the digits 0 . . . 9 randomly, for instance, we would expect the number, $T_3(n)$, of 3s seen after n digits had been generated to be about $n/10$, and we would expect $T_3(n)$ to get closer to $n/10$ as n got very large. A sequence with such a property is said to be **equidistributed**. Of course, that test by itself would not be acceptable to define randomness, since the sequence 01234567890123456789 . . . is equidistributed, but it seems decidedly nonrandom. We could then require another test, perhaps that any pairs of adjacent terms occur about 1% of the time, in the long run, or that the subsequence formed by taking every other term or every fifth term be equidistributed.

The upshot is that there is no agreement about what should constitute the criteria for a pseudorandom sequence. If we require too few tests, we leave the door open to sequences that we would not want to include; but if we require too many tests, we may find that there is no possible sequence that will satisfy them all.

What we will do here is adopt a consensual approach. Most authorities on the matter agree that an acceptable pseudorandom number-generating algorithm is the particularly simple method known as the **linear congruential algorithm**. To generate a sequence $x_0, x_1, x_2, \ldots$ of numbers "randomly chosen" between 0 and $m-1$ by this method, we begin with any number, x_0, called the **seed**, and then generate the rest by the rule

$$x_{n+1} = (Ax_n + B)\,\%\,m$$

For example, if we chose $A = 3$, $B = 1$, and $m = 8$, then starting with $x_0 = 3$, we would have $x_1 = 2$, $x_2 = 7$, $x_3 = 6$, $x_4 = 3$, after which the sequence repeats 2, 7, 6, 3, 2, 7, 6 forever. Starting with $x_0 = 1$ gives 1, 4, 5, 0, 1, 4, 5, 0, . . . , so we have two sequences with **period** (i.e., length of repeats) 4, depending on the seed we choose. Well, these sequences are too short to be of any real use, not to mention that neither of them uses all the numbers from 0 to 7. There are a number of criteria that govern the choice of A and B, given m, some of which we cover in the exercises. Without going into too much detail about the reasons, two generating schemes that work well are

1. $x_{n+1} = (11,549 x_n + 3461) \% 16,384$

2. $x_{n+1} = (9757 x_n + 6925) \% 32,768$

For both of these, the periods are as long as possible, in that for any seed they generate all m possible numbers before repeating. They both pass the tests that most authors agree they should, and in both of them the numbers used for A and B can be interchanged to produce different pseudorandom number generators that are also good.

Many compilers have built-in random number generators, so it is reasonable to ask why we would want to write another routine to generate numbers at random. We presented this technique because it will aid those of you who don't have access to such functions and also because the proper choice of A, B, and m is sufficiently delicate that there have been faulty random number generators that have been in use for years before they were discovered to fail some important statistical test. The ones we give here might even fall into this category, despite the fact that they have passed a number of tests. The best advice is that if you are doing something that requires heavy use of random numbers, make a search of the literature to find generating algorithms that have been thoroughly examined.

Now that we can generate "random" integers in the range $0 \ldots m-1$, it is easy enough to generate random real numbers between 0 and 1. All we need to do is take an integer, r, between 0 and $m-1$, and then produce the real number r/m. There will be m possible numbers produced, and they all will be greater than or equal to 0 and less than 1. The function *RandReal* implements this algorithm.

```
const int MAX = 32767, // m - 1
const double REAL_SIZE = 32768.0;  // m


double RandReal()
// Returns a randomly chosen real number in [0, 1).
// Requires a function Random, which returns a random integer
// in the range 0 .. MAX.
{
     return Random() / REAL_SIZE;
}
```

We could use this scheme to return to integers, if we wished. Suppose that we needed to generate integers randomly chosen in the range $0 \ldots k$, with $k < m$. We could generate a random real number $0 \le x > 1$ from the product $(k+1)x$, and then round that number down to the nearest integer. In C++, we would have

```
int RandInt(int k)
// Generates a number at random in the range 0 . . . k.
// Uses function RandReal, which generates a real number in [0, 1).
{
    return int((k + 1) * RandReal());
}
```

Give yourself some points for cleverness if you can find a way to generate random numbers in the range $0 \ldots k$ without using reals as an intermediate step. One particularly simple way is to generate an integer r with $0 \le r \le m-1$ and then form $r \,\%\, (k+1)$. The problem with this is subtle, though, and it arises from the fact that the low-order bits of integers generated by the linear congruential method are not as random as we would like. In particular, for the two algorithms mentioned earlier, the sequences are alternately even and odd, so the sequence of last bits is 0, 1, 0, 1, 0, 1 . . ., which is decidedly not what we would consider random. If we had chosen $k=1$, then, in an attempt to generate a random sequence of 0s and 1s, we would have been in for an unpleasant surprise. Going to reals as an intermediate step places more emphasis on the high-order bits, and they can be shown to be much more random than the lower-order bits, at least for integers generated by the linear congruential method.

C.2 PROBABILITY DISTRIBUTIONS

One way to generate numbers randomly in the range $0 \ldots 5$ would be to take five fair coins, toss them all, and record the number of heads that came up. This process certainly seems to be random, at least in the sense that we would have no way of predicting the next number we would generate by this process. We find, however, that this process tends to generate 3s much more often than it does 0s or 5s. Upon reflection, this is no surprise, since there is only one way out of all 32 possible arrangements of heads and tails that produces five tails, whereas there are $C(5, 3)=10$ ways to generate a sequence of three heads and two tails. In Figure C.1, we illustrate the results of 50 such coin tosses.

In Figure C.1, we have graphed the values of the random variable x representing the outcomes of the coin toss experiment and their frequencies, namely, the number of times each value occurred in the experiment. The scale for the frequencies, $f(x)$, will clearly depend on the number, N, of trials in the

FIGURE C.1

Results of fifty trials of tossing five coins

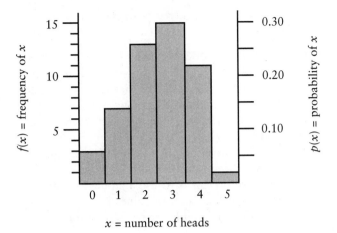

x = number of heads

experiment, so it would be better to graph the **probability** that each event occurred, which is nothing but $p(x)=f(x)/N$. The probabilities will always lie between 0 and 1, of course.

Suppose that x is a random variable that can take any value in the set $\{x_1, x_2, \ldots, x_n\}$, and suppose that the probability that x is equal to x_i is given by a function $p(x_i)$, for $i = 1, 2, \ldots, n$, and that we have the sum $p(x_1) + \cdots + p(x_n) = 1$. Then we say that p is a **discrete probability function** for the random variable x. The set of values for x, along with the probability function for x, is called the **distribution** of x. For the variable x of Figure C.1, for instance, we have the set of values $\{0, 1, 2, 3, 4, 5\}$, and p is defined by $p(0)=0.06$, $p(1)=0.14$, $p(2)=0.26$, $p(3)=0.30$, $p(4)=0.22$, and $p(5)=0.02$.

For any distribution where the set of values is a set of numbers, there are two measures that provide some information about how the random variable behaves. The **mean**, m, of a distribution is the sum of the possible values, weighted by their probabilities, and represents the "average" value of the distribution, while the **standard deviation**, σ, is the square root of the weighted sum of the squares of the differences between the values and the mean. Roughly speaking, the standard deviation represents how closely the values are clustered about the mean, with small standard deviations indicating that the values tend to fall close to the mean. For a given distribution, we may compute m and σ by

$$m = \sum_{k=1}^{n} p(x_k)x_k \qquad \sigma = \sqrt{\sum_{k=1}^{n} p(x_k)(x_k - m)^2}$$

You should be able to verify that for the distribution shown in Figure C.1, we have $m=2.54$ and $\sigma=1.20$, reflecting that the expected value for x is between 2 and 3 and that the values that are obtained are clustered somewhat closely about the mean.

Cumulative Probability Functions

In some cases, we have a fair amount of knowledge ahead of time about the distribution of a random variable, simply by knowing about the process by which the random variable was generated. In other cases, however, we may be able to do no better than to watch a process in action and sample the frequencies of a random variable. If we watch long enough, we may be confident that the resulting probabilities accurately reflect the distribution of that random variable. We might then want to generate our own random variable, with the same distribution as the observed sample, for use in a program that simulates the process we observed.

One way to do this is to use a **cumulative distribution**. Suppose we have a distribution given by a set of values $\{x_1, x_2, \ldots, x_n\}$ and a probability function p. We form the **cumulative probability function**, P, by the rule

$$P(x_k) = \sum_{i=1}^{k} p(x_i) \quad \text{for } k = 1, \ldots, n$$

In other words, the cumulative probability function for the value x_k is found by taking the total of the probability functions for all the x_i for $i \leq k$. For the probability function in Figure C.1, we have $P(0) = 0.06$, $P(1) = 0.20$, $P(2) = 0.46$, $P(3) = 0.76$, $P(4) = 0.98$, and $P(5) = 1.00$, as graphed in Figure C.2.

Now let x be a random variable with value set $\{x_1, x_2, \ldots, x_n\}$ and probability function p, and suppose that P is the cumulative probability function obtained from p. We can use P to generate another random variable, y, with the same distribution as x as follows. We first choose a number, r, at random between 0 and 1. Then if $r \leq P(x_1)$, we set $y = x_1$, and otherwise we set $y = x_i$, where $2 \leq i \leq n$ and $P(x_{i-1}) < r \leq P(x_i)$. As long as r is equally likely to take any value between 0 and 1, this process will guarantee that y has the same distribution as x. Consider the cumulative distribution graphed in Figure C.2. Geo-

FIGURE C.2

Cumulative distribution of the data given in Figure C.1

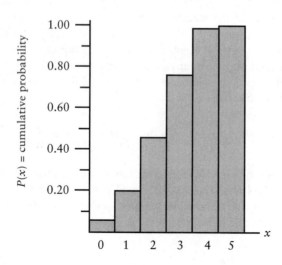

metrically, what we are doing is choosing a point at random on the vertical axis and drawing a horizontal line from that point. We then choose the x value corresponding to the first shaded bar we encounter. This gives the distribution we want because we choose x_i if and only if r satisfies $P(x_{i-1}) < r \leq P(x_i)$, and the chance that that will happen is nothing but the length of the interval from $P(x_{i-1})$ to $P(x_i)$, which is $P(x_i) - P(x_{i-1}) = p(x_i)$.

It is easy to write a function that will generate such random variables. We pick a random number between 0 and 1 and track through the array of cumulative probabilities until we arrive at the first index i for which $P(x_{i-1}) < r$, at which point we stop and return the index i. We would then use the output index to select the value x_i.

```
const int N = (number of values of x);
typedef double ProbArray[N + 1];

void BuildCumulativeArray(ProbArray p, ProbArray P)
{
    P[1] = p[1];
    for (int i = 2; i <= N; i++)
        P[i] = P[i - 1] + p[i];
}

int Y(ProbArray P)
// Returns the index of a value for Y, having the same distribution
// as x.
{
    double r = RandReal();   // Pick a real number between 0 and 1.
    int i = 1;
    while (r > P[i])         // Search the cumulative probability array.
        i++;
    return i;
}
```

Some probability distributions have been studied in depth, largely because many real processes seem to behave according to these theoretical models. We will now describe some of the more common distributions.

Uniform Distributions

A perfectly fair six-sided die could serve as a generator for a random variable with the property that each of the six possible outcomes is equally likely. In general, if a distribution with a value set of size n has the property that for all $1 \leq i \leq n$ we have $p(x_i) = 1/n$, then such a distribution is called **uniform**. Because the linear congruential algorithms 1 and 2 had parameters A and B chosen so that their periods were m, they both produced all possible values before repeating, and so the sequences they generated were uniformly distributed. This means that if we use such a distribution for *Random,* then the variables defined by *RandReal,* and hence by *RandInt,* are also uniformly distributed. This also means that we can use *RandReal* as the basis for the cumulative distribution function previously described.

It is not too difficult to show that if x is a uniform random variable on $[0, 1)$ defined by

$$\text{Value set} = \left\{0, \frac{1}{n}, \frac{2}{n}, \ldots, \frac{n-1}{n}\right\}, \text{ probability function } p\left(\frac{k}{n}\right) = \frac{1}{n} \quad 0 \le k < n$$

then x has the measures

$$m = \frac{1}{2}\left(\frac{n-1}{n}\right) \qquad \sigma = \sqrt{\frac{1}{12}\left(\frac{n^2-1}{n^2}\right)}$$

Since the terms within the parentheses tend to 1 as n gets large, we can see that the mean and standard deviation of such a distribution tend to 1/2 and $1/\sqrt{12}$, respectively.

Normal Distributions

There are a number of random variables, like shoe size and IQ, that seem to satisfy what is known as a **normal distribution**. The coin toss distribution of Figure C.1 approximates a normal distribution that if we repeat the experiment with increasingly large numbers of coins, the resulting distributions tend, when properly scaled, to look more and more like the familiar bell curve of probability theory, graphed in Figure C.3.

The continuous normal distribution with mean m and standard deviation σ is given by the probability density function

$$p = \frac{1}{\sqrt{2\pi\sigma}}e^{-z^2/2} \quad \text{where } z = \frac{x-m}{\sigma}$$

We will not be concerned here, however, with continuous distributions, but will only be interested in those distributions where the value set is finite. In

FIGURE C.3

Normal distribution, limiting case

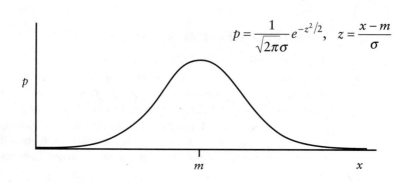

$$p = \frac{1}{\sqrt{2\pi\sigma}}e^{-z^2/2}, \quad z = \frac{x-m}{\sigma}$$

other words, we would like to find a discrete (i.e., finite-valued) distribution that approximates the continuous normal distribution. Help arrives from the result we used to motivate the normal distribution, namely, that the random variable that is formed when we add n independent random variables is approximately normal and gets closer to a normal distribution the larger n is. This result is more precisely stated in Theorem 1.

Theorem 1 *(The Central Limit Theorem):* If $x_1, \ldots, x_n$ are independent random variables, each with mean m and standard deviation σ, then as n increases, the distribution of the random variable z defined by

$$z = \frac{x_1 + \cdots + x_n - nm}{\sigma\sqrt{n}}$$

approaches a normal distribution with mean 0 and standard deviation 1.

In our case, we possess a function, *RandReal,* with mean approximately $1/2$ and standard deviation approximately $1/\sqrt{12}$, so if we set $n=12$ in the central limit theorem, we find that the random variable $z=x_1+\cdots+x_{12}-6$ should serve as a pretty good approximation of a normally distributed random variable with mean 0 and standard deviation 1. The function is implemented as follows.

```
double Normal()
// Generates an approximation to a normal random
// variable with mean 0 and standard deviation 1.
// Uses the function RandReal.
{
   double sum = 0.0;
   for (int i = 1; i <= 12; i++)
      sum += RandReal();
   return sum - 6.0;
}
```

Of course, we may be in a situation where we want a different mean and standard deviation for our normally distributed random variable. It is not difficult to show that if z is a normal random variable with mean 0 and standard deviation 1, then we can produce another normal random variable y with mean m and standard deviation σ by defining

$$y = m + \sigma z$$

Exponential Distributions

In many instances where customers arrive for service in an unpredictable manner, such as customers in line at a bank or terminals waiting for service by a time-sharing computer system, the times between arrivals (not the arrival times themselves) have an **exponential distribution**. In the continuous case, such a distribution has a probability function given by

$$p(x) = \frac{1}{\alpha} e^{-(x/\alpha)}$$

Such a distribution can be approximated by a discrete random variable whose probability function has the property that for all (or almost all) $i = 1$, $2, \ldots, n$, $p(x_{i+1}) = Kp(x_i)$, for some $0 < K < 1$. A typical example is the discrete distribution with value set $\{x_1, \ldots, x_n\}$ and probability function given by

$$p(x_1) = \frac{1}{2}, \quad p(x_2) = \frac{1}{4}, \quad p(x_3) = \frac{1}{8}, \ldots, \quad p(x_{n-1}) = p(x_n) = \left(\frac{1}{2}\right)^{n-1}$$

which we graph in Figure C.4. The last two values are equal to ensure that the probabilities add up to 1, as they must.

The generation process for exponential distributions is particularly nice, and is summarized in the following theorem.

Theorem 2: If z is a uniform random variable that takes values between 0 and 1, then the random variable $x = -\alpha \ln z$ has an exponential distribution given by the probability function

$$p(x) = \frac{1}{\alpha} e^{-(x/\alpha)}$$

This random variable has both mean and standard deviation equal to α.

The following function generates random numbers with exponential distribution, having mean and standard deviation equal to the input variable *alpha*.

FIGURE C.4

Discrete exponential distribution

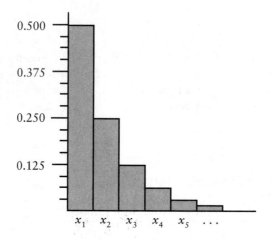

```
double Exponential(double alpha)
// Generates random real numbers which are exponentially
// distributed with mean and standard deviation equal to alpha.
// Uses the function RandReal to generate uniformly distributed
// reals between 0 and 1.
{
    return -alpha * ln(RandReal);
}
```

C.3 SELECTION ALGORITHMS

One reason for simulation is that it might be impractical to test an algorithm on all possible inputs. If, for instance, we had a sorting algorithm and wanted to find how long it would take to sort a list of 12 numbers, it would be foolish even to consider trying the algorithm on all $12! = 479{,}001{,}600$ possible arrangements of the input. What we could do, however, is test the algorithm on a collection of sample inputs.

What we will consider in this section is a natural extension of the notion of choosing a single number at random. We will consider some simple data structures and will describe algorithms that generate randomly chosen instances of those structures. If you find yourself in need of selection algorithms that are not presented here, an excellent handbook is Albert Nijenhuis and Herbert S. Wulf, *Combinatorial Algorithms* (New York: Academic Press, 1975).

Selecting Subsets

To choose a random subset of a set $S = \{x_1, \ldots, x_n\}$, all we need to do is to decide, for each element in the set, whether that element should be included in the subset or not. If we represent the original set as a bit vector, $v[i]$, $i = 1, 2, \ldots, n$, of Boolean values, then every instance of v corresponds uniquely to a subset of S in such a way that x_i is in the subset if and only if x_i is 1.

```
const int SIZE = (the number of elements in the set S);
typedef int Set[SIZE + 1];

void SubsetSelect(Set subset)
{
    for (int i = 1; i <= SIZE; i++)
        subset[i] = (RandInt(1) == 0);
}
```

SubsetSelect could hardly be simpler. It should be clear that this is a good random selection algorithm, in that any subset of S is equally likely to be chosen and the choice of subset is independent of which subsets have been chosen before. The algorithm uses $O(n)$ space (or $O(1)$, if you charge the cost of the bit vector to the calling routine) and runs in time $O(n)$.

A possible disadvantage of this algorithm, however, is that there is no control over the size of the subset returned by the procedure. The sizes of the subsets generated by this process will be more or less normally distributed, with mean $(n-1)/2$, for large enough n. We should not be surprised by this, because there is only one sequence of 0s and 1s that result in the empty set, while there are $C(n, k)$ such sequences that produce a subset with k elements. In most cases, this is not a problem, since we are generally interested in either generating subsets without regard to their size or generating subsets of a fixed size, which is the problem we turn to next.

Selecting a Subset with *k* Elements

Let $S = \{x_1, \ldots, x_n\}$ be a set with n elements, and let $0 < k \leq n$ be a fixed integer. We can then select a subset of S by specifying an array $sub[i]$, $i = 1, \ldots, k$ of numbers in the range $0, \ldots, k$, with the property that if $1 \leq i \neq j \leq n$, then $sub[i] \neq sub[j]$, that is, that the array sub has no duplicate entries. The correspondence between sub and subsets of S is then that x_i is in the subset if and only if the index i is an element of the position array sub.

The problem of k subset selection is thus equivalent to selecting a subset of k integers from the set $\{1, \ldots, n\}$. One way to do this is to have an array, sub, initialized so that for $i = 1, \ldots, n$, we have $sub[i] = i$, and for each of the first k indices, in turn, we swap the element in that index location of sub with the entry in a randomly chosen location at or above that index. At the end of this process, the first k entries in sub will contain a random subset of the set $\{1, \ldots, n\}$.

For example, suppose that $n = 6$ and $k = 3$. Here is the selection process, with the element at the current index in boldface and the element with which it is to be swapped underscored.

Step 1:	**1**	<u>2</u>	3	4	5	6
Step 2:	2	**1**	3	4	<u>5</u>	6
Step 3:	2	5	**3**	4	1	<u>6</u>
Done:	2	5	6	4	1	3

After having performed $k = 3$ swaps, the selected subset is $\{2, 5, 6\}$, found in the first three entries of sub.

```
const int SIZE = (size of set from which we select samples);
typedef int SelectArray[SIZE + 1];

void k_Select(int k, SelectArray sub)
{
   for (int i = 1; i <= SIZE; i++)
      sub[i] = i;
```

```
for (i = 1; i <= k; i++)
{
    // Choose index of entry to swap with i-the entry.
    swap = i + RandInt(SIZE - i);

    save:= sub[swap];
    sub[swap] = sub[i];    // swap the entries
    sub[i] = save;
}
}
```

The proof that *k_Select* works properly is a bit complicated, but it is indeed the case that *k_Select* randomly selects k element subsets of $\{1, \ldots, n\}$ in such a way that each subset is equally likely to be chosen. This algorithm actually serves two purposes, since it is also possible to show that *k_Select* generates uniformly distributed random permutations of the numbers 1 through n, if it is called with $k = n$.

This algorithm uses $O(n)$ space and runs in time $O(n+k)$, since the running time is controlled by the two loops. These time and space requirements may be larger than we wish to accept if, for instance, we are selecting a sample of just 10 numbers from a universe of 32,768. It would be nice if we could find an algorithm that used space and time that were independent of n. A simple method would be the following.

```
while (the number of elements selected is less than k)
{
```

Choose a random number, r, in the range $1 .. n$;

if (r has not yet been selected)

Include r among the selected numbers;

```
}
```

This process requires only enough space to store the k numbers selected. The time this algorithm takes to run is $O(p(s+t))$, where p is the number of times the loop iterates, s is the amount of time it takes to decide whether an element has been selected already, and t is the amount of time it takes to insert an element among the selected numbers. We have little control over p; although it is beyond the scope of this section to show, it is the case that the expected number of times the loop will have to iterate is

$$n \ln\left(\frac{n}{n-k}\right) = k\left(-\frac{1}{\alpha}\ln(1-\alpha)\right) \quad \text{if we write } \alpha = \frac{k}{n}$$

In other words, if we are sure that k will never be larger than αn, for some fixed constant $0 < \alpha < 1$, then we can expect the loop to iterate $O(k)$ times, on the average.

If we expect to produce an algorithm with running time $O(k)$, then, we must make sure that the testing and insertion segments run in constant time. With a data structure that requires fast insertion and membership testing, hashing (see Chapter 9) is the natural choice. We will use an array, *hash,* indexed from 0 to $k-1$, such that each element in the array is a pointer to a linked list. To test or insert a number, *r,* we first find $i = r \% k$ and then search the linked list at index *i* to see if the *r* is there or not. Such a technique will, on the average, require fewer than two tests of the list, and hence insertion and testing will each contribute $O(1)$ time to each iteration of the loop. In other words, this *k* subset selection technique will require $O(k)$ space for the array and the linked lists and will run in time $O(k)$ if the load k/n does not get too close to 1, and in the worst case will run in time $O(k \log k)$.

Enumerating Permutations

We have seen that *k_Select* can be used as a generator for random permutations of the set $\{1, \dots, n\}$. There may be a time when you need to select permutations in a systematic fashion, however, and would like to avoid the possible duplication that could arise from choosing permutations at random. Donald Knuth, in *The Art of Computer Programming*, Vol. 2 (Reading, MA: Addison-Wesley, 1973): 59–60, presents an algorithm that assigns a permutation of $\{1, \dots, n\}$ to each integer m, $0 \le m < n!$, in such a way that different values of m give rise to different permutations. By applying either of the subset selection algorithms to produce a subset of choices for m, we could then use the following algorithm to produce a set of k different permutations of $\{1, \dots, n\}$.

```
const int SIZE = { the sample size} ;
typedef int SelectArray[SIZE + 1];

void DecodePermutation(int m, SelectArray sub);
{
   SelectArray swapArray;
   // Fill the array of swap indices.
   for (int i = SIZE; i >= 1; i--)
   {
      swapArray[i] = m % i;
      m /= i;
   }

   // Initialize the output array
   for (i = 1; i <= SIZE; i++)
      sub[i] = i;
```

```
// Permute the output array by swapping according
// to the values in the swap array.
for (i = 1; i <= SIZE; i++)
{
    int   swapIndex = swapArray[i] + 1,
          temp = sub[i];
    sub[i] = sub[swapIndex];
    sub[swapIndex] = temp;
}
}
```

We may not understand at this stage how it works (see the exercises), but it is clear that this algorithm requires $O(n)$ time and space. Knuth also shows that *DecodePermutation* is also easily invertible in that there is another algorithm, which we might call *EncodePermutation*, that takes a permutation and produces the corresponding integer code.

 ## C.4 EXERCISES

1. Using the linear congruential algorithm 1 with $x_0 = 0$,
   a. Show what $x_1, \ldots, x_{10}$ would be.
   b. Investigate the low-order 2 bits of this sequence by looking at x_i % 4.
   c. Suggest how you would modify the linear congruential algorithm to make the low-order bits of the pseudorandom sequence more reliable.

2. In the linear congruential algorithm, why is it a good idea to make sure that *A, B,* and *m* have no factors in common?

3. The numbers 16,384 and 32,768 are either close to or greater than the maximum integers allowed on some computers, but the linear congruential algorithm requires that all arithmetic be done exactly, with no truncation. How would you implement this algorithm to avoid integer overflow?

4. Many random number generators always give the same sequence of random numbers each time a program using them is run. Why isn't it a good idea? Suggest how you would write a random number generator that would not have this feature.

5. Given integers $a < b$, how could you use *RandReal* to produce a uniform random variable with value set $\{a, \ldots, b\}$?

6. Verify the mean and standard deviation we gave for the uniform distribution given in the text.

7. The probability function of the random variable that counts the number of heads in six tosses of a fair coin is defined by

$$p(0) = p(6) = \frac{1}{64}, \quad p(1) = p(5) = \frac{6}{64}, \quad p(2) = p(4) = \frac{15}{64}, \quad p(3) = \frac{20}{64}$$

   a. Find the cumulative probability function P.
   b. Using the function described in the text to generate random numbers with a given distribution, tell what y values would correspond to the r values 0.067, 0.265, and 0.999.

8. The **Zipf distribution** is defined on a value set $\{x_1, \ldots, x_n\}$ by

$$p(x_k) = \frac{k}{n}\left(\frac{1}{H_n}\right) \quad \text{for } k = 1, \ldots, n \quad \text{and} \quad H_n = 1 + \frac{1}{2} + \frac{1}{3} + \cdots + \frac{1}{n}$$

   The number H_n, called the nth **harmonic number**, is approximately $\ln n$. If the value set is chosen so that $x_k = k$, find the mean of the Zipf distribution. This distribution, by the way, was discovered to fit a number of seemingly unrelated random variables, such as worker salaries, city sizes, and word frequencies in many languages. In the case of word frequencies, it was suggested that the distribution implies a "rule of economy" in linguistics — that short words are more frequent because there is some inner mechanism that makes us tend to use short words. It turns out, however, that the Zipf distribution is merely a statistical artifact (much like the normal distribution, which arises in many cases where a random variable is formed from the sum of other random variables) and so probably doesn't have any deep significance.

9. Trace the action of k_Select with $n=8$, $k=5$, and successive values of $swap$ equal to 6, 6, 2, 3.

10. Using $DecodePermutation$ with $n=3$,
   a. List the permutations that correspond to the f values 0, 1, 2, 3, 4, 5.
   b. See if you can guess the values for $c[1]$, $c[2]$, $c[3]$, $c[4]$, in the $n=4$ case, for all $f=0, \ldots, 24$.

11. Simplify $DecodePermutation$ by observing something about the value of $c[1]$.

12. Reverse $DecodePermutation$ by producing a function

```
int EncodePermutation(SelectArray a)
```

   that takes a permuted array, a, and returns the number m such that $DecodePermutation(m, b)$ makes b into a copy of a.

D

SPECIFICATIONS OF THE ADTs USED IN THE TEXT

In the specifications that follow, each ADT is assumed to have a default constructor (which constructs an empty instance of the object, unless noted), a copy constructor, a destructor, and an assignment operator.

Array

Structure. An array consists of a linearly ordered collection of positions, each of which contains a single element of type T. Each position has a unique *index*, which is an integer in a continuous range from *lower* to *upper*, so for each index i, we will have $lower \leq i \leq upper$, and if a position with index i is a predecessor to a position with index j, we must have $i < j$.

Operations

`Array()`. Pre: true. Post: This array has one position, with index value 0. The value of the element in position 0 is undefined.

`Array (int up, int low = 0)`. Pre: $low \leq up$. Post: This array has $up - low + 1$ positions, with indices in the range $low, \ldots, up$.

`Array (T a[], int sz)`. Constructs an array from an array of elements of type T. Pre: The array a has indices $0, \ldots, sz-1$. Post: This array is a copy of a.

`void SetBounds(int up, int low = 0)`. Pre: $low \leq up$. Post: Sets the upper and lower indices of this array, keeping existing data in the old positions, where possible. Note that the new bounds may lie outside the range of the old bounds (if $low < lower$ or $upper < up$). In that case, the elements in the new range are undefined.

T& operator[] (int i) const. Pre: *lower≤i≤upper*. Post: The array is left unchanged, and a reference is returned to the element in position *i*.

unsigned int Size() const. The array is unchanged, and the number of elements in the array (i.e., *upper−lower*+1) is returned.

int Lower() const. Returns *lower* and leaves the array unchanged.

int Upper() const. Returns *upper* and leaves the array unchanged.

Association

Structure.   An ordered pair (*key, value*) of types *K* and *V*, respectively. The key is set during construction; thereafter it may not be changed.

Operations

Association(K aKey). Pre: true. Post: This association has key *aKey*. Its value is undefined.

Association(K aKey, V aValue). Pre: true. Post: This association has key *aKey* and value *aValue*.

K Key(). Pre: true. Post: Returns the key of this association.

V& Value(). Pre: The value of this association is defined. Post: Returns a reference to the value of this association.

int operator== (Association a1, Association a2). Pre: true. Post: Returns 1 if and only if the keys of *a1* and *a2* are equal.

int operator!= (Association a1, Association a2). Pre: true. Post: Returns 1 if and only if the keys of *a1* and *a2* are unequal.

Note: This ADT is seldom used by itself; it is generally used for the elements of a dictionary or priority queue.

BinaryTree

Structure.   A collection of positions (called **nodes**) arranged in an order such that each position has at most two successors, called *left* and *right*. If the set of positions is not empty, there is a unique position, called the **root**, that has no predecessor and which is the eventual predecessor of every other position.

Operations

BinaryTree(T rootValue). Pre: true. Post: This tree has a single node in the root position, and that node contains *rootValue*.

BinaryTree(T rootValue, const BinaryTree& left, const BinaryTree& right). Pre: true. Post: The root node of this tree contains *rootValue* and the left and right subtrees of the root are *left* and *right*, respectively. This function does not make copies of the two subtrees.

void Clear(). Pre: true. Post: This tree is empty.

BinaryTree Left() const. Pre: This tree is not empty. Post: This tree is unchanged. Returns the binary tree rooted at the left child of this tree's root.

BinaryTree Right() const. Pre: This tree is not empty. Post: This tree is unchanged. Returns the binary tree rooted at the right child of this tree's root.

int IsEmpty() const. Pre: true. Post: This tree is unchanged. 1 is returned if this tree has no nodes; otherwise, 0 is returned.

T& operator() const. Pre: This tree is not empty. Post: This tree is unchanged, and a reference to the value contained in the root node is returned.

BinarySearchTree : BinaryTree

Structure. As *BinaryTree*. In addition, there must be a linear order defined on the underlying set of atoms, and the elements in a BST must obey the property that the atom in each node is greater than the atoms in the left subtree of the node and less than the atoms in the right subtree.

Operations. All the operations of *BinaryTree*, except the merge-constructor. In addition, a BST has the following operations:

void Insert(T e). Pre: true. Post: This tree contains the nodes it did before, along with a new node with value *e*. The binary search tree property is maintained.

void Delete(T e). Pre: true. Post: If this tree did not have a node with value *e*, it is unchanged; if *e* was in this tree before, it has been removed in such a way that the new tree is still a binary search tree.

int Contains(T e). Pre: true. Post: This tree is unchanged. Returns 1 if *e* is in this tree; otherwise, returns 0.

BitVector : Array<int>

Structure. Same as *Array*. The only visible difference is that the array elements are 0 or 1. The big difference is in the implementation—see Exploration in Chapter 1.

Operations. As *Array*. Some authors include the operations Set(int i), which sets $b[i]$ to 1, Reset(int i), which sets $b[i]$ to 0, and Invert(int i), which changes $b[i]$ from 0 to 1 and vice versa.

Dictionary : Set

Structure. A set of atoms. Each atom has an associated *key* of type *K* that determines membership in the set (so there will never be two elements in a dictionary with the same key) and an associated *value* of type *V*.

Operations.   With the exception of *IsEmpty, MakeEmpty,* and *Insert,* none of the *Set* operations are available to users of *Dictionary.*

Dictionary(). Pre: true. Post: This dictionary is created and is empty.

void Remove(K aKey). Pre: true. Post: If there was an element in this dictionary with *key* datum *aKey,* that element has been removed from the dictionary. If there was no such element, this dictionary is unchanged.

V Retrieve(K aKey). Pre: There is an element in this dictionary with key *aKey.* Post: This set is unchanged. Returns the *value* field of the element with key *aKey.*

int Contains(K aKey). Pre: There is an element in this dictionary with key *aKey.* Post: This set is unchanged. Returns the value of the element with key *aKey.*

Note: The underlying set of atoms is often chosen to be associations.

DisjointSet

Structure.   A set of sets $S_1, S_1, \ldots, S_n$ of elements of type T. These sets are disjoint in that S_i and S_j cannot have any elements in common for any $1 \leq i \neq j \leq n$.

Operations

Set(T e). Pre: *e* is not an element of any set in this structure. Post: A set is created containing a single element *e.*

Set Union(Set a, Set b). Pre: *a* and *b* have no elements in common. Post: Returns the union of *a* and *b.*

Set Find(T e). Pre: *e* is in one set in this structure. Post: Returns the set containing *e.*

Digraph

Structure.   A set of positions with no restriction on predecessors and successors.

Operations.   The *Digraph* operations are the same as those of *Graph.*

Note: Some authors disallow the existence of loops by stipulating that no position may be its own successor.

DoubleEndedList : List

Structure.   A list for which insertion, deletion, and inspection are only done at the start and end positions.

Operations. Except for the constructors, no list operations are available to clients. *DoubleEndedList* includes these operations that are not in *List*:

int IsEmpty() const. Pre: true. Post: Returns 1 if and only if the list is empty.

T RetrieveHead() const. Pre: This list is nonempty. Post: Returns a copy of the element at the head.

T RetrieveTail() const. Pre: This list is nonempty. Post: Returns a copy of the element at the tail.

InsertAtHead(T e). Pre: true. Post: *e* is in the list, immediately before the old head.

InsertAtTail(T e). Pre: true. Post: *e* is in the list, immediately after the old tail.

DeleteHead(). Pre: The list is nonempty. Post: The old head element is not in the list; the element following the old head (if any) is the head element.

DeleteTail(). Pre: The list is nonempty. Post: The old tail element is not in the list; the element preceding the old tail (if any) is the tail element.

Note: This ADT is also known as a **deque** (pronounced "deck").

Graph

Structure. A collection of positions (called **vertices**), with a structure satisfying the following two properties for all positions p and q: (1) no position is its own successor, and (2) if p is a successor to q, then q is a successor to p. An **edge** of a graph is a set of two positions, $\{p, q\}$, such that p is a successor to q.

Operations

Graph(). Pre: true. Post: This graph is empty.

int Size() const. Pre: true. Post: The graph is unchanged. Returns the number of vertices in the graph.

int Adjacent(Vertex p, Vertex q) const. Pre: p and q are vertices of this graph. Post: The graph is unchanged. Returns 1 if $\{p, q\}$ is an edge of this graph; otherwise, returns 0.

void DeleteVertex(Vertex p). Pre: p is a vertex of this graph. Post: p is not in the graph (hence, any edge containing p is also no longer in the graph).

void DeleteEdge(Vertex p, Vertex q). Pre: $\{p, q\}$ is an edge of this graph. Post: This graph does not have a $\{p, q\}$ edge.

void InsertVertex(Vertex p). Pre: p is not in the graph. Post: p is in the graph, and p is not adjacent to any edge in this graph.

void InsertEdge(Vertex p, Vertex q). Pre: p and q are in the graph, $p \neq q$, and there is no $\{p, q\}$ edge. Post: p and q are adjacent.

Note: If we associate information of type *T* with every vertex, we can parametrize the graph and include two additional operations:

void Update(T e, Vertex& p). Pre: *p* is a vertex of this graph. Post: The position *p* contains the value *e*.

T Retrieve(Vertex p) const. Pre: *p* is a vertex of this graph. Post: The graph is unchanged. Returns the value contained in *p*.

Note: A related ADT, the **multigraph**, allows loops and multiple edges.

List

Structure.   A collection of positions in linear order. Each position contains an element of type *T*. Any nonempty list has one distinguished position, known as the *current position.*

Operations

List(). Pre: true. Post: The list is empty and the current position is undefined.

List(const List& 1). Pre: true. Post: The list is a copy of *l*.

void Clear(). Pre: true. Post: The list is empty.

void InsertAfter(T e). Pre: true. Post: If the list was empty, it consists of a single position, containing the element *e,* and this position is now the current position. If the list was not empty, it now contains a new position (which is now the current position), and *e* is in that position. The new position is the successor to the old current position, which is circled in the following diagram.

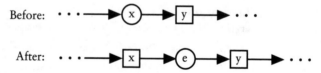

void InsertBefore(T e). Pre: true. Post: If the list was empty, it consists of a single position, containing the element *e,* and this position is now the current position. If the list was not empty, it now contains a new position (which is now the current position), and *e* is in that position. The new position is the predecessor to the old current position, as shown in the following diagram.

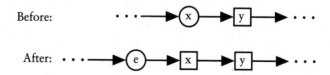

void Remove(). Pre: The list is nonempty. Post: The old current position is removed from the list. If the list had a single position, the current position is undefined. If the list had more than one position, the position preceding the old current position (if any) now precedes the successor to the old current position (if any). If the list had more than one position, the current position is the successor to the old current position, if there was one. Otherwise, the current position is the predecessor to the old current position. One possible case of this operation is illustrated in the following diagram.

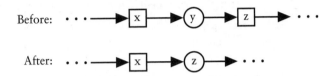

void Head(). Pre: true. Post: The current position is the first position in the list, if any. Otherwise, the list is unchanged (and the current position remains undefined).

void Tail(). Pre: true. Post: The current position is the last position in the list, if any. Otherwise, the list is unchanged (and the current position remains undefined).

List& operator++ (int). Pre: The current position is defined and is not the last position in the list. Post: The current position is the successor of the old current position, if there is one. Otherwise, the list is unchanged.

List& operator-- (int). Pre: The current position is defined and is not the first position in the list. Post: The current position is the predecessor of the old current position, if there is one. Otherwise, the list is unchanged.

T Retrieve() const. Pre: The list is not empty. Post: The list is unchanged and the element in the current position is returned.

void Update(T e). Pre: The list is not empty. Post: *e* is in the current position, replacing the element that was there.

int Includes(T e) const. Pre: true. Post: If *e* is in the list, returns 1 and sets the current position to that of the earliest instance of *e*. If *e* is not in the list, returns 0 and leaves the list unchanged.

int Length() const. Pre: true. Post: The list is unchanged, and the number of elements in the list is returned.

Number

Structure. A *Number* object is an integer of arbitrary size and so has no structure in the conventional sense.

Operations.
Number(). Pre: true. Post: This number represents the value 0.

Number(long i). Pre: true. Post: This number represents the integer *i*.

`ostream& operator<< (ostream& os, const Number& n)`. Pre: *n* is defined. Post: *n* is unchanged. The representation of *n* (in an appropriate base) is inserted in the ostream *os*, and a reference to *os* is returned.

`istream& operator>> (istream& is, Number& n)`. Pre: *n* is defined, and *is* contains the representation of an integer in a given base. Post: *n* represents the number in the *istream*, and the corresponding characters have been extracted from *is*. The operator returns a reference to *is*.

`Number operator+ (const Number& n, const Number& m)`. Pre: true. Post: *n* and *m* are unchanged, and the operator returns a number representing the sum *n+m*.

`Number operator- (const Number& n, const Number& m)`. Pre: true. Post: *n* and *m* are unchanged, and the operator returns a number representing the difference *n−m*.

`Number operator- (const Number& n)`. Pre: true. Post: *n* is unchanged, and the operator returns a number representing the negation, *−n*, of the argument.

`Number operator* (const Number& n, const Number& m)`. Pre: true. Post: *n* and *m* are unchanged, and the operator returns a number representing the product *n*m*.

(The specifications of /, %, ++, and -- are similar.)

`int operator== (const Number& n, const Number& m)`. Pre: true. Post: *n* and *m* are unchanged, and the operator returns 1 if *n* and *m* represent the same number and 0 otherwise.

(The specifications of !=, <, >, <=, and >= are similar.)

`Number& operator= (const Number& n)`. Pre: true. Post: *n* is unchanged, and the operator returns a reference to a copy of *n*.

(The specifications of +=, -=, *=, /=, and %= are similar.)

`int Length()`. Pre: true. Post: Returns the number of digits in the decimal representation of this number.

PriorityQueue : Set<Association>

Structure.   A set of associations with a key field type that is linearly ordered (usually numeric).

Operations

`PriorityQueue()`. Pre: true. Post: This priority queue is empty.

`void Insert(Association a)`. Pre: The priority queue has no element with the same key as *a*. Post: This priority queue is unchanged, except that it now contains *a*.

`Association DeleteMin()`. Pre: This priority queue is not empty. Post: The association with smallest key has been removed from this priority queue.

int isEmpty() const. Pre: true. Post: The priority queue is unchanged. Returns 1 if and only if the priority queue is empty.

Queue : *List*

Structure.   A list of elements of type *T*, where all insertions are performed at one end of the list (called the **rear**) and all deletions and inspections are performed at the other end (called the **front**).

Operations.   Except for assignment, none of the *List* operations are directly available to users of the *Queue* ADT. *Queue* has five operations of its own:

Queue(). Pre: true. Post: The queue is empty.

void Enqueue(T e). Pre: true. Post: The element *e* is at the rear of the *queue*, and the other elements (if any) are in their original order.

void Dequeue(). Pre: The queue is not empty. Post: The element that was at the front position has been removed. The remaining elements are in their original order, and the element that was adjacent to the original front is now in the front position.

T Front() const. Pre: The queue is not empty. Post: The queue is unchanged, and a copy of the top element is returned.

int IsEmpty() const. Pre: true. Post: The queue is unchanged, and the function returns 1 if and only if the queue is empty.

Set

Structure.   A collection of positions with no structural relation. Each position has an associated element of type *T*, and there may not be any two positions with the same associated element.

Operations

Set(T e). Pre: true. Post: This set contains a single position with which *e* is associated.

void MakeEmpty(). Pre: true. Post: This set is empty.

Set operator+ (Set a, Set b). Pre: true. Post: Returns a reference to a set equal to $a \cup b$.

Set operator* (Set a, Set b). Pre: true. Post: Returns a reference to a set equal to $a \cap b$.

Set operator- (Set a, Set b). Pre: true. Post: Returns a reference to a set equal to $a-b$, the set difference of *a* and *b*.

void Insert(T e). Pre: true. Post: If *e* was not in this set, this set now contains *e* and otherwise is unchanged. If *e* was in this set, the original element *e* has been replaced with this one.

void Remove(T e). Pre: true. Post: If *e* was not in this set, this set is unchanged. If *e* was in this set, it has been removed.

int Contains(T e) const. Pre: true. Post: This set is unchanged. Returns 1 if *e* is in this set; otherwise, returns 0.

int operator< (Set a, Set b). Pre: true. Post: Returns 1 if and only if *a* is a subset of *b,* which is to say, if every element of *a* is also an element of *b.*

int operator== (Set a, Set b). Pre: true. Post: Returns 1 if and only if *a* and *b* have exactly the same elements.

SortedList : List

Structure. A list of elements of type *T* (which must be linearly ordered by some *key* member datum), where the elements are arranged so their position in the list is compatible with the key order on the underlying type *T.*

Operations. *SortedList* inherits all the *List* operations, with two modifications:

Insert(T e). Pre: No element in the list has the same key as *e*. Post: The list contains *e* where it should be, and the current position is changed to be the position of *e*. The *List* operations *InsertAfter* and *InsertBefore* are overridden so that they do what *Insert* does.

Update(T e). Pre: The list is nonempty, and *e* has the same key as the current element. Post: The element at the current position has been replaced by *e*.

Stack : List

Structure. A list of elements of type *T,* where all operations are performed at one end of the list, called the **top** of the stack.

Operations. With the exception of assignment, none of the *List* operations are directly available to users of the *Stack* ADT. *Stack* has five operations:

Stack(). Pre: true. Post: The stack is empty.

void Push(T e). Pre: true. Post: The element *e* is at the top of the stack, and the other elements (if any) are in their original order.

void Pop(). Pre: The stack is not empty. Post: The element that was at the top position has been removed. The remaining elements are in their original order, and the element that was adjacent to the original top is now in the top position.

T Top() const. Pre: The stack is not empty. Post: The stack is unchanged, and a copy of the top element is returned.

int IsEmpty() const. Pre: true. Post: The stack is unchanged, and the function returns 1 if and only if the stack is empty.

Note: A number of authors choose to combine *Pop* and *Top* into a single operation that returns the value at the top of the stack and removes that element from the stack.

String : Array<char>

Structure. A *String* object is an array of characters. Each string contains one and only one zero character, which marks the last position in the array.

Operations. All the operations available to users of the *Array<char>* class, except for *SetBounds*. Beyond the inherited operations, *String* includes the following:

String(char* a). Pre: *a* is a zero-terminated array of char. Post: This string is constructed elementwise from the C++ string *a*.

String(char [] a, int sz). Pre: true. Post: This string is constructed from an array that is not necessarily zero terminated.

String(int len). Pre: true. Post: This string has length *len*; the characters in this string are undefined, except that the zero character is in position *len*.

int operator== (const String& str1, const String& str2). Pre: true. Post: *str1* and *str2* are unchanged, and 1 is returned if and only if the strings are equal, which is to say they have the same length and the same characters in each position.

(The operators !=, <, <=, >, and >= are defined similarly, using lexicographic order.)

unsigned int Length(const String& str). Pre: true. Post: *str* is unchanged, and the number of characters (not counting the zero terminating character) in *str* is returned.

ostream& operator<< (ostream& os, const String& str). Pre: true. Post: *str* is unchanged, the nonzero characters of *str* are inserted in *os*, and a reference to *os* is returned.

istream& operator>> (istream& is, String& str). Pre: true. Post: Characters are extracted in order from *is*, up to the first newline character (which is discarded from *is* and not placed in *str*) or until some internal maximum number of characters have been extracted. The extracted characters are placed in *str*, starting in position 0, and are terminated by a zero character. Finally, a reference to *is* is returned.

String operator+ (const String& str1, const String& str2). Pre: true. Post: *str1* and *str2* are unchanged, and a newly created string is returned. The new string has all the nonzero characters of *str1*, in order, followed by all the nonzero characters of *str2*, in order, followed by a zero character.

String Substring(unsigned int start, unsigned int size). Pre: *start*≥0. Post: This string is unchanged. Returns a copy of a string of length *size* that consists of the characters from this string with indices *start, start*+1, . . . , *start*+*size*−1. If *start* is greater than or equal to the length of this string, the empty string is returned. If *start* is less than the length of this string but *start*+*size* is greater than or equal to the length of this string, the returned string will consist of the tail of this string, beginning with position *start*.

String Insert(const String& inner, unsigned int start). Pre: *start*≥0. Post: *inner* is unchanged, and this string has a copy of *inner* inserted, in order, starting at position *start*. The characters in this string from position *start* to the end of this string are shifted so that they occur immediately after the newly inserted characters. If *start* is greater than or equal to the original length of this string, *inner* is appended to the end.

String Remove(unsigned int start, unsigned int size). The pre- and postconditions of this function are the same as those of *Substring*, except that instead of returning a copy of the indicated substring, that substring is removed from this string, and a copy of the result is returned.

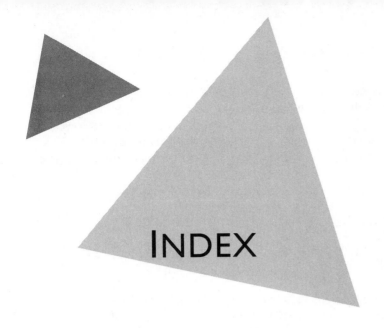

INDEX